#.21- B+T 1-67 (Swearingen)

THE RISE AND FALL OF NAZI GERMANY

THE RISE AND FALL OF
NAZI GERMANY

by
T. L. 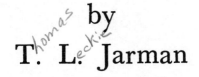 Jarman

NEW YORK UNIVERSITY PRESS

*First published in 1955
by the Cresset Press, Ltd., London.
First United States edition 1956*

SECOND PRINTING 1958
THIRD PRINTING 1964

Manufactured in the United States of America

PREFACE

THE ten years which have passed since Nazi Germany collapsed in ruin and defeat have brought Germany once more into the forefront as a vital factor in the international situation. The rise and fall of Nazi Germany is likely to remain one of the greatest dramas of history. The warnings and lessons of that drama must be appreciated, if the hopes placed in the new German Republic are to be realized. For when I re-read today the letters written during the Nazi period by German friends I can only reflect how plausible their arguments were, how pernicious, and how closely they echoed their master's voice. The story, dark and dire as so much of it is, must be understood by the Germans and their neighbours alike, if the peoples of Europe—and most of all the Germans themselves—are to live in peace and enjoy the fruits of a common civilization.

It was my lot to be in close touch with events in Germany during the Nazi period—and since. I learned to know the political tensions in Germany in the critical years 1931 and 1932 before Hitler came to power, and between that event in 1933 and the outbreak of war in 1939 I was in Germany two or three times each year. Domestic circumstances brought me into intimate touch with the German people, and helped me to understand the German outlook and to assess the chances of peace or war. I was able also in those years to travel widely among the neighbouring countries of Germany, including Russia, Turkey, and the Balkan countries, and to mark their reactions to the growing might of Nazi Germany. Poignant memories haunt me of the last summer of peace, of those bright, hot days in July and August 1939 which I spent in Berlin and Warsaw, Bucharest, Istanbul, and Paris, while Europe still slept and Hitler was putting the final touches to his plans for the destruction of Poland. 'Since those days the Nuremberg trials have shed a brilliant light', as

M. François-Poncet has observed. 'However, those trials revealed nothing which was not already suspected; they simply specified and aggravated what had been sensed and supposed from the beginning.'

Bibliography and footnotes indicate the printed material—already enormous—for the study of Nazi Germany. I am grateful, in particular, to the Wiener Library in London, a collection devoted to the study of National Socialism, and I am also grateful to the *Presse-und-Informationsamt* of the West German Government, in Bonn, for supplying me with a considerable amount of material. My thanks are due, in addition, to the Library of the London School of Economics, to the British Museum Library, to the Bodleian, and also to the Bristol University library which has been a steady source for reference and study over twenty years. Three British historians are outstanding in the field of Nazi studies, and I warmly acknowledge the help I have received from their work—from Mr. Alan Bullock's brilliant and comprehensive life of Hitler, Mr. Hugh Trevor-Roper's study of Hitler's end, and Mr. J. W. Wheeler-Bennett's *Nemesis of Power*.

I also thank friends in many countries for their help at various times, but principally Dr. T. K. Derry, for his ready advice and great assistance in reading the proofs, Dr. William Brown, of the *Freie Universität*, Berlin, for reading sections of my work and giving me the benefit of his comments and suggestions, and my colleague, Mr. W. S. James, of the University of Bristol, for the loan of correspondence. I am, of course, alone responsible for any views expressed. I should also like to thank Miss D. O. Terry and Miss M. Down for their work in typing the manuscript.

T. L. J.

Royal Fort House
University of Bristol
May 1955

CONTENTS

PART ONE
The Background

CHAP.   PAGE

  I.   The German Enigma   13

  II.   The Influence of History   29

  III.   The Beginnings of Megalomania   50

PART TWO
The Rise of the Nazi Party

  IV.   Versailles and Weimar   71

  V.   The Beginnings of the Party   88

  VI.   The Personality and Ideas of Hitler   104

  VII.   Struggle and Opportunity: Economic Slump   121

PART THREE
The Nazi Party in Power

  VIII.   The Nazi Revolution   147

  IX.   The Führer and the Party-State   166

  X.   The Positive Side of the Nazi Régime   185

PART FOUR
Hitler's Foreign Policy

  XI.   Bluff, Preparation, and the Failure of the West   203

  XII.   Growing Strength: Austria and Czechoslovakia   225

  XIII.   Poland—and War   247

PART FIVE
Hitler's War

CHAP.		PAGE
XIV.	Hitler Conquers Europe	267
XV.	Hitler Turns East	286
XVI.	War on Two Fronts	306

PART SIX
The End

XVII.	The End of the Nazis	327
XVIII.	The Nazi Myth and the Future	343
	Bibliography	361
	Index	374

MAPS

1   Germany after Versailles   76

2   Expansion of Germany 1933–1942   285

3   Germany after the Second World War   338

I was born a son of the people; I have spent all my life struggling for the German people. . . .

ADOLF HITLER.

I estimate that at least two and a half million victims were executed and exterminated at Auschwitz by gassing and burning . . . We executed about four hundred thousand Hungarian Jews alone at Auschwitz in the summer of 1944 . . .

RUDOLF HÖSS,
Commandant of Auschwitz Camp.

When such a disaster takes place, there must have been something wrong with those who were led or misled? What is that thing?

H. B. GISEVIUS,
German opposition leader.

PART ONE
The Background

CHAPTER I

THE GERMAN ENIGMA

SIX years of war on a vast scale and the combined efforts of Great Britain, the United States and Soviet Russia were necessary to bring down Hitler's Germany, which had been created only in 1933. A shorter period had been sufficient to defeat the Kaiser's Germany, an empire which had grown from strength to strength since 1871 and was firmly based on the much older kingdom of Prussia. How was it that an Austrian upstart was able to appear among the German people and create a régime stronger than that of the Hohenzollerns; how was it that the corporal of the First World War was to make himself supreme war lord in the Second; how was it that the down-and-out of the Vienna doss-houses was to become ruler of Germany, to overrun Europe, and to menace the world?

These questions, important in themselves, lead to the asking of another, even more important, and fundamental to an understanding of modern European history. How is it that the German people, so orderly and well-disciplined, so industrious and persevering, so advanced in the material ways of civilization, and perhaps the best educated people in the world, can be at the same time so politically immature and so irresponsible, and guilty of the rampant militarism, aggression, and colossal brutality and barbarism that the war revealed to the world? This question indicates the essential paradox in the German situation and opens up the basic enigma or riddle of the German character. It has, not unnaturally, called forth many answers. The paradox accounts for much of the disagreement among foreigners about the Germans; it helps to explain British bewilderment at the apparent contradictions in German policy.

It is, of course, the occurrence of the two world wars which has forced the paradox on British attention. Until after 1870 Germany had seemed remote enough; France, however, was close and, politically, was the traditional enemy. The people of this country knew far more of France and of French civilization than they did of Germany. French history was closely linked with our own; the French language became a general subject of secondary education, whereas German was an extra; and when Englishmen studied European history, that history was largely taken up with the history of France. To many Englishmen, therefore, a knowledge of Germany and things German was lacking. Even to well-educated Englishmen, brought up between the world wars, the realization of the importance of Germany sometimes came only in adult life and as a discovery. The immensity of the German problem became clearer as Hitler made the weight of Germany felt in world affairs.

Some have portrayed the Germans almost as though they were inherently and eternally bad; they seek to find in the Germans of today the same qualities of barbarism as were to be found in the old Germanic tribes who fought out their fierce and treacherous struggles in the primitive forests.[1] Others regard the German people as naturally good, but misled and imposed upon by wicked leaders. Some, again, look for a psychological kink, or see the Germans as good individually, but bad in the mass. Others, yet again, have favoured the theory of the two Germanies—the one, Prussia, whence have come autocracy and militarism, the other, the south and west of Germany, where the older German culture flourished.[2] But, although the military tradition was strongest in Prussia, Hitler was not a Prussian, and the Nazi movement sprang up in Bavaria.

[1] Lord Vansittart, *Black Record: Germans Past and Present* (1941). See also the replies to it—Victor Gollancz, *Shall Our Children Live or Die?*; H. N. Brailsford, *The German Problem*; H. J. Laski, *The Germans—Are They Human?*; H. Fraenkel, *Vansittart's Gift for Goebbels*. Brailsford's pamphlet is a particularly clear and balanced diagnosis of the German problem.

[2] See E. Stern-Rubarth, *Exit Prussia, a Plan for Europe* (1940), and Emil Ludwig, *The Germans* (1942). For an English expression of this view put forward during the First World War see the articles by A. Zimmern in *War and Democracy* (1915), by R. W. Seton-Watson and others.

In 1914 national feeling in the countries of western Europe was simpler and less sophisticated than it is today. Men saw the peoples of other nations in black and white; they distinguished clearly the bad from the good. Few Englishmen knew anything of the Germans at the beginning of the First World War, and it was easy, therefore, for the Press and agencies of national propaganda to present the Germans in the most sombre colours—as barbarous, tyrannical soldiers, in short, as the new Huns. The hatred of Germans as Germans— as the people who had plunged us into world war by invading Belgium—was certainly stronger, and a simpler emotion, in 1914 than in 1939. During and after the First World War, in fact, it came often as a surprise to the soldiers to discover that the French and Belgians did not always figure as the paragons they had been made to seem, but that the Germans were often better than they had been portrayed. Between the wars, as the result of the Allied occupation of the Rhineland and later the opportunities of cheap travel to Germany, Englishmen gradually acquired an acquaintance with, and generally a respect for, the Germans. Many people came to feel that the Germans were much more like us, much closer to us, than the French. All this has helped to strengthen the idea that the Germans are basically good, and that their faults have been due to bad leadership. This was further strengthened by the fraternal feelings of the socialist parties outside Germany for the Social Democrats, who were seen as the champions of a new, democratic Germany against the old forces of militarism and autocracy. When the Second World War came people could distinguish between Germans and Nazis. The Germans themselves, it could be argued, were good even if too easily led; it was Hitler and the Nazis who were to blame.

There was, indeed, considerable controversy in this country as to the nature of the Germans. Were we fighting the Germans or the Nazis? Lord Vansittart, formerly Permanent Secretary of the Foreign Office, made a series of broadcasts, published early in 1941 under the title, *Black Record: Germans Past and Present*. The title indicates the character of the pamphlet; it demonstrated the barbarous behaviour of the

Germans through the centuries, and their continuing menace to Western civilization. It had a large sale, and called forth some notable replies. It was held, and with reason, that barbarous deeds in past history could be laid to the charge of every nation; the German contributions to culture were pointed out; and it was argued that many Germans were themselves against Hitler, as was illustrated by the existence of the concentration camps. But these controversies depended upon whether one took of the Germans a short-term or a long-term view. Taking a long-term view, it was necessary to recognize the good qualities in the Germans and to plan, after the war, to allow those qualities freedom to develop. As Harold Laski put it: 'Germans are what their history makes them. Our business is to beat them in the field. But our business, also, is to use our victory so as to make their history the parent of those qualities in Germans which they possess in the same degree as other nations and can use for the common purposes of mankind.'[1]

But in the short view Lord Vansittart was right: 'I do not say', he wrote in answering the controversies his broadcasts aroused, 'that every individual German is bad; I do say that so vast a majority of Germans in the plural has been made bad by centuries of misteaching, that it will follow *any Führer*, cheerfully and ferociously, into any aggression. Germans in the plural have got to be completely regenerated and retaught —and that can only be achieved by force and time. Experience has amply shown already that the small and weak minority of decent Germans cannot possibly be effective by and of itself. . . .'[2] These words were only too true. The Germans *did* follow their Führer into war, the decent Germans *were* powerless to stop them, and, as the course of events showed, their opposition made no appreciable difference to the progress of the war.

Two wars, however, have not destroyed a certain affinity between the Germans and the English. It is much easier, for

[1] Professor Harold J. Laski, *The Germans—Are They Human?* (Left Book Club pamphlet, 1941).

[2] Lord Vansittart, *Black Record*, Preface, p. viii (Library Edition).

example, for a visitor to feel himself at home in a German than a French family. The Frenchman is a lover of his family, but he keeps it to himself; the German, on the other hand, likes to invite his friends in for a social evening. Beer and sausage, talk and song, around the table, pass the evening away, and the homely party breaks up with a mutual feeling of warmth and goodwill. And the foreigner in Germany is invited to take part: he becomes one of the family circle. There is a *social* element in all this which is hard to define in words, but which is familiar to those who have lived in Germany. The Frenchman lacks the social element; he is an individualist. The foreigner remains an individual, and an individual outside French life. The English and French, says a German observer, 'have little in common. They remain friendly strangers, peacefully disposed towards each other without any real social affinity.'[1] On the other hand, as Ward Price wrote in the *Daily Mail*, 'If Britons accustomed to travel on the Continent were asked in which country they felt most at home, the commonest answer would be—Germany'.[2]

At the same time it is possible to argue that the differences between the English and the French are superficial, whereas there is agreement on certain fundamentals of life; with the Germans, on the other hand, it would be maintained that the affinities are superficial and that they conceal profound differences.[3] The two wars have naturally led to an emphasis on the differences, and the horrors which the Nazis loosed on Europe did not make people anywhere anxious to claim affinity with the Germans. But the paradox remains: the good qualities and the horrors. It requires a philosophic turn of mind to improvise a theory which will include both. The practical Englishman is frequently puzzled by the contradiction.

The Englishman may well be more puzzled if he considers the high approval given in the past by many of his countrymen to things German. Although France has generally been

[1] Herman Levy, *England and Germany* (1949), p. 4.
[2] 14 December 1939.
[3] A. L. Rowse, *The End of an Epoch*, pp. 181-2 ('What is wrong with the Germans?'). Such was the view of Sir Austen Chamberlain, *Down the Years*, p. 229.

better known to us than Germany, there have always been some Englishmen with academic or musical leanings who have studied in Germany and generally they have been much impressed. German scholarship, in the nineteenth and early twentieth centuries, made a great reputation outside Germany. Englishmen like Carlyle, Matthew Arnold, and Lord Haldane all admired the German *Geist* or love of the things of the mind, and approved the thoroughgoing application of the Germans to intellectual pursuits. The historian, H. A. L. Fisher, who studied at Göttingen, Dresden, and Weimar in 1890-1,[1] later described how 'the more eminent professors of Berlin or Göttingen could count upon a band of young English admirers, who, returning to their more civilized but less erudite compatriots, preached the majesty of German knowledge'.[2] And Fisher still recalled when he wrote his *History of Europe* in 1936 the impression the Germany of Bismarck had made upon him. 'It is difficult', he says, 'to overestimate the achievements of the German people during the twenty years of Bismarckian peace, which followed the convulsion of the Franco-Prussian War. Great as had been the pace of economic progress, it had not outstripped the organizing power of the German mind. The foundations of public education had been wisely and truly laid. . . . Nowhere were the advantages to be derived from the marriage of science and industry more quickly, more generally, or more intelligently perceived. . . . Scientific and learned treatises issued every year in prodigal abundance from the printing presses. No people in Europe read more widely or seriously. Music was everywhere— cheaper than in France, more universal than in England, and the best (save for Vienna) to be found in any quarter of the globe.'[3]

In Fisher's day, as he pointed out, German scientific and industrial progress was making itself felt already in the lives of ordinary people. The Germans were pioneers in the chemical and electrical industry; they were also pioneers in building and town-planning. 'While the creators of industrial

---

[1] H. A. L. Fisher, *An Unfinished Autobiography.*
[2] H. A. L. Fisher, *History of Europe*, p. 1,063.   [3] Ibid., pp. 1,056-7

England were permitted to toil and die in a sprawling and disorderly congeries of ignoble hovels', Fisher recalled that 'the Germans thought and planned beforehand'. So were laid the material foundations of the comfortable and attractive home life of the German cities. The start which the Germans gained then they have since maintained. Their towns and cities are well-planned, clean, and orderly. Their houses and flats are practical and comfortable, well-heated in winter by either the old-fashioned stove or modern central heating, and, in summer, allowing the fullest benefit from sun and air by means of large windows and open balconies.

Bismarck, too, was a pioneer in the field of social insurance, and by this means he alleviated the evils of industrialism. In the 1880's he had introduced health insurance, workmen's compensation, and old age, widows', and orphans' pensions. When Lloyd George introduced his health insurance in 1911 he recognized his debt to Germany.[1]

But it was in the field of education that Germany won, perhaps, the highest praise from Englishmen. It is necessary to recall this fact and to emphasize it, because German education has subsequently been blamed both for producing the Nazis and for the prevalent outlook of the older imperial Germany. The attack on German education after Germany's defeat in 1918 was led by H. G. Wells. In his *Outline of History* he wrote of it as 'a systematic exploitation and control of school and college, literature and Press, in the interests of the Hohenzollern dynasty'. Indeed, he went so far as to say that it was 'the greatest of the Hohenzollern crimes that the Crown constantly and persistently tampered with education, and particularly with historical teaching. No other modern state has so sinned against education.'

What, however, had generally struck Wells's predecessors was the excellence of German education. Matthew Arnold, Mark Pattison, and Michael Sadler in the course of their investigations for the old Department of Education, all paid high tribute to the German system. Arnold pressed the need for a State system of organization at home as in the German

[1] H. Levy, *England and Germany*, p. 85.

states, and urged the need of good secondary schools for the middle classes. And it was not only the scholars and academics who recommended the development of education at home on German lines. Scientists and business-men also realized the excellence of the German system and the danger of competition in manufactures. The chemist, Lord Playfair, part of whose education had been in Germany, was active in writing during the '50s and '60s to point out the deficiencies at home which his knowledge of Germany had revealed. 'If we continue to fight with our present voluntary system', warned A. J. Mundella, the Nottingham manufacturer, who knew his firm's hosiery branches in Saxony, 'we shall be defeated.' That was in 1862. But even after the First World War the impression German education had made on Englishmen remained. In 1932 Lord Eustace Percy, a former President of the Board of Education, while on the whole he preferred English to German education, could write: 'Germany has long been recognized as a pioneer nation in the educational field . . . she has standards, she has a philosophy; while other nations, notably England, are content to work out their educational salvation empirically, as the needs of their people seem from time to time to require.'[1] At the same time an American academic observer compared the universities of the United States, England, and Germany. America, he thought, placed 'a naïve trust in education', but 'Germany has in theory and practice come nearest to giving higher education its due position'.[2]

There is the paradox once more. For it is these highly educated Germans, with the impressive tradition of a long-standing and respected educational system behind them, who followed Hitler. They could scarcely have done worse had they been uneducated; in fact, their education had made them all the more dangerous, just as an educated burglar would be more dangerous than an uneducated one. It may

---

[1] Foreword to *The German School System*, by S. Ali Akbar. See also T. L. Jarman, 'German Education and the German Problem', in *Journal of Education*, September 1951. F. Schneider, *Geltung und Einfluss der Deutschen Pädagogik im Ausland*, gives a full account of the powerful influence of German education outside Germany.

[2] A. Flexner, *Universities—American, English, German* (1930).

well be, indeed, that what won English approval was German system and efficiency; and these things alone do more harm than good. Something was missing in German education—something which could humanize. But in any case it is a mistake to attribute too great an importance to education in determining the character of a people. Their schools and universities only represent a part of the national life, and they are a reflection of it as much as a formative influence in its development. A foreigner looking at English education from the outside could draw many false conclusions; he might easily regard the English 'public school' as a nursery of autocracy and aristocracy, of regimentation and militarism—and German teachers of today do sometimes form this view when they see school caps and J.T.C. uniforms, and when they learn of the great powers of a headmaster over his staff and of prefects over the pupils. To us, however, it seems that these features are offset and balanced by others: the team spirit, games, co-operative activity in school societies, and a balance of work and play in the healthy atmosphere of a good school.

The German problem which presents so many puzzling aspects remains, but we can at this stage say one or two things quite definitely. It is impossible to solve the problem with any glib explanation, drawn from German education, or by regarding the Germans as naturally and necessarily bad, for we have seen that before 1914 things German often won high approval, and even between the wars respect for and sympathy with the Germans was not wanting among English people. That there are good Germans everyone who knows Germany must agree. That there are also democratic Germans is demonstrated by the example of Switzerland, where the majority of the people are of German origin and German-speaking. And it gets one nowhere to draw up a catalogue of dark deeds done by the Germans through the centuries, and to argue that the Germans are therefore today what these dark deeds have made them. Similar catalogues could be drawn up for most, if not for all, countries. The early history of the English, the French, and the Scandinavians is marked alike by the darkest deeds of war, barbarism and treachery. No people has an unblemished record. Nevertheless, we may find that certain traits of character have survived in the Germans, or have been revived and strengthened in modern times, that have largely faded into the background in other peoples or have been sublimated in other activities. We may find, also, that certain developments and events in history have influenced and moulded the Germans in a direction unfavourable to peaceful living side by side with their neighbours. As an American anthropologist has pointed out: 'the distribution of innate tendencies among Germans, Danes and Swedes is essentially the same. Differences in social behaviour, then, must be due to historical causes.'[1]

To look first at some traits of the German character. Of course, in discussing the character of the Germans, we must remember that the concept of national character is a vague and indefinite one, particularly in the case of the Germans, who have been divided among so many different German states, and where local and provincial differences have survived in great strength. Many have noticed differences between the Austrian and the Prussian, between the Bavarian or Rhinelander and the north German. Then, again, a people's character may change or develop with the development of its environment; the expansion of its economic system and changes in its way of life will react on the national character.

Certain characteristics, however, do stand out as a result of our knowledge and experience of the Germans. The German is tremendously hard-working, persevering, strong, tough, virile, even crude and rough; he is prepared and eager to suffer and put up with discomfort and inconvenience to achieve his end; he is ready to submit to discipline and leadership, even tyranny, if he feels that it will assist him to reach that end. These qualities—like the system and powers of organization in German education which impressed the foreign visitor —can be either good or bad according to the nature of the end which is sought and the character of the leadership. No people in western Europe is so dependent on the character of

[1] R. H. Lowie, *Toward Understanding Germany*, p. 353.

its leadership as the Germans. Given good leadership, the Germans could be the making of Europe—a solid core of industrious, level-headed, prosperous people like the Swiss or the Scandinavians. Under bad leadership, the Germans just as readily plunge themselves and their neighbours into disaster. The Germans, too, are obedient people; their history is not marked by great revolutions. They love order and legality, and this makes them good civil servants and patient, well-disciplined soldiers. Their obedience is carried so far as to become a vice: they find it almost impossible to criticize the accepted order or to challenge the rightness of State authority. They are not good material for democracy.

One Englishman, who knew the Germans well and spent five years among them as a prisoner, thought the Germans looked with envy on the English as a *Herrenvolk*, a race of masters. 'An inferiority complex is, I think', wrote Captain Payne Best, 'the most marked German characteristic. All the military and martial posturing, the shouting and stamping are just a smoke-screen put up to conceal it. From earliest youth all Germans are brought up to believe that blind and unreasoning obedience to orders is the highest human virtue and that even thought must be directed along lines ordained by higher authority. From earliest youth the education of a German is accompanied by persistent bullying designed to make him feel that he is dirt in the eyes of the man above him; and natural leaders, rare everywhere, are in Germany almost non-existent. Every German has burnt into his soul the memory of countless occasions when he has been shouted at and insulted by someone in authority and, however high the rank he may attain, a certain feeling of inferiority and insecurity never really deserts him. This fact is to my mind the real explanation of Hitler's rise to power and his complete dominance over everyone with whom he came in contact. His leadership was inborn, he had no doubts, and he acknowledged no superior. All other leaders in Germany were synthetic, he alone was real.'[1]

As for the mass of Germans, they have their good qualities,

[1] S. Payne Best, *The Venlo Incident*, pp. 33-4.

but they will follow the leader. 'The vast majority of Germans under Hitler were', Captain Best could write even after the experience of his imprisonment, 'as they have always been, as harmless as a flock of sheep; good-natured, sentimental, hard-working. Unfortunately, unlike sheep, they can be trained to kill and destroy, and with their sheep-like instinct blindly to follow their leader, they can become very dangerous.'[1]

The thoroughness of the German never fails to impress—though it may sometimes raise a laugh. Nothing is done by halves; everything is thought out beforehand down to the last detail. He is an expert, a specialist. He has a zest for collection and compilation, for the encyclopaedia. He is particularly good in philology or history, where careful workmanship and attention to detail are important. Everything is serious; everything is done in dead earnest. The German has little sense of humour, especially where he himself or his country is concerned. He cannot laugh at himself. German professors and students visiting England are always struck by the use of humour in university lectures, for example, and by the lightness of touch here compared with the heavy tone of academic lecturing in Germany. It is this characteristic which makes so much German scholarship seem heavy and unnecessarily involved. The language, too, is florid, elaborate, and cumbrous; it lacks the form of a classical language such as French, and the clarity of French expression. Then the German finds it difficult to set limits, just as in history his country has been rather frontierless. His mind is boundless in its reach and longing, and his claims tend to be boundless also—they lead towards universal dominion.

Then the German is a philosopher. He theorizes by nature. A group of German students will meet on a social occasion and in no time will be engaged in discussing some topic, such as the nature of reality; whereas English students would be casually speaking of cricket or engaging in light-hearted tomfoolery. And as with his obedience and his thoroughness, so with his philosophy—his philosophy is carried to the point at

[1] S. Payne Best, *The Venlo Incident*, p. 77.

which it becomes a vice. The German must carry everything to a logical conclusion. This is often his undoing, for it means applying to human life a logic which makes human life itself illogical and impossible.

The characteristics which are found in the German are to be found also in other races, but in the Germans they appear to be carried to extremes; they are exaggerated. The German is careful, clever and calculating in detail; he can steal a quick advantage by being unscrupulous over a small thing, but he can be exceedingly stupid in big things. It may seem odd to accuse the highly educated, philosophic German of stupidity, but it is difficult to draw any other conclusion when one looks at what the Germans have thrown away. Between 1870 and 1914 they had become one of the greatest peoples in Europe and, by reason of their economic power and military strength, must have become one of the dominant powers in the world *by peaceful means*. This position they could have achieved, had their diplomatic resources been equal to their economic and military ones. But they threw everything away in 1914. Could anything be more stupid? Certainly; the Germans were capable of being even more stupid. They did it again, in 1939.

With their thoroughness and concentration on detail goes an indifference to the interests and feelings of other people which amounts to selfishness. The German thinks so much of himself and his own philosophy or *Weltanschauung* that he ignores the point of view of others. He is convinced of his own rightness; when he comes up against opposition he tends to regard himself as a victim or, in the international sphere, he sees his country as encircled. He falls a prey to self-pity, and may become morbid and brood over his supposed wrongs. He cannot picture the aspirations, desires, wishes, traditions of other nations, such as the Poles or Czechs. He cannot negotiate on a basis of friendly and equal compromise and conciliation; he lacks the basic self-confidence and tact to do this, and suffers from inner disharmony. He must bluster and bully; he calls his heavy guns into action at once.

The German asserts German superiority over others. He

believes in force, and is ready to use force to carry his point. His assertion of superiority appears in the tradition of German philosophy and in his racial theories as well as in militarism.

The characteristics of efficiency and discipline are most closely associated with Prussia. The heel-clicking and stiff bowing on introduction, the rigid features, the close-crop of the hair, the formal manners and lack of natural charm and grace—these things are all Prussian and are typical of the camp and the barracks. When they find that their mechanical efficiency, though it brings success, does not make them liked, the Germans react in two ways. In the one way, they try to convince everyone of their superiority and worth, which makes for formal display, parades, and propaganda; in the other way, they turn away resentfully from the evil and stupid world which cannot appreciate them at their true worth, and this leads to self-pity and persecution mania. Thus at the end Hitler himself maintained that the Germans—and especially the generals—were not worthy of him.

Lack of balance and of sense of humour are marked. The German finds it difficult to tolerate an opposite point of view. His adherence to what he believes to be a logical principle and the attempt to carry it out to the uttermost is what distinguishes the German most clearly from the Englishman. The Englishman acts empirically, he can learn by trial and error, he can laugh and compromise. All this comes to the German only with the greatest difficulty: for by nature and training he must follow his principle and carry it to its logical conclusion. If he thinks the Nordic race is best, he must suppress all other races. If he finds a Jewish problem, then he must exterminate the Jews. Now, ideas of racial superiority and dislike of the Jews are not unknown outside Germany. Indeed, it cannot be doubted that Englishmen of an older generation imagined an inner racial superiority, in India— but it did not prevent them giving peace and justice to the peoples of India. Many people in England and the U.S.A. dislike the Jews, but neither government has introduced the gas-chamber. There is here a profound difference in the conduct of the Germans and that of their western neighbours.

'One looks in vain in their history', an English historian has said, 'for a *juste milieu*, for common sense.'[1]

The Germans cannot, therefore, escape responsibility for the war and the horrors of the régime by putting the blame on the Nazis and their leadership. The leadership must bear the first responsibility, but it was an accepted leadership. It was freely supported by nearly half the German people, and its nationalist principles were approved by many who were not Nazis. 'Nazism', wrote a German professor of Marburg University whose name was on Hitler's first list of dismissed professors, 'far from being a mere incident in German history, arose from conditions peculiar to Germany alone. . . . There are Hitlers everywhere, and have been at all times, but it is Germany's shame that so miserable a figure could become her leader. In order to germinate, the seed of Nazism had to find a favourable soil: it found it in the German Reich and the Germans, such as they had become in their political, spiritual, economic and social history.'[2] But it is a thing of the utmost difficulty to make Germans realize this. At the end of the Second War Germans were eager to blame the Nazis. But then no one admitted to being a Nazi. In this way Germans appeared to avoid any real personal responsibility or consciousness of guilt.

To understand why and how the Nazi régime was established it is necessary to look back into the past of German history and to study the factors which have made the German people what they are. We shall find much in German history to account for the conduct of the Germans in the Nazi period. We can trace, too, the origins and development of State prestige and of racial megalomania, and see, in the feverish agitation which developed against the Treaty of Versailles, German nationalism reach a pathological condition.

In the period between 1919 and Hitler's coming to power in 1933 we witness a veritable struggle for the German soul between the forces of light and the forces of darkness inherent in the whole human drama. Not for nothing is it that the

[1] A. J. P. Taylor, *The Course of German History*, p. 13.
[2] Wilhelm Röpke, *The German Question* (1946), p. 96.

story of Faust is German, and is inextricably interwoven into the literary and psychological pattern of German mentality—the industrious student, the scholar of all-embracing knowledge, the Olympian philosopher, who sells his soul to the Devil for the things of this world. But we must not assume that the success of Hitler was inevitable. And if we do not assume that, then there is hope for the Germans of the future. The Hitler régime represented a triumph of the evil forces in the German mentality over the good, but it is not impossible that, if the Germans can learn the necessary lesson, the good forces at their disposal may develop and become strong enough to triumph in their turn.

For the advent of Hitler was the result of a number of factors which happened unfortunately to work together with great strength for a short period. The Weimar Republic had not long enough, nor had it favourable circumstances, to establish itself and become acceptable as a form of government to all Germans. Had events turned out a little differently, Hitler might have been checked, and the foundations of German democracy stabilized. But it was not to be.

The main factors which, operating together, made possible the triumph of the Nazis are four in number. They are: (1) the historical development of the German people, which was unfavourable to democracy and predisposed them to accept nationalist leadership and military adventure, (2) the personality of Hitler, a demonic man of exceptional will-power and of more than normal influence over others, (3) the economic depression of the 1930's, which brought German discontents to the point of desperation, and (4) the failure of the Western Powers to build an international front determined and strong enough to check Hitler in time. Together these factors were powerful enough to establish in Germany a régime so extreme and fantastic, yet with such strength and such means of charm and attraction, that not only did it make the Germans themselves for the most part willing victims, but it stretched out its hands to link up with fifth columns in foreign lands. The Nazi régime was a new Lorelei turning those who looked to their doom.

CHAPTER II

THE INFLUENCE OF HISTORY

AN examination of German history will help to reveal why the Germans are what they are. For the German problem is not simply the problem of National Socialism; it is much older than that and its roots stretch back far beyond Hitler's seizure of power in 1933, the Versailles settlement of 1919, and even the Franco-Prussian War of 1870. The continuity of the Nazi period with the German past was, indeed, recognized by the National Socialists themselves, though by the selective method of emphasizing those periods or persons in German history which could appropriately figure as their forerunners. Thus the expression the Third Reich drew attention to the existence of the other reichs—the first the Holy Roman Empire which exercised a grand but shadowy authority in medieval Europe, the second the German Empire of 1871. Lastly came the Third Reich, of Adolf Hitler—and the three reichs stand out like mountain peaks, the intervening periods of history, of federalism and attempted democracy, being allowed to remain shrouded in the valley mists. Or, again, Nazi propaganda made use of a picture showing, side by side, the heads of Frederick the Great, Bismarck, Hindenburg, and Hitler, with the inscription: *Was der König eroberte —der Fürst formte—der Feldmarschall verteidigte—rettete und einigte der Soldat.*[1] By this line of succession from Frederick to Hitler, the Nazis proudly claimed their continuity with German greatness in the past, and strengthened their position with the prestige of names respected in German history. With their selection of military figures, the Nazis underlined the nationalistic and military character of their state.

[1] 'What the king conquered, the prince moulded into form, the field-marshal defended, the soldier saved and unified.' Postcards with the inscription and picture were on sale during the Nazi period.

In this country, on the other hand, we pride ourselves on being peaceful in intent and democratic, whereas the Germans have shown themselves in modern times markedly deficient in these qualities. Yet in origin we are German. The Anglo-Saxon conquerors of Britain came from the shores of north Germany, and our language is Germanic. In our affinity with the Germans our common racial origin is still apparent. And it is usually the 'black sheep' of the family who emigrates. The Angles and Saxons who crossed the North Sea to conquer Britain were more adventurous and, if anything, more fierce and warlike than those who stayed behind in Germany. But between those distant times and today the historical development of the German and English has been different, so that now we appear as distinct and different peoples.

Why, then, are the Germans what they are? What are the factors in their history which have prevented the development of democracy and favoured autocratic leadership, and how is it that, in spite of their many good qualities, militarism has so often been dominant?

A number of historical explanations have been put forward for the survival of barbarous characteristics in the Germans. Tacitus, at the end of the first century A.D., described the ancient Germans with their proud, bold, and warlike ways, their tribal leadership, their tribes and tribal assemblies, and their feeling for race and blood.[1] The primitive, barbarous character of this early tribal life was doubtless similar all over Europe, among Germans and non-Germans alike. But then, it is argued, western Europe was conquered by Rome, and Rome failed to conquer the Germans of the deep, forested interior. The Roman frontier lay approximately along the Rhine and Danube, fortified lines linking the two rivers. The Roman Empire brought civilization to western Europe, and it was those western and southern parts of Germany under Roman sway—the Rhineland, Bavaria, and Austria—which subsequently proved to be the most civilized parts of Germany. The rest of Germany escaped the civilizing influence of Rome and—hence the Germans of

[1] *Germania, passim.* He refers to the Angles in section XL.

today. It is a view which would fit in well with the idea of the two Germanies. There may be something in the theory: certainly Europe owes the origin of its civilization to Greece, Rome, and Christianity, all of which influenced it in and through the Roman Empire. But—and this is the great difficulty about this theory—certain other parts of Europe also were unconquered by Rome, but have since become highly civilized, democratic, and peaceful nations. For example, England. The Romans conquered Britain—but the barbarian Anglo-Saxons crossed to the island and destroyed the Romano-British civilization. Historians still argue as to just how far Roman Britain influenced Anglo-Saxon England—but the influence could not have been great. In any case, Scandinavia was right outside the area of Roman conquest, and yet the Scandinavian tribes, warlike and barbarous as they then were, have since developed into nations which are models of civilized life.

Then there is the argument that Christianity, elsewhere brought early by the Romans, penetrated only much later into the heart of Germany. But once more there is the difficulty of Scandinavia. There, also, Christianity came late, but that fact did not warp the development of the Scandinavian peoples.

Such theories, although nothing like complete solutions, do throw a certain light on the German problem. They at least help to explain the differences inside Germany and the strong local and provincial characteristics which have survived from the distant past. It will be more useful, however, to compare the historical development of Germany with that of England. By making that comparison, we may the more clearly reveal the factors which have determined the development of Germany. Let us look first at England.

The Anglo-Saxon invaders of Britain were pagans, fierce and warlike adventurers like the German tribes they left at home. Their coming virtually destroyed the Romano-British civilization and plunged the island into two centuries of savage darkness about which relatively little is known. A picture emerges at length of a number of English tribal kingdoms, distinct and hostile. During the ensuing centuries of warfare, one kingdom after another—Northumbria, Mercia, Wessex—took the lead and exercised an uneasy predominance. By the eleventh century something like an English kingdom was emerging, though provincial differences were still strong and could sometimes plunge the country into civil war. The conquest of the country in 1066 by the Normans imposed a foreign yoke, but with it William the Conqueror brought closer links with Continental civilization, and he was the first of a line in which for the most part strong, effective rulers predominated. In short, he brought the inestimable boon of a strong, central kingship.

In fact, the stage was set for the development of the modern English nation. The Norman invaders were few in number, and before long the peoples coalesced; in spite of the use of Norman-French by the court and Latin by the Church, the language of the conquered people did not disappear, but eventually emerged as a common tongue—English. England was united; in spite of struggles with the feudal barons, the supremacy of the kingship was established, and the royal judges carried the king's law throughout the land. And the kingship passed on by hereditary right; the older Saxon principle of election by the Witan dropped out. A hereditary monarchy established continuity and assisted the development of a system of government. Thus, gradually England became a nation state, whereas in the Holy Roman Empire of medieval Germany the elective principle was a continual weakness. By Tudor times England was a distinct national state with a government able to override the last feudal opposition and the difficulties of religious dissension which the Reformation brought. England was united, well and firmly governed, and able to resist and overcome the menace from the Spanish Empire.

One factor of the first importance in the growth of nationhood was the fact that England was on an island. Its island position gave it unrivalled security, a position held by no Continental nation, though France and Spain were both favoured by the protection of the sea on a large stretch of their frontiers. Inside the island the peoples of Britain were free to develop without direct interference by foreign peoples. The Norman conquest was the last, and England suffered none of those foreign invasions which devastated Continental countries periodically throughout history. England's good fortune in this respect was realized already by Shakespeare when he made John of Gaunt, in *Richard II*, describe our island as:

> *This precious stone set in the silver sea,*
> *Which serves it in the office of a wall,*
> *Or as a moat defensive to a house,*
> *Against the envy of less happier lands.*

Very different was Germany's position, with frontier provinces disputed through the centuries.

England's wars were, in modern times, mainly wars of defence: to prevent the domination of Europe by one power. Thus she fought, and for the same reason, against Philip II of Spain, Louis XIV of France, Napoleon, the Kaiser Wilhelm II, and Hitler. Her struggle with France in the eighteenth century, when English and French clashed in India and Canada, was a fair combat of rival powers, in which France might well have triumphed. If England came out best —that was the fortune of war. In any case, England was never a military power, with great armies organized for territorial conquest of her neighbours in Europe. The Bill of Rights and the Mutiny Act of 1689 had put the existence and size of the standing army firmly under Parliamentary control. We had no conscription until the First World War. Our overseas and colonial wars were fought by small, professional armies. At home in England, national security together with increasing wealth and prosperity, particularly in the nineteenth century, provided the conditions in which Englishmen could develop the qualities of peacefulness and tolerance. Peace at home was conducive to a peaceful attitude of mind and an easy-going way of life.

England, too, was fortunate in seeing the slow, steady, step-by-step development of her system of government from medieval parliament into modern democracy.[1] There was one break in that evolution, with the Civil War and the execution of the King. But the war was a mild affair compared with the horrors of the religious wars in France or the Thirty Years' War in Germany; in any case, it is 300 years ago, and since then the evolution has been steady and largely peaceful.

The struggle between King and Parliament in the Civil War and the Revolution of 1688 (an exceedingly moderate, model revolution) assured the supremacy of Parliament, but the new system had sprung from the old; it was a system in which both king and Parliament had place and function.

The Industrial Revolution changed the face of England; it vastly increased its population and created new social classes, manufacturers and workers. Such radical social changes brought political changes also; but violence and disorder were relatively slight. By successive steps in 1832, 1867 and 1884 the franchise was widened, until parliament became a democratic assembly in the modern sense—though the vote for women came only after the First World War. The English Parliament and English political philosophy became models for the world. 'We were all', wrote an Italian statesman with reference to the period before 1914, 'disciples of the English liberal philosophers. John Stuart Mill's book *On Liberty* moulded the liberal thought of two generations before the war. We regarded it not only as a monument of English wisdom, but also as a synthesis of the practical British spirit.'[2] Fortunate indeed had been the British people in its political evolution. The working together of the factors of strong monarchy at an early stage, island position, economic prosperity, and steady democratic development produced a people inclined by outlook towards peace, democracy and toleration —things which we regard today as normal.

[1] Von Ranke, the historian, caught a glimpse of this truth as early as 1857, when he visited England. In a letter from London to the King of Bavaria he described his participation in an election on the hustings, and also the medieval atmosphere of the Cambridge colleges, and said: 'They are complementary. Democratic and conservative tendencies are balanced—neither will drive out the other.' L. von Ranke, *Das Briefwerk*, p. 424. See E. Eyck, *Politische Geschichte Englands* (1951) for a German liberal account of British political development.
[2] Francesco Nitti, *Bolshevism, Fascism and Democracy* (1927), p. 32.

How different was the development of Germany. German history does not show normality, but extremes. The early tribal divisions did not disappear, as in England, in the course of the political evolution of the nation. No strong national kingship emerged for long enough to establish itself; the territorial divisions, instead of disappearing, became more numerous. By the end of the Middle Ages there were some 300 states, large and small, in Germany—duchies, counties, ecclesiastical territories, free cities, a medley of territories which makes a map of medieval Germany a complicated and bewildering patchwork. It was in the Middle Ages that the fatal future of German political development was decided. A German historian writing in 1933 of medieval Germany appropriately used the title *Deutschlands Mittelalter Deutschlands Schicksal*.[1]

It is important, however, to emphasize that, at the beginning, there was no essential difference between Germans and English. Angles, Saxons, Frisians, Franks, Burgundians, Alemannians, and Thuringians all made themselves felt in central Europe as the Roman Empire declined, and of these the Angles and some of the Saxons pushed over the North Sea to conquest and settlements in Britain—during the *Völkerwanderung*, the migration of peoples in the third, fourth, and fifth centuries. The divisions in Germany which persisted and became worse at a later date cannot be attributed to any special tribal differences in early times. Germany was not distinguished in this from France or England. 'Like all other nations of modern Europe', says a British historian of Germany, 'the Germans appeared on the threshold of history as a number of separate and often hostile stems . . . in this respect German history is no different from that of England or France.'[2]

Again and again there arose in Germany some ruler who succeeded temporarily in bringing together the scattered Germanic peoples under one head. Of the Franks, Clovis at the end of the fifth century and Charlemagne at the end of the eighth established a wide hegemony in north-western Europe.

[1] 'Germany's Middle Ages, Germany's Destiny.' By H. Heimpel.
[2] G. Barraclough, *Factors in German History*, p. 4.

Charlemagne in the year 800 was crowned by the Pope at Rome, thus reviving the tradition of the Roman Empire. But each time the empire, after the death of the forceful personality which had held its different races and lands together, disintegrated. Five great duchies—Saxony, Franconia, Thuringia, Swabia and Bavaria, based in name on the old tribal divisions—appeared in the ninth century. Headed by dukes or military leaders under the nominal suzerainty of the Frankish crown, the duchies appear to have become feudal units rather than tribal territories. The Saxon, Otto I, asserted himself as German king over the dukes, and was crowned at Rome in 962. Holy Roman Empire and German kingship were thus combined, but their power was shadowy and not destined to take on lasting reality. More than once, however, it looked as though a strong German kingship might establish itself. In the eleventh century, for example, under the Salian Franks the German kingship could compare with that of England or France. All were consolidating their crown lands, developing a money economy and administering their territories through royal officials. In the second half of the twelfth century Frederick Barbarossa, of Hohenstaufen, showed himself a powerful ruler in Germany and Italy (and left a tradition behind him comparable to that of the legendary King Arthur in our own island). But each time civil war and political anarchy supervened in Germany and the reality of central government disappeared.

The relation between the Empire and the Papacy was fatal to Germany. It led many German emperors to march into Italy, and waste men and treasure in their attempts to maintain the allegiance of their Italian dominions. Worse still, it led to papal interference in Germany. The popes were not prepared to leave the appointment of bishops to temporal rulers—yet this was often a vital matter to a medieval ruler, for a bishop was, with lands and castles, an important feudatory. The struggle—the investiture controversy—led to civil war in Germany. Worst of all, the popes supported the theory of election for the German kingship. Thus the German kings, instead of being able to establish a hereditary monarchy

THE INFLUENCE OF HISTORY

which would have helped to secure continuity in the work of government, were compelled to submit to election by the princes before being crowned emperor by the pope. This practice was formalized by imperial law in 1356; it 'legalized anarchy and called it a constitution'.[1]

The central power in Germany was henceforth, and indeed was already, but a shadow: real power, such as it was, lay with the princes—dukes, counts, bishops, imperial towns— each in his own territory. Of about 300 principalities in Germany at the end of the Middle Ages many were small and individually weak. Sometimes the smaller lords and knights banded together for self-protection, and the cities also formed associations, the greatest of which was the Hanseatic League in the north. Whereas, by the end of the Middle Ages, England and France were each establishing a strong, centralized nation-state, Germany remained divided and a prey to disorder. Robust and vigorous as German medieval life was, especially in the cities, politically the country was weak. Germany was little more than a geographical expression. Political development was fatally retarded: dreams there were of universal empire, but statehood was lacking.

In contrast with the island frontiers of England, Germany could be regarded as frontierless. Their status as Holy Roman Emperors drew the German kings across the Alps to assert their claims in Italy. And on both east and west as well, Germany lacked clear frontiers; and this meant insecurity. The Rhine was no longer a frontier, as it had been in Roman times, for German territories stretched far to the westward: in this area rendered debatable by German weakness the French kings, especially as they grew stronger at home, were all too ready to interfere. On the east, among the Slav tribes and where there was waste land of uncleared forest and marsh, the Germans themselves pushed outwards in a wave of conquest and colonization during the twelfth, thirteenth, and fourteenth centuries. They acquired the new lands of Mecklenburg, Brandenburg, and Pomerania; they pushed into Silesia; and the Teutonic Knights—originally a crusading

[1] Bryce, *Holy Roman Empire* (ed. of 1922), p. 246.

order—conquered East Prussia and lands eastward, temporarily, as far as Estonia. This vast expansion eastward indicates a new direction of Germanic influence vital for the future, and a new family became of importance in Brandenburg—the Hohenzollerns.

For Germany the centuries passed in an incredibly complicated series of dynastic struggles, while the greater princes strove to consolidate and enlarge their territories. One family —the Habsburgs in Austria—emerged as the most powerful of the princely houses, and in that family the title of emperor remained from the fifteenth century until the end of the Holy Roman Empire in 1806. But while they built up a strong connection of family territories, the Habsburgs could not unite Germany—too often their family interests ran counter to those of Germany. For a moment, under Charles V (1519-56), a vast empire appeared again: this time it included Austria, the Netherlands, Spain and the New World. But it could not last, nor did it produce any lasting authority in Germany. The princely powers, the forces of disintegration, were too strong.

To those older forces of German disintegration and weakness there was added, in the time of Charles V, yet another. To the existing political and dynastic divisions the Reformation added a difference in religion. There were fierce peasant risings also—the peasants stimulated by religious ferment— and their savage suppression riveted the feudal and autocratic authority of lords and princes even more firmly in Germany. Civil war broke out between Catholics and Protestants, and in the next century there followed the dreadful Thirty Years War. The religious conflict, which passed so lightly over England, was devastating in its effect on Germany. A bitter, bloody, German struggle brought also foreign interference—Danish, Swedish and French—and horrible deeds of savagery were perpetrated, both by Germans and by foreign mercenary troops. Swedish and French national interests were pushed at the expense of Germany, and the unhappy country became the scene of what was latterly—for the religious origin of the struggle was lost sight of—a European struggle between the Bourbons of France and the Habsburgs of Austria. The

Germans were decimated, towns sacked and ruined, peaceful peasants destroyed, while rival armies and robber bands lived on the countryside. The outcome, in the Peace of Westphalia of 1648, was, apart from the loss of German territory to France and Sweden, the strengthening of the territorial princes—and perhaps it is not altogether fanciful to suppose that the savagery of the Thirty Years War left some permanent effect on the German character.

The lands of the princes were now virtually independent states—Prussia emerging as, next to Austria, the strongest—and the treaty gave them the right of forming alliances, not only with each other, but also with foreign powers. Each prince might thus follow his own foreign policy: while at home he administered his territory by means of a bureaucracy of officials and kept order with a mercenary army. At the same time the autocratic character of the ruling houses was strengthened. The earlier limitations on autocracy were generally avoided or destroyed, especially in Austria, Prussia, and Bavaria. There had been in these territories states-general, assemblies which in more favourable circumstances might have developed into parliaments. But the princes were now generally strong and cunning enough to filch from the states-general, under one pretext or another, the vital control over taxation. Once the princes had possessed themselves of the power to levy and collect the taxes, the possibility of parliamentary—and later democratic—evolution was gone. Thus in the seventeenth and eighteenth centuries, at the very time when parliamentary control of government was firmly established in England, even its embryonic forms were destroyed in Germany.

Two outstanding developments of the eighteenth century for Germany were the rise of Prussia and the French Revolution. The state of Prussia, the Hohenzollern ruler of which early in the century took the rank of king, was formed of the union in 1618 of the old Brandenburg with the East Prussia of the Teutonic Knights. By war and inheritance the Prussian rulers acquired a chain of territories stretching from the Polish frontier westwards to the Rhine. Able rulers between 1640 and 1786, notable among whom was Frederick the Great (1740-86), built an efficient military state, with a powerful army and people reared on the principles of obedience, duty, work, and sacrifice. Prussia stood out as a great power in its own right, able to hold its own in Europe; it emerged as the German rival of Austria, and was from now on to play a dominant role in German development.

The French revolutionaries, when war came with their monarchical neighbours, looked to the Rhine frontier as a goal. Prussia and Austria were not able to prevent this for the time being and later, in addition, by a number of arrangements with Napoleon, the map of Germany was redrawn. The more than 200 states were reduced to forty by forcing the smaller territories, Church principalities, and imperial towns into a number of medium states. In 1806 the Emperor, Francis II, gave up the imperial crown and took instead the title Emperor of Austria. So, finally, the Holy Roman Empire, which had long ceased to be a reality, came to an end in name also. Once more the weakness of Germany had been revealed. The French invader had done very much as he chose with German territory. Indeed, the course of modern history was showing, even more vividly than the course of medieval, the weakness and insecurity of Germany. In 1760 the Russians had entered Berlin; in 1806 the French marched into the city in triumph. The Prussian capital was indeed open to attack on either side. It was not therefore surprising that the Prussian kings should be, more than ever, convinced of the need of a powerful Prussian army.

The wars with France led indeed to a national recovery in Prussia and to a remarkable and widespread growth of national feeling in Germany as a whole. Not unnaturally, there was a national reaction to French occupation, but even so the particularist interests of the princes—including those of the King of Prussia and the Austrian Emperor—were against national unity. The Allies at the Congress of Vienna in 1815, in accordance with the dynastic principle of legitimacy, confirmed the existence of the German states: thirty-nine, a number of them now kingdoms, remained as sovereign powers, loosely linked together in a Germanic Confederation, with a federal Diet of representatives of member governments, but not of peoples. Inside this confederation Prussia and Austria were rivals, and the mutual rivalries, together with the autocratic character of the princely governments, prevented the growth of a true federation as had been the case with Switzerland, which developed into the modern federal democracy of twenty-two cantons. The greater part of the Swiss are German. How different the future of Germany might have been if a German federation could have grown up like the Swiss!

There were, however, certain powerful factors making for German unification. The *Zollverein* or Customs union of 1834, the development of a railway system, and the industrial revolution after 1850 with a vast increase in population—all these reduced the importance of state boundaries and made for unification. And there was in Germany a certain liberalism —in spite of the politically retarded condition of the country. In 1848 the wave of revolutions which swept Europe affected the German states. The demand for liberal constitutions was accompanied by a demand for national unity. The German liberals, with some support from the rulers of some of the smaller states, called a parliament from all the states to meet at Frankfort (1848-9), and the assembly offered the crown of a united Germany to the King of Prussia. He refused: a sovereign ruler by God's grace could not accept a crown from a popular assembly. The failure of the liberals to unite Germany by peaceful means was a turning-point in modern German history.

In the end Prussia produced the man who could unite Germany by diplomatic finesse and by force—a fierce, ruthless, *Junker* reactionary from Brandenburg. Bismarck, as Prussian minister-president, came to power in 1862, and set himself the task of destroying liberalism in order to strengthen conservative Prussia and maintain her position as a great power: in the process he united Germany. 'The great questions of the day', he said, 'will not be settled by resolutions and majority votes . . . but by blood and iron.' As a youth in a student-corps at Göttingen he fought some twenty-five duels; as a man he engineered three wars.

He first of all expanded the Prussian army, in the face of liberal opposition, and carefully made his plans and preparations. Bismarck was a master of diplomacy and intrigue. His three wars brought him success. First, in 1864 Prussia defeated Denmark after a dispute over the border duchies of Schleswig and Holstein. Then, in 1866 Prussia provoked Austria over the administration of the duchies and defeated Austria—and her supporters among the German states; she annexed a number of the German states, including Hanover, and excluded Austria from the North German Confederation which was now formed. This left Prussia the dominant power in Germany. Next it was to be war against the ancient invader, the traditional enemy. Here was the making of a love of war, a military tradition. The gods of war were inspiring the German soul. In 1870, after Bismarck had skilfully turned existing differences to his advantage, Prussia defeated France in the Franco-Prussian War, making Prussia appear the champion of all Germany against the age-old hostility and interference of France. Thus the remaining princes were won over, though not without misgiving and opposition, and the King of Prussia himself, who regarded the title of emperor as an unsubstantial and unnecessary frill, agreed nevertheless to Bismarck's proposals. The King was made German Emperor, and the new German Empire, the Second Reich, was proclaimed by the victorious Bismarck at Versailles in January 1871. At long last Germany was united—but Prussia and Prussianism had triumphed over Germany.

'The whole Empire', said Treitschke soon after its foundation, 'is an extended Prussia. . . . Prussia is the dominant factor. . . . The conditions are such that the will of the Empire can in the last instance be nothing else than the will of the Prussian state.'[1] And it was this now dominant Prussia which was at the same time the most highly disciplined and, from the point of view of human social development, the most backward part of Germany. How far the savage struggles of the

[1] *Politik*, II, p. 346.

early wars and conquest of the Slav population influenced the later Prussian stock and character may be a matter of dispute. But Treitschke, in an essay published in 1862, had asked: 'Who can understand the innermost nature of the Prussian people . . . unless he has familiarized his mind with those pitiless racial conflicts whose vestiges, be we aware of them or not, live on mysteriously in the habits of our people.'[1] The hard, stern background of early Prussia is referred to by two modern English historians when they described Brandenburg in the fifteenth century as 'sour and sandy soil on which brutal manorial chiefs and brutish serfs fought a dour and relentless battle with nature and with each other'.[2] After the Thirty Years War the position of the peasantry was greatly depressed and Prussia became a land of large estates owned by the Junkers (i.e. landlords, or squires) and worked by serf labour. Prussia developed as a highly organized, military state: it was said in the eighteenth century that 'Prussia was not a country with an army, but an army with a country'. The position has been well summed up by a modern German writer: 'Absolutism and feudalism were the destiny of all Germany. But while outside Prussia they were mitigated by the more complex and more organic character of society, by a certain passive *laisser faire*, by a good-natured slackness, and in not a few cases by a truly liberal spirit, in Prussia they were rationalized, mechanized, and made into a system, until the Prussian state had become a regular clockwork in which the individuals were simply cog-wheels. Here in Prussia everything had to be done on the model of the smart shouldering of arms and the parade march.'[3] And Prussian success—in the military and economic spheres— won admiration. It won over many of the liberals. It was a triumph of will and power, of force. After 1879, when Germany became protectionist in fiscal policy, 'and thanks also

[1] H. von Treitschke, *Origins of Prussianism (Das deutsche Ordensland Preussen,* trans. E. and C. Paul), p. 19.
[2] J. A. R. Marriott and C. Grant Robertson, *Evolution of Prussia,* p. 17.
[3] W. Röpke, *The German Question,* p. 148. How Germanic life was modified and made more pleasant by 'good-natured slackness' appeared clearly in pre-1914 Austria. See Wickham Steed, *The Habsburg Monarchy;* and Stefan Zweig's autobiography, *The World of Yesterday.*

to the unexampled increase in population, there began now the colossal growth of industry, of transport, of the great towns, of the great stores, of the industrial districts, of the mass parties, of State care for mass welfare; of monopolies, trade union federations, and banks—and the old Germany began to disappear and to give place to a Greater Prussia drunk with success. . . . That this was a selling of one's soul was scarcely noticed.'[1]

Coupled with the manifest victory of German arms in Bismarck's wars was the survival of a Prussian, aristocratic, military tradition. The swagger of the young officer—the conservative aristocrat whose outlook was still largely that of a feudal landed class—set the tone. Duelling, honour esteemed in the special sense of prestige, the picking of quarrels and the avenging of one's 'honour' with swords or pistols, these things, once common to the military upper class everywhere, continued in Germany when elsewhere they had died out. The scars of old duelling wounds were held in high regard, though the foreigner generally looked on the German so marked with a mixture of curiosity and disgust. Militarism, the military character of the Prussian state, was part of its social structure. In the eighteenth century the Junkers formed the officer class; landlord and peasant in civilian life, officer and man in military life, in either case social subjection was the principle. And when, in the nineteenth century, the officer class was widened to include reserve officers drawn from the new middle classes of business and professional life, these men showed great pride in their association with the old, traditional social superiority of the regular officers. Thus the military habit of thought maintained its hold; a civilian, democratic way of life failed to assert itself. Whereas all states had armies, they were not necessarily militaristic. But in Prussia the army was traditionally the dominant element in social life.[2]

It was Bismarck, above all, who stamped the Prussian

---

[1] Röpke, op. cit., p. 168.

[2] K. Buchheim, *Leidensgeschichte des Zivilen Geistes*. See the extracts in Hans Kohn, *German History—Some New German Views*, pp. 44-64.

military character upon the whole of Germany. Bismarck himself, later on, admitted his responsibility for the wars which had brought Prussian success. He even, in a way, reproached himself: 'Without me three great wars would not have happened and 80,000 men would not have perished.'[1] But the wars which followed as an indirect consequence of Bismarck's quarrel with France, produced an incomparably greater slaughter. As Dr. Erich Eyck, perhaps the most distinguished Bismarckian scholar of our day, has said: 'In one point, and that perhaps is the most important of all, Bismarck's heritage has outlasted all the changes of the age. The militarism he impressed upon the German nation by his doctrine of "blood and iron" and its brilliant and triumphant realization remained overwhelmingly strong and proved stronger than the bitter disappointments of the First World War and the Weimar Republic, in which at least a part of the people tried to do without it.'[2]

'The greatest and most important figure of his time', Bismarck has recently been called. 'If the age in which he lived can be associated with the name of one person, there can be no doubt that it is the Age of Bismarck. There was nobody whose speeches were heard with the same attention by the whole world.' And Eyck continues: 'His spell over the German people was almost boundless and no name filled a gathering of German students more quickly with enthusiasm than the name of Bismarck.' Yet to us his intolerance makes him an unattractive figure. As Eyck, himself a refugee from Hitler, says: 'Bismarck was not able to do justice to an adversary, even if the differences were only slight—and he did not at all care to do so. The passage of years did not mellow his judgment. He had no respect for the majesty of truth . . .' and Eyck argues that from him the German people 'learned to consider lack of morality as a quality of a great statesman. The machiavellian doctrine of the *raison d'état*, which justifies every infringement of written and unwritten law, began to

[1] Quoted by E. Eyck, *Bismarck and the German Empire*, p. 174.
[2] Ibid., p. 184. For a penetrating discussion of Eyck's views, see 'The Bismarck Problem', by Professor Franz Schnabel, in Kohn,op. cit.,Chapter 3.

spread and to take deeper roots until even Hitler's broken treaties and brutal cruelties were accepted not only as excusable, but as proofs of his greatness.'[1] Indeed, in spite of the vast difference in their social origin, there were similarities in the methods of Bismarck and Hitler—and both were accepted with enthusiasm by the German people. As a recent German writer has put it: 'The majority of Germans see today in Hitler a terrible destroyer of his country. But if we seek a better way we must learn to understand fully that the destruction started with Bismarck's work and that the Wilhelminian epoch externally so glamorous contained the seed of death.'[2]

The new Imperial Constitution which Bismarck worked out was autocratic in nature. There was in pre-1914 Germany a Reichstag elected by manhood suffrage, but it did not control government as did the English Parliament. Although by 1912 the Social Democratic Party (i.e. the German Socialist or Labour Party) was the largest in the Reichstag, and the party had in its programmes and policy denounced war, it could not influence the policy of the Government. And the Social Democrats were without experience. The chancellor was responsible not to the Reichstag, but to the emperor, and the other ministers were responsible to the chancellor. In Prussia, the largest and most powerful of the German states, the system of voting was arranged so as to give the majority to the upper, conservative classes. Germany was still a federation of the twenty-five states, but real power lay with the dominant state—Prussia. Prussia itself was in the hands of the landlord class, and later of the powerful industrialists. Bismarck's system gave the people no opportunity for political education and experience. There was in the German system of government between 1871 and 1914 little hope of true democratic development and of popular responsibility.

German unity had come by force and war. This fact was to give an underlying character to the new empire. German

[1] E. Eyck, *Bismarck After Fifty Years* (Historical Association, 1948, General Series: 98).
[2] C. H. Müller-Graaft, *Irrweg und Umkehr, Betrachtungen über das Schicksal Deutschlands*, quoted in Kohn,op. cit., p. 41.

unity and material greatness had been won by a series of victories, and those victories lived on in the memory of many who survived into the Hitler period. As recently as the years immediately before 1939 the aged Field-Marshal von Mackenson used to review on the Petersburg the remaining veterans of those three wars. A leading German professor, a contributor in 1910 to the *Cambridge Modern History*, wrote of German unification: 'War, ever the most potent factor in the founding of states, has brought unity to the German people.'[1] And thinking, in 1910, of Germany's future and the lesson of her history, he wrote: 'In view of her geographical and military position, set in the centre of the international construction of Powers and impelled by the inward necessity for further development, this country is subjected to a stronger tension of conflicting forces than any other Power, and therefore needs to put forth her strength the more effectively if she is to hold her own. It is only the fullest exercise of her strength which has sufficed since the days of the Saxon and Hohenstauffen Emperors to vindicate the existence of the Germans as a nation. Long centuries of weakness and dismemberment have taught them that, without this determined display of force, the heart of Europe will become an object of attack and spoliation for their neighbours. In the new empire, Emperor, princes, and people, all parties and all ranks, are agreed that these lessons of the centuries, taught by the heights and depths of the nation's history, shall not have been given in vain.'[2]

Thus, it is in the light of the historical development of Germany and the lasting military character of Prussia—for historical research does not reveal a plan for world conquest in 1914—that we must view Germany's share of responsibility for the First World War. Germany was not alone to blame. The immediate cause was the determination of Austria-Hungary, subsequent upon the assassination at Serajevo of the heir to the Austrian throne, to crush Serbia, and it was

[1] Herman Oncken, 'The German Empire', *Cambridge Modern History*, Vol. XII, p. 134.
[2] Ibid., p. 173.

Austria which opened hostilities. But Serbia was not alone. Russia supported her, and France was the ally of Russia. Germany was to blame in that she did not restrain her ally Austria, and, in order to gain the advantage of rapid military action, declared war on Russia and France. Germany was best prepared for war, but Austria-Hungary, France, and Russia also were great military powers; their competition in armaments had been intense and all efforts at disarmament had come to nought; the interests of the great powers had clashed for years past; colonial and Balkan rivalries had demonstrated in successive crises how dangerous the European situation was and how near to war. It was the unhappy legacy of Bismarck that, although he himself maintained the European peace after 1871 until his fall, he divided Europe into two armed camps. He had fatally alienated France by the annexation of Alsace-Lorraine, and the protective measures he took in forming the Triple Alliance with Austria-Hungary and Italy led to the formation of the Dual Alliance between France and Russia.

In the pre-war years Germany had done little or nothing to ease the tension in Europe.[1] The military character of the country and the language used by its writers had gone far to convince many people abroad of Germany's warlike intentions. The swift victories of 1864, 1866, and 1870 and her vast economic development gave her a position of pre-eminent military power. Her heavy-handed methods in diplomacy and the threat of war, the building of a great navy which she did not need and which brought her into conflict with Great Britain, and the aggressive character of the Kaiser William II's speeches, all these things added to the tension. Even Great Britain, which had stood outside the European quarrels, was alienated and alarmed, and, after the *Entente Cordiale* of 1904, came closer to France and Russia.

German unity, and with it political power, had come late and suddenly. Industrialization, economic power, and with

[1] See Joseph Antz, '*Der Fall Foerster*', in *Frankfurter Hefte*, August 1954. He gives a clear, interesting analysis of the German Professor F. W. Foerster's criticism of German policy.

it military strength, increased rapidly, for Germans of every class had an unlimited capacity for work. Germans looked also to their heritage of literature and music, scholarship and science, all of which had had a splendid flowering in the nineteenth century. All this was stimulating, exciting. It turned German heads. Germany at last was great. The ancient claims of empire were still recalled; new opportunities beckoned. Germany might be greater yet. There was the danger in the years before 1914: a great nation with economic and military strength of the first order, but a people politically immature and unable to control the leaders who might be tempted to misuse that strength. The German state was a threat to Europe. 'Have a care', said Mommsen, 'lest in this state, which has been at once a power in arms and a power in intelligence, the intelligence should vanish, and nothing but the pure military state should remain.'[1] Mommsen's warning came true in 1914, and again in 1939. Indeed, with the course of the First World War, militarism grew in Germany. Among the bourgeoisie there were 'sanguine hopes of great German conquests, and hence newly strengthened sympathy for militarism'. In 1916 Field-Marshal Hindenburg and General Ludendorff became virtual military dictators; their orders were carried out even against the wishes of Chancellor and Kaiser. Such was the confidence of the people in the leaders of the Army that when defeat came they could not credit it. 'Soon there were many who no longer believed that Ludendorff lost the war, but now thought that Erzberger, when he signed the Armistice . . . had been a traitor.'[2] There was the origin, and the psychological strength, of the stab in the back legend. German faith in their military leaders of the First World War was to help the Nazis to create the movement which led directly to the Second.

[1] Quoted in *Why We are at War* (1914), by members of the Oxford Faculty of Modern History.
[2] Karl Buchheim in Kohn, pp. 61-3.

CHAPTER III

THE BEGINNINGS OF MEGALOMANIA

THE danger inherent in German political development was matched by the danger implicit in German thought, which shows an exaggeration and irresponsibility which are the counterpart of the political immaturity which a study of German history reveals. An over-emphasis on the powers of the state, an obsession with war, a concern with German expansion to include all Germans outside the frontiers, and a belief in the superiority of the Aryan, Nordic, or Teutonic race —all these are marked features of modern German thought.[1]

It is, of course, always difficult to draw the line between a legitimate patriotism and exaggerated, aggressive nationalism. German national feeling received a powerful impulse from the philosopher Fichte, who, after Prussia had been defeated by Napoleon in 1806, issued his *Addresses to the German People*. He saw in the purity of the German language an indication of a sound and healthy nation. The Germans, he thought, were sounder than the Latinized peoples of Europe in that German was less mixed with Latin and Celtic languages. He emphasized the conception of *Volk* or nation, but it was a lofty conception of the divine making itself manifest in the spiritual development of human society. Such a conception in itself is not to be condemned, but it can be twisted and abused, as later Germans too often have demonstrated. Hegel, who, when Fichte died in 1814, followed him in the chair of philosophy at the University of Berlin, laid an emphasis on the State as the central concept of political thought, and his teaching exercised a great influence both in and outside Germany.

[1] With regard to German writing of history, the Swiss historian Dr. Walther Hofer says it is open to criticism on three grounds: 'Power is idealized. . . . War is made heroic and moral. The national idea is . . . made absolute.' Hans Kohn: *German History—Some New German Views*, p. 193.

'The State', wrote Hegel, 'is the actuality of the ethical idea. It is ethical mind . . . knowing and thinking itself.' It is 'an absolute unmoved end in itself' and 'this final end has supreme right against the individual, whose supreme duty is to be a member of the State'.[1] Thus he regarded the State as a supreme authority, almost in a personal sense. Of war between states he wrote as of a means of purifying 'the ethical health of peoples' corrupted by a long peace, in the same way that 'the blowing of the winds preserves the sea from the foulness which would be the result of a prolonged calm'.[2] And again, of the State he said: 'The state is the world which mind has made for itself. . . . As high as mind stands above nature, so high does the state stand above physical life. Man must therefore venerate the state as a secular deity' (*Irdisch-Göttliches*).[3]

All this is set out in technical philosophical language, and could scarcely be used directly by the vulgar popularizers of tyranny. Its author was described by a British philosopher as showing in his life a 'deeply idealistic, poetical, and religious view of the world'.[4] Yet to Hegel can be traced the threads of thought which have led both to nationalist megalomania and to the idea of the dictatorship of the proletariat. As has so often happened, the Germans grossly exaggerated certain elements in the Hegelian or Idealist theory of the State. The State—even ultimately the Nazi State—became a standard of right and wrong. German students took all too easily from their professors a doctrine which fitted in so well with the development of modern Prussia and later the Bismarckian Empire. The doctrine of State supremacy and of war as its necessary instrument seeped down into the German nature. So it was not altogether unreasonable for Professor Hobhouse, reconsidering his Hegel after the bombing of London in the First World War, to see in that event the tangible outcome of Hegelian philosophy: 'With that work began the most penetrating and subtle of all the intellectual

[1] *Philosophy of Light* (trans. T. M. Knox, 1942), pp. 155-6.
[2] Ibid., p. 210.
[3] Ibid., p. 285.
[4] E. Caird, *Hegel* (1883), p. 90.

influences which have sapped the rational humanitarianism of the eighteenth and nineteenth centuries, and in the Hegelian theory of the god-state all that I had witnessed lay implicit.'[1]

The man who did most to provide a theoretical basis for the Prussianization of Germany was Heinrich von Treitschke. He was by birth a Saxon and in his youth of liberal outlook, but he became a full-hearted supporter of Prussia. For him 'the will of the Empire can in the last instance be nothing else than the will of the Prussian State'.[2] Treitschke in his own person showed how strong was the influence of Prussia and its powers of attraction—to size, military strength, coal and iron, Treitschke would now himself add an intellectual justification. He was early elected a deputy in the new imperial Reichstag, and in 1874 became professor of history in the University of Berlin. There, between that date and his death in 1896, he delivered his lectures to large and enthusiastic audiences.

His *Politik*, an important work based on his lectures, set out his ideas. The keynote is the State as power, and this is recognized and accepted as harsh and hard. The State is indifferent to a subject's feelings; it is concerned only with his obedience. 'It does not matter what you think, so long as you obey.'[3] And since the State is power, 'then the organization of the army must be one of the first cares of the constitution'.[4] In service to the State, through the army, the individual must forget himself, and realize how small a thing is his life alone and something only to be fully realized when merged in the whole. 'The grandeur of war is in the utter annihilation of puny man in the great conception of the State.'[5]

What is most striking and most sinister is that Treitschke, far from regarding war as an occasional regrettable necessity, went out of his way to justify and glorify it and to make it of

---

[1] L. T. Hobhouse, *Metaphysical Theory of the State* (1918), p. 6. Cf. J. A. von Rantzau's essay, 'The Glorification of the State in German Historical Writing', in Hans Kohn, pp. 157-74. He criticizes Hegel and Ranke as 'worshippers of the State'.

[2] *Politics* (Eng. trans. by Blanche Dugdale), Vol. II, p. 375.

[3] Ibid., Vol. I, p. 23-4.

[4] Ibid., Vol. II, p. 389. See also pp. 406.

[5] Ibid., Vol. I, pp. 66-7.

permanent importance in the policy of the State. 'The army is not always upon active service, but the silent labour of preparation never ceases.'[1] Even more, Treitschke regarded war as an institution divinely ordained, and thought that to banish it from the universe would be to mutilate humanity. Periods of peace he regarded as 'exhausted, spiritless, degenerate periods'. But that they would utterly corrupt mankind he did not believe. 'It is not worth while', he said, 'to speak further of these matters, for the God above us will see to it that war shall return again, a terrible medicine for mankind diseased.'[2]

Nor are governments immoral if they provoke war lightly. Indeed, he said that the State must have a sensitive and highly developed sense of honour, just as he praised duelling for officers and deplored its disappearance among the English. 'If the flag is insulted, the State must claim reparation; should this not be forthcoming, war must follow, however small the occasion may seem; for the State has never any choice but to maintain the respect in which it is held among its fellows.'[3] 'No courts of arbitration will ever succeed in banishing war from the world.' The idea of lasting international peace he ridiculed. 'War', he said, 'is both justifiable and moral, and the ideal of perpetual peace is not only impossible but immoral as well.'[4]

Treitschke taught those ideas which were becoming characteristic of German thought and were later to reappear in all their crudity and with dynamic effect among the Nazis. His lecture courses, given year after year, had great success; he was an important influence over the youth of the new Germany, and his lectures were attended not only by students, but also by officers and officials. Indeed, Treitschke's lectures both influenced the future and illustrated the ideas which were gaining strength in the Germany of his time. His lectures were based on his earlier essays, dealing, many of them, with current German politics. For that reason his *Politik* reflected the views which had become dominant, and consequently the book was

[1] *Politics* (Eng. trans. by Blanche Dugdale), Vol. II, pp. 396-7.
[2] Ibid., Vol. I, p. 68.   [3] Ibid., Vol. II, p. 595.   [4] Ibid., pp. 598-9.

enthusiastically received by German readers.[1] When Balfour wrote in 1916 an introduction to the English translation of the *Politik*, he clearly stated the issue inherent in the clash between the German liberals and Bismarckian Prussia: 'It is permissible to conjecture that if the political creed of Treitschke's youth had borne the practical fruit which he so passionately desired, the subsequent history of the world would have been wholly different. If "liberalism", in the Continental sense, had given Germany empire and power, militarism would never have grown to its present exorbitant proportions. The greatest tragedy of modern times is that she owes her unity and her greatness . . . to the unscrupulous genius of one great man, who found in the Prussian monarchy, and the Prussian military system, fitting instruments for securing German ideals.'[2] Balfour later on referred to Treitschke's description of war as a 'medicine for mankind diseased'. Already in 1916 that medicine had, as Balfour put it, 'been supplied in overflowing measure'.[3] Since then it has overflowed again.

Another renowned German who stressed the importance of force was Nietzsche. Born in 1844, and much influenced by the Bismarckian unification of Germany, the egotism and megalomania in Nietzsche's character and teaching grew worse until madness overtook him. The man who wrote an autobiography called *Ecce Homo* with chapters entitled 'Why I am so Wise' and 'Why I am so Clever' lingered on for eleven years as an imbecile, during which very time his ideas were beginning to exercise a powerful influence over men's minds. Once more it was the characteristic German obsession with power that made the keynote of Nietzsche's teaching. In *The Will to Power* he wrote: 'Society has never regarded virtue as anything else than as a means to strength, power, and order. . . . The State, or unmorality organized, is from within: the police, the penal code, status, commerce, and the family; and from without: the will to war, to power, to

[1] H. W. C. Davis, *Political Thought of Heinrich von Treitschke*, Preface and p. 35.
[2] *Politics*, Introduction, pp. viii-ix.
[3] Ibid., pp. xxviii-xxix.

conquest and revenge.'[1] In other ways, however, Nietzsche stood somewhat outside the characteristic lines of German nationalistic thought. He was not altogether an admirer of the German people. He thought of the German philosophers as 'unconscious swindlers', and among these he included Fichte and Hegel; he attacked Wagner and Treitschke. He was not a racialist in any narrow sense, nor was he anti-Semitic. But he too falls in with the objective of German expansion and domination. 'The future of German culture', he wrote, 'rests with the sons of the Prussian officers.' For they, he thought, were the most manly. 'We require an intergrowth of the German and Slav races, and we require, too, the cleverest financiers, the Jews, for us to become masters of the world.'[2] And, unlike Wagner, he did not try to effect some kind of reconciliation between his philosophy of power and Christianity: Christianity Nietzsche called 'the one great curse, the one enormous and innermost perversion. . . . I call it the one immortal blemish of mankind.'[3] For him, Christianity was the moral code of weaklings and slaves; only such as these longed for freedom and happiness.

Nietzsche's object was to break through this slave morality, and thereby set free the will to power restrained and restricted by it. Moral values must disappear, or, rather, there must be a transvaluation of values: gentleness must become severity, what is soft must become hard. Man must become superman, and be lonely, hard, and engaged in continual strife. Man must be trained for war; those who are weak or sick must be eliminated, for the superman will not weaken himself by feeling pity. 'Society is not entitled to exist for its own sake, but only as a substructure and scaffolding, by means of which a select race of beings may elevate themselves to their higher duties, and, in general, to a higher existence.'[4] 'There is', he wrote, 'no such thing as the right to live, the right to work,

[1] II, p. 184. References are to the *Complete Works* in English translation, edited by Dr. Oscar Levy, 18 vols. See also *The Antichrist*, p. 128, and *Beyond Good and Evil*, pp. 226-7.
[2] *Peoples and Countries* (a fragment, included with *The Genealogy of Morals*), pp. 222-4.
[3] *The Antichrist*, p. 231.
[4] *Beyond Good and Evil*, p. 225.

or the right to be happy: in this respect man is no different from the meanest worm.'[1] Nietzsche elevated the savage and brutal elements in barbarous mankind: 'It is impossible not to recognize at the core of all these aristocratic races the beast of prey; the magnificent blond brute, avidly rampant for spoil and victory.'[2] Again and again he equated the natural man with the beast of prey. The complete man was the complete beast. Christianity, he argued, in attempting to tame the barbarian, was simply weakening the healthy animal by making it ill.[3] The qualities of the strong, hard, barbarian Teutons he hoped to see revived in a new aristocracy of supermen. All this has the authentic German touch; in his stress upon power, war, and aristocratic leadership, Nietzsche helped to mould what have become German features.

'Ye shall love peace as a means to new war', he wrote, 'and the short peace more than the long. You I advise not to work, but to fight. You I advise not to peace, but to victory. . . . Ye say it is the good cause which halloweth even war? I say unto you: it is the good war which halloweth every cause. War and courage have done more great things than charity.'[4] He expressed very clearly his belief in leadership and his hatred of the masses: 'I am opposed to parliamentary government and the power of the Press, because they are the means whereby cattle become masters.'[5] He gave, too, a striking picture of the kind of conditions from which, in fact, future dictators, Mussolini and Hitler, were to spring: 'The corrupted ruling classes have brought ruling into evil odour. The State administration of justice is a piece of cowardice, because the great man who can serve as a standard is lacking. At last the feeling of insecurity becomes so great that men fall in the dust before any sort of will-power that commands.'[6]

Disciples of Nietzsche have tried to show that Nietzsche did not mean what he appears to say. 'Power' and 'war' were

---

[1] *The Will to Power*, II, p. 208.
[2] *Genealogy of Morals*, p. 40.
[3] See *The Antichrist*, pp. 150-1, and *Beyond Good and Evil*, p. 118 and pp. 223-4.
[4] *Thus spake Zarathustra*, p. 52.
[5] *The Will to Power*, II, p. 206.   [6] Ibid., p. 205.

to be taken, they say, in a spiritual sense. But the fact remains that the Nazis made of Nietzsche one of the philosophic supports of their way of life. Great attention was given to him in German periodicals in the 1930s and many short books appeared to explain him to ordinary Germans. Hitler himself paid several visits to the Nietzsche-Archiv, the Nietzsche library and museum in Weimar, and was photographed gazing in rapt veneration at a bust of the philosopher. Nazi writers could exclaim: 'When we call out to youth, marching under the swastika, "Heil Hitler!"—at the same time we greet with this call Friedrich Nietzsche!'[1]

There were many other contributors to the remarkable complex of German nationalist thought. The anti-Semitic element was clearly represented by Eugen Dühring, a lawyer, philosopher and economist, who was a lecturer in Berlin University immediately before Treitschke. Like Wagner and Treitschke, he attacked Jewish interests in the German Press. Treitschke wrote of it being 'nothing short of an outrage that Jewish influence should predominate today in our political Press'.[2] But Dühring went much further than criticism of Jewish Press interests. Among his philosophical and economic works, Dühring wrote *Die Judenfrage als Racen-, Sitten-, und Kulturfrage* (The Jewish Question as a Question of Race, Morals, and Culture) and asserted that society was in many places paralysed by moral poison. In this social degeneration he traced the influence of the Jews. 'What is the role', he asked, 'of the Jews in this corruption? . . . Where the Jews are to the fore, there is most corruption. This is a basic fact of all cultural history and cultural geography.'[3]

Of the protagonists of the Aryan or Nordic race theory the outstanding pioneers were, strangely enough, a Frenchman and an Englishman, Count de Gobineau and Houston Stewart Chamberlain. De Gobineau, an aristocrat, educated in Switzerland and spending much of his active life abroad in diplomatic posts in Eastern as well as in Western countries, was

[1] Quoted by Crane Brinton, *Nietzsche*, p. 209. See his whole chapter, 'Nietzsche and the Nazis', with the photograph referred to above.
[2] *Politics*, II, p. 31.
[3] *Die Judenfrage*, p. 7.

apparently a man of attractive qualities, a poet, and a sculptor, but imbued by his studies with a profound pessimism as to the outcome of human affairs. He saw mankind already in process of degeneration—a view not perhaps surprising in one who realized how slight was the layer of civilization in western Europe, and how deep were the levels of poverty, misery, and barbarism in the Orient and in South America. The key to history and civilization he found in race. When he published, in 1853-5, his volumes entitled *Essai sur l'inégalité des races humaines*, de Gobineau, in his dedication to George V, King of Hanover, stated his conviction that 'the racial question dominates all the other problems of history and holds the key to it, and that the inequality of races suffices to explain the whole unfolding of the destiny of the peoples'. A new racial group, he maintained, can radically transform a country previously sunk in torpor, and as an example of such transformation he named the Anglo-Saxon invasion of Britain, 'when Providence carried into that island some of the peoples ruled by Your Majesty's illustrious ancestors, and reserved for the future to these two branches of the same nation the rule of the same sovereign house' (i.e. Hanover).

De Gobineau commenced his study by considering the reasons for the fall of civilizations and, having dismissed most of the reasons generally suggested, found a new and deeper reason in what he claimed to be the permanent differences between races. He distinguished three basic races: black, yellow, and white. Of these three races, he set himself to show the superiority of the white race. The mixture of races, he argued, although it produced some good results in the realms of art and literature and was also the means of strengthening weaker races, had at the same time inevitably weakened the stronger races; it had led to confusion and weakness, and would lead ultimately to ruin—for this fatal process of intermixture had long been under way. The Brahmans of primitive India, the heroes of the *Iliad*, the Scandinavian warriors, 'such glorious phantoms of the finest races already vanished', were far more powerful agents of civilization than the mongrel races of today. Hence de Gobineau's pessimism—for the mixing of races, 'however bad it makes the present, prepares a future even worse'.[1]

As for the past, he wrote, 'history shows us that all civilization flows from the white race, that no civilization can exist without the co-operation of this race, and that a society is only great and brilliant in proportion as it preserves for a longer period the noble group which has created it'.[2] Of the white race the Aryans are the finest branch and, he asserted, no true civilization has existed in Europe except where they have been dominant.

To support his views, he proceeded to make a wide and detailed examination of the historical origins and migrations of the peoples. Far back in the mists of antiquity he distinguished in central Asia the Aryans—'this illustrious human family, the noblest among the white race'. Their name, Aryan, is the finest a race can have, for it means 'honourable' (and de Gobineau supposed that the root Ar was still preserved in the German word Ehre for 'honour'). The Aryans then 'were men of honour, worthy of esteem and respect, and ready, if men did not grant that respect, to take it. If this interpretation is not to be found strictly in the word, it is to be found in the facts.'[3]

This supremacy of the Aryans, in intelligence and energy, persisted, and de Gobineau singled out the German branch for special note. 'Placed upon a sort of pedestal, and separating himself from the environment in which he works, the Aryan German is a powerful creature . . . everything he thinks, says, and does, is thus of major importance.'[4] Wherever he marched and settled in Europe he brought vitality and the prospect of betterment. Thus the break-up of the Roman Empire at the hands of the Germanic tribes from the north, far from being a disaster, was a benefit to mankind. The Roman of the fourth century, degenerate by reason of his mongrel race, was well replaced, thought Gobineau, by the vital and powerful German.

Looking at Europe in his own day, Gobineau saw a

---

[1] *Inégalité des races humaines*, Vol. I, pp. 221 and 218.
[2] Ibid., p. 220.   [3] Ibid., pp. 367-70.   [4] Ibid., Vol. II, p. 365.

decadence which he regarded as the result of the fatal working of racial intermixture—in Italy, Spain, south-eastern Europe, and Russia. Pockets of Aryanism still postponed general decay —for example, in Switzerland, in the Tyrol, and in the Caucasus. 'The greatest abundance of life, the most considerable agglomeration of forces', however, he marked out as existing in the territories enclosed by a line stretching from the north of Sweden and enclosing Denmark, Hanover, the Rhineland as far as Basle, enveloping Alsace and Lorraine, and following the course of the Seine to cross the Channel, enclose Great Britain, and reach northwards to Iceland. In this north-westward part of Europe he found the last remnants of the Aryan race. 'It is there that beats the heart of society and, consequently, of modern civilization. This situation has never been analysed, explained or understood up to the present.'[1] Though Gobineau did not here view the modern Aryan in a narrowly German sense—and in fact the area he indicated excluded most of modern Germany—there were others who would in future place the Germans in the centre of the picture.

Gobineau's theories were taken up in Germany. Richard Wagner, the composer, was impressed by his racialism and met Gobineau in 1876, when the two men formed a friendship. Wagner thought that, although the Latin peoples and also the English had surpassed the Germans in cultural development, the Germans by reason of greater racial purity surpassed other people in the greatness of the leaders they produced. But he feared the Jews as a disintegrating element among the Germans, and, coupled with them, he attacked the Press and democracy. He attacked them as un-German, and stressed in his writings and his romantic operas everything German. He created for his musical public a romantic conception of age-old Germanic culture, of Teutonic gods and heroes. Wagner did try to combine his German racialism with Christianity, for the Germanic heroes who in future, he hoped, would strive against racial degeneration were to accept a kind of Germanized Christianity. But the danger to

[1] *Inégalité des races humaines*, Vol. I, pp. 491-2.

non-Germanic peoples in these vague, idealistic theories was never far below the surface.[1]

Wagner's popular success in creating a romantic ideal of Germanism coincided with the political and economic triumph of a Prussianized Germany after 1870. Indeed, it was the great wave of triumphant nationalism and 'beer-mug patriotism' that carried Wagner's operas to the height of their popularity. And personally linked to Wagner and his circle were the outstanding pioneers of Germanism, those who sought their model in the blond, Teutonic barbarian—de Gobineau, Nietzsche, and the Germanized Englishman, Houston Stewart Chamberlain, who wrote Wagner's life and, many years later, married his daughter.

Chamberlain was an extraordinary figure. The son of an admiral and nephew of a field-marshal and two generals, he was himself intended for the British Army. But his health made this career impossible, and he turned instead to studies and became as life went on an ever stronger exponent of Germanism; during the First World War he became a naturalized German. Born at Southsea in 1855, he went later to school in Versailles and then to Cheltenham College. He was removed from school for health reasons, and worked under a German tutor. He studied botany, geology, astronomy, and medical sciences at Geneva. Thence he went to Germany— to Dresden, where he plunged into the study of Wagner's writings and music. His own knowledge and powers developed: he could write freely in French and German as well as English, and in 1899 he produced his great work in German, *Grundlagen des Neunzehnten Jahrhunderts* (Foundations of the Nineteenth Century).

As the title indicates, the author's object was 'to reveal the bases upon which the nineteenth century rests'. He studied the history of the past: he examined the legacy of the ancient world and the story of its heirs, finding a turning-point about the year 1200 in the awakening of the Teutonic peoples, for

[1] Professor Maurice Boucher, in his *Idées politiques de Richard Wagner*, p. 6, has pointed out the mixture of conflicting ideas in Wagner. He could be claimed as a precursor of the Third Reich or of a pacific and humanitarian version of Communism.

'the inhabitants of northern Europe have become the makers of the world's history'.

Like de Gobineau, he regarded the Teutonic barbarians not as destroyers of the Roman Empire, but as saviours. 'It is untrue', he wrote, 'that the Teutonic barbarian conjured up the so-called "Night of the Middle Ages"; this night followed rather upon the intellectual and moral bankruptcy of the raceless chaos of humanity which the dying Roman Empire had nurtured; but for the Teuton, everlasting night would have settled upon the world.'[1] Unlike the pessimistic de Gobineau, however, Chamberlain, though he paid tribute to his 'brilliant work', looked forward to hopeful development in the future under Teutonic guidance. 'If', he says, 'we do not allow ourselves to be led astray in our sound judgement by Utopian conceptions of gradual improvement of mankind as a whole, and of political machinery working ideally, then we are justified in the hope and belief that we Teutonic peoples, and the peoples under our influence, are advancing towards a new harmonious culture.'[2]

Indeed, Chamberlain seems divided between the two views —or perhaps is seeking to reconcile them—that the original Aryan or Teutonic blood or race is of supreme value and the apparently opposite view that new and worthy races can be created. And, in contrast to Gobineau, he allows for the effect of historical and geographical conditions as well as the quality of the human material and the circumstances of selection and breeding in the production of races. 'The sound and normal evolution of man', he wrote, 'is therefore not from race to racelessness, but on the contrary from racelessness to even clearer distinctness of race.'[3] He admits that Slavs have largely interbred with Germans, but that has not weakened the Germans. What the Germans have become, the French learnt in 1870; they have learnt also to know the power of German science and scholarship. 'That is the valuable result of the creation of race by nation-building.' Race may be ennobled

[1] *Foundations of the Nineteenth Century* (trans. by J. Lees), Author's Introduction, p. xvii.
[2] Ibid., Author's Introduction, pp. xcvii-xcviii. Also Vol. I, p. 262 and p. 315.
[3] Ibid., p. 296.

or may degenerate, 'but the firm national union is the surest protection against going astray'.[1] Here Chamberlain is clearly paying tribute to the German State as a means of preserving Germanic racial qualities and passing them on unharmed or improved to the future.

But whatever the contradictions in his theories, Chamberlain thought race the most important factor in historical development. Men must be judged like race-horses and dogs. 'Nothing is so convincing', wrote Chamberlain, 'as the consciousness of the possession of race. The man who belongs to a distinct, pure race never loses the sense of it.' Chamberlain was not anti-Semitic in the ordinary sense, though he saw the Jews as an alien people over against the Germans. He praised the Jews for their racial purity, and quoted with approval Disraeli's novels *Tancred* and *Coningsby*, in the latter of which Sidonia says: 'Race is everything; there is no other truth. And every race must fall which carelessly suffers its blood to become mixed.'[2]

By the term 'Teutonic peoples', Chamberlain meant 'the different north-European races, which appear in history as Celts, Teutons (*Germanen*), and Slavs, and from whom— mostly by indeterminable mingling—the peoples of modern Europe are descended. It is certain that they belonged originally to a single family . . . but the Teuton in the narrower Tacitean sense of the word has proved himself so intellectually, morally and physically pre-eminent among his kinsmen that we are entitled to make his name summarily represent the whole family. The Teuton is the soul of our culture. . . . If we look around we see that the importance of each nation as a living power today is dependent upon the proportion of genuinely Teutonic blood in its population. . . . True history . . . begins at the moment when the Teuton with his masterful hand lays his grip upon the legacy of antiquity.'[3]

Of course, great claims have been made elsewhere for other races. Four years before the appearance of *Foundations of the*

---

[1] *Foundations of the Nineteenth Century*, p. 297.
[2] Ibid., p. 271. Also p. 269 and Author's Introduction, pp. lxxvii-lxxix.
[3] Ibid., p. 257.

Nineteenth Century another Chamberlain, by name Joseph, Colonial Secretary, said: 'I believe in the British race. I believe that the British race is the greatest of governing races that the world has ever seen.'[1] Rhodes put forward the widest claims. And the imperialist enthusiasm of Kipling had its day. The American struggle on the frontier with the Red Indians was a demonstration of a struggle for survival of a fierce and bloody kind. The Germans, however, seemed unable to outlive a period of early barbarism, whereas a feeling of moral responsibility came to influence the thoughts of those in power in England. Lord Curzon, Viceroy of India, said in 1904 of the British government in relation to the races of India: 'Subduing them not to the law of the sword, but to the rule of justice, bringing peace and order and good government to nearly one-tenth of the entire human race.'[2] Rhodes, too, thought of a permanent union of colonies and mother country as meaning 'eventually permanent peace in the world'.[3]

Houston Stewart Chamberlain idealized his barbarian heroes beyond measure—'those splendid "barbarians" glowing with youth, free, making their entry into history, endowed with all those qualities which fit them for the very highest places'. He pictured them as in eternal struggle with the non-Germans as heirs of the legacy of the ancient world. 'In the nineteenth century', he wrote, 'as in all former centuries, but, of course, with widely differing grouping and with constantly changing relative power, there stood side by side in Europe these "Heirs"— the chaos of half-breeds, relics of the former Roman Empire . . . —the Jews, and the Germans. No arguing about "humanity" can alter the fact that this means a struggle. When the struggle is not waged with cannon-balls, it goes on silently in the heart of society.' It goes on by marriages, by increased communications enabling further mixture of races, by the shifting of wealth. 'But this struggle, silent though it be, is above all others a struggle for life and death.'[4]

[1] *Foreign and Colonial Speeches* (1897), pp. 88-90.
[2] *The Times*, 21 July 1904. For these and other quotations, see G. Bennett, *The Concept of Empire*.
[3] Statement of faith as postscript to his will cf 1893, preserved by the Rhodes Trustees.
[4] *Foundations of the Nineteenth Century*, pp. 575-8.

Though Chamberlain had no following in his country of origin, in Germany his book was a great success and had a strong influence. Three editions were sold out in three years; it had gone through eight by 1909. Sixty thousand copies had been sold in Germany, and it was felt that an English translation was called for. In writing an introduction to the English edition, Lord Redesdale remarked upon how Chamberlain's learning as expressed in the book had 'ripened for the good of the world'.[1] How that was so is not exactly clear! But Chamberlain met and influenced the Kaiser, William II, who admitted the strong effect of Chamberlain's book upon him. They exchanged enthusiastic letters on the subject of Germany. 'Your Majesty and your subjects', wrote Chamberlain, 'have been born in a holy shrine. . . . God builds today upon the Germans alone. This is the knowledge, the certain truth, that has filled my soul for years.' And the Emperor replied: 'You sing the High Song of the German. . . . I invoke God's blessing . . . upon my comrade and ally in the fight for Germans against Rome, Jerusalem, etc.'[2]

The Wilhelmine era, as it was called, began with the accession in 1888 of William II. Two years later the Kaiser dropped Bismarck, and began to exercise a large degree of control over his chancellors. William was a flamboyant character, determined to cut a figure as the head of the great German Reich, and during this period the spirit of aggressive nationalism, imperialism, and anti-British feeling grew apace and gained ever stronger hold over Germany. Organizations, official and unofficial, were created to push German aims and ideals. There were the Press Bureau of the Foreign Office and the Publicity Bureau of the Naval Ministry; there were the Colonial League, the Navy League, and the Pan-German League, all of which had prominent members and powerful industrial backing. The Pan-German League, which was built up in the years 1886-94, put forward the widest claims, and its propaganda chief, Professor Ernst Hasse, published

[1] *Foundations of the Nineteenth Century*, Introduction, p. vi.
[2] See Wickham Steed, 'From Frederick the Great to Hitler: The Consistency of German Aims' (1938), in *International Affairs*, Vol. 17, pp. 667-8.

in 1905 his *Deutsche Politik*, in which he laid claim to Holland, Belgium, and western Russia. A British Foreign Office minute of 1906 by Eyre Crowe stated that 'There can be no doubt as to the immense popularity of the Pan-German movement and of the agitation carried on by the German Navy League. Both these organizations are inspired by bitter and often scurrilous hostility to Great Britain.' The minute was written on a dispatch from the British Minister in Munich which described the aims of the Pan-German League or Union. 'The Union begins by claiming all German-speaking peoples as of German kith and kin. It aspires to the ultimate inclusion of the German-speaking cantons of Switzerland, of the Baltic provinces of Russia, of parts of Belgium and Luxemburg, and most important of all, of Holland with her littoral and her colonies.' And the dispatch quoted the Union's weekly publication: 'The elevation of Germanism into Pan-Germanism is the necessary step in the evolution which has by successive stages witnessed the Brandenburg and Prussian States, the Zollverein, the North German Confederation, and, lastly, the German Empire.'[1]

Eyre Crowe of the Foreign Office, whose mother and wife were German and who was in close touch with German opinion, summed up the position in a lengthy and important memorandum in 1907. The German argument, as he put it, was: 'A healthy and powerful state like Germany, with its 60,000,000 inhabitants, must expand, it cannot stand still, it must have territories. . . . Necessity has no law. The world belongs to the strong.'[2]

Among German writers who produced nationalistic works[3] on war the most outstanding was General Friedrich von Bernhardi. He wrote in 1911 *Deutschland und der nächste Krieg* (Germany and the Next War). He echoed Nietzsche and Treitschke in his defence of war. He stressed the need of German expansion. 'Strong, healthy, and flourishing peoples

[1] *British Documents on the Origins of the War* (ed. Gooch and Temperley), III, pp. 350-5.
[2] Ibid., p. 405. The memorandum occupies pp. 396-420.
[3] For example, O. R. Tannenberg, *Grossdeutschland: die Arbeit des 20sten Jahrhunderts*, and E. Weber, *Krieg oder Frieden mit England?*

increase in numbers. From a given moment they require a constant expansion of their frontiers, they require new territory for the accommodation of their surplus population. Since almost every part of the globe is inhabited, new territory must as a rule be obtained at the cost of its possessors, i.e. by conquest which thus becomes a law of necessity.'[1] He regarded Great Britain as barring the way, and hence as an enemy. Peace with her was unlikely to last. Germans must instead keep in view the possibility of a war with England and arrange their political and military measures to face a dangerous future. In a later work, published in 1914, he described war as 'the highest expression of true civilization', and declared 'that war is a political necessity, and that it is fought in the interest of biological, social and moral progress'.[2] 'World power or downfall' were the alternatives confronting Germany in 1914.[3]

Both Bernhardi and Houston Stewart Chamberlain lived to see the downfall of their hopes in 1918. But both looked forward to a revival of German might. Continuity with the past was remarkable and alarming. Bernhardi in a new book, *Vom Kriege der Zukunft* (The War of the Future), complained that 'our present government has handed us over, tied and bound, to the power of our enemies'. But he hoped that Germans would once more 'look on war as it really is. It is most unlikely that I myself shall ever live to see that great day . . . yet I write comforting words for the future. . . . Germany will arise again; she has a great future before her.'[4] And in 1923 Chamberlain wrote to Hitler: 'You have mighty things to do. . . . My faith in Germanism had not wavered an instant, though my hope—I confess—was at a low ebb. With one stroke you have transformed the state of my soul. That in the hour of her deepest need Germany gives birth to a Hitler proves her vitality; as do the influences that emanate from him; for these two things—personality and influence—belong together. . . . May God protect you!'[5]

[1] Op. cit. (trans., A. H. Powles), p. 14.
[2] *Britain as Germany's Vassal* (trans., J. Ellis Barker), p. 105.
[3] See *The New Bernhardi*, published in 1915 in London.
[4] Op. cit. (trans., F. A. Holt), pp. 271-2.
[5] Quoted by Wickham Steed in *International Affairs*, Vol. 17, p. 669.

Hitler was to show himself the supreme megalomaniac. As Duesterberg, former deputy-leader of the nationalist organization, the *Stahlhelm*, later on, after the Second World War, expressed it:

Had not Nietzsche pointed to the Superman as the final human objective? And Hitler felt himself the Superman, for whom there was neither law nor morality, for whom Germany was only the springboard for his vast ambitions. He was to be the greatest statesman, the greatest general, the man-become-God for all time. What was a Hannibal, a Caesar, Alexander the Great, Frederick the Great, and Napoleon against him! What was Christ for Hitler! A little, long-forgotten Jew?[1]

[1] T. Duesterberg, *Der Stahlhelm und Hitler*, p. 9

PART TWO

The Rise of the Nazi Party

CHAPTER IV

VERSAILLES AND WEIMAR

HITLER emerged in the troubled post-war years as the fanatical champion of German nationalism, of that exaggerated nationalism which had already proved to be so powerful a factor in modern German history and German thought and the development of which had proved a menace to the freedom of the European nations. The violence of German nationalism was checked in 1918: at Versailles in the following year the Allies imposed a treaty of peace which they intended as a safeguard for the future; at Weimar the Germans themselves drew up a constitution for the new democratic republic. A little more than a month separated the signing of the Treaty of Versailles and the adoption of the Republican Constitution. They were produced at the same time—an unhappy time for Germany, and an unhappy fate was to link their fortunes in the future. Both became principal objects of Hitler's venom.

The defeat of Germany at the end of the First World War was the greatest possible shock to that highly organized military nation. Behind all the alleged injustices, wrongs, and grievances which German propaganda was to play up to the full lay concealed the unmentioned but fundamental grievance—that Germany lost the war. As a result of defeat Germany failed to gain that 'place in the sun' upon which the nationalists had set their hearts, and which the ordinary German had been taught to expect as a right. Instead the country was plunged into the political and economic chaos which was the inevitable concomitant of defeat. The advance of the Allies on the Western Front and the collapse of Bulgaria, Turkey, and Austria-Hungary had been followed by political revolution at home.

The revolution itself was a comparatively moderate affair.

By September 1918 military collapse was imminent, and at the beginning of October the commanding generals, Hindenburg and Ludendorff, were pressing for immediate armistice negotiations; they were also supporting a widening of the Government with a view, apparently, to shifting the onus of defeat from themselves to the Social Democrats, who would be needed to make a stable parliamentary majority. Early in the month a coalition Government was formed under Prince Max of Baden, and he begged the Social Democrat leaders, Ebert and Scheidemann, to join and bring their party behind the new Government. Ebert favoured such a course; Scheidemann was against it. 'No one', thought Scheidemann, 'could be expected at a moment of absolutely certain collapse to enter a bankrupt concern.'[1] But the Party Executive decided on participation, and the Social Democrats joined the government. On 3 October Prince Max sent his request for an armistice to President Wilson, and during the next month a number of communications passed between them.

Then on 3 November revolution broke out: the sailors at Kiel mutinied after a court-martial for refusal to sail on a desperate expedition into the English Channel; the disturbances spread among the factories, and workers' and soldiers' councils were formed on the Russian model. A demand grew up that the Kaiser should abdicate. President Wilson had intimated that the Allies would sooner negotiate with a democratic Germany than with the old order. Prince Max, realizing at last that he would be unable to resist this demand, himself advised abdication. On 9 November a general strike broke out in Berlin. Prince Max resigned, and handed over the reins of government to Ebert. On hearing of this, the Kaiser, who was at military H.Q. at Spa, fled to Holland on 10 November. Ebert, who now found himself in charge of a collapsing nation, formed a provisional government of six (including three minority or Independent Socialists, who later withdrew), and the Allied armistice terms were accepted on 11 November.

[1] L. Scheidemann, *Memoirs of a Social Democrat* (trans., J. E. Michell), II, p. 485.

Thus there was an armistice—but long months were to pass before a treaty of peace was signed and a new democratic constitution brought into force. Meanwhile, Germany was distracted: disturbances, revolutionary outbreaks, uncertainties of every kind. Look, for example, at the front page of the *Frankfurter Zeitung* for one relatively quiet day in 1919.[1] The German citizen who cast his eye over the page learned that the peace terms were now being printed, in a book of about 350 pages, and he read reports of President Wilson's intentions for the Saar, of the annexation of Danzig, that Germany was to lose all her colonies, and that Kiaochow (formerly leased to Germany by China) had been promised to Japan; from Berlin he received a report of Polish provocation, and of an impending Polish military attack on Posen and Upper Silesia; he read a letter from Prince Max of Baden to the Chairman of the British Red Cross appealing on behalf of German prisoners of war still in captivity, and pointing out that their treatment was deteriorating in French and Belgian camps; and he found, what perhaps touched him most closely of all, an account of the revolutionary struggle which had been going on in Germany's second largest state, Bavaria, since early in April. By private line from Bamberg came the news that the Government forces were now closing their ring around Munich, held by the Spartacists or Reds—but it had looked as though Red action in Bavaria might have been the signal for Communist uprising throughout Germany or even, as the newspaper had suggested the previous day, throughout western Europe.

It is not surprising that amid all this the minds of the Germans were distracted and distraught. And, in view of subsequent propaganda, certain things must be made clear before any further discussion of the Peace Treaty and the foundation of the German Republic. Since the First World War there has been intensive examination of the question of responsibility for that war, and there has been a tendency to lessen the share of responsibility attributed to Germany. But that is not to say that Germany was guiltless—as Hitler

[1] *Frankfurter Zeitung*, 2 May 1919.

pretended.[1] Whatever the exact share of responsibility may have been, there can be no doubt that Germany's share was considerable, and she could not therefore expect, if defeated, to escape lightly. She had shown very clearly herself what kind of a peace she would make when victorious—the treaties in 1918 of Brest-Litovsk with Russia and of Bucharest with Rumania, settlements by which Russia lost nearly a quarter of her land in Europe, was saddled with heavy financial liabilities, and was forced to disband her army, while Rumania both lost territory and fell under German economic domination. Germany was defeated in the field after four long years: the German generals realized that military collapse was inevitable and were taking steps towards an armistice *before* revolution at home took place. The 'stab in the back' explanation was invented later. As Scheidemann afterwards wrote: 'The guilty consciences of those laden with guilt later invented the "dagger thrust". The collapse was not the consequence of the revolution; it was the other way about: without the collapse, the revolution that broke out six weeks later would probably not have occurred.'[2] Indeed it would have been difficult to make any treaty which would have been satisfactory to Germany. Germany had fought the world so long as she saw the prospect of victory; Ludendorff's March offensive, after Germany had settled with her enemies in eastern Europe, came within reach of breaking the Allied Western Front. Only when Ludendorff had failed did he think it time for peace. For Ludendorff thought there could only be victory or defeat. The demand for peace by compromise he thought a crime.[3]

The Treaty of Versailles, which was signed on 28 June 1919, was the result of the labours during the preceding months of the Peace Conference in Paris, at which President Wilson of the United States, Clemenceau of France, and Lloyd George of Great Britain were the dominant figures. The Germans were not allowed to take part in the oral discussion—which

[1] Baynes, *Hitler's Speeches*, II, p. 1,156.
[2] *Memoirs of a Social Democrat*, II, p. 506.
[3] Scheidemann, op. cit., II, p. 469.

fact was the basis of the future description of the treaty as 'dictated'—but even without them the conference was not particularly peaceful. American idealism clashed against French realism with its overriding demand for security against Germany, and the French desire for a weak Germany found little support from a British tendency to let bygones be bygones and to visualize the eventual recovery of Germany as an important factor in the European economy. A series of violent crises occurred among the Allies themselves. If they made a bad treaty, that is not surprising; what is surprising is that they made a treaty at all (and, as it was, China did not sign and the U.S.A. did not ratify).

Not unnaturally the terms—when they were handed to the German delegation called to Versailles to receive them— were a heavy blow. The new Socialist Government found it difficult to get anyone who would go to Versailles to sign,[1] and armed opposition was considered; but the generals could only warn of disaster. The treaty, therefore, was signed. Under its terms Germany lost Alsace and Lorraine to France and also the ownership of the Saar mines, while the Saar territory was to be put under the government of a League of Nations commission; Germany lost several small frontier territories to Belgium, Posen to Poland, and part of Silesia (after plebiscite); northern Schleswig (after plebiscite) was returned to Denmark; German colonies were taken away and placed under League of Nations mandate; German armed forces were radically reduced, her fleet handed over, and the Rhineland permanently demilitarized and occupied by Allied forces for a term of years; part of her merchant fleet was given up; and, what proved most important of all, reparations payments of unfixed amount were to be paid as compensation to the Allies for the damage caused by German arms. It was undoubtedly the reparations provisions of the treaty which were most open to criticism. J. M. Keynes, then the Treasury representative at the Conference, pointed out that Germany

[1] See, for example, the *Berliner Tageblatt* of 25 June, which described the difficulty under a principal headline, '*Wer wird unterzeichnen?*'

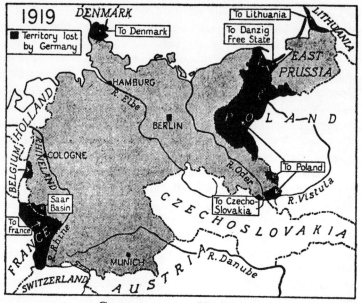

GERMANY AFTER VERSAILLES

would be unable to pay all of the vast sums demanded,[1] and he resigned his official position.

There are, in fact, only two ways in which payments can ultimately be made between states: one is in gold, the other by goods and services. When the payments are large, the small reserve of gold in a central bank is useless, and if payment is attempted by goods and services these compete with the industries of the receiving country and cause economic dislocation and consequent unemployment. In fact, Keynes did mention two possible methods of payment: (1) that German labour might be sent to France to reconstruct the zones devastated in the war; (2) that Germany might be built into a great industrial state again able to flood the markets of the world with exports and to create a surplus over her imports, out of which surplus reparations could be paid. But such suggestions were not easy of practical application: France had French labour, even unemployed,

[1] See his *Economic Consequences of the Peace* (1919), p. 134 and p. 154.

to set to work at home, and to build Germany once more into a great industrial state was what France wished to avoid. And so Keynes's advice and suggestions came to nothing. Reparations bedevilled relations with Germany for years; the attempt to make Germany pay led to French armed intervention in the Ruhr in 1923, and vastly embittered relations. During the years which followed an appearance of annual payments was kept up, but only because during these years of temporary recovery Germany was able to make large borrowings from the United States—indeed, it is estimated that, over all, Germany borrowed more than she paid. The whole intricate business finally broke down during the world slump of the 1930s, when even Great Britain, which was not actuated by the motives which might well have encouraged Germany to avoid payment, was unable to maintain her own payment of war debts to the United States.

But this is to look too far ahead. The immediate German reaction to the peace terms was one of anger, indignation and—real or pretended—disillusion. On the day of signature an article in the *Berliner Tageblatt* described the treaty as 'the document of disgrace'. Two days earlier the newspaper's special correspondent at Versailles had written:

> The world knows that we were forced by bloody pressure to undertake obligations beyond our strength and which effected an indelible disgrace to our feelings. Not on us falls the shame, if, under the threat of bombing and hunger, we are forced to set our signature to a document which binds us to the impossible and covers us with slander. By order of the Council of Four it is to be printed on Japan paper and bound in Morocco leather, so that it may for ever rest in the archives of France—a priceless, collector's edition. We are waiting to see if world history will suffer itself to be bound in morocco, and if the 'Big Four', who were strong enough for a forsaken and ruined Germany, will be strong enough to maintain for ever their work of wrath.[1]

The Nationalists in the National Assembly issued on the day of signature a statement violently denouncing the treaty,

[1] *Berliner Tageblatt*, 26 June 1919. Paul Bloch, *Nun muss Frieden sein*. The Council of Four: Wilson, Lloyd George, Clemenceau, and Orlando (Italy).

and attributing it to the democratic revolution. 'One cannot refuse to brand this treaty', ran their statement, 'as the fruit of revolution, which has disarmed the German people.'[1] At the same time, *Vorwärts*, the newspaper of the Social Democratic Party, condemned the treaty, but wrote more moderately. In a kind of manifesto, *An die Partei*, on its front page, the Socialist newspaper said:

> For almost five years German Social Democracy fought for the ending of the war and for a peace which should make possible between nations friendship and cultural emulation . . . a peace without annexations and indemnities. . . . Unfortunately until 9 November 1918 not Social Democracy but the Pan-Germans controlled the policy of our country. Therefore, there has come about, as the outcome for us of this war, the saddest peace that world history has ever seen, a peace which threatens to make the nations lasting enemies. . . .[2]

In the evening edition of the same day, the newspaper expressed the hope that the peace would not represent the lasting and final form of things, and referred scathingly to the nationalists:

> We dream not of a bloody *Revanche* like the Pan-German fools, who are now experiencing their 'justice' on their own bodies, but we hope and trust confidently in the victory of right. . . . Before us lies a struggle for the victory of right, not a battle with bloody weapons, but a battle of the spirit . . . on the day of triumph for wrong, we greet the coming peace of right, for which we are going to struggle shoulder to shoulder with our working-class brothers on the other side of the frontiers.[3]

On the following day the *Berliner Tageblatt* published a remarkable article by the Finance Minister, Dr. Dernburg. Like the rest, he condemned the treaty: 'Peace is signed, our cup is drained to the dregs.' But at the same time he made a striking admission:

[1] Reported by the *Frankfurter Zeitung*, 29 June 1919 (second edition).
[2] *Vorwärts*, 28 June 1919 (morning edition).
[3] Ibid. (evening edition).

The Right has certainly made for itself a comfortable position, in refusing to accept responsibility for results which must surely be of the worst kind for Germany's future. But we have to remind the Right that our enemies, both during the armistice period and in the making of the treaty, have worked after a Pan-German model. Not one, no not one, of the rapacious and oppressive clauses is without its precedent in the proposals which the Right and many of the National Liberals made during the war in preparation for a German victory.[1]

He went on to say that he felt the terms of the treaty could not be carried out; that German economic life would fail to recover, and that as a result Allied demands would not be satisfied. Therefore, he urged, its most oppressive terms must be modified as quickly as possible. To this end, he looked to the promised eventual entry of Germany into the League of Nations, and for an equality of status for Germany which could lead to discussion and argument. Meanwhile, he advised the Germans to abandon revolutionary ideas, devote themselves to hard work at home and co-operation between classes, and look once more to taking their place among the nations.

Wise counsel indeed! If all Germans could have come in time to think like that, how different the future would have been! There has, of course, been immense controversy about the treaty, both in Germany and outside. But whatever the shortcomings of the settlement may have been, whatever the sufferings which fell upon the Germans (to some extent also their sufferings must be discounted for Germans are masters of the art of organizing sympathy), certain things about the peace settlement stand out clearly enough. Germany was left intact as a sovereign state: she was not broken up into lesser units; she was not destroyed—nor did disarmament expose her to serious risks; no nation attacked her, once she set herself to the task of carrying out the terms of the treaty. Twenty years later she was ready to fight another world war. And it is by no means certain that a milder peace treaty would have avoided that war. The German philosopher-historian, Oswald

[1] *Berliner Tageblatt*, 29 June 1919.

Spengler, said: 'The legend that a mild peace would prevent a second world war would only have originated in heads that had never studied the German mind.'[1] Both Italy and Japan were on the winning side in 1918, but both became aggressors. The Germans at Brest-Litovsk and Bucharest, and in their various statements of war objectives, had given an idea of what a German peace would be like.[2] As the Social Democrats had put it in their manifesto, '*An die Partei*', in *Vorwärts*, they had struggled for nearly five years for a genuine peace, but power had not been in their hands. That obvious admission gave the show away: the Germans fought for four years, and as long as they had a chance of victory; then at the last moment they appeared to embrace Social Democracy, and expected a peace which would leave things much as before. Nevertheless, the Allies were perhaps, in view of subsequent events, not altogether wise. The treaty may have been just, but not altogether expedient. For somehow or other, if there was to be lasting peace, the Allies had to find some means of reconciliation with the Germans. With that object in view, the Social Democrats, then in power in Germany, many of them, like Ebert and Scheidemann, of working-class origin, who had striven for years for reconciliation between the nations, were the most hopeful people with whom to work. It was indeed a tragedy that the new democratic government had to bear the burden of the hated peace treaty; and that defeat and democracy were so closely associated in German minds.[3]

While the Peace Conference in Paris had been thrashing out the terms of the treaty, the provisional government in Germany was coping with further revolutionary outbreaks and with the task of framing a new democratic constitution. The majority of the Social Democrats were solidly nationalist in sympathy, some like Ebert himself having wished to retain the institution of monarchy, and they were determined to

[1] Quoted by Knight-Patterson, *Germany from Defeat to Conquest*, p. 591.
[2] See ibid., Chapter 2.
[3] The Germans were quick to notice—for example, in the *Frankfurter Zeitung*, 11 May and 29 June—that there were also some criticisms of the treaty in England and France.

save what they could of the ordered life of the old Germany. They were at once challenged by the extreme Left—some of the minority group or Independent Socialists and the Spartacus group (later the Communists). These latter aimed to make Germany, backed by Soviet Russia, a spearhead of world revolution. 'I saw', said Scheidemann, 'the Russian folly staring me in the face—the Bolshevist tyranny, the substitute for the tyranny of the Czars! No, no, Germany should not have that on top of all her other miseries.'[1] A number of bloody clashes took place: in Berlin, in Bavaria, and elsewhere. It was during the Berlin disturbances that two leading Communists, Liebknecht and Rosa Luxemburg, were killed in the streets while under arrest by the soldiers. To subdue the revolutionary workers, the provisional government had to co-operate very closely with the military authorities and use the armed forces and volunteer bodies of ex-officers to put down the mob. The Social Democrat leaders had before them the example of what had happened in Russia: they realized how Kerensky and the moderates of the first revolution had been overthrown by the second revolution of Lenin. They were determined to prevent any second revolution in Germany. They were ultimately successful. But success meant retaining most of the conservative forces of the old Germany: the influence of the generals, the former imperial civil service, the industrialists, and the great landlords in Prussia was still strong. There was a political, but no social revolution in Germany. The country simply lost its Emperor, and the states their dynasties; the country changed the form of its state from a monarchy to a republic.

After elections in January 1919 the new National Assembly was convoked in Weimar. The impression grew up abroad that Weimar had been selected in homage to Germany's greatest poet; that its selection meant a change from the military spirit of Berlin and Potsdam to the liberal traditions of Goethe. This, however, was not really the explanation. Ebert felt that at any cost the new Assembly must not meet in the present Red atmosphere of Berlin. Enquiries were made in

[1] Scheidemann, *Memoirs of a Social Democrat*, II, p. 581.

several towns, and it was found that Weimar possessed a good theatre which could very well be used for parliamentary meetings. And so Weimar was chosen.[1]

But at Weimar the Social Democrats—forming now a coalition government with the Centre and Democrat Parties—attempted to create a really democratic constitution for Germany. Seven months the work went on—draft and re-draft, meetings in committee, meetings in full session of the National Assembly, conferences with the states. Preuss, Minister of the Interior, a professor of law and a member of the Democrats, had the principal hand in the drafting. The constitution was promulgated on 11 August 1919. Germany remained a federation, with a Reich government and parliament for the whole nation, and governments and parliaments in each of the states. The new constitution, in fact, so far as political theory could provide, set up ultra-democratic machinery. 'The Germans', as an English writer pointed out in a study of the new post-war constitutions of Europe, 'have made use of all the devices new and old by which a democracy can express itself, and have sought at the same time to find room for the application of new theories. Cabinet government has been borrowed from England, the idea of a strong, popular president from America, direct legislation from Switzerland. The President and the Reichstag are to occupy a position of equal importance; both are representative of the sovereign people, each is to act as a counterpoise to the other; in cases of dispute the decision rests with the people. A referendum can be brought about by the decision of the President, or of a minority in the Reichstag, or on the demand of a section of the people themselves. The complication does not end here. The Reichstag is the chief legislative authority, but it is not the only representative assembly; a Reichsrat or second chamber has been established to represent the interests of the member-states and to serve as a check on the actions of the Reichstag, and an Economic Council to give expression to the needs of the industrial life of the nation.'[2]

[1] Scheidemann, *Memoirs of a Social Democrat*, II, p. 614.
[2] A. Headlam-Morley, *New Democratic Constitutions of Europe* (1929), p. 44.

The people was declared to be sovereign. 'The German Reich', the Constitution stated, 'is a republic. Political power emanates from the people.' Election to the Reichstag and to the state parliaments was to be by universal suffrage, with men and women being able to vote at the age of twenty. Unlike the method of election to Parliament in this country, there was an elaborate system of proportional representation, which was framed to prevent the wasting of votes and to allow representation to small parties standing for the point of view of tiny minorities. In accordance with liberal principles, the individual was guaranteed full democratic liberty. 'All Germans are equal before the law'; 'Personal liberty is inviolable'; 'The house of every German is his sanctuary and is inviolable'; 'Every German has a right . . . to express his opinion freely'; 'All Germans have the right to form associations or societies'; 'All inhabitants of the *Reich* enjoy complete liberty of belief and conscience'; and so on.

All this had the authentic Western, liberal stamp. Foreign opinion at the time was, not unnaturally, guarded. Foch and Clemenceau perceived the old German spirit taking on a new form.[1] In England *The Times* published a noncommittal leader which said: 'For English people the most interesting question is how far the Constitution holds out the promise of a real democratic change in the spirit and practice of German government.'[2] A French professor of constitutional law, not unsympathetic to the ideal of the new Constitution, stated: 'The political institutions of Germany are as strongly impregnated with the *democratic idea* as possible. The majority is sovereign. But there are minorities, to the right and to the left, that aspire to dictatorship.'[3]

That admirably summed up the position. The new Constitution represented what was best in Germany, and the coming years were to see a struggle for the German soul

---

[1] Their opinions are quoted in Knight-Patterson, *Germany from Defeat to Conquest*, p. 265.

[2] 16 August 1919.

[3] René Brunet, *The German Constitution* (trans., J. Gollomb, 1923—with text of Constitution).

between that best and the dark forces of ruthless nationalism which threatened it and ultimately overwhelmed it.

From the start the Republic was beset from both sides, from Left as well as Right, and the beginnings of German democracy were stormy. While the National Assembly was meeting at Weimar the revolutionary outbreaks in Berlin and elsewhere continued sporadically. In March once more Noske, the Social Democrat Minister of Defence, was successful in putting down a Communist rising in Berlin; in Bavaria ever since the first days of revolution the Communists had been struggling to gain complete control. Eventually a civil war broke out between the extremists and the moderate Socialists. The *Reich* Government did not interfere, but left the two Bavarian factions to fight it out; on 1 May the troops of the moderate Government entered Munich, where the extremists, after a fanatical resistance and the murder of the hostages they had seized, were overcome. Bloody retaliation followed.

During 1919 the threats to the Republic had come from the Left, and it was the Communists who had instigated armed insurrection. In 1920 the threat came from the Right. In March a nationalist, Dr. Kapp, supported by certain generals, some of their troops, and certain irregular forces, known as Freikorps, seized Berlin and declared Kapp as Imperial Chancellor. But the President, Ebert, and his Chancellor, Bauer, had escaped in time from Berlin, and fought back by calling the workers out on a general strike. It was a great success, bringing all business to a standstill in Berlin; important also was the fact that Kapp did not get support from the high officials of the *Reich* and state ministries or from the upper middle-class leaders.[1] After a few days Kapp fled to Sweden, his troops left the capital and the Government returned. But now the general strike movement itself got out of hand—and in the east end of Berlin there was talk of setting up a new German Communist republic. Communist risings took place in western Prussia, Bavaria, Wurtemburg, in Leipzig, and, most serious of all, in the Ruhr. Eventually, by an energetic use of the military forces available, the Government regained control.

[1] A. C. Grzesinski, *Inside Germany*, p. 101.

But conditions remained unsettled, and another symptom of the highly unsatisfactory character of German public life was the number of political murders which took place, in many cases the murderers escaping. The most notorious of the murders were those in 1921 of Erzberger, a former Minister of Finance who had concluded the Armistice in 1918, and in 1922 of Walter Rathenau, Minister for Foreign Affairs and a great industrialist, whose death aroused horror far outside the borders of Germany, and who was murdered by nationalist fanatics as a Jewish protagonist of peace, reconstruction, and democracy.

The Republic was attacked also by nationalist intellectuals, whose ideas were in line with the exaggerated Germanism of the nineteenth and early twentieth centuries. Once more the characteristic megalomania appears. Spengler, whose considerable historical work, *The Decline of the West*, set a certain fashion at the end of the war in the study of the rise and fall of civilizations, wrote other works in which he dealt with the crisis of his own time. 'In the heart of the people', he wrote, 'the Weimar Constitution is already doomed. Its completion was received with utter indifference.' What he looked for was a combination of a newly-interpreted Socialism with the old Prussianism. 'Let no one hold back who is born to rule. I appeal to the young. Become men! We want no more ideologues, no talk of education and world-citizenship and the spiritual mission of Germany. We need hardness and Socialist supermen. Socialism means might, might, and again might.'[1] And Moeller van den Bruck published his *Das Dritte Reich* in 1923, which foretold the third *Reich* of the Nazis although its author committed suicide before Hitler's movement had become of importance. He condemned the liberalism which, he asserted, had brought the defeat in 1918 and the Republic of Weimar. He called for a spiritual rebirth of the German national spirit; he called for a leader. Conservative traditions must be revived: Germany must return to 'a form far more truly German than western parliamentary government and party systems—leadership'.[2]

[1] *Preussentum und Socialismus*, p. 99. [2] Op. cit. (trans., E. D. Lorimer), p. 228.

Peace and democracy—the nationalists and Hitler tried their hardest to associate these things in the German mind with defeat. In one of his early speeches Hitler claimed that he and his supporters 'were the first to declare that this Peace Treaty was a crime':[1] not quite an accurate claim, for, as we have seen, in Germany the treaty was almost universally denounced. What Hitler did was to excite and inflame the existing feeling against the treaty. With the full force of his wild, brutal speeches he attacked the new German republic and the treaty it had signed. In a speech of April 1923, he attacked the 'Peace Treaty of Versailles as the perpetual curse of the November-Republic'. He cried:

> With this armistice begins the humiliation of Germany. If the Republic on the day of its foundation had appealed to the country: 'Germans, stand together! Up and resist the foe! The Fatherland, the Republic expects of you that you fight to your last breath', then millions who are now the enemies of the Republic would be fanatical Republicans. Today they are the foes of the Republic not because it is a Republic but because this Republic was founded at the moment when Germany was humiliated, because it so discredited the new flag that men's eyes turned regretfully towards the old flag.
>
> It was no Treaty of Peace which was signed, but a betrayal of peace.

And he went on to state the first and fundamental task of his new National-Socialist movement:

> It desires to make the German once more National, that his Fatherland shall stand for him above everything else. It desires to teach our people to understand afresh the truth of the old saying: He who will not be a hammer must be an anvil. An anvil are we to-day, and that anvil will be beaten until out of the anvil we fashion once more a hammer, a German sword.[2]

In those words was implicit the history of Germany during the next twenty-two years. Hitler revealed himself as the implacable enemy of the new democratic order in Germany and

[1] Baynes, I, p. 18 (speech of April 1922).   [2] Baynes, I, pp. 56-7.

of the Treaty of Peace with which it was associated. The Weimar Republic was born in troubled times, and it faced a troubled future. It did represent an attempt at a rational and peaceful control of German affairs; it did represent what was a middle way between the extremes of nationalism on the Right and Communism on the Left. And already, in those early years, Hitler saw that way as doomed. 'There are', he said in 1922, 'only two possibilities for Germany: do not imagine that the people will for ever go with the middle party, the party of compromise.' The people will turn, he argued, to 'either the Left: and then God help us! for it will lead us to complete destruction—to Bolshevism, or else it is a party of the Right which at the last, when the people is in utter despair . . . is determined for its part ruthlessly to seize the reins of power—that is the beginning of resistance'.[1]

[1] Baynes, I, p. 14.

CHAPTER V

THE BEGINNINGS OF THE PARTY

THE beginning of the National Socialist movement may be said to date from the day in September 1919 when Adolf Hitler became No. 7 of the committee members in the little group known as the German Workers' Party (*Deutsche Arbeiterpartei*). The group used to meet in the smaller and poorer Munich cafés. Without Hitler it would have remained a mere discussion group; with Hitler it grew and was transformed. Hitler was able to make brilliant use of the endemic unrest in the Bavarian capital to create a movement, which he succeeded later in making the mightiest political force in Germany and, indeed, in the world.

Hitler was still, in the early days of the movement, on the strength of his regiment; he received pay and rations until 1 April 1920. During 1919, while stationed in Munich, Hitler was assigned to political work in the army—to counteract the effect of socialist and democratic ideas among the troops. He was given a course of lectures on German politics, and was sent to investigate the activities of the German Workers' Party. At the meeting he attended, he spoke himself and won approval. In this way he came to join up with the strange little group whose meetings he first attended as an army agent. Among the members of the Party was the locksmith, Anton Drexler, who had started the movement and who aimed at giving it both a national and working-class character, and there was the journalist Karl Harrer: both were pushed into the background before long as Hitler himself rose to prominence. There were the writer Dietrich Eckart, a well-to-do man, and thus a financial blessing to the movement in its early days of poverty, and the civil engineer, Gottfried Feder, with his economic theory of the tyranny of interest; and there were Ernst Röhm, an officer on the staff of the

Army District Command in Munich, and later Alfred Rosenberg, the philosopher of the movement.

From the start Hitler made himself felt, although he had to struggle along with only a few marks to pay for multigraphing invitations to the Party's meetings. At first he spoke to small groups. He spoke in the famous Hofbräuhaus Keller in October to only 111 people. But early in 1920 he took over the propaganda work of the Party, began to organize things on a much larger scale, and presently could fill the largest halls, where according to Bavarian fashion the audience sat at rough-hewn tables and drank beer. To arrange such big meetings with the scanty funds available, Hitler had to overcome the opposition of the cautious inside the movement. His success in developing a bold policy was clear indication of his growing influence.

The new movement must also have a programme; Hitler, Drexler and Feder worked it out together. The first mass meeting was held on 24 February 1920 in the Festsaal of the Hofbräuhaus in Munich, and Hitler, in spite of considerable opposition, read out the programme, point by point, to the audience of about 2,000. As a result, the twenty-five points were held to have been accepted, and they came to be regarded as the Party's official programme.

The programme[1] demanded the union of all Germans in a Pan-German state according to the principle of self-determination, equal rights with other nations, the abrogation of the treaties of Versailles and St. Germain, and living space for the settlement of surplus population. The programme laid down special claims to citizenship for Germans, and excluded Jews and foreigners living in Germany; it asked for the expulsion of aliens who had come to Germany since 1914. On the economic side it asserted the duty of every citizen to work, declared that all unearned incomes should be abolished, and that the gains of war profiteers should be forfeited. It demanded that the State should take over trusts, and share in the profits of large industries. It asked for a greatly increased

[1] A translation is printed in Baynes, I, pp. 102-7. See also Konrad Heiden, *History of National Socialism*, pp. 10-16.

scale of provision for the aged, and for the proper maintenance of a sound middle class: to this latter end the large stores were to be brought under public control and rented to small tradesmen, and small tradesmen were to be preferred in obtaining all public supplies. It demanded agrarian reform, such as the expropriation without compensation of landowners when land was needed for national purposes and also the prevention of all speculation in land; and it declared that there should be the death penalty for traitors, usurers, and profiteers. It asked for educational reforms: school curricula to be made more practical, and free education for specially talented children; it asked for health reforms—maternity welfare centres, and compulsory games—and for a national army. The Press should be purified of foreign financial or other interests. There should be religious freedom; the Party itself stood for positive Christianity, and combatted Jewish materialism. And lastly, in order to secure these objects, the leaders of the Party asked for a strong central authority in the State.

The Party programme expressed the spirit of the time. It was a compromise between the nationalism of Hitler and the socialist idealism of Drexler and others. The programme served the needs of the moment; it appealed to socialist and idealistic elements. But it never possessed the importance which it might have had in a party founded on reason and argument. The real driving force in the Party's development was not the programme, but the personality of Hitler. And Hitler's one dominant aim was nationalist. Nevertheless, Hitler was to be embarrassed on more than one occasion by the socialism of his movement. But for the moment the programme served its purpose, and Hitler could exploit it to the full: it promised something for all. The Party now enlarged its name. In August 1920 the German Workers' Party added a prefix and became the National Socialist German Workers' Party (*Nationalsozialistische Deutsche Arbeiterpartei*). The name came to be commonly abbreviated as Nazi Party. There was now a party and a programme, and a Hitler to put them across. Hitler thus stepped into history as a master demagogue; he knew how to appeal to his audiences—and they grew in zeal and numbers. 'To be a leader', he said, 'means to be able to move masses.'[1]

Hitler's task was not only to move the masses, but to create a mass movement. His great meetings, in the Hofbräuhaus or the Zirkus Krone (the first in the Circus was early in 1921, with over 6,000 present), served a double purpose: they appealed to the crowd and won support, but at the same time they served as a powerful instrument of mass psychology. For they gave to his followers and supporters the feeling of belonging to a vast movement, whose success was certain by reason of its own size, power, and passionate strength of purpose; the meetings were a colossal exercise in mass suggestion. Hitler realized also the importance of organized terror and brutality—both in the defence of his own meetings from Red interference and in attack on the meetings of other political parties. The origin of the force of Brownshirts lay in the need for throwing-out squads to maintain order at the Nazi meetings. At first they wore swastika armlets. A little later he was able to put his men into brown uniforms, and teach them the special Nazi salute with extended arm and hand. This uniformed force was the S.A.—the *Sturmabteilung* (storm troops). Hitler expended much care in the design of a flag— a red flag with a black swastika in a white circle. Such were the symbols of the movement.[2] By their dress, discipline, and unmeasured violence in action the Nazis gained wide attention; they threw their Red opponents out of the Hofbräuhaus on one famous occasion (in November 1921) which became legendary in the history of the Party. On another occasion (October 1922), at a demonstration in the town of Coburg, 800 Nazis fought a running engagement in the streets with the Communists and Socialists.[3] It was a marked demonstration

[1] *Mein Kampf*, p. 474.

[2] *Mein Kampf*, pp. 406-11. See also pp. 397-8 and pp. 441-7. Photographs of Nazi rallies early in 1923 show the participants in civilian clothes, some in Bavarian national costume and with Swastika armlets. Large impressive Nazi flags were much in evidence (*Berliner Illustrierte Zeitung*, 4 February 1923). Also see ibid., 11 February, for a picture of Nazi children with swastika flags, and an article deploring the political indoctrination of youth by both Nazis and Communists.

[3] Kurt G. W. Ludecke, *I Knew Hitler*, pp. 85-92, gives a graphic account of it. Compare the tactics of the Blackshirts in Italy, 1919-22.

of Nazi determination to use violence to smash their opponents. And on this, and many other occasions, it succeeded. But to carry out its work of propaganda and action the Party must have funds and influential friends. From this point of view, the situation was not unfavourable. In the general reaction against Red violence in Bavaria, army officers and influential men, such as members of the Bavarian Government and judges, did not look askance at a party of the right which would fight the Communists. Captain Röhm, for example, on the staff of the District Command, was a man of ability who had influence in the army itself and with the Freikorps. Men who had belonged to such defence organizations, Röhm now pushed into the Nazi movement. Then Röhm's commanding officer, Major-General Ritter von Epp, was a supporter of the Party. He helped to raise funds to buy the Party a newspaper, the *Völkischer Beobachter* (Folkic, or Racist, Observer), in December 1920. With such support from the army—always so powerful a factor in German politics—Hitler had a strong initial advantage. And the very fact that Hitler was allowed to hold his great meetings and provoke political violence by his incendiary speeches shows that the Bavarian Government was either powerless or sympathetic, certainly not eager to suppress terrorism so long as it was directed against the Left.

Hitler also strengthened his hold over the Party. His methods had caused some resentment: Harrer resigned, and Drexler and others had severely criticized Hitler himself. But the Party could not do without him. In July 1921 the committee was thrust aside, Hitler was made President, and the rules of the organization were amended to give him unlimited power. He made his former sergeant-major, Max Amann, the manager of the business side of the Party, and Dietrich Eckart editor of the new newspaper. New offices were acquired, and slowly furniture and files, a typewriter and the telephone were installed. Through Eckart, who had a large circle of acquaintances in Munich and other parts of Germany, Hitler was introduced to wealthy people who could help the movement. There were the Bechsteins, the piano manufacturers. Then

Hitler visited the Wagners at Bayreuth, and Houston Stewart Chamberlain. Gradually Hitler became known. Other wealthy people helped him. Putzi Hanfstängl, of the rich Munich art publishers, who had studied in America and rowed in the Harvard boat, helped him—by advancing a loan in dollars, and charming him, when he could not sleep, by playing Wagner on the piano. Another Munich publishing family, the Bruckmanns, took to him, and the industrialist Aust introduced him to gatherings of business-men, to which he spoke and some of whom contributed to Party funds. From such sources, and from membership fees and collections at the mass meetings, came the early funds. Occasionally someone like Thyssen, of the great steel firm, Vereinigte Stahlwerke, made a large donation. But even so it is not easy to form a clear picture of how Hitler and some of the other Nazis lived during these years. There was a casual air about the early affairs of the Party. Kurt Ludecke, an adventurer who threw in his lot with Hitler, said that the Party organization in Munich 'lived from day to day financially, with no treasury to draw on for lecture-hall rents, printing costs, or the thousand-and-one expenses which threatened to swamp us . . . we never had money enough. Everything demanded outlays that were, compared to our exchequer, colossal. Many a time, posting the placards for some world-shattering meeting, we lacked money to pay for the poster.'[1] Ludecke himself, on Hitler's behalf, went to attempt to raise funds in the United States. He tried, but without success, to get money from Henry Ford, who was reported to be anti-Jewish. And he contacted the Grand Wizard of the Invisible Empire, the head of the Ku Klux Klan.[2]

Although Hitler had lost some of the earliest members of the organization, there were around him a growing number of men whose names, later on, were to be known throughout Europe. Apart from Eckart, Rosenberg (who later published his racial philosophy in the *Mythus des 20 Jahrhunderts*), and Röhm, there were now Hess and Göring. Rudolf Hess was a serious and devoted follower. A German, born in Alexandria,

[1] *I Knew Hitler*, p. 78.   [2] Ibid., pp. 180-96.

he had flown as a pilot in the First World War. Afterwards he became a student at Munich University, and while there fell under Hitler's spell. Hermann Göring, who had led the famous Richthofen Fighter Squadron and won Germany's highest decoration for bravery, had also been drawn to Munich with some idea of university studies. He, too, was moved to join the Nazis, and soon became commander of the S.A. There was Julius Streicher, a teacher in an elementary school in Nuremberg, who ran *Der Stürmer* (The Stormtrooper), a violently anti-Semitic paper. There were others also, who if less well known had nevertheless a certain notoriety: Hermann Esser, a young man of the worst moral reputation, Heinrich Hoffmann the photographer, Christian Weber, a chucker-out in a café, and Ulrich Graf, butcher and wrestler, who acted as personal bodyguard to Hitler.

Hitler, with his friends and followers around him and the Party movement behind him, felt his power and influence growing. He began to see himself and his movement as a real force in German politics. The condition of Germany four years after the Armistice was still unstable. The German Government had but narrowly survived the challenges from Left and Right, and the murders of Erzberger and Walther Rathenau demonstrated how bitter and ruthless was the opposition to the Republic. In Bavaria there were many changes of government, and democratic government itself was continually threatened. Things parliamentary were a subject for parody. A Munich cartoonist sketched a deputy who wound up his three-hour speech at last by saying: 'We cannot tell the Government too often: the people want deeds not words!'[1] The nationalist organizations, of which there were a number, worked loosely together, and in the summer of 1922 there were plans to overthrow both the Bavarian Government and the German Government in Berlin. Hitler and the S.A. were ready to march with the others, but this time the *Putsch* was called off. But the idea was in the air. In Italy, Mussolini showed the way. Again and again the Blackshirts, like the Nazis, had clashed with the Reds. And in October 1922 the

[1] *Simplicissimus*, 5 November 1923.

March on Rome of the Fascist squads had demonstrated that they meant business and induced the King to call on Mussolini to become head of the Government.

Hitler had now to play his part in the complicated inter-action of German federal politics and Bavarian state politics. The Bavarian Right-wing nationalist and Roman Catholic governments disliked the republican régime in Berlin; some Bavarians looked for a restoration of the Bavarian monarchy, and some even for a separation from Germany and a union with Austria. Hitler's aim, however, was quite different: he wanted a nationalist government in Berlin, and would hear nothing of Bavarian separatism. Thus the Bavarian Govern-ment was not unwilling to make use of Hitler's S.A. as an instrument against the Left Wing, but went no further with him; while Hitler wanted to use the Bavarian leaders, and the troops stationed there, to help him against the republican régime in Berlin. 'We want to call to account the November criminals of 1918. . . . No, we do not pardon; we demand— vengeance! The dishonouring of the nation must cease. For betrayers of the Fatherland and informers, the gallows is the proper place.'[1] The friction between Berlin and Munich gave Hitler his opportunity.

Meanwhile, the growing inflation and the French occupa-tion of the Ruhr were rendering the German situation des-perate. And a desperate situation provided the conditions in which success might be possible for the Nazis; under such conditions the Germans might be driven to accept a desperate remedy. The political uncertainty in Germany and the repara-tions for which the Allies asked (fixed in May 1921 at the equivalent of £6,600,000,000) gravely affected the country's economic position. The mark dropped seriously in 1921, and went on dropping. By late 1923 the mark was valueless. The following table indicates its fantastic collapse:

1 dollar = 4 marks, at the 1914 rate
January 1922: 1 dollar = 191 marks
January 1923: 1 dollar = 17,972 marks
November 1923: 1 dollar = 4,200,000,000 marks

[1] 18 September 1922: Baynes, Vol. I, p. 107.

The Germans found difficulty in making their reparations payments, and in January 1923 they were in default. The French thought the Germans could pay if they wanted to pay, and were determined to make them do so. So Poincaré moved French troops into the Ruhr Valley, an area containing four-fifths of Germany's remaining resources in coal and iron: French policy was to stay there until Germany decided to pay up. The result was that from January to August the Ruhr was the scene of an undeclared war. The German Government used the weapon of passive resistance: a general strike of the Ruhr workers, supported and financed by the Government. The French tried to run the Ruhr by force, and at the same time encouraged German separatists to aim at a separate Rhineland republic. Meanwhile, the hapless German people suffered; they queued for money outside the banks and for food outside the shops. They went out into the countryside to seek potatoes and to gather firewood. Children were evacuated from the occupied territory, the Scandinavian countries organized relief, and the illustrated Press made events in Rhineland and Ruhr known all over Germany. Hatred for the French and nationalistic feeling in Germany were accentuated. In the end the French won an empty victory: Germany made new undertakings to resume reparation payments, but meanwhile the catastrophic inflation had destroyed middle-class stability and assisted Hitler's movement of the extreme Right. Monetary savings of all kinds lost their value, and a disaster of this kind which hit at the thrifty, right down from the upper middle class to the workers, destroyed not only economic but psychological stability as well.

Hitler had now, as speedily as possible, to attempt to unite all the nationalist forces in Bavaria behind himself and also to secure the tacit assistance of the Bavarian Government and the District Command of the German Army in Bavaria. Then there might be a march on Berlin. He had no use for a movement of national unity against the French—unless he were in control. Many nationalists, including Röhm, did not see things as clearly as Hitler. They looked simply to any means of strengthening Germany against the French, and thought of the S.A. as simply an auxiliary to the army. Hitler thought the French, and the building of a German army to settle scores with them, could wait; the S.A. must first be used as a political force—to give Hitler control of Germany. He was thinking, he admitted later, of a *coup d'état*.[1] So Hitler redoubled his efforts. Meetings and demonstrations went on with increasing excitement. Röhm, early in 1923, was active in bringing about an alliance between the Nazis and four other nationalist organizations, the *Reichsflagge* (Reich Flag), the *Kampfverband Niederbayern* (Fighters' League of Lower Bavaria), the *Vaterländische Vereine München* (Fatherland Leagues of Munich), and the *Bund Oberland* (Oberland League). But the Bavarian Government was aware of this, and was suspicious; it naturally did not wish to commit itself to a movement which might be a failure. General von Lossow, the commanding officer in Bavaria, was also noncommittal, though Hitler called on him frequently. It was, in fact, still hard going for Hitler. A great Nazi concentration of some 20,000 storm-troopers on 1 May, which was intended to smash the Socialist and trade union May Day demonstration, had to be called off when the army intervened. A fiasco for Hitler; but nevertheless no action was taken against him for his threatened breach of the law. Hitler had failed; but he could try again. There was a pause in Nazi activities, but in September they were renewed. At a great rally in Nuremberg Hitler appeared side by side with Ludendorff—the hero of the nationalists. When Stresemann, the Chancellor, on 26 September called off the passive resistance in the Ruhr, Hitler fiercely attacked his action as surrender to the enemy. Stresemann's action was wise in itself, but it stirred the nationalists to extreme action: the S.A. men were made ready. The Bavarian Government, realizing that crisis was near, declared a state of emergency, and appointed the Right-wing politician, Gustav von Kahr, as state commissioner with full power. Nazi meetings were banned. At the same time the Reich Government itself was menaced: from Left and Right, in many parts of Germany. For example, in Saxony and Thuringia

[1] Speech at Munich in 1936: Baynes, Vol. I, p. 154.

the state governments included Communists as well as Socialists, and in Bavaria there was Hitler and also the uncertain von Kahr, who might take an independent course of action in keeping with his Bavarian monarchist and particularist sympathies. Von Kahr, indeed, made to a Press conference ambiguous statements, such as: 'The monarchy will not be recalled, but it may grow and come of itself.'[1] The Reich President, Ebert, gave emergency powers to the Minister of Defence, Gessler, and the Commander-in-Chief, General von Seeckt, whose aim was to maintain order and so prevent civil war.

Putting it briefly, there were three main forces involved: the Reich; the Bavarian Government of von Kahr together with the district commander of the army, General von Lossow; and Hitler. In their struggle with the central government, either von Kahr or Hitler might use the other for his own ends. Relations between the Reich and Bavaria grew worse in October, when Berlin demanded the suppression of the *Völkischer Beobachter* and the arrest of certain nationalists for their abusive attacks on Stresemann, Seeckt, and Gessler. Von Kahr refused to take orders from Berlin, won over von Lossow, and organized armed resistance. Would Munich march on Berlin, or Berlin on Munich?

But still von Kahr delayed. And meanwhile the Reich Government was dealing not unsuccessfully with its difficulties. If the national crisis were passed, the Bavarian leaders would never dare to act. Or at least they would content themselves with some move towards Bavarian independence, which was not at all what Hitler wanted, and abandon any idea of a national revolution for all Germany. Hitler must force von Kahr's hand.

Several plans were made, and given up under the effect of changing events. But on the evening of 8 November 1923 von Kahr spoke at a big meeting in the Bürgerbräu Keller, in the outer part of the city beyond the River Isar, and Lossow and Seisser, commander of the state police, were present with him. It was an important meeting; most of the Bavarian

[1] *Vorwärts*, 2 October 1928.

Cabinet and many nationalist politicians were there. Hitler thought that this meeting was to declare Bavarian independence. He must act at once, and the gathering together of Bavarian leaders at their meeting offered an opportunity. As von Kahr was speaking, S.A. men surrounded the hall. This action was made easier by the fact that Hitler had some useful influence with the police: among his supporters was the former Munich police chief, Pöhner, and also Frick, an official in the police department. When this preparatory action was complete, Hitler rushed into the hall, and with a band of armed men moved towards the platform. The 'beer-hall *Putsch*' had begun.[1]

Hitler raised his revolver, fired two shots at the ceiling to demand quiet, and, while Kahr and those around him were still dumbfounded at the sudden interruption, shouted from the platform:

> The National Revolution has begun. Six hundred armed men are covering the hall. No one may leave. . . . The Bavarian Government is deposed. The Reich Government is deposed. A provisional Reich Government has been formed. The barracks of the army and of the police are occupied; the troops and the police are already moving under the swastika flag.

Hitler's bluff worked. Next, leaving Göring to speak to the crowd, Hitler drew Kahr, Lossow, and Seisser into a side-room, where he and Pöhner begged them to join the national revolution. Hitler was half-mad with excitement; he brandished his revolver and threatened them: four bullets, he said, were left—three for them and one for himself—if they failed to support him. Trapped as the trio were, they played for time. Then Ludendorff arrived—summoned only a short time before in the name of Germany—and his arrival turned the situation in Hitler's favour. Together they all returned to the

---

[1] A full account was given in the subsequent court proceedings, *Der Hitler-Prozess vor dem Volksgericht in München* (2 parts; Knorr and Hirth, Munich, 1924). Also vividly described by Ludecke, *I Knew Hitler*, Chapter 10. He was not an eyewitness, but built up his own version of the facts shortly afterwards from detailed conversation with Göring and others, adding further touches from later talks with Rosenberg, Röhm, Amann, Pöhner, and Hitler himself.

platform, and Hitler announced—to loud cheers—that all would co-operate with him in a new, national government for Germany.

Meanwhile the men of the S.A. and other allied nationalist organizations had been mobilized and informed that the long-expected national revolution was beginning. Röhm seized the War Ministry, close to the city's principal avenue, the Ludwig-strasse, and proceeded to set up defences with barbed wire and machine-guns. The main nationalist forces marched through a city of cheering crowds to the Bürgerbräu Keller where, on the floor and in the gardens, they made their quarters for the night. So far so good: Hitler and his nationalist allies appeared to be in control of the city.

But after the meeting at the Bürgerbräu, Hitler made the mistake of leaving to deal with matters elsewhere. Once he was gone, Kahr, Lossow, and Seisser had managed to slip away. Now they began to see things in a different light. Angry messages came by telegraph from Berlin. Crown Prince Rupprecht, the representative of the deposed Bavarian royal family of the Wittelsbachs, sent an appeal to officers not to join. In spite of much sympathy among young officers for Hitler and Röhm, the higher-ups stood firm. Army discipline held, and Kahr and Lossow now began to organize counter-action.

On the next morning, 9 November, Hitler and his forces were still in the Bürgerbräu, and Röhm was still holding the War Ministry, although he was now besieged by regular troops. Ludendorff, who was convinced the army would never fire on their old leader, and Hitler now decided on a march into the city to win back Kahr, Lossow, and Seisser and the Munich populace; they counted on a great popular demonstration to allow them to establish control over the city. But while Hitler was making his plans for a march, the authorities had brought in regular troops from outside. Together with the police, they took up positions and put up machine-guns. Tension was acute—but even at the War Ministry each side hesitated to open fire, for there were very mixed feelings on both sides.

Then, soon after eleven o'clock, the march started. A column of several thousand men, with rifles slung across their backs, left the Bürgerbräu, and marched across the river by the Ludwig Bridge—brushing the police aside—towards the centre of the city. Hitler, Ludendorff, and other leaders were at the head, and the swastika flag was flying. The column reached the centre of the city, passing through the Marienplatz, thronged by the crowds, towards the Odeonsplatz and the Ludwigstrasse, which was blocked by troops. Near the Feldhernhalle the Bavarian state police barred the way. The column approached at about 12.30. 'Halt!' shouted the police, but the Nazis tried to brush them aside as they had done at the bridge. 'Don't shoot. Ludendorff and Hitler are coming', cried one of the Nazis. But a volley rang out. Sixteen Nazis were killed: Hitler fell to the ground, Göring was wounded, Ludendorff marched on, erect and fearless, and was arrested. In panic, the crowds and the procession broke up and dispersed. Hitler was pushed into a car by his friends and driven off, to be arrested later. Göring was got across the Austrian frontier by his wife, and into hospital at Innsbruck. In the afternoon, Röhm surrendered, in the War Ministry. The *Putsch*, the national revolution, was over.

The basic reason for Hitler's failure was that an opposition, which Hitler in his enthusiasm had never clearly visualized, had materialized. He had counted on carrying the Bavarian authorities; and the army with them, by a bold and sudden stroke; he had not counted on the need for fighting a civil war.[1] Thus when the police volley rang out and his fellow-Nazis collapsed around him, his dream was broken.

Now the Nazi Party was suppressed, and, in February 1924 Hitler, Ludendorff, and others were put on trial for high treason before a special court in Munich. They were accused of having attempted to overthrow by violence the Bavarian Government and the Reich Government. But the position was a difficult one: the chief witnesses for the prosecution,

[1] Yet with the long run of revolts and disturbances civil war was in the air. 'Haven't you had enough of war?' cried a mother on finding the nursery divided by barricades. 'We're not playing soldiers; only civil war', answered the children (in *Simplicissimus*, 12 November 1923).

Kahr, Lossow, and Seisser, had been implicated; the Bavarian authorities were not anxious for publicity; Franz Gürtner, Minister of Justice, was a friend of Hitler, and saw to it that the judges were lenient. Hitler took full advantage of this situation. It afforded him a valuable publicity. The President of the Court referred to his military decoration and bravery in the field. Hitler himself was allowed to give a full account of his career and his aims. He showed good spirit, took the lead, and in a trial which lasted over three weeks spoke out boldly and became a national figure in the Press. He took full responsibility for attempting to overthrow the republic—but then, he pointed out, Kahr, Lossow, Seisser had all been with him in this, they had all talked it over together. Hitler said that it was remarkable that he who had shown blind obedience for six years in the Army should now be found opposing the State. The reason went back to his youth in Vienna: 'I left Vienna as an absolute anti-Semite, as the deadly enemy of the whole Marxist conception.' He had formed the opinion during the war that, unless radically dealt with, Marxism would be the ruin of Germany. The German revolution of 1918, he declared, was treason—'a common crime, a stab in the back of the German nation'. Therefore the National Socialist movement was resolved that Marxism must be fought to the end. He went through the events of recent months leading up to his *Putsch*, and concluded:

> I alone bear the responsibility. But I am not because of that a criminal. There can be no high treason against the traitors of 1918. . . . I feel myself not a traitor, but a German who wished the best for his people.[1]

Indeed, Hitler won much sympathy at the trial, and he was treated very lightly. The outcome was that Ludendorff was acquitted, and Hitler received the minimum sentence of five years' fortress detention. A number of other sentenced Nazis joined him there—in the obsolete fortress at Landsberg—and Hitler spent a period of comfort and healthy living, with

[1] *Der Hitler-Prozess*, Part 1, p. 28. See also Hitler's closing speech, Part 2, pp. 85-91.

ample food, rest, and exercise in the garden. And in fact, Hitler served only part of his sentence—less than nine months. He was allowed to receive visitors, to read and write, and the time was sufficient to get him well into the writing of his book —*Mein Kampf*. In that book Hitler was to tell the story of his early days of struggle, and how the passion of German nationalism developed in him; he was to describe his despair at the Armistice and revolution in 1918, and his determination to strive for the destruction of Marxism and to work for the creation of a new Germany.

CHAPTER VI

THE PERSONALITY AND IDEAS OF HITLER

'DARKNESS surrounded me', Hitler wrote in *Mein Kampf* when he described his feelings on hearing, while in hospital in Pomerania, that Germany had accepted the Armistice. 'Darkness surrounded me as I staggered and stumbled back to my ward and buried my aching head between the blankets and pillow.' Hitler wept. Germany had been betrayed, it seemed, and all had been in vain—'in vain all the sacrifices and privations, in vain the hunger and thirst for endless months, in vain those hours that we stuck to our posts though the fear of death gripped our souls, and in vain the deaths of two millions who fell in discharging this duty'. Surely, he thought, those heroes must return and take vengeance on the new rulers of Germany who had brought the war to this disastrous end. 'Was it for this? . . . Was this meant to be the fruits of the sacrifice which German mothers made for their Fatherland when, with heavy hearts, they said goodbye to their sons, who never returned? Has all this been done in order to enable a gang of despicable criminals to lay hands on the Fatherland?' The soldiers at the front had fought without counting the cost—but behind the lines the Socialists had betrayed them, and surrendered. 'Was this then what the German soldier struggled for? . . . Was it for this that he lived through an inferno of artillery bombardments, lay gasping and choking during gas attacks, neither flinching nor faltering, but remaining staunch to the thought of defending the Fatherland against the enemy? . . . And at home? . . . What a gang of despicable and depraved criminals!'[1]

During the following days and nights in hospital Hitler lived through a fever of despair. His hatred of Germany's enemies increased, especially, as he said himself, 'hatred

[1] *Mein Kampf* (English unexpurgated edition, 1939), pp. 176-8.

for the originators of this dastardly crime'. When Germany's defeat took clearer shape in the Treaty of Versailles, Hitler found something tangible to attack. He was like a man possessed. Often moody, silent, and awkward, he would spring to life whenever the subject was mentioned. Gradually his fanaticism and his tireless pursuit of nationalist objectives won him attention. Sometimes out of curiosity, rich people would invite him to their houses. Once on such a visit in Garmisch, on a Sunday afternoon in 1921, he arrived in his dirty trench-coat and sat for an hour or so, silent and awkward. Then the conversation turned to the treaty. As if by a miracle, Hitler sprang up and began one of his long tirades. Next day his new friends went to hear him speak at a public meeting in Munich. His attack on the Treaty of Versailles won him applause. And already he was beginning to exercise his charm over wealthy and influential women. A certain countess, whose family helped him during these early days, was heard to say after the meeting: 'Isn't he great? My admiration for him is so strong that I wear his picture in my locket.'

Yet so far Hitler had given few signs of greatness. All that marked him out was a certain eccentricity among his fellows; otherwise he had failed to find regular employment and make any kind of position for himself, and his origins and early life were humble and obscure. He was born in 1889 at Braunau-on-the-Inn, a little Austrian town on the frontier with Germany, where his father was a Customs official. Of peasant stock in a countryside where intermarriage and also the birth of children out of wedlock were common, Hitler's father was an illegitimate son, and, taking his mother's name, was known for many years as Alois Schicklgruber. But he was subsequently legitimized and used the name of Hitler. Adolf Hitler himself was never known by any other name. The domestic life of Hitler's father was not happy or regular; he was married three times, and had two families. Adolf Hitler was the third child of the third marriage; his mother was his father's second cousin, and twenty-three years younger than her husband.

Hitler was sent to the Realschule, a secondary school in

Linz. His father wanted to make him a civil servant, but Hitler hankered after becoming an artist. The record is uncertain, but it seems that Hitler was unsuccessful at school. Then his father died in 1903. Hitler's mother managed to keep him at school; and it seems that he studied art, but he failed to gain admission into either an academy of art or of architecture. His ambitions were frustrated, and at the end of 1908 his mother died and Hitler was left to fend for himself. He betook himself to Vienna.

The years in Vienna, from 1909 to 1913, were the hardest and unhappiest in Hitler's life. It is certain that he suffered deeply —not only from unemployment and poverty, but also from isolation, a poor, untrained young man as he was, alone and friendless in the great capital city of Vienna, where the splendid buildings and commercial prosperity contrasted with his own misery. His accommodation was of the poorest, in doss-houses or in the home for men in the Meldemannstrasse in the 20th District. An account has been given of Hitler sitting on his bed while his clothes were being cleaned of lice, and also of his shovelling snow in the streets and suffering from the cold, for he had no overcoat.[1] He worked at various jobs as a casual labourer and a builder's assistant, and also painted cards and small views which he sold. He lived a hand-to-mouth existence. Those few who recalled him later on have portrayed him as disliking regular work, excitable and despondent by turns, but with energy and ambition which could be called up on occasion. He did not smoke or drink; he was then too shy and awkward in his ways to have any success with women. He spent much of his time reading newspapers and talking politics. And he read widely but unsystematically, borrowing books on many different subjects from the public library.

In 1913 he moved to Munich. He said himself that he was happy there, but his mode of life seems to have been much the same. Then, in the next year, came the war. Hitler volunteered at once, though an Austrian, for service in the Bavarian Army. The war for Hitler was salvation: it was the way out

[1] R. Olden, *Hitler the Pawn*, pp. 45, 46.

of failure and frustration. Though he never rose above the rank of corporal, he won the Iron Cross and is reported to have been a brave soldier. The war hardened and confirmed his ideas, and in its aftermath he was launched upon his extraordinary political career.

Hitler began clearly to form for himself his romantic sense of his mission to rebuild Germany—a romantic conception, but one he was to carry out with the greatest realism. In the midst of national disillusion and decay Hitler found for himself an objective to which he could devote all his energies. And not only could he create this sense of purpose for himself; he could give it to others. One of his early followers described his emotions on first hearing Hitler at a mass meeting in 1922: 'His words were like a scourge. When he spoke of the disgrace of Germany, I felt ready to spring on any enemy . . . glancing round, I saw that his magnetism was holding these thousands as one. . . . I was a man of thirty-two, weary of disgust and disillusionment, a wanderer seeking a cause; a patriot without a channel for his patriotism, a yearner after the heroic without a hero. The intense will of the man, the passion of his sincerity, seemed to flow from him into me. I experienced an exaltation that could be likened only to religious conversion. . . . I felt sure that no one who had heard Hitler that afternoon could doubt that he was the man of destiny, the vitalizing force in the future of Germany. . . . I had given him my soul.'[1]

Such was Hitler's personal force of magnetism. His ideas were shouted to vast audiences in his hundreds of speeches. He also put his ideas into writing in his remarkable book.

Hitler's *Mein Kampf*, the first volume of which was published in June 1925, is remarkable because it set out then ideas and policies which later, in spite of the greatest difficulties and obstacles, Hitler was able to carry out in practice. The book is an exposition of Hitler's fundamental ideas and at the same time a revelation of its author's personality. The reader feels the force, drive, and ruthless use of both prejudice and reason; the ideas are those of a powerful and

[1] Ludecke, *I Knew Hitler*, pp. 22-5.

original character, if not of an original thinker. The material, however, is badly arranged and scattered, for the author jumps from one subject to another with little attempt to provide a systematic study or a steady framework for his ideas. The book is repetitive, and too long. Scornful as he shows himself again and again of the academic type of mind, the university professor, and the bourgeois thinker, his own work shows clearly enough the intellectual failings of the self- and half-educated man. His thought is undisciplined, he is careless of anything which does not support his case, and he exaggerates wildly. Yet force and logic are there—particularly effective when he is criticizing the weaknesses and follies of others.

On the first page of his book, Hitler clearly expressed his fundamental aims: first, Germany and Austria must be re-united, and this on the simple racial principle that 'people of the same blood should be in the same Reich'; next, when all Germans are embraced by one Reich, if that territory is insufficient to assure them a livelihood, 'then can the moral right arise, from the need of the people, to acquire foreign territory. The plough is then the sword; and the tears of war will produce the daily bread for generations to come.' These sweeping aims, so simply stated, Hitler saw not as the expression of an academic or theoretical policy but as the essence of his personal life and mission. He saw his birthplace, the little frontier town of Braunau-on-the-Inn, as the symbol of a great task. Braunau, on the frontier of Austria and Germany, called him to what seemed his life's work—'in the pursuit of which every possible means should be employed'.

'Every possible means'—again on the first page, and indeed in the first paragraph—this phrase indicates the methods of complete ruthlessness which the author was prepared to use to achieve his ends. Page after page shows Hitler's belief in power, in both will power and physical force. Like the many Germanic thinkers before him, though he only mentions by name the military writer Clausewitz and Houston Stewart Chamberlain, he was imbued with the conception of life as a struggle and of power as the means to victory. Life was a 'world of everlasting struggle, where one creature feeds on the other and where the death of the weaker implies the life of the stronger'.[1] Hitler regarded the great days of German history as a demonstration of the successful development of power politics, for 'Germany herself was a magnificent example of an empire that had been built up purely by a policy of power. Prussia, which was the generative cell of the German Empire, had been created by brilliant heroic deeds and not by a financial or commercial compact. And the Empire itself was but the magnificent recompense for a leadership that had been conducted on a policy of power and military valour.'[2] Like so many Germans, Hitler was entirely won over by the success of Bismarck in creating a united Reich and laying the foundations of a mighty Germany; he was ready wholeheartedly to approve Bismarck's methods. Nothing succeeds like success; if war brought success, then nothing succeeded like war. 'The Second Reich', wrote Hitler, 'was founded in circumstances of such dazzling splendour that the whole nation had become entranced and exalted by it. Following an unparalleled series of victories, that Empire was handed over as the guerdon of immortal heroism to the children and grandchildren of the heroes. . . . When its foundations were laid the accompanying music was not the chatter of parliamentary debates, but the thunder and boom of war along the battle front that encircled Paris. . . . Bismarck's State was not founded on treason and assassination by deserters and shirkers, but by the regiments that had fought at the front. This unique birth and baptism of fire sufficed of themselves to surround the Second Empire with an aureole of historical splendour such as few of the older states could lay claim to.'[3]

Struggle and battle must lay the foundation. Then, and only then, thought Hitler, could economic development and prosperity follow. 'And what an ascension then began! A position of independence in regard to the outside world guaranteed the means of livelihood at home. The nation increased in numbers and in worldly wealth. The honour of the State and therewith the honour of the people as a whole were secured and protected by an army which was the most striking

[1] *Mein Kampf*, p. 550. See also p. 124.   [2] Ibid., p. 139.   [3] Ibid., p. 193.

109

witness of the difference between the new Reich and the old German Confederation.'[1] To take up the work again where it had been abandoned, as Hitler thought, shamefully by the November revolutionaries was the task of the National Socialist movement. 'If in its historical development the German people had possessed the unity of herd instinct by which other peoples have so much benefited, then the German Reich would probably be mistress of the globe today.'[2] And in its struggle for national expansion the movement must be ever conscious that Germans 'are members of the highest species of humanity on this earth, that we have a correspondingly high duty and that we shall fulfil this duty only if we inspire the German people with the racial idea, so that they will occupy themselves not merely with the breeding of good dogs and horses and cats, but also care for the purity of their own blood'.[3]

These political ideas and the way they are expressed all bear the unmistakable stamp of Hitler's strong personality; indeed, they are feelings rather than thoughts, and they are part and parcel of his being. There is an emotionalism about Hitler's character which is betrayed, not only by the fanaticism and hysteria which he displayed in his career, but also by what he wrote. He shows himself as a romantic in his idealization of the German race and of military valour as displayed in war—as a romantic, but at the same time as a deadly realist in his judgement of possibilities and policies and in the ruthlessness of the means he advocated for achieving his ends. Throughout the account he gives of his life he provides glimpses of the direct personal impact upon him of the great events he experienced or studied. Among his father's books he discovered a popular history of the Franco-Prussian War. These two volumes of an illustrated periodical of the years 1870-1 became his favourite reading, and he developed an enthusiastic interest in war.[4] He watched the Boer War, 'even though from so great a distance', with enthusiasm, for here was a war on the horizon of his own life.[5] Perhaps, after

[1] *Mein Kampf*, pp. 193-4.   [2] Ibid., pp. 332-3.   [3] Ibid., p. 526.
[4] Ibid., p. 20.   [5] Ibid., p. 142.

all, events would show that he too had been born in an age comparable with those he read of in history, and was not destined to live out his days in an age of peaceful competition among the nations. At the Realschule his history teacher awoke an interest in the glorious past—'when we listened to him we became afire with enthusiasm and we were sometimes moved even to tears'. History became Hitler's favourite subject; he was filled with admiration of German greatness in the past and with dreams of German greatness in the future.[1] His visits to Wagner's operas—he recalls his first visit to *Lohengrin*—and his wish to be an artist, what he saw of architectural beauty in Munich and Vienna, the first glimpse of the Rhine when the whole troop train burst into the strains of *Die Wacht am Rhein*, a return when wounded in 1916 to the sacred soil of Germany—all these experiences were unforgettable to Hitler and deepened his passionate feeling for the Germanic homeland.

During his years of poverty and suffering in Vienna, when, untrained and unskilled, Hitler had to plunge into a personal struggle for survival, he formed some of his strongest impressions. 'Vienna', he wrote, 'was a hard school for me; but it taught me the most profound lessons of my life. . . . In Vienna I acquired the foundations of a *Weltanschauung*. . . . That *Weltanschauung* and the political ideas then formed have never been abandoned, though they were expanded later on in some directions. . . . There in Vienna stark reality taught me the truths that now form the fundamental principles of the Party which within the course of five years has grown from modest beginnings to a great mass movement.'[2]

In Vienna he was reinforced in his Germanism. He developed a strong dislike for the multi-racial Austro-Hungarian Empire and its Habsburg rulers. Looking at things simply as a German, he appreciated none of the cultural interest of this capital where German, Slav, and Magyar cultures met. Instead, he wrote: 'This conglomerate spectacle of heterogeneous races which the capital of the Dual Monarchy presented, this motley of Czechs, Poles, Hungarians, Ruthenians, Serbs and

[1] *Mein Kampf*, pp. 25-6.   [2] Ibid., p. 116.

Croats, etc., and always that bacillus which is the solvent of human society, the Jew, here and there and everywhere—the whole spectacle was repugnant to me. The gigantic city seemed to be the incarnation of mongrel depravity.'[1] The keynote of Hitler's thought and feeling is his Germanism. That is why he detested and deplored the mixing of the German element with the Slav and other racial stocks. That is, perhaps, why he was happier when, later, he moved to Munich—a German city. More and more he pondered on the position of the Germans in the world and their possible future. Somehow they must find means of moulding the world to make the position of the Germans secure and to allow their unhampered expansion.

Hitler considered the problem which faced the Kaiser's Government in Germany before 1914. There was an annual increase in population, which implied an increasing pressure on land and the available resources of the country. There were four possible ways of dealing with the problem: (1) birth control, (2) internal colonization, (3) acquisition of new territory for settlement, (4) increased exports. Which policy should the Government have followed? Hitler dismissed the first, for he thought it would weaken the race and that a race so weakened would be ousted by a stronger. The second policy, of increasing the productivity of the soil at home (more farmers and better farming), could only put off the evil day. The fourth policy was the one adopted; it proved inadequate and brought Germany into conflict with England. The right policy, Hitler argued, was the third: to acquire new territory and settle it with men and women of German stock, so building up a healthy peasant class as the basis of the nation and making for it the best protection against the social evils of the time. As the territory of the world was already divided among the existing powers, the policy would involve war and conquest. 'One must not allow existing political frontiers', he wrote, 'to distract attention from what ought to exist on principles of strict justice'—the specious claim of strict justice meaning, of course, what was of advantage to the Germans,

[1] *Mein Kampf*, pp. 114-15.

and ignoring the interests of other races. The object of the policy, which 'would have been reached only by war', was Russia. 'If new territory were to be acquired in Europe it must have been mainly at Russia's cost, and once again the new German Empire should have set out on its march along the same road as was formerly trodden by the Teutonic Knights, this time to acquire soil for the German plough by means of the German sword and thus provide the nation with its daily bread.' To safeguard the German rear, an alliance should have been made with England. To gain that end, the German Government should have been ready to abandon colonial and naval ambitions and to avoid German competition with British industries—'no sacrifice should have been considered too great if it was a necessary means of gaining England's friendship'.[1]

Hitler's analysis of German foreign policy before 1914 makes it very clear what Hitler felt that policy ought to have been. It is strange that foreign statesmen did not read *Mein Kampf* more carefully. There was, to some extent, a feeling that circumstances had changed, and that Hitler as head of the German State would not do what Hitler the agitator had written in the early years of the Nazi movement. Nor would Hitler necessarily still advocate a policy which he had considered right for the German Government before 1914. It is stranger still, therefore, that foreign statesmen did not observe and ponder closely that Hitler, in the second part of *Mein Kampf*, comes back to the subject and clearly advocates for the future the conquest of territory at the expense of Russia —a policy which must inevitably mean the rearmament of Germany and European war. 'The task to be accomplished', he wrote in 1925, 'is the same today.'[2]

Hitler devoted two chapters, 'The German Post-war Policy of Alliances' and 'Germany's Policy in Eastern Europe', to the subject of the foreign policy he advocated—a policy of military power. First Germany must, by rearmament, regain her freedom of action. Then, to cover her rear while she expands eastwards, Germany must settle her accounts with

[1] *Mein Kampf*, pp. 120-32.   [2] Ibid., p. 497.

France. 'France', he argues, 'is and will remain the implacable enemy of Germany'—though he admits that if he were French he would not act towards Germany otherwise than Clemenceau acted. The French, too, 'obsessed by negroid ideas', are becoming 'a threatening menace to the existence of the white race in Europe'.[1] For allies, Germany must look to England,[2] for England does not wish to see the military power of France dominant in Europe any more than she wished to see Germany dominant, and to Italy, where 'the great man beyond the Alps' had redeemed his country from Marxism.

But Russia is the crucial power, and to the relations of Russia and Germany Hitler devoted special attention. This relationship Hitler foresaw was likely to prove 'the most decisive point in determining Germany's foreign policy'.[3] He demanded a healthy and natural proportion between the numbers and growth of population and the territory it inhabited. 'Only a sufficiently large space on this earth can assure the independent existence of a people.'[4] Germany has not got this: she must therefore expand; she must have space, or *Lebensraum*. A struggle to regain the frontiers of 1914, as advocated by some, would be useless; much more is needed. 'We National Socialists must stick firmly to the aim that we have set for our foreign policy; namely, that the German people must be assured the territorial area which is necessary for it to exist on this earth. . . . The territory on which one day our German peasantry will be able to bring forth and nourish their sturdy sons will justify the blood of the sons of the peasants that has to be shed today. . . . State frontiers are established by human beings and may be changed by human beings. . . . But when we speak of new territory in Europe today we must principally think of Russia and the border States subject to her . . . today there are 80 million Germans in Europe. And our foreign policy will be recognized as rightly

---

[1] *Mein Kampf*, pp. 505, 509, 532, and 548.
[2] Hitler said in 1925: 'I believe that our world programme, in the far future, needs England more than any other country.' Ludecke, *I Knew Hitler*, p. 267.
[3] Ibid., p. 522.
[4] Ibid., p. 523.

conducted only when, after barely 100 years, there will be 250 million Germans living on this continent.'[1]

In Vienna Hitler's other ideas also developed—his belief in the superiority of the Aryan race and his hatred of the Jews, his consciousness of social problems of urban and industrial life, his reaction to democratic methods of government. His antipathy towards the Jews sprang up as the result of personal encounters. He appeared to feel a natural antipathy or repugnance. He described their first impact upon him: 'Once when passing through the Inner City, I suddenly encountered a phenomenon in a long caftan and wearing black sidelocks. My first thought was: Is this a Jew?' As he wandered about the city it seemed to him that everywhere he found Jews. 'Especially the Inner City and the district northwards from the Danube Canal swarmed with a people who even in outer appearance bore no similarity to the Germans.' To Hitler they were personally objectionable. 'That they were water-shy was obvious on looking at them and, unfortunately, very often also when not looking at them at all. The odour of those people in *caftans* often used to make me feel ill. . . .'[2] Thus Hitler reacted in a direct, personal manner; he reacted much as a member of the white race reacts against the black and in so doing creates the colour-bar. But Hitler went much farther. He read anti-Semitic literature and pondered upon the social and cultural standards of the cosmopolitan capital. He became convinced that the Jews were behind all forms of vice: prostitution, the white slave traffic, and degenerate tendencies in the Press, in art, in literature, and the theatre. He also found that the Jews were leaders of the Social Democratic Party. This, for Hitler, was a real discovery: 'thus I finally discovered who were the evil spirits leading our people

[1] *Mein Kampf*, pp. 531-49. Hitler was remarkably consistent in his views with regard to Russia. In a private conversation in 1932 with Ludecke, he spoke of 'Winning for Germany the room she deserves' and of a 'German Reich stretching from the North Sea to the Urals' (*I Knew Hitler*, p. 423). See also F. Hesse, *Das Spiel um Deutschland*, p. 288. He outlines Hitlers views with regard to Russia at the time of the invasion 1941. They were identical with those of *Mein Kampf*, *sie waren also zwanzig Jahre hindurch bei Hitler lebendig geblieben und bilden das A und O zum Verständnis seiner Aussenpolitik.*

[2] *Mein Kampf*, pp. 58-60.

astray'. He tried to argue with them. But, it seems, even Hitler met his match: 'sometimes I was dumbfounded. . . . I gradually came to hate them.' Especially he hated Jewish Marxism with its international outlook, and this hatred led him to make the wildest utterances: 'Should the Jew, with the aid of his Marxist creed, triumph . . . this planet will once again follow its orbit through ether, without any human life on its surface. . . . And so I believe today that my conduct is in accordance with the will of the Almighty Creator. In standing guard against the Jew I am defending the handiwork of the Lord.'[1]

Hitler accepted the view, which he had doubtless picked up in his private reading, of the superiority of the Aryan race. 'Every manifestation of human culture', he says, 'every product of art, science and technical skill, which we see before our eyes today, is almost exclusively the product of the Aryan creative power. This very fact fully justifies the conclusion that it was the Aryan alone who founded a superior type of humanity; therefore he represents the archetype of what we understand by the term: MAN.'[2] The Jews he regarded as parasites, uncreative themselves, who had insinuated their way into Aryan communities; he accused them also of aiming at world dictatorship. On the way to this goal they had already gained a large measure of economic control through finance; and had also through Marxism gained control of the worker, both in the Socialist parties and in the trade unions. He argued that the Kaiser's Germany failed because it ignored these influences. The task of the Nazi movement must be to extirpate these alien racial influences and create a 'German State in a German nation'. The *Völkisch* (folk) conception of the world must confront the Marxist. 'The *Völkisch* concept separates mankind into races of superior and inferior quality' and it postulates 'the victory of the better and stronger and the subordination of the inferior and weaker'.[3]

Hitler's unemployment and poverty in Vienna made him acutely aware of social problems. It was this experience which

[1] *Mein Kampf*, pp. 60-66. [2] Ibid., p. 243.
[3] Ibid., p. 321. See also pp. 253-76 and p. 539.

added the social element to the national in his *Weltanschauung*, and so brought into being National Socialism. Hitler sometimes went hungry to buy books and study, but, as he said, 'the blinkers of a narrow *petit bourgeois* education were torn from my eyes'. He not only studied like the academic economist, but he was forced to feel the contrast between great wealth and poverty. 'Abject poverty', he wrote, 'confronted the wealth of the aristocracy and the merchant class face to face. Thousands of unemployed loitered in front of the palaces of the Ring Strasse; and below that *Via Triumphalis* of the old Austria the homeless huddled together in the murk and filth of the canals.'[1] Hitler came to realize that mere charitable relief for the existing generation would be of little avail. He looked instead for some long-term policy of social reform which would remove the underlying causes of social degradation. Thus he was brought into contact with socialist ideas, with Marxism and the Social Democratic Party. But that Party he condemned; with its internationalist character, it was anathema to Hitler the nationalist. Then, as a building workman, he was ordered to join a trade union. He refused, and his mates threatened to throw him off the scaffolding. Hitler came to see the workers as the dupes of a great international movement of political poison and physical violence. But he realized, a little later, that trade unions were necessary to protect the workers against unscrupulous and socially irresponsible employers. He realized, too, that if the masses could be dominated by a socialist movement, they might also be dominated by a nationalist movement, so long as it did not neglect social problems. Marxism must be countered by a positive movement, but one equally ruthless.[2] With his advocacy of fundamental social reform Hitler coupled a thoroughgoing denunciation of the social failings of the Kaiser's Germany, failings which he thought had contributed to the downfall of 1918. He condemned the worship of Mammon and the commercialization of Germany, the decline of morals and public decency, he deplored prostitution (advocating early marriage and State assistance for large families) and

1 *Mein Kampf*, pp. 33-4.   2 Ibid., pp. 33-52.

the spread of syphilis, poverty and the consequent tuberculosis, he urged the cleansing of cultural life and its freeing from exoticism, he called for a reform of education to make it less academic and to provide for physical training, he discerned a decline in religion and declared faith to be essential to the masses.[1]

At the same time, Hitler developed a strong dislike for democracy and parliamentary institutions. Although he admitted a certain admiration for the British system, Hitler was disillusioned by what he found when he attended the Austrian Parliament. He found a multi-racial body; some of the members spoke, not in German, but in Slav vernaculars. Sometimes there were tumultuous scenes; at others the members were half asleep. Hitler pours scorn on the proceedings. Over against democracy he placed the leadership principle. 'A man of real political ability will refuse to be the beadle for a bevy of footling cacklers; and they in their turn, being the representatives of the majority—which means the dunderheaded multitude—hate nothing so much as a superior brain. . . . The majority represents not only ignorance, but also cowardice. And just as 100 blockheads do not equal one man of wisdom, so 100 poltroons are incapable of any political line of action that requires moral strength and fortitude.'[2]

Gradually Hitler came to the conclusion that a National Socialist mass movement led by resolute and determined leaders must be created to counter democracy and Marxism. Personal responsibility must replace the parliamentary principle. A national movement must bring about the ruthless destruction of Marxism and the creation of a new, nationalist Germany. There must be a thorough clean-up of revolutionary socialist forces.[3] As he had said in a speech in 1922: 'The Marxists taught: If you will not be my brother, I will bash your skull in. Our motto shall be: If you will not be a German, I will bash your skull in. For we are convinced that we cannot succeed without a struggle. We have to fight with ideas, but, if necessary, also with our fists.'[4] But Hitler asked

[1] *Mein Kampf*, pp. 200-27. See also pp. 338-64. [2] Ibid., pp. 80-1. [3] Ibid., p. 554.
[4] November 1922 at Munich; *Hitler's Words* (ed. G. W. Prange), p. 122.

himself the question: 'Is it possible to eradicate ideas by force of arms? He remembered Bismarck's failure to suppress socialism. He came to the conclusion, however, that ideas could be destroyed if the movement against them had behind it an even stronger idea. Thus National-Socialism must be a positive force; something which could be substituted for Social Democracy.[1] And there must be propaganda, which 'must not investigate the truth objectively', but 'must present only that aspect of the truth which is favourable to its own side'. The propaganda must appeal to sentiment rather than reason, and there must be constant repetition. Elsewhere, also, Hitler observed that 'the big lie is more credible than the small lie, since they themselves [i.e. his opponents] often tell small lies in little matters but would be ashamed to resort to large-scale falsehoods'.[2]

Hitler saw his National Socialist Party as a movement which by the force of will power would become a National Socialist State. First the leaders must exercise their will power; then the masses could be won over and made nationally-minded. But as the party became a mass movement it must not sacrifice the leadership principle and become corrupted by democracy: if the Party 'takes part in the parliamentary institution it is only for the purpose of destroying this institution from within; in other words, we wish to do away with an institution which we must look upon as one of the gravest symptoms of human decline'.[3] The State is a means to an end, and that end is the preservation of the race:[4] to achieve that end, the movement must secure control of the State. 'The National Socialist State . . . must grow out of an organization which has already existed for a long time. This organization must possess National Socialist life in itself, so that finally it may be able to establish a National Socialist State that will be a living reality.'[5] And Hitler showed throughout a remarkable and rare blend of cynicism and idealism. In condemning the vices and weaknesses of both the Kaiser's Germany and the Weimar Republic, he stands

---

[1] *Mein Kampf*, pp. 140-55. [2] Ibid., p. 198 and pp. 161-3.
[3] Ibid., p. 289. [4] Ibid., p. 330. [5] Ibid., p. 488.

out almost as a stern prophet of order, discipline, moral rectitude, and the triumph of spirit over matter: 'Man should take care not to have too low an estimate of the power of an ideal. . . . It was not preoccupation about their daily bread that led men to sacrifice their lives, but the love of their country, the faith which they had in its greatness, and an all-round feeling for the honour of the nation. . . . That is why we must face the calculators of the materialist Republic with faith in an idealist Reich.'[1]

Thus, as M. François-Poncet has expressed it, Hitler 'craved power for himself, but for Germany too. Better he did not distinguish between himself and Germany, he identified himself with her . . . he bore Germany an exclusive and passionate love.' With this obsession he was a menacing character. 'He was no normal being. He was rather a morbid personality, a quasi-madman, a character out of the pages of Dostoevski, a man possessed.'[2]

[1] *Mein Kampf*, p. 365.
[2] *The Fateful Years*, pp. 291-2. M. François Poncet was French Ambassador at Berlin, 1931-8.

CHAPTER VII

STRUGGLE AND OPPORTUNITY: ECONOMIC SLUMP

WHEN Hitler was released from prison in December 1924 he was faced with the task of rebuilding the Nazi Party, which had disintegrated during his absence. In his final speech at his trial, Hitler had pointed to Bismarck, Mustafa Kemal in Turkey, and Mussolini in Italy as men who had acted arbitrarily and unconstitutionally—but whose action had been justified by its results.[1] In the same way, he argued, he would have been justified had he succeeded. He appealed for a final verdict to the judgement of history.[2] But for the time being he had failed—failed to seize power by force. Now he must find a new method—slower, but surer. And it is a measure of the strength of Hitler's belief in himself and his mission that he persevered. After a momentary despair at the failure of his *Putsch*, Hitler devoted himself to the task of writing while in prison and, on his release, set himself to the work of re-creating his movement.

Though the Party was weak, Hitler, when free again, was the only possible leader. While in prison, it seems, Hitler had welcomed and intentionally encouraged the personal and political quarrels in the movement, Party divisions which would prevent the development of a strong organization under a new leader who might replace him, and divisions which would allow Hitler to act as umpire. Just as in 1923 he had not wanted a united reaction from Berlin to French action in the

---

[1] *Der Hitler-Prozess*, Part 2, p. 85. There had been much interest in the popular Press in the idea of the strong man as the saviour of the country in troubled times. Pictures of Caesar, Napoleon, Lenin, Kemal, Mussolini, and Primo de Rivera were published. Hitler may have been influenced by them: 'In chaotic Europe —not merely in Germany—there is today a growing belief in the Dictator as Messiah', *Berliner Illustrierte Zeitung*, 4 November 1923; cf. issues of 28 October and 30 December.
[2] *Der Hitler-Prozess*, p. 91.

Ruhr so long as he was not in power, so now he did not wish a strong national party unless he was in control. And there were many differences among Nazis and nationalists. Rosenberg, for example, was on bad terms with Streicher and Esser, two most unpleasant members of the group, and Ludendorff, though living in Catholic Bavaria, was fiercely anti-Catholic. Rosenberg, Gregor Strasser, and Ludendorff, however, did co-operate with north German nationalists in a national bloc (known as the German Freedom Movement, for the Nazi Party as such was banned) and won thirty-two seats (1,918,300 votes) in the spring elections for the Reichstag of 1924, but such were the Party quarrels that in December they had only fourteen seats (907,300 votes). Early in 1925 Ludendorff and Strasser left the bloc, and it was dissolved. Röhm, too, who had been released and had thrown himself into building up an S.A. again, was disgusted with Hitler's attitude, and threw up his post. Eckhart had died; Göring was abroad. Hitler had to assert himself once more, and follow a new line of action. As he had said, while still in prison, to Ludecke, 'When I resume active work it will be necessary to pursue a new policy. Instead of working to achieve power by an armed coup, we shall have to hold our noses and enter the Reichstag against the Catholic and Marxist deputies. If outvoting them takes longer than outshooting them, at least the result will be guaranteed by their own Constitution!' Hitler, at the same time, referred with approval to the thirty-two members in the Reichstag—and Hitler's approval surprised Ludecke, for when the elections had been held Hitler had violently disapproved of the Nazis' participation. But Hitler evidently was beginning to realize that slow, steady work at building up a popular movement might do far more than a *Putsch*, and he continued: 'Sooner or later we shall have a majority —and after that, Germany. I am convinced this is our best line of action, now that conditions in the country have changed so radically.'[1]

But it would be a long, hard struggle, for conditions had indeed changed. First of all, Hitler himself was suspect almost

[1] K. Ludecke, *I Knew Hitler*, pp. 217-18.

everywhere. After he had tried to revive his activities by holding a meeting in February 1925, and had showed much of his old influence over the crowd, the authorities in Bavaria banned him as a speaker—and this ban was applied by many other German states over a period of two or three years. And, in the second place, conditions in Germany were improving, and with the improvement Hitler's influence waned and his ephemeral debating triumphs at his trial were forgotten.

The German Republic had, in fact, survived all its trials and difficulties. Dr. Schacht had been appointed as a special commissioner to deal with the inflation problem only a few days after Hitler's *Putsch* in Munich had failed. Schacht succeeded in creating a new stable currency, the Rentenmark, and by the middle of 1924, while Hitler was in prison, the inflation was over. In August, to solve the reparations problem, the Dawes Plan, drafted by an American general, was negotiated, scaling down reparations payments and putting the whole thing on a business footing. Meanwhile, America was prepared to make loans to Germany—and this helped to keep the wheels of German industry turning, although, since reparations payments turned out to be less than German borrowings abroad, it was the beginning of the fantastic procedure whereby America and the Allies financed their own compensation for war losses. The French occupation of the Ruhr was wound up, although the last French troops did not leave until July 1925. At the same time negotiations were going on for a wider political settlement. Later in 1925, on 1 December, the Locarno Pact was signed in London. The Franco-German and Belgo-German frontiers were mutually guaranteed by Great Britain, Italy, and the three Powers directly concerned. The statesmen, Stresemann, Briand, and Austen Chamberlain, worked well together: there was a new optimism in Europe, 'the spirit of Locarno'. The evacuation at the beginning of 1926 of the first zone of Allied occupied territory in the Rhineland (the final stage of evacuation was in 1930) and Germany's admission into the League of Nations in September 1926 presaged well for the future. All these things strengthened the German Republic.

Then, in 1925, President Ebert—the Social Democrat leader who had been President since the beginning of the Republic —died. In the presidential election which followed, the result was indecisive, but Ludendorff, who had been put forward by the Nazis, was completely defeated, for he obtained only 211,000 votes out of a total of nearly 27 millions. A second election was held, Ludendorff withdrawing. Hindenburg now appeared as the candidate of the Right, and was elected. Thus a field-marshal, conservative, nationalist, monarchist, became head of the German Republic. His election temporarily shook confidence abroad. But in Germany, if anything, it strengthened the Republic by giving it a powerful figurehead, and doing something to reconcile to it conservative opinion. Hindenburg remained President until his death in 1934.

From 1924 onwards a period of recovery set in for Germany. Once more industry began to make profits and pay wages: there was employment, and money to be made. There was food, chocolate cakes, and cream again, and beer. In the February of 1925 the Munich Carnival was held for the first time since 1914, and in the city where the Nazis had marched people went wild, dancing and singing all night long. People began to travel abroad again, the war began to fade into the background, optimism revived. Stresemann hobnobbed with the Allied statesmen at Geneva. The order of the day was peace and international conciliation. Hitler and his rabid nationalism were forgotten. 'Until the Beer-hall *Putsch*', wrote Ludecke, 'Hitler had been riding a wave of national despair, with the support of the Army. In this new era of fake calm, however, he found himself practically deserted by his "big" friends, who were advising "loyal co-operation" with the "consolidated Republic".'[1]

In these years, however, even Hitler himself did not do too badly. Though Party fortunes were at a low ebb, Hitler's personal and domestic life was more secure and comfortable than it had ever been. He wrote articles for Party newspapers and was paid for them, and probably he received money from Party funds—anyhow, he lived in the homely comfort of the

[1] *I Knew Hitler*, p. 304.

Bavarian countryside. There he dwelt in the mountain villa, Haus Wachenfeld, on the Obersalzberg, above the village of Berchtesgaden, close to the Austrian frontier. As he was still an Austrian citizen, he could, if necessary, at any time have escaped from the German police by crossing the frontier. At the same time, he was not too far from Munich—130 miles by rail—and could return there when required. Hitler owned the party's paper, the *Völkischer Beobachter*, and its business manager, Max Amman, kept Hitler busy with the preparation of *Mein Kampf* for the press and with his newspaper articles. At home Hitler lived almost a family life. He had brought his widowed half-sister from Austria to keep house for him. She brought with her a pretty, blonde, seventeen-year-old daughter, Angela—Geli for short—for whom Hitler formed a romantic attachment. He led a pleasant life—pleasant, even luxurious as compared with the lives of many of his Nazi followers, and in these years of the party doldrums Hitler's private life did not pass without criticism.[1]

Party difficulties continued: a possible rival emerged. There was the powerful personality of Gregor Strasser, who, though a Bavarian by birth, built up a strong following for himself in north Germany. As a Reichstag Member, he was paid and had a free pass on the railways; he had parliamentary immunity and could speak anywhere, unlike Hitler, who was still under the ban. Helped by his brother Otto, he ran the Berlin paper, *Berliner Arbeitszeitung*, and the fortnightly *Nationalsozialistische Briefe*. And with the Strassers worked a little Rhinelander with a crippled foot, a young man who had studied philosophy and literature at six universities—Dr. Joseph Goebbels. The Strassers were socialists: they looked for the nationalization of industry and land, and they began to develop something like a party within the Party. At one meeting, in Hanover (November 1925), Goebbels was reported to have said: 'I demand that the petit bourgeois Adolf Hitler be expelled from the National Socialist Party.'[2] But three months later Hitler called a conference in the south, at Bamberg, won over Goebbels ('ambitious, an opportunist and a liar',

---

[1] K. Heiden, *Der Führer*, pp. 222-4.   [2] O. Strasser, *Hitler and I*, p. 97.

said Otto Strasser of him), and managed, for the time being, to reconcile Gregor Strasser. By 1927 Goebbels was Hitler's representative, *Gauleiter*, in Berlin: there he was to fight his long struggle to establish National Socialism in the Red capital. At the same time he founded *Der Angriff*, a rival paper to the Strassers', and worked for Hitler as against any possible recovery of independence by the Strassers. Another cause of anxiety for Hitler was the S.A. Its officers thought of themselves as a military organization. They were a potential reinforcement of the Regular Army.[1] They spent their time in exercises, manœuvres, and drinking, and cared little for politics; they disliked taking orders from Hitler as head of the political side of the movement.

Slowly, in spite of all these difficulties, the Party grew and developed its organization. At the end of 1925 its recorded membership was 27,000; by the end of 1929 it had grown to 178,000. In July 1926 Hitler held a mass rally, or *Parteitag*, at Weimar, in Thuringia, a state in which he was allowed to speak. Hitler stood in his car and took the salute as 5,000 Nazis marched past.

In August 1927 the second *Parteitag* was held, and 30,000 S.A. men were reported on parade. This time it was in Nuremberg, for, meanwhile, Hitler had been allowed to speak in Bavaria again—from May 1927 (from September 1928 in Prussia). These *Parteitage* grew out of the annual general meetings of Party delegates—as prescribed by German law for political parties, and the election of their officers. Thus Nazis from all over Germany came together—though in the Nazi Party election was only nominal. But the meetings had a real purpose, as Hitler explained later on. They brought him into contact with leaders from other parts of Germany and served to unite the mass of Party members with the leaders, and they had a psychological value in giving inspiration for carrying on the struggle and a confident expectation of victory. Party members returned home to their little towns

[1] Memorandum of the Chief of the Imperial General Staff (1928 and 1930), pointing out that the German generals thought of a possible future expansion of the Army by incorporating the partly trained members of the patriotic associations: *Documents on British Foreign Policy*, Second Series, Vol. I, p. 598.

and villages refreshed: 'they turned homewards filled with a new, blind trust and a new and unprecedented confidence'.[1] Blind trust—that was the characteristic which Hitler chiefly valued in his followers. They must say: 'My leaders know what they want! For if they do not know what they want, how am I to know, how could I give my decision?' The Nazi principle was political leadership. The leader must impose his decision from above. 'The ruling principle is: Never must a resolution be passed by a majority decision! Never! . . . There is no decision possible for which one man does not assume responsibility. That is the ruling principle of our movement.'[2] So on the foundation of this *Führerprinzip* (leadership principle) the Nazi organization gradually extended itself throughout Germany. The provincial area was the *Gau*, its leader the *Gauleiter*, and the *Gau* was in turn divided and subdivided. At the top of the organization Hitler was supreme; each *Gauleiter* was appointed by him.

By 1928 the central Party organization, with its offices in Munich, had its departments for foreign affairs, the Press, the building up of party factory cells to win over the working classes, agriculture, economics, race and culture, legal questions, and so on. The fine headquarters at the Brown House, 45 Briennerstrasse, were opened in 1931. From time to time new Party organizations were created, and linked up with the parent organization. Such new creations were the Nazi Teachers' Association, the Union of German Nazi Lawyers, the Union of Nazi Physicians, the German Women's Order, the Hitler Youth, and the Union of Nazi Pupils for the pupils at higher schools.[3] But the Nazi Party was still a small thing —without importance in the German political scene. In the elections of May 1928, Goebbels, Göring (now back from Sweden and in Hitler's movement once more), Strasser, Frick, and von Epp and eight others were elected to the Reichstag on the Nazi list, but the Nazi votes polled were only 810,000. The Social Democrats increased their poll to reach over

[1] As explained by Hitler in speeches at Weimar, 1936, and the Nuremberg *Parteitag*, 1933: Baynes, I, pp. 198-200.
[2] Ibid., p. 200.
[3] K. Heiden, *History of National Socialism*, p. 111.

9 millions; the German National Party of conservatives lost votes, but still had over 4 million. The Nazis were thus still insignificant in comparison with the great parties. And Germany in the heyday of the Republic was a country of modernism and freedom, of modern painting and modern architecture, functional buildings and flat-roofed dwellings. Freedom degenerated into licence; youth enjoyed the sunshine while it could. Bars for homosexuals, cafés where men danced with men, a new liberty between the sexes, nudism, camping, sunbathing, pornographic literature in the corner kiosks—all these things were accepted as part of the new life. In August 1928 Stresemann was in Paris: he was there as the guest of the French, to sign on behalf of Germany the Kellogg Pact renouncing war. Goodwill was in the air—but Hitler still foretold disaster. The new prosperity, he maintained, was based on slight foundations.

This time Hitler turned out to be right. But he had to wait. Meanwhile, he seized, as a matter of tactics, whatever opportunity he could. In August 1929, Stresemann accepted the Young Plan—Owen D. Young, the American banker, had acted as chairman of the committee of experts appointed to work out arrangements for a final settlement of reparations. The plan fixed fifty-nine years as the period over which Germany was to pay reparations. This had not been fixed by the Dawes Plan. The Young Plan, however, was not unfavourable, as the payments to be made were scaled down. But Hitler attacked it. He linked up with the powerful industrial magnate, Alfred Hugenberg, leader of the German National Party: a fierce agitation developed, and the Nazi and Nationalist Press carried on a violent campaign against the Government and the Young Plan. The agitation failed, and the laws embodying the Plan eventually passed through the Reichstag and were signed by President Hindenburg (13 March 1930), but Hitler had achieved valuable publicity, and considerable contributions were made to Nazi funds by leading industrialists.[1] The ever closer links between Hitler and the wealthy capitalists, however, antagonized once more the

[1] F. Thyssen, *I Paid Hitler*, p. 118 and Chapter 5.

socialist element in the Party. This time (in 1930) Hitler lost Otto Strasser, who broke away, though Gregor stayed with Hitler. Otto Strasser announced in the newspapers the break with Hitler under the heading, 'Socialists leave the Nazi Party', and formed his own Union of Revolutionary National Socialists, or Black Front.[1] Although he survived an attempt on his life by S.A. hooligans, his movement dwindled away in the coming months.

On 3 October 1929 Stresemann died: the leader of the moderates in Germany, the representative of the policy of reconciliation by the carrying out of the peace terms, was gone. Three weeks later, on 24 October, came the Wall Street crash, the collapse of security prices on the American Stock Exchange: the world economic slump had begun. From New York an economic chain-reaction spread throughout the world, and gravely affected Germany. Hitler's opportunity was at hand.

The world economic slump of the years following 1929 was catastrophic. Just because it was a world slump, because world economy had come to be so closely linked with the American economy, its effects were graver and more far-reaching than any previous slump. It caught business-men and economists by surprise. For by 1925 the world had recovered from the economic destruction and dislocation of the war, and production and consumption per head were higher than in 1913. By 1929 production in the United States had reached a level never previously attained, and it looked as if a period of unbroken prosperity lay ahead. Then came the Wall Street crash. The prices of securities slumped because in the preceding period of confidence and mass production America had over-produced: stocks had piled up, farmers could not sell their crops profitably, and the great factories found themselves clogged with surpluses; profits fell and disappeared; men were paid off. Unemployment was the most marked, and the most clearly remembered, symptom of those tragic years. The world was faced also with the paradox of poverty in the midst of plenty: the world had never had

[1] O. Strasser, *Hitler and I*, pp. 128-9.

greater stocks of material goods of all kinds at its disposal, yet men stood idle in queues for relief instead of going home at the end of the week with good wages in their pockets. It was several years before economic readjustment could bring a solution; slowly unemployment, cuts in production, and deliberate destruction of surplus goods reduced output, and so raised prices and made them remunerative again to producers. In the United States President Roosevelt's New Deal helped with public works and relief to tide the country over the crisis. During the worst period of the slump, however, there were, in round figures, 12,000,000 unemployed in the United States, 6,000,000 in Germany, and 3,000,000 in Great Britain.

Germany, in particular, was seriously affected by what happened in America because, during the years of recovery, it was the American loans that had been used to restore German industry and help her to pay reparations. Now American lending to Germany ceased, and as the slump developed in America, German unemployment rose steeply:

> 1,320,000 in 1929 (September)
> 3,000,000 in 1930   „
> 5,102,000 in 1932   „

In the early months of 1932 unemployment had reached, and reached again early in 1933, the peak figures of over 6,000,000. Here once again, as in the inflation, was something which affected great masses of the German people, and spread through all circles an insecurity and lack of confidence in the future. Once more there was abroad the desperation which looked for desperate measures. In 1928 and 1929 Hitler was still insignificant and his Party powerless, but the economic crisis gave it a powerful stimulus; the growth of the Nazi Party coincided with the years of economic depression. Its sudden and rapid climb to a position of dominant, political importance is clearly shown by the figures of Nazi votes and seats in the Reichstag elections:[1]

[1] At the end of this chapter a table is given of elections for the Reichstag, 1919-33. Lord D'Abernon, British Ambassador to Germany 1920-6, published *Lord D'Abernon's Diary* in 1929-30. The final volume contained only two references to Hitler, and those concerned his actions in 1923. A biographical footnote in

810,000 votes . . . 13 seats . . . 1928
6,409,000 votes . . . 107 seats . . . 1930 (September)
13,779,000 votes . . . 230 seats . . . 1932 (July)

The elections of September 1930 made the Nazi Party the second party in Germany, and Hitler a figure seriously to be reckoned with; the next election, 1932, made the Nazi Party the largest in the Reich.

The years of crisis slipped by. In March 1931 the German Foreign Minister put forward a scheme for a Customs union between Austria and Germany. The scheme might have done something to alleviate the economic difficulties of the two countries, but it was contrary to the peace treaties, and ran into the strongest opposition from France. The failure of the scheme was a blow to Austria, which had suffered peculiarly from the results of the war, and in May her largest private bank, the Kreditanstalt, reached the verge of collapse and had to be aided by the Government. Financial crisis followed in Germany, and in July the Darmstädter und National-Bank closed its doors, although President Hoover in America had already taken the initiative in arranging a moratorium on reparations and war debt payments. The German Government, to deal with the crisis, temporarily shut all banks and stock exchanges. Further international action led to the freezing of short-term credits to Germany, and this, in turn, helped to bring financial crisis to Great Britain, whose bankers, unable to withdraw their short-term loans to Germany, found themselves in difficulties elsewhere. The world was in the grip of forces beyond its control.

The full extent of the changes, political as well as economic, which the world slump would bring were not, of course, immediately evident. Even in the summer of 1931, when the banks were failing, life went on and, for example, in Berlin

Vol. II, p. 50, spoke of Hitler as 'fading into oblivion'. It was thought in Germany that Russia, in order to create a state of confusion, must have sent funds to the Nazis for their 1930 election campaign. Report of Sir Horace Rumbold, British Ambassador, 18 September 1930: *Documents on British Foreign Policy,* Second Series, Vol. I, p. 510. For a British Socialist view of the influence of the world slump, see H. N. Brailsford, *The German Problem,* p. 11: 'Before that year [1929] Hitler was a nuisance: after it, he became a danger . . . a mood of desperation seized the people. The demagogue had a plan . . . a big minority voted Nazi.'

the English visitor found life normal enough. Indeed, he was impressed by the building and improvements which had taken place in the good years. Shops and offices along the Unter den Linden were bright and lively, the *Ubahn* brought the crowded trains of city workers to their daily routine, men and women on holiday were visiting the capital, young people were swimming and sun-bathing at Krumme Lanke and the Wannsee, the pinewoods and lakes around the city were as lovely as ever. It was difficult to realize just how serious the position was. Yet beneath the surface there was tension and deep anxiety. All the time Germans remembered the inflation and how their savings had melted away. They watched the growth of the extreme parties, Nazi and Communist. For the election of 1930 had seen a great increase in strength for the Communist Party also. Their seats increased from fifty-four to seventy-seven with a poll of over $4\frac{1}{2}$ millions. (And in the November elections of 1932 they had 100 seats with a poll of nearly 6 millions.) 'Bad economic conditions play straight into the hands of the extreme elements of the State, whether they are National Socialists or Communists', wrote the British Ambassador.[1] Moderate people feared to attend political meetings because of the danger of physical violence, and even the most optimistic feared a clash between the two extremes. 'It cannot go on like this', it was said. 'There must, sooner or later, be a show-down.'

The world slump brought far-reaching political changes in Great Britain and the United States, where democratic government was well-established and traditional; in Germany, where it was something of recent date, the economic crisis was a threat to the very foundations of the Weimar Republic. Those foundations, though the Republic had survived so far, had never been very firm. As the first post-war election in 1919 had shown, the Social Democratic Party, even at the moment of its greatest strength, could not of itself form a majority government. To form a government it depended on its bourgeois allies, the Catholic Centre Party and the

[1] Sir Horace Rumbold, 16 January 1931; cf. 4 March 1931: *Documents on British Foreign Policy*, Second Series, Vol. I, pp. 551, 573; also Vol. II, pp. 79-84.

Democrat Party. Weimar Germany saw a series of coalition governments. This involved political bargaining and compromise, which tended to make government weak and ineffectual in a time of crisis which would be liable to break up the party compromises. On the other hand, of course, the opposition parties could not easily form any alternative coalition to defeat the democratic forces; it was inconceivable that the two main opposition parties, the German National Party and the Communist Party, should agree to make a coalition to form an alternative government. But for some time the Catholic and conservative Von Papen, who was nominally a member of the Catholic Centre Party, had toyed with the possibility of detaching the Catholics from the Social Democrats and building instead a coalition government of the Catholic Centre with parties of the Right.[1] The fundamental political problem of the depression years was to find some combination of forces which would provide a government with a majority in the Reichstag.

At the end of March 1930 Müller, the last Social Democratic Chancellor, who had presided over a coalition with the Catholic Centre, Democrats, and People's Party, had resigned because of disagreement among his supporters over contributions to the unemployment insurance fund. Dr. Brüning, leader of the Catholic Centre, had become Chancellor, but he had been unable to count on a secure majority in the Reichstag. So many difficult problems had to be dealt with and so many interests were involved that political bargaining became very complicated. Could wages and unemployment relief be cut? Should taxes be increased or a capital levy imposed? Should tariffs be raised? What financial assistance could be given to landowners and farmers? In July Brüning failed to persuade the Reichstag to pass his whole financial programme. In reply he got the President to use the emergency powers given him by the Constitution; the financial programme was made law by Presidential decree. It was a serious step Brüning had taken—and it was

---

[1] Von Papen, *Memoirs*, pp. 105-6 and 141. Cf. Report of Sir Horace Rumbold, 28 March 1930: *Documents on British Foreign Policy*, Second Series, Vol. I, p. 473.

challenged at the time—but it was forced on him by the lack of political agreement among the parties, and by the serious nature of the economic crisis.

Hitler was ready to exploit the situation to the full. Economic disaster and political weakness gave him his opportunity. Disorders at public meetings and in the streets increased. The newspapers almost daily reported murders and deeds of violence—many perpetrated by the Nazis. Everything was done to make a propaganda use of acts of violence against the Nazis. When, in February 1930, the young Horst Wessel, a Berlin S.A. leader, was shot by the Communists, Nazi propaganda idealized him as a martyred hero, and his verses, the *Horst Wessel Lied* (Horst Wessel Song), were sung on the march. The S.A. was still, however, a problem to Hitler:[1] later in the same year they mutinied in Berlin, and the Nazis had ignominiously to call in the police to restore order. But Hitler's personal intervention and promises of better pay pacified them. The Nazi election successes in September pushed the incident into the background, but Hitler brought back Röhm, who had been serving as an officer in the Bolivian Army, to be S.A. chief-of-staff and to bring them under control. And meanwhile Heinrich Himmler was building up for Hitler a specially chosen corps in black uniform, an élite, which would prove a counter-balance to the S.A.: the S.S. (*Schutz Staffeln*, or protective detachments).

The S.A., indeed, presented a nice problem. The S.A. must be strong enough and bold enough to crush political opposition and intimidate the moderates—'Possession of the streets is the key to power' ran one of the slogans—but they must not be so bold, now that Hitler was following a policy of legality, as to push him into hasty action or engineer a *Putsch* for themselves. For Hitler was now strong enough to count on ultimate success if he acted with caution. About him were resolute and unscrupulous assistants—Göring, Goebbels, Röhm, Frick. Nazi public meetings were now bringing a big financial return. A Sportpalast meeting in Berlin gave 14,000

[1] Sir Horace Rumbold's Report, 5 September 1930: *Documents on British Foreign Policy*, Second Series, Vol. I, p. 506.

marks profit.[1] And Göring had many invaluable social contacts. In fact, most important of all, Hitler was now in close touch with wealthy industrialists, and ample funds were becoming available.[2] For the industrialists began to see in Hitler their champion against Communism and the trade unions, just as officers and ex-officers of the Army saw in him the man who would re-create Germany's military might and find jobs for unemployed soldiers. No one was satisfied with the political situation. President Hindenburg and those around him were looking for some means of finding a stable government—either based on a Reichstag majority or on the presidential authority. Hindenburg was an old man, eighty-four in 1931. Those around him, his son Oskar, Oskar's friend, General von Schleicher, a powerful influence in the Defence Ministry, and von Papen, had much influence with him. Hitler, with his mass support in the country, was a vital factor in their considerations: a possible path was opening out before Hitler.

The year 1931 saw Hitler in direct contact with the men who counted politically. In the autumn Röhm put him in touch with Schleicher. Schleicher was the means of persuading both Chancellor Brüning and President Hindenburg to receive Hitler. But neither was impressed by him, and the attempt to bargain for Nazi support in the Reichstag broke down. But Nazi popular successes continued—for example, during 1931 in the state elections for Oldenburg, Hamburg, and Hesse. Further talks with Hitler followed early in 1932, but again they came to nothing. The immediate subject of discussion was the prospect of a presidential election. Could

[1] The British Ambassador asked Dr. Curtius and General Gröner if they could explain where Hitler got his funds. Both ministers mentioned the great Nazi meetings at which the entrance fee was 50 pfg. or more. At a recent Sportpalast meeting the takings were 16,000 marks. Expenses of hiring the hall, etc., were 2,000 marks. Thus the Party cleared 14,000 marks. And meetings were being held all over Germany. Report of Sir Horace Rumbold, 5 November 1930: *Documents on British Foreign Policy*, Second Series, Vol. I, p. 533.

[2] F. Thyssen, *I Paid Hitler*, pp. 132-3, refers to his own contributions, and those of the Munich printing and piano chiefs, Bruckmann and Bechstein. Hitler's speech to the Industry Club at Düsseldorf, January 1932, made a deep impression, and a number of large contributions followed: speech in Baynes, Vol. 1, pp. 777-829.

the parties agree to prolong Hindenburg's term of office? Would Hitler back him if Hindenburg stood for re-election? There was no agreement, and the election took place in March and April. Hindenburg was opposed by Hitler (who for the purpose was given German citizenship by the state of Brunswick, where the Nazis were influential). On the first poll Hindenburg was just short of the clear majority required over all other candidates; on the second poll he was elected by a substantial majority, but nevertheless the election demonstrated the growing mass support for Hitler. Though Hindenburg had over 19 million votes, Hitler had polled 13,417,460. Something of a reaction followed, however, against the Nazis, for the S.A. was suspected of having had its own plans to seize power. As a result of growing pressure from state governments, led by Prussia (which was a stronghold of the Social Democrats) and Bavaria, the Reich Government dissolved the S.A. and S.S. Hitler himself stuck to his policy of legality, and the uniforms disappeared from the streets.

There was no drive, however, behind the action against the Nazis; nor was there unity. Schleicher followed a tortuous policy. Perhaps he could detach the S.A. from Hitler and bring it under Army control? Or perhaps he could make a deal with Hitler and bring him into the Government? As a result of his underhand actions, he raised such a campaign against General Gröner, Minister of the Interior, a strong opponent of the Nazis and the minister responsible for dissolving the S.A., that Gröner resigned. Schleicher now turned against Brüning, and influenced Hindenburg against him. Schleicher told Hindenburg that the Army had lost confidence in Brüning. He also promised support for a new man, Papen. Brüning depended on presidential decrees to govern. Now Hindenburg withdrew his support, and asked Brüning for his resignation. Brüning resigned on 30 May 1932. Hindenburg called on Papen.

But if Brüning had had a difficult position with the Reichstag, it was nothing as compared with that of Papen. The Catholic Centre, angered by the treatment of Brüning, disowned Papen, and he had great difficulty in forming a government. When formed, it rested only on presidential support and that of the army. Papen looked to the Right. Was there a possibility of forming a coalition with the Nazis? It was a question worth considering. It was the only way for Papen and Schleicher (now Minister of Defence) to get any popular, mass support, and if Hitler was forced to share responsibility, they thought, he would be forced to moderate his tone. For Hitler himself coalition offered the only possible way to power, so long as he had not an absolute majority and would not risk a *Putsch*. Meanwhile, playing for Nazi support, Papen lifted the ban on the S.A. This led to renewed disorders and street fighting in Berlin, the Ruhr, and Altona. Many people were killed, and the disorders gave Papen the pretext for dissolving the Prussian State Government and making himself Reich Commissioner for Prussia. Prussia had had a steady Government by Social Democratic and Centre coalition ever since the revolution, but the coalition had lost its clear majority at the last elections, and so was in a difficult situation. Now it was dissolved. The Prussian ministers, the Social Democratic Party, and the trade unions made no resistance. This was significant: the Left was not likely to resist a seizure of power by the Right. Then came the elections at the end of July—dissolution of the Reichstag and new elections being part of the price Papen paid for Nazi support.

This gave the Nazis a chance once more to work for a clear majority: they made a stupendous electioneering effort, Hitler using air transport to reach vast meetings all over Germany. The utmost effort was made by every possible means to win the German people: to win, cajole, promise, threaten, hypnotize. Along the streets of the capital the swastika flag was to be seen everywhere, the Nazi papers, the *Beobachter* and the *Angriff*, were piled in heaps at the newspaper kiosks, and posters and slogans screamed the Nazi message of national honour and social justice, bread, and a greater Germany, while uniformed Nazis moved among the crowds. The mass meetings were great spectacles, prepared with every trick of Goebbels and the other propaganda experts. At Brandenburg Hitler arrived by plane, roaring over the field where 60,000 had collected to hear him. As he left—to hurry off to meetings the same day in Potsdam and Berlin—he paused to pat the head of a child who handed him flowers. That evening in Berlin 100,000 people packed into the great Grunewald Stadium, and another 100,000 waited outside to listen to the loudspeakers. Banners waved against the evening sky. Men of the S.S. in close rank were drawn up by the speaker's stand, and S.A. bands played military marches with tremendous power. As Goebbels spoke, 'suddenly a wave surged over the crowd, it leaned forward, a word was tossed from man to man: Hitler is coming! Hitler is here! A blare of trumpets rent the air, and 100,000 people leaped to their feet. . . . Hitler had stepped through a passage-way to the tribune, bathed in light, hatless, brown-shirted, briskly saluting. When the tumult subsided at length, like a thunderstorm receding, he threw defiance and appeal, with his whipping, cracking speech, over loudspeakers and microphones into the falling darkness of the night.' After his speech, Hitler, standing erect and his arm outstretched, was carried away in his huge, black Mercedes, amid a continuous roar of cheering. As his car left, a column, thousands strong, of S.S. men carrying torches marched through the arena. Fireworks shot overhead, the bands broke out again, and 'the crowd rose to its feet to join in the most tremendous rendition on record of *Deutschland über Alles* and the Nazi *Horst Wessel* song'.[1]

The Nazis doubled the votes they had obtained the last time. Now they polled 13,745,000 votes, which gave them 230 seats in the Reichstag. The Nazi Party was thus by far the largest party in the country, but still the absolute majority eluded them. Hitler, however, was pushing himself forward as a serious candidate for the chancellorship. But Nazi violence as displayed in many outbreaks was causing much nervousness: at Potempa, in Silesia, a working man, alleged to be a Communist, was kicked to death by five Nazis, and this raised nation-wide excitement. (They were condemned to death, but, after a personal intervention by Hitler, were reprieved.) There was a reaction against the Nazis.

[1] Described by Ludecke, who was at both meetings: *I Knew Hitler*, pp. 342-6.

The other parties, and also Papen himself, thought that Hitler had shot his bolt. Nazi votes, they thought, had reached their peak in the July elections; the Nazi tide was on the turn. When Hitler met Papen and Schleicher on 13 August, they offered Hitler the vice-chancellorship only. Hitler raged against them, but in vain. He was summoned to the President and asked by him if he would enter Papen's Government. Hitler asked for full power, but Hindenburg replied that his conscience would not allow him to hand over power to a single party. An account of the meeting appeared in the Press —all the world knew: Hitler had demanded 'entire and complete control of the state', and he had been refused.[1]

Even now, when power had escaped him by a hair's-breadth, Hitler did not lose heart. He held the Party together, and made renewed contacts with the Government. Both Papen and Schleicher underestimated Hitler. So did some of Hitler's supporters, including Strasser and Ludecke, the latter thinking it was weakness on Hitler's part to hold back after his election victory while the S.A. were spoiling for a march on Berlin. But Hitler, with unerring political instinct, was playing a skilful game. He realized how useful Hindenburg with his great prestige could be to him; it was essential to acquire power legally and make use of that prestige. 'I need Hindenburg—I need that feeble-minded old bull', Hitler told Ludecke in private. 'Say what you will', Hitler continued, 'his prestige is still priceless—a fabulous reputation that must be exploited. Here's a symbolic picture I don't intend to miss: Hindenburg representing the Old Germany and I the New, the Old Germany reaching out its hand to the New—the old Field-Marshal of the World War and the young Corporal from the trenches pledging themselves to the swastika at the Court of Frederick the Great! . . . I'll stage such an act in Potsdam as the world has never seen! If I force a showdown, the old idiot might resign, and I can't afford it.' Then Hitler went on to make his meaning even more precise: 'I need his prestige for the transition period, until I've solidified my power. With his prestige behind me I can proceed step by

[1] *Berliner Tageblatt*, 13 August 1932 (evening edition).

step: I can get rid of Versailles, I can rearm, I can get allies. I don't care what they think and write about me abroad; better for them to keep on underrating me until I get strong. I'll be ready to strike before they know it, the fools!'[1] And a little later in the conversation Hitler referred to the lesson of caution he had learnt at Munich in 1923. 'What if the Reichswehr should shoot again? No, *mein Lieber*, the Feldherrnhalle was enough. I've learned since then. . . . If you can achieve something by cunning, don't try noble deeds; they might knock your teeth out.' But behind the cunning there would be force when the time was ripe: 'If it's going to take bombs to show these gentlemen in London, Paris, and New York that I mean business—well, they can have them. Don't be afraid. I'll go the limit, when the time comes, but not before. . . . I've learned to wait. . . . I have only one thought: to make Germany great. . . . I can see a German Reich stretching from the North Sea to the Urals, but without a Stalin!'[2]

Papen, however, was convinced that the Nazis were losing ground: he thought that new elections would show this. He dissolved the Reichstag, and the elections in November showed that he was right. The Nazis lost 2 million votes and their seats were reduced to 196; the Communists gained ground, reaching a total of 100 seats, the greatest they ever had, but the Nazis were still the largest party in the Reichstag. Papen rejoiced at the Nazi setback: again he offered Hitler the vice-chancellorship. Hitler, however, was wary and showed great skill in manœuvre; he waited. Papen was prepared to carry on, fight another election to show up the Nazis still further, or rule, if necessary, as a dictator. But now the arch-intriguer, Schleicher, began to work against Papen. Tortuous negotiations went on. Papen was induced to offer his resignation; Schleicher put himself forward as a possible alternative chancellor; Hitler was called twice, on 19 and 21 November, to

[1] Ludecke, *I Knew Hitler*, pp. 412-14; cf. p. 539. Hitler had a certain mystic respect for Hindenburg as the representative of former German military might.

[2] Ibid., p. 423. One only has Ludecke's word for this private conversation, but his book was published in 1938, and how clearly Hitler's words foretold his later policy!

meet Hindenburg and was now offered the chancellorship if he could secure a majority in the Reichstag, but this he could not do, and Hindenburg would not have him as a presidential chancellor (if he were to be that, why replace Papen?), for that would lead to party dictatorship.[1] Papen was ready to resume office, declare a state of emergency, and govern by decree backed by military force. Hindenburg agreed—but then, once more, Schleicher, as representative of the army, declared that the army had lost confidence in Papen, and would not in the circumstances envisaged guarantee order. Hindenburg, unwilling to face civil war, gave way, and on 2 December called Schleicher to be chancellor—the last chancellor of the democratic régime.

Schleicher now tried his hand at the task, at which others had failed, of making a stable government. He approached the Nazis through Gregor Strasser, with whom he was already in contact. Schleicher failed to make a deal, but his method of approach cast doubt on Strasser. A violent quarrel broke out between him and Hitler, and Strasser threw up his job as head of the Party organization and went off to Italy. The affair shook Hitler: the Party fortunes were at a low ebb, and it was short of money. But once again the Führer's personal influence prevailed, and he held the Party together. In a New Year message to the Party Hitler declared: 'I am absolutely resolved not to sell the birthright of our movement for the mess of pottage of sharing in a government, but without power.'[2] Meanwhile, Schleicher was trying to win support from other parties and the trade unions. He broadcast to the nation his plans for dealing with unemployment, controlling prices, and subsidizing land settlement in the eastern districts of Germany. He was not trusted, however. He alarmed the industrialists, and could not win over the workers and he was condemned by the landlords of the eastern districts for his policy of 'agrarian Bolshevism'. Then on 4 January 1933 Papen and Hitler met in the house of von

[1] *Berliner Tageblatt*, 19 and 21 November 1932. The issue of 25 November prints the official communiqué rejecting Hitler.

[2] *Völkischer Beobachter*, 1 January 1933.

Schröder, a Cologne banker. Papen was convinced that, with the Nazi Party as the largest in the Reichstag, something must be done to make it shoulder responsibility in a Government, but that the Nazis would be, in turn, held in check if they entered a *coalition* government. The possibility of replacing Schleicher was perhaps discussed, and the possibility of a coalition between Nazis and Nationalists. Accounts differ as to what was said,[1] but the important thing was that Hitler had re-established useful contact with Papen. Soon afterwards Hitler met Hugenburg, the leader of the Nationalists, and negotiations began for a coalition. Meetings later took place between Papen and Oskar von Hindenburg, Hitler and Göring. Now Schleicher found himself in the same position as Papen eight weeks earlier. On 28 January he asked Hindenburg for permission to dissolve the Reichstag, and Hindenburg refused. Schleicher therefore resigned. Next morning the Nazi *Völkischer Beobachter* carried a heading in letters an inch high: 'Our demand after Schleicher's fall: the Chancellorship for Hitler.' Hindenburg turned again to Papen, who sought to bring Nazis and Nationalists together. At this final moment there was still for Hitler the fear that Schleicher, with the army behind him, might intervene. But nothing happened, and Papen succeeded in his negotiations by agreeing to serve as vice-chancellor under Hitler. On the morning of 30 January Hitler was summoned to meet the President. Two hours later Hitler was Chancellor.

This was indeed the miracle of National Socialism. 'I cast my eyes back', Hitler had said just a year earlier, 'to the time when with six other unknown men I founded this association, when I spoke before eleven, twelve, thirteen, fourteen, twenty, thirty, fifty persons; when I recall how after a year I had won sixty-four members for the movement. . . . I must confess that that which has today been created when a stream of millions of our German fellow-countrymen is flowing into our movement, represents something which is unique in German history.'[2] Again, four years later he said: 'It is truly a

[1] Cf. Schröder, in *Nazi Conspiracy and Aggression*, Vol. II, pp. 922-4, and Papen, *Memoirs*, pp. 227-30.
[2] Speech in 1932, Baynes, Vol. I, p. 824.

miracle to trace this development of our movement. To posterity it will appear a fairy tale.'[1] And now, on this historic, magic Monday night of 30 January 1933, the S.A., S.S., and Stahlhelm staged a gigantic torchlight march through the streets of Berlin. Through the Brandenburger Tor and along the Unter den Linden and the Wilhelmstrasse marched the endless Brownshirt columns, hedged in by the cheering crowds. From the Chancellery windows Hitler watched, and Hindenburg from those of the nearby Presidential Palace: the old Field-Marshal nodding and tapping with his cane, the delighted Hitler with arm outstretched in the Nazi salute. For hour after hour the marching columns passed. . . . Germany was launched on the road to Armageddon.

ELECTIONS FOR THE REICHSTAG, 1919-33[2]

Seats gained by the Parties

Party	1919 (Jan.)	1920 (June)	1924 (May)	1924 (Dec.)	1928 (May)	1930 (Sept.)	1932 (July)	1932 (Nov.)	1933 (March)
Social Democratic	163	113	100	131	152	143	133	121	120
Independent Socialist	22	81	—	—	—	—	—	—	—
Communist	—	2	62	45	54	77	89	100	81
Catholic Centre	71	68	65	69	61	68	75	70	73
Bavarian People's	18	19	16	19	17	19	22	20	19
Hanoverian	3	4	5	4	3	3	—	1	—
People's	22	62	44	51	45	30	7	11	2
Democrat	74	44	28	32	25	14	4	2	5
Economic	—	—	9	17	23	23	2	1	—
Independents	4	4	5	—	—	51	7	10	6
Nationalist	42	65	106	103	79	41	40	51	53
National Socialist	—	—	32	14	13	107	230	196	288
Total	419	462	472	485	472	576	609	583	647

[1] Speech in 1935, Baynes, Vol. I, p. 138.
[2] Based on the table given by G. Scheele, *The Weimar Republic*, p. 149. Note that the total numbers of seats in the Reichstag varied with the total votes cast at each election. The country was divided into thirty-five large electoral areas, in each of which the electors voted for party lists. Every 60,000 votes given in an area to a party list secured the election of one member on that list; odd votes were not wasted, but were transferred to Reich party lists. (See Articles 22, 23, and 25 of the Weimar Constitution.)

PART THREE

The Nazi Party in Power

CHAPTER VIII

THE NAZI REVOLUTION

THE Nazi Revolution did not precede, but followed Hitler's becoming Chancellor of the German Reich. Hitler was called upon in legal fashion by the President to assume the Chancellorship; he did so as the result of bargaining with Papen, and political bargainings in one form or another had been going on for a long time. Papen thought that, as a result of his bargain, he would be able to control and moderate Hitler. The Nazi leader came to power as the result of the failure of the other parties in Germany to combine against him—that is, of their failure to realize in time how small were their own disagreements when compared with the magnitude of the menace which threatened them. The Nazis, before Hitler came to power, never won more than slightly over 37 per cent. of the votes cast in an election. But the other parties were hopelessly divided in their opposition: the Social Democrats were not strong enough alone, the Communists hated the Social Democrats almost more than the Nazis, the Nationalist Party in its nationalistic outlook sympathized with the Nazis. Thus Hitler was able to strike his bargain with the influential Papen and Hugenberg, the leader of the Nationalist Party; Hitler became head of a coalition government. At first, therefore, he had to go carefully; it took him just five months to consolidate his position and make himself dictator.

In Hitler's coalition Government Papen was Vice-Chancellor; he was also Reich Commissioner for Prussia, and these two offices appeared to give him sufficient power to hold Hitler in check. Of the remaining posts only two were held by Nazis: Frick was Minister of the Interior, and Göring Minister without Portfolio (and also Minister of the Interior for Prussia). Two posts were given to men of Hindenburg's choice: the diplomat von Neurath became Foreign

Minister, and General von Blomberg Minister of Defence. The other posts went to the Nationalists, Hugenberg, Seldte (leader of the Nationalist private army, the *Stahlhelm*, comparable to the S.A.), and others of their party. It certainly looked promising enough for Papen; he had persuaded Hindenburg to overcome his fears of making Hitler Chancellor, and now with the new coalition Government it seemed evident that the wild man was under firm control. But Papen had a lot to learn.

The Nazi-Nationalist coalition held 247 seats in a Reichstag of 583. Hitler's first task was to find a secure parliamentary majority. Hitler might have gained the support of the Catholic Centre; negotiations were opened, but Hitler saw to it that they broke down. It was his aim to fight an election with the State machinery on his side; it had long been his aim not to revolt against the State, but to take over all the machinery of state, and use it to make the Nazi revolution. Papen was beguiled into the trap and persuaded Hindenburg to dissolve the Reichstag: Germany was to go to the polls once more. 'The struggle is a light one now', wrote Goebbels, 'since we are able to employ all the means of the State. Radio and Press are at our disposal. We shall achieve a masterpiece of propaganda. Even money is not lacking this time.'[1]

Hitler presented the Nazi Party as an alternative to the weakness and futility of the old régime, of the democratic system which had rested chiefly on the Social Democrat and Catholic Centre parties. 'In fourteen years the system which has now been overthrown has piled mistake upon mistake, illusion upon illusion.' The other parties, he argued, had failed in foreign policy, and had brought economic ruin at home. He even avowed that his Government was more Christian than the Centre, whose members had sat with Socialist atheists. How different, he argued, the Nazis would be! 'I ask of you, German people, that after you have given to the others fourteen years you should give to us a period of four years.'[2]

Neither funds nor force were lacking in the Nazi campaign. Göring played a prominent part in raising funds; he called

---

[1] Goebbels, *My Part in Germany's Fight*, p. 240, diary entry for 3 February.
[2] Speeches at Stuttgart and Cologne, Baynes, Vol. I, pp. 239 and 250.

a meeting of the great industrial leaders, including Krupp and Dr. Schacht, and a subscription list from the leading German firms was drawn up. To ensure that the force of the State also was on the Nazi side, Göring used all his ruthless energy. As Minister of the Interior for Prussia, he was in charge of the Prussian police and Prussian state administration; since Prussia was by far the largest state, Göring in fact was in charge of nearly two-thirds of Germany, and was of greater importance than the Reich Minister of the Interior (who, in any case, was the Nazi, Frick). Göring proceeded to purge the Prussian civil service and police; he dismissed those officials whose loyalty to the new Government was doubtful and replaced them by Nazis. He formed an auxiliary police into which he drafted large bodies of men from the S.A. and S.S., and supplied them with arms. He warned the regular police that they must co-operate with S.A., S.S., and the *Stahlhelm*. And, above all, he told the police to use their firearms 'without regard for the effect of their shots'. With Göring in charge of the coercive machinery of the Prussian state, German citizens were helpless; the law afforded no redress to Nazi violence.[1]

The main Nazi attack was directed against the Communists, which was good propaganda and sound tactics. It was announced that, in a raid on the Communist headquarters, the police had found the plans for a Communist revolution. But these were never published, in spite of promises by Hitler and Göring to do so. Then on the night of 27 February the Reichstag building caught fire and was burnt out.[2] This was but part, so went the official explanation, of a campaign of Communist terrorism. A young Dutch Communist, van der Lubbe, was caught in the act of starting fires. Actually, it appears certain,[3] the Nazis themselves had used an underground

[1] Göring's police orders are given in Baynes, Vol. I, p. 220. See also ibid., pp. 220-2, for extracts from Göring's speeches touching on violence in the revolution.

[2] See the detailed account by K. Heiden, *The Führer*, Chapter 22.

[3] *Nuremberg Proceedings*, Vol. IX, p. 434, and Vol. XXII, p. 418. Compare W. Frischauer, *Göring*, p. 120, and Butler and Young, *Marshal without Glory*, p. 128. Ludecke heard the news on the boat returning from New York: 'Immediately there flashed through my mind: Clever! Well done! I took for granted, of course, that the Nazis had done it': *I Knew Hitler*, p. 505.

passage leading from the palace of the President of the Reichstag (Göring) to the Reichstag building to fire it, and used
the Dutchman as a cover-up. The subsequent trial at Leipzig
was embarrassing to Göring: the judges acquitted the
accused Communist leaders (the German, Torgler, and the
Bulgarian, Dimitroff, who with great audacity scored well off
Göring during the trial). Van der Lubbe only was executed.
Hitler had wanted the immediate hanging of the Dutchman
outside the Reichstag—and is said to have wanted a St.
Bartholomew's Night of vengeance throughout Germany. The
coalition Government, however, demurred; Hugenberg and
Papen wished the army to intervene, but Blomberg opposed
its intervention in politics.

The Nazis were restricted, but not stopped. The burning of the Reichstag served its purpose. Hitler issued a
presidential decree 'for the protection of People and State':
to protect the people, it suspended the clauses of the
Weimar Constitution guaranteeing personal liberty. Göring
arrested the Communist Deputies of the Reichstag and a
number of Social Democrats as well. Nazi violence against
the Communists increased—meetings were broken up, newspapers suppressed, leaders and speakers beaten up. The
Communist Party was not banned, however; it was wiser to
leave it to split the working-class vote at the election, and so
avoid any accession of strength to the Social Democrats.
Hundreds of people were injured and fifty-one officially admitted killed during the election campaign. Moderate people
everywhere were intimidated, either by reports of the intended
Communist revolution or by the Nazis' terrorism itself. Hitler
was able to dramatize his election campaign as a struggle to
save Europe from Bolshevism. In an interview with the *Daily
Express* correspondent, he denied charges that the Reichstag
fire was a put-up job. 'But I will tell you another thing',
Hitler said. 'Europe, instead of suspecting me of false play,
should be grateful to me for my drastic action against the
Bolshevists. If Germany went Communist, as there was every
danger of her doing until I became Chancellor, it would not
have been long before the rest of civilized Europe fell a prey

to this Asiatic pest.'[1] Hitler concluded the interview by saying: 'We must crush Communism out of existence.' But he said that normal freedom would then be restored—an empty promise. Göring epitomized the ferocity behind the campaign when he declared at one of his meetings: 'Fellow Germans, my measures will not be crippled by any judicial thinking. . . . I don't have to worry about justice. . . . This struggle will be a struggle against chaos, and such a struggle I shall not conduct with the power of the police. A bourgeois State might have done that. Certainly, I shall use the power of the State and the police to the utmost, my dear Communists, so don't draw any false conclusions; but the struggle to the death, in which my fist will grasp your necks, I shall lead with those down there—the Brown Shirts.'[2]

The German nation polled on Sunday, 5 March, after weeks of oratory, threats, street violence, vast meetings, demonstrations, and torchlight parades, which all helped to create the impression of an invincible mass movement advancing to victory. Nearly 90 per cent of the electors voted. The Nazis polled 17,277,200 (increasing their vote by 5½ millions) out of a total of 39,343,300, which gave them 288 seats in a Reichstag of 647 members. With their allies, the National Party of fifty-three members (with a poll of 3,136,800), the Nazis thus had a bare majority. The remarkable thing about the election results, however, was how steady had been the reaction of the great opposition parties to the Nazi campaign: the Social Democrats lost one seat only, polling over 7 millions; the Catholic Centre increased their votes, and polled nearly 4½ millions; and even the Communist Party, though it lost 1 million votes, polled nearly 5 millions. As far as the figures went, the Nazi victory was by no means overwhelming. But it was sufficient. If the Communists were absent—and most of them were under arrest—the Nazis would have a majority in the Reichstag without the support of the National Party. And that would make Hitler independent of Papen and Hugenberg.

Hitler's task was to make himself supreme by destroying, or

[1] Interview with Mr. Sefton Delmer, *Daily Express*, 3 March 1933.
[2] Speech on 3 March, Frankfurt-on-Main: *Nuremberg Documents*, 1856-PS.

reducing to a subordinate position, those other institutions or organizations which could in any way challenge, check, or hamper his power as head of the Reich government. This process was one of *Gleichschaltung*, or co-ordination: the whole life of Germany was to be brought under the control of the Nazi Party. Hitler had to deal with the Reichstag and the political parties, with the trade unions, and with the federal states, or *Länder*.

At first Hitler showed himself conciliatory, for he wanted the Reichstag to pass an Enabling Bill to give the Government special powers. To do this, which meant an alteration of the Constitution, would require a majority of two-thirds. To win the support of all the conservative forces, he staged a splendid ceremony at Potsdam, just as he had said privately he would,[1] to mark the reconciliation of old and new in Germany. The ceremony on 21 March was to mark the opening of the new Reichstag, but the Garrison Church at Potsdam evoked memories, not of Weimar and a democratic Germany, but of the military spirit of the Kaisers. The Army and the S.A. formed guards of honour as President and Chancellor arrived. Inside the church were the surviving high officers of the old imperial Germany, headed by Field-Marshal von Mackensen, and all in uniform. The Nazi Deputies in their brown shirts, the Nationalist members, and the Catholic Centre were drawn up in rows. The Kaiser's chair was empty, but behind it sat the former Crown Prince, representative of the Hohenzollerns. Hindenburg, bowing low to the ex-Crown Prince, spoke briefly of the mandate given by the people to the new Government, of its heavy tasks, and of his hope for a united, free, and proud Germany. Hitler, in civilian morning dress, followed. He spoke of 1918 and the collapse of the nation, and said: 'In a unique revival, in the last few weeks our national honour has been restored and, thanks to your understanding'—addressing Hindenburg—'the union between the symbols of the old greatness and the new strength has been completed. . . . We pay you homage, *Herr Generalfeldmarschall*. . . . Providence places you over this revival of our

[1] See p. 139.

nation.'[1] Hitler shook Hindenburg by the hand; and the old warrior stepped down alone into the crypt to lay a wreath upon the tomb of Frederick the Great. Then the roar of guns in salute broke the silence and, a little later, in the clear spring sunshine outside, the troops and detachments of the S.A. and the Stahlhelm marched past in review.

Two days later, on 23 March, the Reichstag met in its temporary accommodation at the Kroll Opera House. The building was surrounded by S.S., and inside were men of the S.A. But Hitler, in proposing the Enabling Bill, spoke in a conciliatory tone; he had, indeed, already made certain worthless promises to the leaders of the Catholic Centre, and he now made more to the members of the Reichstag as a whole. 'The Government', he said, 'offers to the parties of the Reichstag the opportunity for friendly co-operation.' Only the Social Democrats dared to oppose—their leader, Otto Wels, having the great courage to stand up in the hostile throng and say that his party would vote against the Bill. The Communists were in gaol; the Catholic Centre voted for the Bill. The result was announced by Göring: for the Bill, 441; against, 94. When Hitler, with the Cabinet, appeared on the balcony, the crowd went wild with delight. Again and again it shouted, *'Heil Hitler!'* By the new law, the Government was given the power for the next four years to make laws without the Reichstag; such laws were to be drafted by the chancellor, and they might modify the constitution. Hitler was independent of the Reichstag—he was a dictator.

The policy of *Gleichschaltung* was soon applied to the political parties and the trade unions. Many of the local trade union offices had, indeed, already been pillaged by the Nazis, but on 2 May, after the people of Berlin had been dazzled on May Day by a gigantic Nazi demonstration and spectacle on the Tempelhof field, the trade union offices all over the country were occupied by men of the S.A. or S.S. The union officials were often beaten up and thrown into prison or concentration camp. The union organizations were then taken

[1] *Dokumente der deutschen Politik*, I, pp. 20-4. This volume also contains the text of the Enabling Bill and that of the presidential decree of 28 February (after the Reichstag fire), *zum Schutz von Volk und Staat.*

over by the Nazis, and re-formed into the new German Labour Front. The Nazis followed up their blow to the trade unions by one against the Social Democratic Party itself. On 10 May its property—buildings, offices, newspapers, and funds—was seized. In June this Party was formally banned. The Communists had not been allowed to take their seats; their Party property was also confiscated. The other parties, though less roughly handled, saw the danger of a similar fate. At the end of June and the beginning of July the small Democrat Party, the People's Party, and the once-important Catholic Centre Party all liquidated themselves. Hugenberg, in spite of his protests, could not save his own Nationalist Party; it also liquidated itself at the end of June, and Hugenberg was forced to resign his ministerial post. Seldte, the leader of the Stahlhelm, joined the Nazi Party, and his organization was eventually merged in the S.A. On 14 July the Government issued an official order declaring that 'The National Socialist German Workers' Party constitutes the only political party in Germany'.

Meanwhile—indeed, ever since the election victory of 5 March—the process of *Gleichschaltung* had been applied to the federal states. Prussia was already under Göring's control. On March 5, on the initiative of Göring, the Government of Hamburg was seized by a coup. On 9 March General von Epp acted for Hitler in Bavaria, where there had been since Hitler's becoming Chancellor of the Reich some talk of secession and restoring the Wittelsbach monarchy; Epp turned out the Bavarian Government and filled up the posts with Nazis. Between 5 and 16 March the other federal states passed under Nazi control, Frick, as Minister of the Interior, sending in *Reichskomissars* to replace the state governments by Nazi ministers. Early in April Hitler appointed for each state a *Reichstatthalter*, or governor, with powers to appoint and remove the state government and dissolve the state parliament. At the same time Papen was pushed aside altogether in Prussia (where he had been nominally superior to Göring), Hitler making himself *Reichstatthalter*, with Göring as Minister-President. On 30 January 1934 a new law abolished the elective state parliaments altogether, and transferred their once sovereign powers to the Reich; the *Reichstatthalters* and state governments were made subordinate to the Minister of the Interior of the Reich.[1] Thus, under Hitler, German administration reached a degree of centralization previously unknown. As Frick explained the new law: 'The historical task of our times is the creation of a strong, national, unitary state to replace the former federal state. . . . The state governments from today on are merely administrative bodies of the Reich.'[2]

Hitler was now dictator, with the machinery and powers of a great state in his hands. But as a former Nazi revolutionary he was still surrounded by revolutionaries—men who were violent and fanatical, good fighters in a revolutionary movement, but inconvenient and embarrassing when once the revolution had succeeded. One makes a revolution with one set of men; one governs with another—as Mussolini was reported to have said later on to Hitler. Then there were many in the Nazi Party, and many who had joined it later in its time of success, who had hoped to get something out of it. Some of them were disappointed, and some did not do as well as they had hoped. At first there were excitement and expectancy, then anti-climax. Disappointment and discontent were rife and had to be reckoned with, and there were also the old rivalries and jealousies among the Party leaders which had shown themselves as early as Hitler's imprisonment in 1924. There were, too, the very natural fears of the established civil servants in their ministries, of the Foreign Service, and of the higher officers of the Army for the new men who were being placed in positions of authority. The capitalist elements of Germany, the great industrialists and also the small traders and shopkeepers, feared the radical, socialist demands of the Left wing of the National Socialist Party. Outside of Germany there was the reaction of foreign states to be watched—for example, the nervous reaction of France, Poland, and Russia. There were protests from abroad

---

[1] *Dokumente der deutschen Politik,* II, p. 101.

[2] *Völkischer Beobachter,* 31 January. See F. L. Schumann, *Hitler and the Nazi Dictatorship,* pp. 264-7.

about the atrocities inside Germany, for it was soon reported that terrible things were happening—secret arrests, beatings and torture, imprisonment without trial. Göring's secret police were gaining notoriety. Prisons and concentration camps began to fill up, and against the Party the ordinary person had no redress. Ordinary Germans, who had not suffered, were apt to excuse themselves with a shrug of the shoulders. 'You know the times we live in', they said.

Nevertheless, the Nazi movement had behind it a powerful revolutionary force, which had gathered to itself a large mass support in the country. It was wrong to suppose, as Socialist and Communist elements in foreign countries tended to do, that the Nazi régime was a dictatorship imposed by force on an unwilling people. It was even more wrong to imagine that the German people were awaiting an opportunity for revolt. The extraordinary thing is that Hitler had been able to carry through his policy of *Gleichschaltung* without serious opposition. Reichstag, parties, trade unions, the federal states had all given way without a struggle. Hitler himself was surprised by the collapse of the opposition. The Nazis had shown great energy, determination, and will power; unfortunately, the moderate, reasonable, liberal elements had shown nothing comparable, and even the Communists and the Social Democrats, with their theoretical attachment to the idea of social revolution, had not dared to make a stand. Indeed, the violent elements in the Communist Party were attracted by the Nazis. And Röhm, it seems, welcomed them into the S.A. 'It's easier to control Communist elements inside the S.A. than by closing the ranks against them', he said. 'They can't undermine the S.A.—some of my best men are former Communists. Let them call them "Beefsteaks" [i.e. red inside, brown outside, as Berlin put it]. I like them radical.'[1] Hitler's success was a measure of what could be achieved by an unscrupulous and determined leader, and how easily the masses could be cajoled, seduced, and led away. Hitler had nothing to fear from the German people. But he had to fear a crisis in his own Party.

[1] As reported by Ludecke, *I Knew Hitler*, p. 597.

Hitler was faced with three problems: the problem of the second revolution, as it was called; the old problem, which had given trouble before, of the relation between the S.A. and the Army; and the new problem raised by the declining health of Hindenburg. And these problems were not distinct and separate; they were interconnected.

Hitler himself was not interested in the details of government and administration; nor was he an economist or socialist. Promises of social and economic reform were useful to beguile the masses, but the work of managing the economic system he was prepared to leave to industrialists and economic experts so long as they provided employment and produced the goods. Hitler wanted time: time to consolidate his régime and to prepare for the great tasks of foreign policy which were his main interest. But he was being pushed by the forces in his party pressing for a second revolution, and he was aware of a divergence in the Party between the conservative, national and capitalist element and the socialist element. Hitler himself sounded a note of warning. In a speech on 1 July 1933 to S.A. and S.S. leaders, he explained that the first three stages of the revolution—preparation, the seizure of power, and the achievement of totalitarianism—were over. The chief requisite now was order. The idea of a second revolution or 'revolution in permanence' could not be tolerated. 'I will suppress every attempt to disturb the existing order as ruthlessly as I will deal with the so-called second revolution, which would lead only to chaotic conditions.'[1] And a few days later he addressed the Reichstatthälter, assembled in Berlin. Once again Hitler said: 'The revolution is not a permanent state of affairs, and it must not be allowed to develop into such a state. The stream of revolution released must be guided into the safe channel of evolution. . . . We must therefore not dismiss a business-man if he is a good business-man, even if he is not yet a National Socialist; and especially not if the National Socialist who is to take his place knows nothing about business. In business, ability must be the only

[1] Baynes, Vol. I, p. 287; and see also Seton-Watson, *Britain and the Dictators* pp. 222 et seq.

authoritative standard. . . .'[1] And again, a week later, in speaking to the Nazi *Gauleiters*, he said that there must be no 'radical breaking up of existing conditions which would endanger the foundations of their own life'.[2] Others in the Party, and especially in the S.A., thought otherwise.

Goebbels had often attacked the reactionary forces of the right; Gregor Strasser, though he was now living privately since throwing up his job in the Party, looked on Hitler's advent as the first stage in a revolutionary process; his brother, Otto Strasser, stood for simultaneous attack on bourgeois capitalism and international Marxism, and had broken with Hitler because he regarded him as a reactionary. Most important of all, however, was Röhm, because he was Hitler's friend and comrade since the early days and was now chief-of-staff of the S.A. with between 2 and 3 million men under his command. But revolutionary Nazis did not agree among themselves, and were kept apart by personal jealousies and fear. Ludecke, according to his own account, had tried several times, and especially in 1932, to bring Röhm and Strasser together, but without success. Ludecke's personal story in 1933-4—an old Party member imprisoned first on Göring's orders and then put away in a concentration camp on Hitler's orders, finally being forced to escape over the frontier—is some indication of the intrigues going on in the Party. In June 1933 (shortly before the Gestapo arrested him on Hitler's directions) Ludecke had a long talk with Röhm, and the two men discussed the prospects of 'a house-cleaning of the Party' and an extension of the revolution. One difficulty was that Röhm could always be attacked by his enemies in the Party on the ground of his private vices. 'Those hypocrites!' Röhm exclaimed. 'I've suffered enough from that. . . . Homosexuality isn't a reason for removing an able and honest leader from any position, so long as he is discreet. Such a more or less natural abnormality is nobody's business. . . . Haven't I worked all my life for this land and given Hitler all I had? Where would he be without me? Hitler had better look out

[1] Speech of 6 July 1933: Baynes, Vol. I, p. 865.
[2] Speech of 13 July 1933: ibid., pp. 484.

—the German revolution is only beginning!' Then Röhm
tossed over to Ludecke a copy of a Nazi monthly, in which
a bold message from Röhm himself headed, '*S.A. und deutsche
Revolution*', was published: 'One victory on the road of German revolution has been won. . . . The S.A. and S.S., who
bear the great responsibility of having set the German revolution rolling, will not allow it to fall asleep or to be betrayed
at the halfway mark. . . . If the Philistines believe that the
national revolution has lasted too long . . . it is indeed high
time that the national revolution should end and become a
National-Socialist one. . . . We shall continue our fight—with
them or without them. And, if necessary, against them. . . . We
shall watch relentlessly to keep the half-hearted and the oppor-
tunists from hanging themselves like so much lead on the
Führer's sacred, socialistic will. . . . We are the incorrup-
tible guarantors of the fulfilment of the German revolution.'
Bold words! Rash words! And Hitler had read the article,
so Röhm avowed, and Röhm had said more to Hitler than
he had thought proper to put in print. Röhm had a clear, if
rather naïve, view of things. 'The cowardly surrender of the
opposition surprised Hitler', he said, 'more than it surprised
me. He can't get over it. Why doesn't he put the money-bags
where they belong! If he didn't know it before, he knows
now that I'll never allow our revolution to fizzle out. Of
course, he's in a quandary and, as usual, shuns a clear-cut
decision. . . . But if he thinks he can squeeze me for his own
ends for ever, and some fine day throw me on the ash-heap,
he's wrong. The S.A. can also be an instrument for checking
Hitler himself.'[1] Röhm, too, had a view of the wider, world
situation: he saw the possibilities—the German Army High
Command hand in hand with big business and looking for a
military alliance with Russia; or Hitler as dictator with the
Army under his thumb marching eastwards against Russia. For
his own part, Röhm (and Ludecke) thought to work with Russia
and against capitalism in Germany and the West.[2] Again, in a

---

[1] Ludecke, *I Knew Hitler*, pp. 595-7. Röhm's article is in the *National Sozialistische
Monatshefte*, No. 39, June 1933.
[2] *I Knew Hitler*, pp. 647-9. Views expressed in February 1934 at a secret meeting with Ludecke, who had slipped out from Oranienburg Concentration Camp.

speech in April 1934, Röhm expressed his view that the German revolution was 'not a nationalist, but a National Socialist revolution, with special stress on the word "Socialist". . . . There are still men in official positions today who have not the least idea of the spirit of the revolution. We shall ruthlessly get rid of them if they dare to put their reactionary ideas into practice.'[1]

It was, indeed, a clear picture Röhm had given. Röhm and his S.A. were after the fruits of Socialism, the spoils and pickings of revolution—though this was not altogether unnatural when one recalls the long years of depression and unemployment, and how the S.A. had offered hope to unemployed workers and professional men and ruined members of the middle classes. Hitler was interested in power, and to secure the power he had achieved he must retain the support of the Army and ensure his succession to the Presidency. The Army was now bitterly jealous of the S.A., and feared it, for the S.A. was many times larger than the Army, and Röhm wished to use it as the basis for a new people's army. And the Right-wing conservative forces behind the President hated and feared the radical, socialist element in the Party headed by Röhm. Hitler was indeed in a quandary. For the S.A. could still be useful to him; he could use it to bring pressure, blackmail, if necessary, on the Army and the Right-wing forces of industry and finance; he could use it as a bargaining counter in foreign policy—for example, by offering to reduce its strength when Mr. Eden visited Berlin in February. And perhaps, too, Hitler suffered genuine qualms in turning on his old friends; he certainly had a strong sentimental feeling for the early days of struggle, the *Kampfzeit*. But Hitler was a realist: at all events he must retain on his side the real forces of the country, the Army and large-scale industry.

Hitler tried conciliation, as he had done before with Röhm and with the Strassers. He made Röhm a minister in the Reich Government in December, and wrote him a most friendly, personal letter at New Year, 1934. Hitler thanked

[1] Quoted by Seton-Watson, *Britain and the Dictators*, pp. 223-4.

him and his leadership of the S.A. for 'making it possible for me to win decisively in the struggle for power'; he thanked him for his 'imperishable services' and declared: 'How grateful I am to destiny for being allowed to number such men as yourself among my friends and comrades-in-arms.'[1] But Röhm was not satisfied. Göring had been made a general and Hitler had promised Blomberg a field-marshal's baton. 'And I!' said Röhm to Ludecke. 'I am still minister without portfolio.' Then, referring to the New Year letter from Hitler: 'He can't fool me. . . . Yes, we still need him. Unfortunately, half the nation already sees a demi-god in him. But we must push him soon, lest the others push him first. . . . If Hitler is reasonable, I shall settle the matter quietly; if he isn't, I must be prepared to use force—not for my sake, but for the sake of our revolution.'[2] On 4 June Hitler spent five hours with Röhm. 'I implored him for the last time', Hitler reported later, 'to oppose this madness of his own accord', and to 'use his authority so as to stop a development which in any event could only end in a catastrophe'.[3] But apparently Röhm was neither won over nor intimidated. For the immediate future, Hitler ordered the S.A. on leave for July, and Röhm himself went on sick leave on 7 June—but not without a message to his men which contained a challenge to the enemies of the S.A.: 'At the hour and in the form which appears to be necessary they will receive the fitting answer.'[4] To Röhm there seemed no immediate danger. Like so many others, he, too, underestimated Hitler.

But the intrigues went on in Germany, and tension grew. Schleicher had appeared again in the background. The full story of what went on is not known, and probably never will be. However, it seems certain that Hitler managed to reach an understanding with the generals: the Army should remain the national source of power and the S.A. be kept in a subordinate place; Hitler, in spite of conservative hopes of a

[1] *Völkischer Beobachter*, 2 January 1934: trans., Ludecke, p. 649, and Baynes, Vol. I, p. 289.
[2] Ludecke, *I Knew Hitler*, pp. 648-9.
[3] Speech to the Reichstag, 13 July 1933: Baynes, Vol. I, p. 316.
[4] *Frankfurter Zeitung*, 10 June 1934: trans., Baynes, Vol. I, p. 287.

restoration of the Hohenzollern monarchy when Hindenburg died, should succeed to the presidential power.

Then, on 17 June at the University of Marburg, Papen made a bold speech. It was a warning to Hitler of the anxieties of the Right, of the conservative and respectable forces in Germany, and indeed voiced the doubts and fears of decent elements throughout the nation. He dealt severely with the idea of the second revolution:

> Whoever toys irresponsibly with such ideas should not forget that a second wave might be followed by a third, and that he who threatens to employ a guillotine may be its first victim.
>
> Nor is it clear where such a second wave is to lead. There is much talk of the coming socialization. Have we gone through the anti-Marxist revolution in order to carry out a Marxist programme? . . . Would the German people be better for it, except perhaps those who scent booty in such a pillaging raid? . . . At some time the movement must come to a stop and a solid social structure will arise. . . . There is no upbuilding amid everlasting eruptions.[1]

He went on to ask for confidence and understanding rather than propaganda. 'It is time', he said, 'to join together in fraternal friendship and respect for all our fellow countrymen, to avoid disturbing the labours of serious men and to silence fanatics.' Papen's speech was something of a sensation. Goebbels, as Minister of Propaganda, took steps to ban its publication. Papen saw Hitler and threatened resignation. Hitler also received a warning from the President and a threat to declare martial law. A few days later, appearing publicly in Hamburg, Papen received an ovation. In the last week of June tension reached breaking-point.

On 30 June Hitler struck. Behind him he had the S.S., and the Army. It was in the Hotel Dreesen at Godesberg on the Rhine, on the afternoon of the 29th, that Hitler made up his mind. That very night he flew from Bonn to Munich to confront Röhm in person. Early on Saturday morning, the 30th, with Goebbels, who had rapidly put his radical views

[1] Text of speech given by Oswald Dutch, *The Errant Diplomat*, pp. 191-209.

aside, and other Nazi leaders, and well guarded by the S.S., in armoured cars, Hitler drove out to the hotel where Röhm was staying at Wiessee. The S.A. leaders on whom they could lay hands were dragged out of bed, accused of plotting a *coup d'état*, carried back to Munich, where Hess was waiting for them, and shot by S.S. guards in the old Stadelheim Prison. The notorious Heines, found sleeping with a youth, was shot there and then, according to one account. Röhm, shut in a cell with a loaded revolver, refused to commit suicide, and was shot by one of the S.S. In Berlin Göring and Himmler directed operations. Executions of S.A. leaders went on during the Saturday and Sunday. Karl Ernst, seized when setting out on a voyage with his wife, is said to have died shouting, '*Heil Hitler!*' He thought that Hitler had been betrayed. At the same time, a number of others, some of them supposedly dangerous, were disposed of individually in their homes, offices, or elsewhere—the ex-chancellor General von Schleicher and his wife, his friend, General von Bredow, Gregor Strasser, and two of Papen's staff, von Bose and Edgar Jung. Papen himself narrowly escaped, though placed under house arrest for several days. Prominent Catholics were shot, including Dr. Klausener, leader of Catholic Action. There were many executions in other parts of Germany. Hitler's old opponent, von Kahr, former premier of Bavaria and now a man of seventy-three, was dragged from bed in the night; his body was later found hacked to pieces. Willi Schmidt, the Munich music critic, was done to death by reason of his name; the S.S. were looking for a different Schmidt. How many died altogether is not known: estimates varied from the official figure of seventy-seven to a figure of over 400. There may have been many more. 'Like a black panther on a dark night', Hitler was reported as saying, 'so I spring on my enemy by surprise and destroy him.'[1]

Whether there was any real or definite plot against Hitler cannot be decided for certain. No valid evidence was produced, it is unlikely that all these very different people could

[1] T. Duesterberg, *Der Stahlhelm und Hitler*, p. 86. He gives the number of victims as 1,100.

have been involved in the same plot, and the fact that Röhm was on holiday and caught completely unawares does not indicate that he was on the point of making an immediate coup. But by his action, Hitler relieved the pressure on him from Left and Right, and disposed of men who might have been dangerous. Hitler defended his action in a speech on 13 July to the Reichstag—to a Reichstag which since the *Gleichschaltung* of the political parties consisted of Nazi members only. He made the most of the known vices of the S.A. leaders, Röhm and Heines, of their homosexual practices, and also accused them of drunkenness, extravagance, and luxurious living on Party funds. But these things had for a long time been no secret. Hitler did not, however, hide what was their real crime—the threat of a second revolution. He spoke of them as 'uprooted', and said that they had become 'revolutionaries who favoured revolution for its own sake and desired to see revolution established as a permanent condition'. They had found 'in Nihilism their final confession of faith'. Hitler made a grandiloquent plea in his own defence: 'Mutinies are repressed in accordance with laws of iron which are eternally the same. If anyone reproaches me and asks why I did not resort to the regular courts of justice, then all I can say to him is this: in this hour I was responsible for the fate of the German people, and thereby I became the supreme justiciar of the German people. . . . And everyone must know for all future time that if he raises his hand to strike the State, then certain death is his lot.'[1] In other words, stripped of its grandiloquence, what Hitler was saying meant that, like a Chicago gangster, he had succeeded, and, having succeeded, he now disposed of his fellow-gangsters lest they might prove dangerous.

Some people hoped that Hitler's action would at last open German eyes. This, however, was a complete error. People said instead: 'Leave me in peace with your terror stories. I don't want to know of them. . . . Hitler saved us from a far worse civil war.'[2] Hitler, too, doubtless wanted to forget.

[1] Speech to the Reichstag, 13 July 1934: Baynes, Vol. I, pp. 321-2.
[2] T. Duesterberg, *Der Stahlhelm und Hitler*, pp. 89-90.

Months later there was still on the walls in the Dreesen Hotel a photograph of Hitler and a group of Nazis, which had originally included Röhm. But now Röhm was covered by a figure cut from another photograph and pasted skilfully over the dead S.A. leader. Röhm was hidden lest Hitler on subsequent visits should remember.

It remained for Hitler to put the final touches to his position of absolute power. On 2 August President von Hindenburg died—at a lucky moment for Hitler. At once a law, dated 1 August, was issued, uniting in the person of Hitler the offices of President and Chancellor. Hitler was thus in theory as well as fact head of the State. The title 'President' was, perhaps, too republican in flavour for Hitler. He did not use it, but was known as *Führer und Reichskanzler*. But he wanted its powers; with the presidential function he became commander-in-chief of the German armed forces. Officers and men now took the oath of allegiance to Hitler, mentioned by name in the form of words: 'I swear by God this holy oath that I will give unlimited obedience to the Führer of the German Reich, Adolf Hitler.'[1] On 19 August by plebiscite the German people were asked to approve. Out of 45 million voters, over 38 millions voted 'Yes'. The Nazi revolution, Hitler's revolution, was complete. Hitler's sense of personal power grew. For him there was neither law nor morality—for him all that was old-fashioned sentiment.[2]

[1] Quoted in *Germany*, Vol. II (official handbook), p. 343.
[2] Duesterberg, p. 90.

CHAPTER IX

THE FÜHRER AND THE PARTY–STATE

THE Nazi Revolution made Hitler the head of a one-party state on the Italian or Russian model. There was, however, no formal abrogation of the Weimar Constitution, through the democratic forms of which Hitler and the Nazis had come to power. But the *Machtübernahme*—the taking over of power by Hitler in 1933—was the end of the ill-starred Weimar experiment in democracy, and marked the triumph of a completely different *Weltanschauung* or philosophy of life, though one in some ways more in keeping with older authoritarian traditions in Germany. In the Nazi philosophy—if indeed it merits the name of philosophy—were blended a number of strains: the idealist theory of the State, with state and race placed in a position superior to that of the individual, militarism, the personal intuitionism of Hitler, and the *Führerprinzip* or leadership principle. What this amounted to in practice was that Hitler was supreme throughout Germany; he combined in his own person the highest functions of the State and was its *Führer*. As Dr. Hans Frank said to a congress of German lawyers: 'There is in Germany today only one authority, and that is the authority of the *Führer*.'[1] Or *Might is Right*, as a former member of the Berlin Bar who had escaped to safety called his book on the Nazi State.[2]

Many thousands of words were poured out by Hitler in his speeches to explain the Nazi State, many thousands more were written by Nazi lawyers and professors: enthusiastic speeches and the written word represented an attempt to create a faith of the Nazis' own invention. Common blood

---

[1] *Völkischer Beobachter*, 20 May 1936. See Professor Baynes's notes and bibliography on the 'Constitution of the National Socialist State', Baynes, Vol. I, pp. 413-21. Text of laws, decrees, and constitutional speeches in *Dokumente der deutschen Politik*.

[2] F. Roetter, *Might is Right*.

unites a people, it was held, and such a people has its own *Volkgeist* or national spirit. To that innate spirit the leader must appeal, and his success in so doing proves his right to leadership. People and leader are in tune. 'Once you heard the voice of a man, and it struck deep into your hearts; it awakened you, and you followed the voice.'[1] So spoke Hitler. 'We have faith in our people', he cried at Würzburg in 1937, 'and beyond that in our Movement which represents this people of the future. . . . If Providence had not guided us I could often never have found these dizzy paths . . . no man can fashion world history unless upon his purpose and his powers there rests the blessing of this Providence.'[2]

In such speeches Hitler created an atmosphere of fanatical mysticism. His audiences would respond and fall completely under his spell. Once he had carried his massed listeners away, they would have worshipped and applauded even had he spoken to them in an unknown tongue or reeled off mathematical formulae unintelligible to them. It was the magic of Hitler: to make words and sounds more powerful far than meaning, and to inflame to the uttermost national prejudices more potent, in any case, than rational thought.

German critics—those who succeeded in getting out of Germany and putting their criticism into writing—have made this clear. As the former Hamburg civil servant, Dr. Marx, ironically put it: 'The National Socialist idea is not to be desecrated through exhaustive rational exploration. No ideological myth survives vivisection with what Dostoevski called the "learned knife". The National Socialist idea must be kept in the twilight which prevails at places of worship. It is the Party, not the state, that conducts the service.'[3] Another German writer, a refugee professor, Dr. Neumann, declared outright: 'National Socialism has no rational political theory. But has it an anti-rational one', he went on to ask, 'and is there such a thing as an anti-rational theory?' And he answered his own question: 'A political theory cannot be non-rational. If it claims to be

---

[1] Speech of 13 September 1936: Baynes, Vol. I, p. 207. See also pp. 438-49 and 198-205.
[2] Ibid., pp. 410-11.
[3] F. M. Marx, *Government in the Third Reich*, p. 77.

non-rational, it is a conscious trick.' Then he took as an example a description of National Socialism by a Nazi professor at Heidelberg: 'And there has arisen . . . blood against formal reason; race against purposeful rationality; honour against profit; unity against individualistic disintegration; martial virtue against bourgeois security; the folk against the individual and the mass.' Words, words, words—so typical of the Nazi hysteria. 'The so-called non-rational concepts, blood, community, folk', wrote Neumann, 'are devices for hiding the real constellation of power and for manipulating the masses. The charisma of the Leader, the superiority of the master race, the struggle of a proletarian race against plutocracies, the protest of the folk against the State are consciously applied stratagems.'[1] Indeed, these were the screens behind which was hidden the reality of power—the personal dictatorship of Adolf Hitler. And the personal leadership of the *Führer* was recognized every time Germans met or took leave of each other in the words which became throughout Nazi Germany the ordinary form of greeting—*Heil Hitler!* As an educated middle-class German put it: 'Having a great man as our leader, we do not feel a lack of freedom. We have an unlimited confidence in him and his leadership.'[2]

The supremacy of the *Führer* applied in every sphere of Party and State: political policy and decisions were his; he was supreme in the making of laws; he exercised supreme control over foreign policy, determining and moulding it, making agreements and alliances, deciding on war or peace; he was supreme commander of the armed forces; his authority was behind the whole executive, administrative and judicial machinery of the country. Indeed, what had formerly been the most important institutions of central government lost much of their importance and were transformed. The Cabinet was dominated by Hitler and the other Nazi ministers in it, and, in any case, was used less and less as the central instrument of government. The Reichstag did not

---

[1] Franz Neumann, *Behemoth—Structure and Practice of National Socialism*, p. 379. The passage he quoted was by Ernst Krieck, Nazi philosopher.

[2] Extract from a personal letter.

disappear, but the parties did. So the Reichstag became a Nazi assembly, composed of selected old Party men. It met only once or twice a year to hear a speech by Hitler or to endorse, though without discussion, a law which had already been drawn up. It was therefore a body without importance in the machinery of government; it could not act, it could only advise and applaud. It was well described as 'the most highly paid male chorus in the world'.

The *Führer* used the Nazi Party and the machinery of the State as instruments by means of which he could carry out his will. *Führer*, Party, State, stood in that order. 'It is not the State which gives its orders to us, but we who give orders to the State!' cried Hitler at the Party Congress in 1934. 'It is not the State which created us; we fashioned for ourselves our State.'[1] The exact relationship of his two instruments, the Nazi Party and the State, and their relationship to the German people was not easy to determine. The Nazi Party took up the task of creating a Nazi State for the German people: had this process ever reached completion, the three might have reached identity. But in the short period of Nazi government this process could not have been perfected. At one moment Hitler could declare, 'The Party is the people', and seven lines further on in the same speech could contradict that by adding: 'The Party is a body of picked men. It represents in its constitution a selection from the people of its political elements.'[2] The second statement was nearer the truth than the first. The contradiction arose, perhaps, because Hitler realized that political forms would be ephemeral, and sought something of eternal validity; he sought a lasting reality in the German people: 'What I have called into life in these years cannot claim to be an end in itself—all can and will be transient. For us the permanent element is that substance of flesh and blood which we call the German people. Party, State, Army, economic organization—these are but institutions and functions which have only the value of a means to an end . . . and that end is again and always the people.'[3]

---

[1] Baynes, Vol. I, p. 662.　　[2] Speech of 8 July 1936: Baynes, Vol. I, p. 203.
[3] Speech of 20 February 1938: ibid., p. 428.

The relationship of Party and State was, however, very close. 'Party and State are distinguished', it was said, 'but not separated; they are united, but not fused.'[1] The Law of 1 December 1933 for securing the unity of Party and State expressed it by declaring that the National Socialist Party was the pillar of the German state and was 'indissolubly linked to it'.[2] At the same time two Party leaders, Hess, the *Führer's* deputy, and Röhm, chief of staff of the S.A., were made members of the Cabinet, thus creating two new links between State and Party. Goebbels explained that every Party member who held an office in the State must regard himself first of all as a National Socialist, and must carry out his actions on Nazi principles and in close co-operation with Nazi officials.[3] Thus government and civil service came to be penetrated by Nazi principles as members of the Party were appointed to public positions, and the remnant of democratic objectivity from Weimar days began to disappear. Hitler defined clearly enough the relation of State and Party at Nuremberg in 1935: 'The function of the state is the continuance of the administration. . . . The function of the Party is: (1) The building up of its own internal organization so as to create a stable, self-renewing, permanent cell of National Socialist teaching. (2) The education of the entire people in the meaning of the conceptions of this idea. (3) The introduction of those who have been so trained into the State to serve either as leaders or followers.'[4]

The government, administration, and Party organization of Nazi Germany made up as complicated a system as has ever been known; perhaps only to be rivalled by that of Soviet Russia, cast as the Soviet network is over so vast a geographical area. Germany was already divided into states, and the states into provinces and districts, but these political and administrative areas did not coincide with the Party areas or *Gaus*. The Army had its own geographical areas or *Wehrkreise*. S.A., S.S., and the Hitler Youth were also organized into different areas. Why the Germans, with their love of

---

[1] Carl Schmitt, *Staat, Bewegung, Volk* (1934), p. 21, quoted by Baynes, p. 415.
[2] *Dokumente der deutschen Politik*, I, pp. 90-1.
[3] As stated by Baynes, Vol. I, p. 416.   [4] Ibid., Vol. I, p. 444.

efficiency, tolerated these complexities, is something very puzzling. It was partly that they took over existing administrative machinery and added to it that of their own Party. Nazi political and social machinery did, however, give full scope to the German love of organization, and it also provided employment for many members of the Party. All those in positions which provided possibilities of expansion made full use of them; they built up their own offices, added to their staffs, and created organizations which sometimes stretched out through local offices into the whole country. Personal rivalry and jealousy, together with this natural tendency to expand, led to the creation of what were almost separate personal empires. Such were the power complexes centring on Himmler (police), Göring (second Four-Year Plan for economic development), Goebbels (propaganda) and Ley (*Arbeitsfront*—labour). Inside their respective spheres, the great Nazi leaders exercised considerable independence. Hitler, the demoniac dreamer, although ultimately supreme, was content to leave the detailed work of administration to others, although he breathed life and spirit into the whole unwieldy structure. A trained observer wrote in 1937 that 'it would require a lifelong study of administration to understand the complicated political structure of the National Socialist Party, and even an expert would be driven mad if he tried to unravel the relationships of Party to State. . . . Only one man ever understood the complicated machinery, it is said, and he suggested so many reforms and prunings that he was sent to Dachau concentration camp.'[1] Nevertheless, the system worked, with ruthless efficiency. German productive and military powers were developed rapidly and to such effect that in six years Germany was ready to challenge the world. Doubtless the vital organs of national policy, economic, police, and military, were thorough and efficient. The rest was a useful façade to employ Party men and keep them contented, to maintain morale, and put out propaganda on the widest scale at home and abroad.

[1] S. H. Roberts, *The House that Hitler Built*, p. 72. F. L. Schumann, *Hitler and the Nazi Dictatorship*, pp. 65-78, gives an account of the Party machinery.

Hitler had, to carry out his various functions as Party leader and head of the State, four chancelleries. As President, or *Führer*, he used the presidential chancellery under Dr. Meissner, who managed to maintain his position there under Ebert, Hindenburg, and Hitler.[1] As Chancellor—that is, as prime minister or head of the government—he used the State Chancellery, the *Reichkanzlei*, under Dr. Lammers. As leader of the Nazi Party, Hitler had the Party Chancellery under Hess (later under Martin Bormann). To deal with Hitler's more personal activities there was a fourth chancellery, the Chancellery of the *Führer*, under Philip Bouhler.

The unchallenged supremacy of Hitler and the nature of the Party reduced the importance of the Government or Cabinet (*Reichsregierung*). Ministers were no longer independent, free to argue and discuss, and with a following in a freely elected Reichstag and outside in the country; they became the instruments of Hitler and Party policy. The Cabinet contained many of the leading Nazis—Hitler, Hess, Göring, Himmler (from 1943), Goebbels, Rosenberg, Frick, Darré—but it also contained members who had not belonged to the Party, and others who were high officials, such as the heads of the Reich and presidential chancelleries. The functions of the Cabinet as a central body in the administration of the country grew less; its meetings became infrequent. The power to frame laws could be delegated to smaller groups of ministers or, after the commencement of the war, to the smaller Ministerial Council for Defence of the Reich, and Hitler himself held the power to draft laws under renewals of the Enabling Act. A pivotal figure in these arrangements was Dr. Lammers, head of the Reich Chancellery. He was the link between Hitler, the Cabinet, and the individual ministers or groups of ministers. Another factor weakening the Cabinet as a central governing body was the creation of a number of other authorities answerable directly to Hitler. Such was the appointment in 1936 of Göring as Plenipotentiary for the Four-Year Plan. Similarly, in 1936 Baldur von Shirach was made Reich Youth Leader. During the war

[1] See Otto Meissner, *Staatssekretar unter Ebert-Hindenburg-Hitler* (1950).

such authorities increased in number and were reported by 1943 to be over sixty.

The connexion between Cabinet and Party was close but by no means complete. Although Hitler had written in *Mein Kampf* of building up the Party as a State within the State, an organization ready at a given moment to take over the functions of government, there was in fact no complete taking over of ministerial posts by Nazi Party leaders. There was, thus, no complete identity between Cabinet posts and the corresponding posts in the Party leadership. In some cases there was this identity: Goebbels was Minister for Public Enlightenment and Propaganda, and at the same time propaganda chief of the Nazi Party; Himmler was leader of the S.S. and Chief of the German Police (later Minister of the Interior), so controlling the police of Party and State; Darré was Minister of Agriculture and leader for farming in the Party. In other cases, such important ministers as Göring (Air), and Ribbentrop (Foreign Affairs) did not at the same time hold positions of leadership in the Party. In the early days of power the conduct of foreign affairs offered a peculiar and most confusing picture. The diplomat Neurath, not a Party member, was Minister of Foreign Affairs, while Rosenberg, a jealous rival, ran the Party's Foreign Affairs Department, and the still more jealous Ribbentrop ran a bureau, under Hess, which came to be known as the 'Ribbentrop Bureau'. It took an active interest in foreign affairs, and Ribbentrop was later to become Minister at the expense of Neurath and Rosenberg.

The vast organization of the Nazi Party itself was also complicated.[1] Under the *Führer* stood the *Reichsleiter*. These *Reichsleiter*, nineteen of them in 1937, were the highest Party leaders, and included Hess, Hitler's deputy and head of the Party Chancellery, Goebbels, Himmler, Rosenberg, Ley, Frick, and Darré. Several of these were also ministers in the Cabinet. Others of the Nazi leaders were much less well known to the public, but held important administrative

[1] *Organisationsbuch der N.S.D.A.P.* gives details, diagrams, and coloured plates of the many Nazi uniforms and badges. See also *Nationsozialistisches Jahrbuch*.

offices in the Party's organization: Amman was head of the Party's publishing company, Schwartz was the treasurer, and Buch was in charge of Party discipline and of courts to decide disputes between Party members. Himmler was head of the S.S. and, after the death of Röhm, Lutze was head of the S.A. Ley was head of the Labour Front. General von Epp headed the Colonial Department of the Party, and Baldur von Shirach the Department for Youth Organization and Education. Among them all, these men ran a complex of departments and offices covering both the administration of the Party and all the fields of human activity.[1] The Party function was educational and propagandist; the Party departments were, in most cases, not directly executive. They existed to propagate the Nazi mythus and to see to it that the Nazi view was influential in the actual carrying out of policy by the ministers of the Government and the other governmental organizations created. In some cases, as we have seen, the same Nazi Party leaders were active in both spheres; in others there was a duplication. The central administration of the Party remained in the Brown House in Munich, but, of course, the Party offices spread to other parts of the city and outside, and to Berlin.

Schwartz and Amman showed great talent as administrators. Schwartz was in ultimate control of the whole Party organization and all its affiliated organizations. He maintained at one time a card index of 14,000,000 cards with details of all members of the Party and its formations. Party finances rested on membership dues, lotteries, public collections, State grants, and licence fees paid for the right to manufacture uniforms and emblems for the Party. Amman built up a gigantic publishing enterprise. By 1939 the *Völkischer Beobachter* appeared in six editions and was by far the largest German daily newspaper, with a daily sale of over 1,600,000 copies. He also published a number of other Nazi papers and periodicals, and *Mein Kampf* and other leading Nazi books with an enormous circulation, and he had taken over one of Germany's largest publishing firms, the Ullstein Verlag, and

[1] See p. 127.

with it the publication of a number of important papers, one being the *Berliner Illustrierte Zeitung*.

Membership of the Party was distinguished from membership of the many organizations and formations attached to it. Actual membership of the Party was under 1 million at the beginning of 1933; four months later it was claimed to be 3 million. Then a stop was put to further applications for membership. But exceptions were made, and in 1937 and again in 1939 the conditions of admission were altered and became easier. Boys and girls who had served in the Hitler Youth for four years were, after a careful process of selection, transferred to the Party. By 1943 it was claimed that there were 6½ million members. With a membership of that size, the Party had evidently become something larger than the political *élite* which, earlier on, it had claimed to be. But the idea was retained in that members could, for certain offences, be expelled from the Party. As membership of the Party was an essential qualification for most higher positions—in Government employment, for example—expulsion was a serious matter, not to mention the danger of arousing the interest of the political police.

Throughout the Reich the Party was organized into thirty-two *Gaue* or party regions, increased later to forty-two with the addition of the new territories of the Saar, Austria, and the Sudetenland. The term *Gau*, derived from the Latin *pagus*, had for the Germans a romantic flavour of pre-Christian Teutonism, though the actual Party regions were based on the Weimar electoral divisions. Each *Gau* was controlled by a *Gauleiter*, appointed by Hitler. The *Gau* was divided into *Kreise*, or districts; in the whole Reich in 1939 there were 822 of these districts. Each *Kreise* was under its *Kreisleiter*, also nominated by Hitler. Below the *Kreise* came the *Ortsgruppe*, or local group, which might be a country district, small town, or section of a city; of these groups there were 27,989. Each was under its *Ortsgruppenleiter*. Next came the *Zelle*, or cell; these were 92,696 in number. The Zelle had its *Zellenleiter*. At the foundation was the *Block*—that is, the block of houses —and of these there were 481,875. Each had its *Blockwart* or warden, who was the Nazi agent directly in contact with the people living in these houses, and who was able to keep a careful eye on them and report any suspicious activity or careless talk to the police. The lower officials were voluntary workers, but the posts of *Gauleiter* and *Kreisleiter* were paid positions, with offices for their districts, staff, and considerable organizations. All the more important departments or branches in the central Party organization had representatives or officers in the *Gau*, and some had them also in the *Kreis*. Thus a vast Party network was spread throughout the country. *Gauleiter* and *Kreisleiter* appointed the holders of certain local government positions, and every child, youth, or grown man was touched somewhere by the Party—by the Hitler Youth, or the Labour Service, or the Labour Front.

Much of this machinery was constructive in the sense that it was used to conduct the ordinary work of government or to further the positive aims of National Socialism, but the Party also possessed a formidable negative apparatus of control, coercion, and destruction—the S.A., the S.S., the Gestapo, and the concentration camps. Secret police, detention, imprisonment, and execution are typical of police-states, but in Germany they were organized with all the natural German thoroughness and efficiency. The cruelty was therefore all the worse: it was not the cruelty involved in being in the hands of uncouth and primitive guards and in lack of proper facilities, food, clothing and housing, as often is the case with atrocities committed by backward peoples; it was a refined brutality without parallel in modern times.

The S.A., the Nazis' para-military organization, increased rapidly in size after Hitler came to power. From a membership of 300,000 at that time, it increased to something like 1 million men by the end of 1939. It was much more numerous than the Army, so long as the Army was kept to the Versailles limit of 100,000 men. The S.A. gave a degree of military training, and Röhm had nursed great ideas for it, as, for example, incorporating its units into the Army as complete S.A. units, with its own officers given equivalent military rank, a swamping of the Army which the generals had feared.

But the S.A. lost something of its former importance after the shooting of Röhm and his fellows in 1934. The famous storm troopers, who had kept order at the early Nazi meetings and had broken up those of the opposition parties, were no longer needed for those purposes once opposition had been crushed and when no rival parties were allowed. The S.A., for a time, came to be thought of as a social and sports organization, and there was question as to how far there were real tasks remaining for it. But a decree of January 1939 increased its importance once more by giving the S.A. throughout Germany the task of pre- and post-military training— that is to say, of military training before and after the period of conscription introduced in 1936. There were other paramilitary organizations, in some ways comparable to the S.A. —namely, the Motor Corps (N.S.K.K. or *N.S. Kraftfahrkorps*) and the Flying Corps (N.S.F.K. or *N.S. Fliegerkorps*).

The S.S., which had originated in the specially picked men of Hitler's personal bodyguard and had been developed by Himmler, was the *élite* of the Nazi fanatics. But these fanatics were not wild men in the ordinary sense; they were selected men of strong physique and intelligence, carefully trained, and devoted to the carrying out of the *Führer's* purposes. The men of the S.S. were trained men, but they were more than that: they made up a racial *élite*, and through them the policy of building a super-race was developed.[1] When an S.S. man married, he and the woman he married had to meet special racial and eugenic standards; their children would be born in a special S.S. mothers' house and under the care of an S.S. doctor; the family might live in a special S.S. settlement; an S.S. boy would have open to him certain educational advantages and would do his military service with an S.S. unit. The S.S. had its own elaborate organization, its own courts for dealing with breaches of discipline, and its own Press, which published the weekly *Das Schwarze Korps* (The Black Corps). The ordinary S.S., spread throughout Germany, was stated in 1939 to number 240,000. Apart from

[1] S.S. Standartenführer Gunter d'Alquen stressed this aspect in *Die S.S.*, pp. 8-10.

this, Himmler built up an armed branch, known as the *Waffen* (weapon) S.S., which was greatly enlarged after the outbreak of war. Thus Hitler had in the S.S., with its political and military forces, an instrument of tremendous power. The S.S. was respected—and feared. The S.S. was the most active and merciless agent of coercion: in police duties, the concentration camps, and the expulsion and murder of Jews.

The S.S. was closely connected with the police. Immediately after Hitler's coming to power, the police forces which were controlled by the different states were reorganized; in Prussia—that is, the greater part of Germany—they were reorganized by Göring (as Prussian Minister of the Interior), and in the other states by Himmler. Göring made it possible for the police to arrest anyone and hold him, without trial, in a concentration camp; he also purged the Prussian police of those of known or suspected democratic sympathy, and he built up the famous Gestapo (*Geheime Staatspolizei*—secret state police). In April 1934 Himmler, already political police leader in the other German states, was made head of the Prussian Gestapo also; in 1936 he became police chief in the Reich ministry of the interior. Himmler was chief or *Reichsführer* of the S.S., and so the S.S. and the police forces of all Germany passed under the immediate control of the same man. Himmler, after his appointment in 1936, divided the German police into two branches: (1) the *Ordnungspolizei* (order police), under Daluege, which comprised all the ordinary police forces throughout the country, including armed police forces in barracks, motorized formations, fire police, water police, and an emergency technical formation, (2) the *Sicherheitspolizei* (security police), under Heydrich, which comprised the criminal police and the Gestapo (political police), though the distinction between ordinary and political criminals might not always be clear.

The combination of police and S.S. organizations which Himmler had under his control was indeed a formidable one. The leaders of the police were high-ranking S.S. officers. Apart from Himmler himself, Daluege and Heydrich both held rank roughly equivalent to that of general in the Army. More and more, as time went on, members of the police forces were admitted to membership of the S.S. The relation was close. Yet Himmler maintained check and counter-check. He had his own security service inside the S.S., and this service, with its branches throughout the country, acted as an intelligence service for the Party. This *Sicherheitsdienst des Reichführers* (security service of the Reichsführer, i.e. Himmler, *Reichsführer* of the S.S.) came under the chief of security police, but had its own separate central and local offices. This organization spied on the Gestapo itself, as well as on Nazi officials, central and local. With such a network of police and security organizations stretching into every corner of the Reich and beyond, it was all but impossible for opposition to take shape and organize itself.

And if more was needed, there was still a supreme agency of terror in the concentration camps. In these camps the S.S. possessed a permanent weapon of intimidation. Those who were arrested by the Gestapo and sent to Buchenwald, Dachau, Sachsenhausen, or any other of the camps, disappeared into a little-known, mysterious world spoken of with dread or turned aside with an uneasy jest when the subject came up in conversation outside. And the terror was increased by officially inspired campaigns of rumour about what happened inside. The prisoners lived in huts or barracks, surrounded by electrified fences covered by searchlights and machine guns, and guarded by numerous watch-towers. Factories, quarries, and mines were run in connexion with the camps, and prisoners worked long hours and had to do, in addition, barrack-square drill. Routine and treatment were left to the S.S. men in charge, and they appeared to have been selected from the most brutal elements. The Gestapo had the power to arrest a person and imprison him without judicial proceedings; or, if he had been tried for some recognized offence in the ordinary courts and acquitted, or sentenced and had served his time in prison, he could still be seized and placed in protective custody—that is, in a concentration camp. A typical Gestapo order was as follows:

Order for Protective Custody. Based on Art. 1 of the decree of the Reich President for the Protection of People and State of 28 February 1933, you are taken into protective custody in the interest of public security and order.

Reason: Suspicion of activities inimical toward the State.[1]

This method of terror—extra-legal arrest and imprisonment in concentration camps—was explicitly recognized by Göring and Frick,[2] and employed against, not only Communists, but all those whom the Nazis regarded as their enemies. Thus the *Bibel Forscher*, a group of Bible research workers and Jehovah's Witnesses, because they were pacifists, were put away in concentration camps.[3] Social Democrats suffered, particularly if they were pacifists or prominent in international movements, and, of course, against the Jews the concentration camps were a ready weapon.

The concentration camps were thus a carefully planned instrument to crush opposition and deter all forms of criticism or discontent. People outside were intimidated by the threat. Inside, the S.S. were free to inflict the most savage treatment. The Camp Commandant of Dachau in 1933 laid down a series of rules which included as punishments hanging, flogging, and solitary confinement. Among the offences punishable by hanging was the collection of 'true or false information about the concentration camp'. But in spite of that, a mass of evidence[4] exists as to the brutalities practised in these camps, even before the war; after the outbreak of war things became very much worse. In the early months of the Nazi régime concentration camps were set up in most of the larger towns, but in the latter peacetime years the

---

[1] *Nuremberg Documents*, 2,499-PS.

[2] Ibid., 1,723-PS (order by Frick as Minister of Interior). Göring, *Aufbau einer Nation*, p. 89.

[3] *Nuremberg Documents*, D-84 (Gestapo instructions, 1937).

[4] See the White Paper (Cmd. 6120) of 1939, *The Treatment of German Nationals in Germany, 1938-9*. Very interesting, because written by a Nazi who found himself for some months of 1933-4 in camps at Brandenburg and Oranienburg (Sachsenhausen), is Ludecke's account, *I Knew Hitler* (1938), pp. 607-47. Part I of the catalogue of the Wiener Library, *Persecution, Terror and Resistance in Nazi Germany*, contains a list of books on the concentration camps.

number of camps appears to have been reduced. At the beginning of the war in 1939, according to a report by the S.S. general, Pohl, there were six camps, Dachau with 4,000 prisoners, Sachsenhausen with 6,500, Buchenwald with 5,300, Mauthausen with 1,500, Flossenburg with 1,600 and Ravenbruck with 2,500.[1]

Probably the most cruel fate in Nazi Germany was that of the Jews. The Communist might switch his allegiance and join the S.A., but the Jew could not change his race. And the whole race was marked out for persecution. If there could be said to be a Jewish problem in the sense that there was a high percentage of Jews in the professions—for example, in law and medicine—it was a barbarous way of dealing with the problem to attack the whole race. But the anti-Semitism of the Nazis went deeper than this: it rested on the mystical feeling for German blood and soil and that the Jew polluted the blood, and it was strengthened by Hitler's early personal prejudice. As soon as Hitler came to power the open attacks on the Jews began. They were held up to scorn in the Press and on the stage; sometimes they were seized and paraded in open carts through the streets; an official boycott was organized against their shops and businesses, and the words *Wer beim Juden kauft ist ein Volksverbrecher* (Whoever buys from a Jew is a traitor) were placarded in public places. Julius Streicher's paper, *Der Stürmer*, ran a continuous nation-wide campaign against them, accusing them of every kind of crime, moral and political, and covering them with filth and slander. In September 1935 two new laws were announced at Nuremberg: they came to be known as the Nuremberg laws. They stated that only a person of German or kindred blood could be a citizen, and they forbade marriage between Jews and Germans. Thus the Jew was thrust out from citizenship, and deprived of all the rights of Germans. He was shut out of a number of professions, including the civil service and teaching, and his position—and also that of people of mixed, partly Jewish race—was deplorable. As revenge for the murder of a German diplomat in Paris by a young Jew in November 1938,

[1] *Nuremberg Documents*, R-129 (Report from Pohl to Himmler, 1942).

an organized[1] pogrom took place throughout Germany, and many synagogues were burnt. These disturbances, although organized by the Nazis, might easily be thought by decent people—as was thought at Neunkirchen in the Saar, where the synagogue was destroyed—to be the work of hooligans who got out of hand. A law of 12 November made the lot of the Jews much worse still; they were debarred from ownership in whole or in part of any enterprise; they might not work as artisans; and they had to give up their property. Large numbers did indeed manage to leave Germany. In 1933 there were 503,000 Jews in Germany; by the outbreak of war in 1939 it was estimated that 226,000 had left the country.

The Christian Churches in Germany Hitler was not able to reduce to complete subservience. Neither the Lutheran Church nor the Roman Catholic Church could accept the pagan teachings of Rosenberg and the extreme Nazis, nor could they tolerate a doctrine which was based on racialism and persecution. A long struggle developed inside the Lutheran Church between those who, under the leadership of Reichs-bischof Müller, supported Hitler and compromised with their faith, and those others who stuck firm to Christian teachings. Many of the pastors, such as Dr. Niemöller, went to concentration camps for conscience' sake. The Nazis made great play with the argument that the Churches were free so long as they did not interfere in politics, but stuck to religion; the Nazis did not explain, however, whether the Christian doctrine of the brotherhood of man—both Jew and Gentile—was religion or politics. With the Papacy Hitler was able to make a concordat in July 1933, and the priests were to abstain from politics—but trouble soon arose over the training of the young. There was a direct clash between what they were taught by the Church and what they learnt in the Nazi organizations. For the Nazis Germany was the new god—and that was something neither Catholic nor Protestant could accept. Leading Catholics such as Cardinal Faulhaber, the

[1] The orders of Heydrich were discovered at the end of the war, *Nuremberg Documents*, 3,051-PS. See also the confidential report of an S.A. brigade leader in the Palatinate, listing the synagogues destroyed by fire or wrecked by other means: *Nuremberg Documents*, 1,721-PS.

Archbishop of Munich, and Count von Galen, Bishop of Münster, were outspoken in their criticism of Nazi teaching. But the Churches, in spite of the bravery of many devoted Christians, were not strong enough to put any serious obstacle in the way of Nazi progress. The Christian protest was not completely stilled, but against the Churches also there was ever present the menace of the Gestapo and the concentration camps.

Hitler himself, though he had been brought up a Catholic and appealed from time to time in his speeches to God and Providence, showed little but contempt for religion. But he was astute in his dealings with the Churches. He did not make a frontal attack on them; rather, he encouraged decay from the inside, and drew away the young by providing them, in the Nazi Party and its organizations, with a more exciting alternative to the Churches. 'We must prevent the churches', said Hitler, 'from doing anything but what they are doing now—that is, losing ground every day. Do you really believe the masses will ever be Christian again? Nonsense! Never again. That tale is finished. . . . We need not hurry the process.' Because of its power as an institution, Hitler had a certain respect for the Roman Catholic Church. 'The Catholic Church', he said, 'is a really big thing. Why, what an organization! It's something to have lasted nearly 2,000 years! We must learn from it. Astuteness and knowledge of human nature are behind it.' But the day of the Church was almost over, Hitler thought, and if the priests opposed him he would know how to deal with them. 'I shall certainly not make martyrs of them. We shall brand them as ordinary criminals. I shall tear the mask of honesty from their faces. And if that is not enough, I shall make them appear ridiculous and contemptible.' This was indeed his method when, later on, priests were accused of currency offences and immorality. As for the Protestants, 'you can do anything you like with them', he said; 'they will submit . . . they are insignificant little people, submissive as dogs, and they sweat with embarrassment when you talk to them.' For Christianity, a religion of love and international brotherhood, Hitler had no use. It could be left, he thought, to decay in the new, Nazi Germany, where the sentiment of German nationalism would take its place. Hitler turned with hope to the German peasantry, in the matter of a basic faith as in that of racial expansion eastwards. 'It is through the peasantry that we shall really be able to destroy Christianity because there is in them a true religion rooted in nature and blood.'[1]

[1] Quotations are from Rauschning, *Hitler Speaks*, Chapter IV, in which he recounts a conversation of 1933 with Goebbels, Frau Goebbels, Frau Raubal, Streicher, and others.

CHAPTER X

THE POSITIVE SIDE OF THE NAZI RÉGIME

THE victims of the Gestapo and the concentration camps were few when numbered against the millions of the German population. It was unwise to ask too many questions about those who disappeared; the ordinary German, if he sometimes felt qualms of conscience, shrugged his shoulders and convinced himself that there was nothing he could do about it and that, so long as he went about his business and kept his mouth shut, it would not happen to him. And such, indeed, was the case for the ordinary, hard-working, non-political citizen. Nothing could be more false, indeed, than to imagine that under the Nazi régime the Germans were a people browbeaten and cowed by fear of the secret police, and driven to work against their will by the methods of terror employed by a ruthless dictator. This was the mistake—coupled with the equally false idea that the German workers were suffering unbearable economic hardships—which obsessed many supporters of the Labour Party in this country. Those who thought in this way were also likely to regard Russia as a people's paradise. In fact, it was more correct to see the roles as reversed: in Russia the use of force was more evident than in Germany and poverty and squalor were prevalent everywhere in Russia, in keeping with an Asiatic rather than a European way of life. Once the Nazis were in power and all open opposition had been overcome, terrorism was kept in the background.

The most striking thing about Nazi Germany was the new spirit which animated the country: a new hope, a new self-confidence and pride, a new energy and determination filled a people who since 1918 had suffered the heavy blows of defeat, the collapse of the currency, and, finally, the prolonged economic depression of the world slump.

Deutschland erwache! (Germany awake!)—that had long been a popular slogan with the Nazis. Now that they were in power it seemed, indeed, as if Germany had awakened. Germans found a new faith in the greatness and future of their country. As a German headmaster wrote in 1937 in reference to the plebiscites which produced mass votes in favour of Hitler's policies: 'In fact 98% have voted for Hitler *of their free will*. And they would do it at any time. So would I.'[1]

Order and discipline were re-established, at least outwardly, and Germans, with their long-established respect for authority and the force behind it, regarded the creation of a strong government as a good thing in itself. The menace of Communism had gone. Ever since the Armistice, Germany had been, from time to time, threatened by uprisings engineered by the Communists. To many moderate Germans it had seemed, in the years immediately preceding 1933, that they were faced with a choice between the Nazis and the Communists—a choice of evils, perhaps, but it seemed that Hitler was the lesser evil. Germans, and many people also outside Germany, looked on the disappearance of the Communists as a good thing. For long enough, backed by the sinister power of Soviet Russia, they had menaced the way of life of the Western states. First Mussolini in Italy, now Hitler in Germany, had crushed that menace. To many people in the West it appeared that Germany was a bulwark of Europe against the Communist East: Nazi Germany barred the road to Soviet expansion westwards. Inside Germany, and outside, people could feel but little sympathy for the Communists. If the Communists had been treated with brutality, they had certainly asked for it; they had themselves been the strongest exponents of violence in politics. It was the best possible line for the Nazis to follow to make it appear that their terror was directed against the Communists; with terror against Communists in the foreground—and Jews were often labelled as Communists—brutality against Social Democrats, liberals, pacifists, and others might well be overlooked. If the Nazis practised terror, it was to be taken for granted

[1] In a personal letter.

that the Communists, had they seized power in Germany, would have applied a far greater terror. Men still recalled 1917 in Russia, and the horrors which followed.

Germany in the years 1933-9 was an open country in a sense in which Soviet Russia has never been. Germans, those who were not politically suspect in any way, could travel abroad; the currency they could take out was limited, but exchanges could be arranged with foreigners visiting Germany. The Nazi leaders did not fear that if Germans visited foreign countries they would come back with their own national allegiance weakened. The foreign visitor was welcome in Germany; he could travel all over Germany, and enjoy the amenities of the country or study its new régime; he could make his own arrangements, travel alone without being a member of a conducted party, and was free to live if he wished, in a German family. Indeed, what the visitor to Germany saw was generally overwhelmingly in Germany's favour. He found what was apparently the most orderly and well-directed country in the world; people were at work and appeared to be contented, all the amenities of life were there: opera, theatres, the cinema, cafés and restaurants, hotels, books, sports, hiking and sun-bathing in summer, skiing in winter. The young, or those who saw Germany for the first time, were liable to feel that all this was provided, had been created, by the Nazis: they forgot that Germany had had much to offer before the Nazis, and that many of the advantages of German life could be found also in Scandinavia and Switzerland. And they overlooked the dark side of the Nazi system. Moderate Socialists who went to Germany, for example, with the party holidays of the W.T.A. (Workers' Travel Association) were inclined to return feeling that the case against the Nazis had been exaggerated, and that Germany was a fine country.

Even Germany's enemies could be won over. Lloyd George, who had brought the Germans to their knees in 1918, was persuaded to visit the country in 1936, and at Berchtesgaden he had two friendly interviews with Hitler. Hitler, as he had said in *Mein Kampf*, admired the great popular orator, and

Lloyd George in his turn saw in Hitler a true national leader. Here was a German putting into practice a large-scale policy of public works to provide employment, similar in its scope to the Liberal leader's policy, *We can Conquer Unemployment*, for which he had failed to gain a backing at home. His biographer has written that Lloyd George, 'weary of the flabby inaction of those in power in Britain, was ready to applaud the constructive achievements of the German statesman, who was actually doing the job of restoring a nation that had sunk far lower in economic and spiritual collapse than any other in modern times'.[1] Lloyd George could not foresee the future; he did not realize 'at the time the extraordinary craftiness of Hitler's character, the unscrupulous depths below his geniality and protestations of peaceful friendliness'. At the time he was impressed by what he saw and heard in Germany, and he recognized in Hitler 'an amazingly capable and magnetic leader, and that his early work on behalf of Germany, marred though it was by ruthlessness, tyranny and injustice, was in many respects inspiring, constructive, and beneficent'.[2]

At the basis of Nazi success was Germany's economic recovery. The Nazis did find a solution to the unemployment problem, however unsatisfactory the future might show that solution to be. That the men could get jobs again, and were back at work—that in itself was a source of pride to the Germans when they were told of the faltering and fumbling methods of foreign countries to deal with the problem. The reduction of the German unemployment figures by 5 million was a remarkable achievement, and of the greatest propaganda value also. When Hitler had come to power, there were 6 million unemployed out of Germany's 20 million workers; by the end of 1936 only 1 million were listed as unemployed.[3] That was what the *Führer* had brought about.

---

[1] Malcolm Thomson, *David Lloyd George*, p. 436. Cf. the account by P. Schmidt, *Statist auf diplomatischer Bühne*, pp. 336-40.

[2] Thomson, pp. 435-7.

[3] See C. W. Guillebaud, *Economic Recovery of Germany*, p. 46 (employment and unemployment figures quoted from *Konjunktur-Statistisches Handbuch*, 1936), and p. 86.

He had asked for four years: he had kept his pledge. That alone was enough to swing over the German workers at least to a tacit support. It is true, of course, that some people had lost their jobs—Communists, Socialists, pacifists and others —that some political refugees had managed to leave the country, and that others were prisoners in concentration camps. Perhaps 1 million people had been absorbed by the expansion of the army and by the labour-service camps and by absorption into the various Nazi organizations. Further, marriage allowances paid by the Government encouraged women to give up jobs in shop and office and stick to the home. The Nazi policy for women was *Kinder, Kirche, Küche* (children, church, kitchen), and this not only relieved the congestion of the labour market, but also won them much political support from German women. The great thing, however, was that the men—the mass of the workers, skilled and unskilled—were back at work.

What the conditions of the German workers were like was a matter hotly disputed between the Nazis and the Labour movements abroad. The Nazis maintained that wages had remained largely constant, and that in addition many benefits were now provided for the workers which were not available before. Outside Germany Labour newspapers calculated that German real wages had fallen considerably, even by as much as 40 per cent. Certainly there was need for assistance to the poor on a fairly large scale, especially in winter. The *Winterhilfe*—the street collections by Brownshirts for winter help to the poor were obvious to all—was a large-scale and carefully organized Nazi campaign to arouse a feeling of social unity and to provide help for the unfortunate. But, on the other hand, the German worker had many advantages. Rents were controlled, there were slum clearance and building of working-class houses, and special facilities were organized for cheap holidays as well as cheap rates for sports and other entertainments. The German worker worked hard, and he certainly had little spare cash: this applied also to many of the middle and professional classes. But in Germany the basic necessities were there, and entertainment was good, simple,

and cheap. The German worker forgot his claims to democratic citizenship and freedom, the 'freedom to starve', as it
had been contemptuously described, and contented himself
with work and the new self-respect it gave him.

How was the miracle brought about? The means was the
expansion of credit in order to finance a programme of public
works and rearmament. It is true that Hitler came to power
as the trade cycle in Germany appeared to be turning in a
favourable direction, and that he was able to take over certain
relief measures with which a beginning had been made by
the two previous chancellors, von Schleicher and von Papen.
But Hitler made a much greater effort on the widest front to
deal with unemployment, and outlined on 1 May 1933 his
Four-Year Plan, followed by a law for the reduction of unemployment on 2 June. The plan provided for considerable
public expenditure, the finance of which was to come from
the issue of special employment-creation bills, on public works
—housing, roads, the development of agricultural and sub-
urban settlement, river regulation, and public utilities. These
were direct measures for creating employment. Then there
were indirect measures by stimulating private enterprise to
undertake work which would involve increased employment.
Private. expenditure for replacement and renewal of equipment in industry and agriculture was freed from income tax
and other taxes, and these concessions were extended later
to apply to all capital expenditure. Income tax relief was
allowed for the employment of domestic servants—these being
treated as an addition to the taxpayer's family. Then there
were the marriage bonuses—on condition that the wife did
not resume her work; this might mean that the husband
slipped directly into a job. The bonus was in the form of an
interest-free loan; it was repayable in small instalments, but
these were reduced as each child was born. All monetary and
capital operations were placed under the control of a committee whose chairman was Dr. Schacht, the President of
the Reichsbank.

Public works were an essential part of the Nazi policy for
dealing with unemployment. In itself, this was not new, and

it was a policy adopted in other countries also. During the Weimar period loans had been used to finance public building, and in the United States Roosevelt's New Deal made extensive use of organized public undertakings to relieve unemployment. But Hitler had the apparatus of dictatorship in his hands. As Dr. Schacht said in a speech at a trade fair at Königsberg in 1935: 'The secret of financing Germany's political and economic tasks lies in a centralized and rigid concentration of the whole public and private activities of the German Reich . . . only possible within a State based on authoritative rules.'[1] Hitler could fix wages and use certain measures of compulsion. It was easier in Germany to organize those who were unemployed into work-gangs and move them from place to place wherever they were most wanted. Thus towns could be planned, housing estates created, and new factories built as a nucleus around which the residential quarters were arranged. Hitler, with his youthful interest in art and architecture, took a personal interest in the new building schemes, and attention was also given to layout and landscape gardening. And certainly the public buildings of the Nazi period were erected in a simple, attractive style of neo-classic, in keeping with modern demands and at the same time graceful and impressive. New official buildings in Berlin, the German Art Museum in Munich, and the theatre in Saarbrücken were fine examples. They appeared to indicate a period ahead of peaceful and constructive effort. Indeed, it was often urged to foreigners that they proved that Hitler's intentions were peaceful; he would not erect, it was argued, these splendid and expensive public buildings only to see them destroyed in the bombing which might be expected early in another war. Hitler himself used a similar argument. Speaking in 1937 to British delegates to an International Commission of Front Line Fighters, he said: 'They do not believe that I want peace. They ask me what I will do when the four years' plan is over. I have enough work ahead of me for twenty years.'[2]

[1] Quoted by W. F. Bruck, *Social and Economic History of Germany from William II to Hitler*, p. 212.
[2] Baynes, Vol. II, p. 1,348. Cf. ibid., p. 1,220, Reichstag speech of May 1935.

Perhaps most striking of all Hitler's public works, and best known, were the *Autobahnen*, or great motor roads. The scheme, financed like the main Plan itself by the issue of employment-creation bills, was commenced early in September of Hitler's first year of power, and was an immediate method of taking men off the dole and putting them to useful work. A new organization was created, the Reich *Autobahn* group, under the engineer and old Party member, Dr. Todt. Plans were made, the country mapped out, and the labourers collected. They were housed in huts, ate in a mess, and lived a semi-military existence. But they worked hard, and produced splendid, new arterial roads. These roads were wide and straight, with parallel tracks, providing one-way traffic in each direction, separated by a broad stretch of grass and shrubs. There was no cross-traffic on these roads; bridges or viaducts were used when other roads or railways had to cross. Cars coming on to or leaving the *Autobahn* did not do so at right angles, but moved on or off gradually at special points. The building of these great roads certainly helped to relieve unemployment; it was a large-scale and long-term programme, which stimulated the motor industry and the iron and steel industry also, for the building of the numerous bridges created a demand for steel. The roads were also of propaganda value: they impressed foreigners, and they impressed the Germans themselves. In addition, they were of strategic value: important roads led to the Austrian, Czech, Polish, and Belgian frontiers, and such roads were well calculated to serve the needs of modern mechanized armies.

There was a further scheme, commenced in September 1933, for subsidizing the repair of houses and the conversion of houses into flats. The State paid so much to the householder on condition that he spent two to four times as much himself—either from his own or borrowed moneys. And what he used himself was treated as capital invested with a rate of interest paid by the State. Such advantages made an important stimulus to repairs and alterations leading to increased employment in the building trades. Then, again, there were special programmes of capital development by the railways and Post Office which were an additional stimulus to employment. And influence was brought to bear, both personal influence and propaganda by State and Party, on employers to employ as many men as possible.

At a rather later stage, rearmament became of great importance. What had begun in secret could be brought into the open as soon as Hitler announced in March 1935 that Germany was withdrawing from the Disarmament Conference and reintroducing conscription. Rearmament was now pushed on with great haste—and indeed there was, in some ways, a war atmosphere in Germany. Employers and workers were urged to exert themselves in a great patriotic drive for production: to make Germany strong and a power among the nations. Now the drive was directed to the production of all the equipment of military power. Weapons and munitions of all kinds had to be manufactured, and factories and tools were constructed or adapted for the purpose. Barracks, hutments, aerodromes were laid out and built, the planes and all the necessary equipment manufactured and set up. Military expansion was, of course, enormous: it covered the transformation of a country which had until recently been limited by the disarmament clauses of the Versailles Treaty into the greatest military force of its time. And, again, the expansion was financed by the Government issue of bills, known as special bills. That the great programmes of public works and rearmament could be successfully carried out demonstrated how great were the reserves of labour power and resources which waited to be used fully for the exercise of will power and ingenuity. The new production was of capital goods, factories, machines, buildings, roads, and unproductive goods, arms and weapons of destruction; it did not lead to any considerable increase of consumption by the general public. Production was financed by the creation of bank credit and not by the printing of paper money, but in either case the tendency would be inflationary. But inflation was prevented by rigid control of both wages and prices.

Economic policy was closely allied to Hitler's nationalist aims, with their attendant programme of military expansion.

Military expansion could only be based on economic expansion, on the fullest development of the heavy industries which offered employment to the workers and provided the basic materials of war. Here, then, was a dilemma for the Nazis: a nationalist policy meant making Germany independent of foreign countries, yet economic expansion must necessarily mean the import from abroad of raw materials not found, or not found in sufficient quantities, in Germany. The policy of *Autarky*, the economic self-sufficiency of the nation, was followed in every possible way. *Ersatz*, or substitute, goods produced by the skill of German chemists were used wherever possible in place of goods formerly imported. Such research had been going on long before the Nazis, and was now intensified: much use was made of *Buna* (synthetic rubber) and substitutes for wool and petrol. The materials to be imported from abroad were reduced as far as possible and a drive undertaken for the production of foodstuffs at home; only materials essential to the country's development plans were to be admitted, and elaborate quotas, licence arrangements, and exchange restrictions were worked out. Bilateral agreements were made with a number of individual countries for trading purposes.

At the same time every effort was made to increase German exports in order to provide the foreign currency and credits to pay for the essential imports. At first the Reichsbank's gold reserves had been used for payment, until they dwindled down. Then the Government mobilized all holdings of foreign currency, and Germans who concealed their possession of foreign assets were made subject to heavy penalties. Germans were prevented from taking money out of the country for travel or other purposes, and foreign businesses with branches in Germany were prevented from taking out their profits. Then Dr. Schacht (Minister of Economics) devised a system of currency manipulation: the value of the mark was varied to suit particular kinds of transaction. A specially favourable rate was allowed to the foreign visitor to Germany. Other rates were allowed in various trading agreements which encouraged importers to buy German goods and pay for them in the much-needed foreign currency, even if they paid rather less than they would have had to pay at the normal rate of exchange. The world economic depression, however, had compelled other countries also to adopt restrictive methods; they might, for example, cut down their own imports from Germany. But, in spite of the many difficulties, Germany managed to 1935 to achieve a small export surplus. And, at the same time, Dr. Schacht developed a system of barter, especially with South America and the Balkan countries, which, while it supplied Germany with raw materials, also tended to give her political influence in the small states of south-eastern Europe.

The Cambridge economist, C. W. Guillebaud, writing in 1938, rightly used the expression, 'the economic recovery of Germany'. 'By the autumn of 1936', he wrote, 'the success of the first Four-year Plan was no longer in doubt. Unemployment had ceased to be a serious problem and there was practically full employment in the building and engineering industries.... The seemingly hazardous policy which was embarked on in 1932-3 had been vindicated by the result. Initially, the State orders provided the demand for work at a time when effective demand was almost paralysed and savings in the aggregate were non-existent; the Reichsbank supplied the money funds needed for investment; investment drew the unemployed into work; and work created the incomes, and therewith the savings, out of which the short-term indebtedness previously incurred was able to be carried and, in a certain measure, to be funded. The scepticism of the outside world, which, almost without exception, had refused to believe in the possibility of the German experiment succeeding, was proved to be unjustified. Recovery was no longer on paper; it was there for everybody to see.'[1]

In September 1936 Hitler launched Germany on a second Four-Year Plan with Göring at its head, and for this purpose Göring was given powers overriding those of the Cabinet Ministers concerned, including Schacht, the Minister of Economics. The plan aimed at carrying on the effort to make

[1] C. W. Guillebaud, *Economic Recovery of Germany*, p. 101.

Germany independent of foreign supplies of essential food-stuffs and raw materials; the country must be made self-sufficing in case of war, and unaffected by external economic changes in time of peace. Further intensification of agricultural production, expansion of fishing and whaling, development of new substitute materials, utilization of waste products (e.g. collection from house to house of tins, razor blades, toothpaste tubes, etc.), the building of the Hermann Göring works at Salzgitter to make use of low-grade iron ores not previously used—all these were means of making the fullest use of modern scientific methods to exploit to the full the materials found in Germany or easily accessible to her. The plan meant prolonging the effort throughout Germany and the postponing of increased consumption, which would have now been possible had the drive for armaments been curtailed, and it meant increased State control through Göring and his agencies over the economic life of the nation. But the wheels of industry were kept turning fast and with the booming output the Germans were well content; wages and prices were kept stable, and inflation prevented. As Guillebaud put it: 'When it is remembered that in March 1938 Germany was in a state of full employment (in the usual sense of this term), that there was an extreme scarcity of labour, and that many of the most important industries were working to capacity, with heavy overtime, this relative stabilization of wages and prices must be regarded as a very remarkable achievement. It is certainly unique in economic history down to the present time.'[1] Indeed, as each year passed the German factories grew busier: the great blast furnaces in the Ruhr and the Saar poured out their glowing, molten lava at night as well as day, and the railways rattled and rumbled with the passage of their freights. A mighty nation was at work.

Even a dictator cannot afford to ignore altogether the wishes of the people, and the success of the Nazi régime depended to a large extent on the goodwill of the workers. The Nazis laid a firm foundation in the way they dealt with unemployment, and they strengthened their position by

[1] C. W. Guillebaud, *Economic Recovery of Germany*, p. 218.

building up the *Arbeitsfront* (Labour Front). They were not content simply to dissolve the old trade unions and seize their property; they put in place of the unions this new and powerful organization under Dr. Ley which had behind it the coercive apparatus of the Nazi State, but which appealed to the workers through its propaganda on social and patriotic grounds. Strikes and lock-outs were made impossible—they were condemned as political sabotage—and the *Arbeitsfront*, which included the employers as well as workers, provided machinery for industrial conciliation and arbitration. That industrial disputes could be settled without strikes meant a considerable economy, and aided the Nazi drive for increased production. Co-operation between employers and workers—instead of the old class war—was extolled as a means of benefiting everybody. This was a sound social argument; but co-operation strengthened the national economic system, which, ultimately, Hitler would use for his own dark ends.

The Labour Front had also more visibly attractive ways of appealing to the workers. Wages, if low, could be supplemented, with the German genius for careful and elaborate organization, by providing special facilities—for holidays and travel, for entertainment, for sport. Inside the Labour Front there was the department known as *Kraft durch Freude* (Strength through Joy), and this was an excellent means of providing cheap holidays for the lower-paid workers, who might otherwise have had to stay at home. Workers who wished to take advantage of the scheme made weekly contributions. As the number who did so ran into millions, things could be organized in mass and the cost of the holidays to each person could be low. Hotels were booked up, special trains and buses run, and liners chartered. And there was considerable variety. A worker and his family might go for a day's steamer cruise on the Rhine or a week's sea trip to Norway or Madeira; he might spend a seaside holiday at one of the Baltic resorts or he might visit Italy. The Germans knew how to enjoy themselves in simple ways—in the sun and fresh air, and with beer and song, and dancing on deck to the ship's band. Then, apart from *Kraft durch Freude*, there were other remarkable trips run by travel agencies or travel companies, and numerous foreigners took advantage of these. The organization and efficiency of German travel arrangements were unsurpassed and, together with the amazingly low cost, were at the same time a means of bringing in the much-needed foreign money and impressing the outside world with what the Nazis were doing. For example, the Hamburg-Nordamerika Line sent its cruising liner *Monte Rosa* from Hamburg via the Norwegian fiords to Spitzbergen and the Ice Frontier—a three-week trip for the equivalent of £12. The ship was well filled, decks were turned into dormitories, food was plentiful and good (and with special provision for vegetarians—Hitler himself was a vegetarian), and everything was clean and comfortable. Anything at all comparable run by an English steamship company at the time cost five times as much.

Arrangements were also made to bring within reach of workers the theatre and classical concerts. Sometimes blocks of seats at the theatre would be reserved at special rates. The Ministry of Propaganda itself took a hand in making cheap seats available whenever a propaganda purpose might be served. In this way, either through *Kraft durch Freude* or the ministry, cheap seats were to be had in the theatre or at the opera. In the country or in isolated places, film shows and concerts were arranged, and orchestras were brought to play in factories. Once more the Nazis were, even if for their own ends, doing a real work of popular education. New sports were also brought at low cost to the workers. Football and handball were thought to be popular enough, but swimming, sailing, and skiing, and instruction in them, were provided, and the workers taking advantage of such facilities were again to be numbered in millions.

Quite apart from the workers, for whom careful consideration was given, the Nazis waged a constant struggle for youth, for woman as the mother, and for the physical well-being of the whole German race. 'You ask me what I have done for the women of Germany', said Hitler to a meeting of women. 'Well, my answer is this: that in my new Army I have provided you the finest fathers of children in the whole world.'[1] Gone was the theoretical equality of rights between the sexes of the Weimar days—when men were unemployed and women sad because deprived of marriage and children. 'To-day', said Hitler, 'we see countless radiant and smiling faces', for women 'must be saying to themselves, "What a healthy splendid race of men it is that is growing up in Germany!" Now that we have reintroduced general military service, that is a wonderful education from which the coming generations of young Germans will profit—a wonderful generation which we are drawing to ourselves through the Hitler Youth, the S.A., and the compulsory labour service.'[2] This youth was Germany's future. 'It is a glorious sight, this golden youth of ours: we know that it is the Germany of the future when we shall be no more.'[3] And, again, Hitler said: 'All that we do we do in the last resort for the child. Often we think we are caring for ourselves, for the folk of our own day, yet the deepest meaning of all our work and of our life is only this: that we may safeguard the life of our people.'[4]

To this end, the Nazis applied a rigorous policy, partly racial, partly eugenic in character. Marriage and sexual inter-course with Jews were forbidden (by one of the Nuremberg laws of 1935), but everything was done to encourage early marriage between healthy Germans and the consequent increase of the population. The status of the mother was especially honoured, marriage bonuses and family allowances were given, the unmarried mother of sound German children was not unfavoured, birth control was discouraged, and laws against prostitution and venereal disease strictly enforced. The law on healthy marriages required medical examination, and forbade marriage where either partner suffered from certain infectious or hereditary diseases. Other laws provided for sterilization in certain cases, and the 'mercy killing' of weakly babies and the elderly infirm was reported.[5]

At every stage of development the Nazis sought to mould

[1] Quoted by S. H. Roberts, *The House that Hitler Built*, p. 229.
[2] Speech of 13 September 1935, Baynes, Vol. I, p. 532.
[3] Speech of 8 September 1934, ibid., p. 530.
[4] Speech of 10 September 1937, ibid., p. 532.
[5] See *Germany* (official handbook), pp. 450-4, for some details of these eugenic measures.

and influence the young with the object of creating a race of splendid Germans, a true *Herrenvolk*. Little boys and girls had their own Nazi organizations, and at fourteen the boys joined the *Hitlerjugend*. The Nazi youth movement undoubtedly captured the imagination of the children; it was a real punishment to remain, for any reason, outside. Children wanted to march and sing and salute, they wanted to go to the Nazi camps, they wanted to enjoy the wonderful, exciting life that was organized for them. And no other youth movement was allowed to compete for their loyalty. Children became, from an early age, the devoted followers of the *Führer*, like those who demonstrated at a great cinema meeting in Cologne and chanted in unison: '*So war es* [So things were]. We were slaves; we were outsiders in our own country. So were we before Hitler united us. Now we would fight against Hell itself for our leader.' Then for the young men there came six months of compulsory labour service in a camp before their two years' military service. The labour service had as its object to let manual labour break down the barriers of social class, mould the character still further to the Nazi pattern, and strengthen the physique of the potential soldier and worker. Outdoor manual labour and military drill (with spades instead of rifles) were the means. The physical training of the young began to make its mark on the whole nation; the Germans carried off many of the prizes at the Olympic Games held in 1936 in Berlin, and the foreign visitors were impressed both by German athletic prowess and by the splendid spectacle offered in the German capital. There was before their eyes a new Germany: of youth, of power, of faith—though its future was in the hands of one man whose megalomania would lead its people to disaster. But for the moment this was hidden: each September at Nuremberg the *Parteitag*, or rally, was held, with the most magnificent pageantry. The marching of thousands of disciplined, uniformed figures, the massed bands, the forest of flags, the simple glories of the vast stadium on the Zeppelin Field lit at night by hundreds of searchlights meeting in a dome overhead—all had their effect, intense and hypnotic, on German and foreigner alike.

PART FOUR
Hitler's Foreign Policy

CHAPTER XI

BLUFF, PREPARATION, AND THE FAILURE
OF THE WEST

NAZI Germany was two-faced. The successes at home, the splendours of the régime, the spiritual force and drive of a movement which had remade a nation—that was one face. The other showed itself in the destruction of freedom, the horrors of the concentration camps, and in the tireless preparations for war. At first, Hitler tried to show the one face only; the grim face was hidden. He had to deceive the outside world as to his true intentions, and to do this he talked of peace and pointed to the great constructive effort which was being carried out in Germany. His successes on the economic and social front at home served therefore to bluff the foreigner. But they also served to build up in his own people the power, material and psychological, for the coming struggle. Hitler understood also, better than anyone, the value of indirect, underground, subversive activities. He was determined to soften up his enemies, to weaken them by a war of nerves, before he struck. 'The place of artillery preparation for frontal attack', he said, 'will in future be taken by revolutionary propaganda, to break down the enemy psychologically before the armies begin to function. . . . How to achieve the moral breakdown of the enemy before the war has started . . . that is the problem that interests me.'[1]

Hitler knew well enough the difficulty of keeping the grim face hidden. 'Possible foreign complications give me head-aches', Hitler said in a private conversation a little more than four months before he came to power. 'Can I also fool these gentlemen abroad for any length of time? That's the question. What will England say, France, the United States, once I'm Chancellor? . . . Will I be able to rearm Germany before

[1] Rauschning: *Hitler Speaks*, p. 19.

they get on to me with a preventive war? That depends largely, I suppose, on whether they have the leadership and guts to strike—if they can get the people to go to war again, and that I doubt.'[1] Already Hitler suspected a lack of will in the democratic states. Nevertheless, he went on to argue that, because of the vulnerability of the Nazi régime in its early stages, 'it would be better to ally myself with Italy and Japan, and play along with England even if I can't get her friendship'. Then he said: 'The economic power of the Versailles states is so enormous that I can't risk antagonizing them at the very outset. If I begin my régime with socialism, Paris, London, New York will be alarmed, the capitalists will take fright and combine, and I'll be whipped before I know it. A preventive war will ruin everything. No; I've got to play ball with capitalism and keep the Versailles Powers in line by holding aloft the bogy of Bolshevism—make them believe that a Nazi Germany is the last bulwark against the Red flood. That's the only way to come through the danger period, to get rid of Versailles and rearm. I can talk peace and mean war.'[2]

Hitler was completely devoted to foreign policy and the great object of national expansion which he planned. But, as he said, 'I must above all recognize that it is not the primacy of foreign policy which can determine our action in the domestic sphere—rather, the character of our action in the domestic sphere is decisive for the character of the success of our foreign policy. . . . The essential thing is the formation of the political will of the nation as a whole: that is the starting-point for political action.'[3] When he had to justify himself to foreigners, Hitler argued plausibly that it was against Bolshevism, not against other nations that political action must be directed. 'We are teaching the German youth

---

[1] K. Ludecke, *I Knew Hitler*, p. 410. In the chapter headed 'Alone with Hitler', Ludecke describes a private interview on 12 September 1932. Although Ludecke's account cannot be checked, the words attributed to Hitler (set down by Ludecke in 1937) describe exactly the policy Hitler followed and was to follow in the years 1933-9.
[2] Ibid., p. 422.
[3] Speech of 27 January 1932 to the Industry Club at Düsseldorf: Baynes, Vol. I, pp. 814-16.

to fight,' he said to Mr. Ward Price of the *Daily Mail*, 'but to fight against internal evils, and particularly against the Communist danger, of whose formidable proportions people in Great Britain have never had and have not yet any idea.'[1] Otherwise, said Hitler in 1933, he looked for peace. 'We wish to live in peace with England; we wish to live in peace with France; we wish to live in peace with Poland.'[2] 'Germany', said Hitler in an interview with the foreign Press, 'is the bulwark of the West against Bolshevism. . . . Germany will continue to fight Communism.'[3] There was the enemy against whom the Germans would march. And to satisfy the West still further, he made a number of peace speeches. For example, at the Nuremberg Rally of 1936 he said: 'All through these long years we have never had any other prayer than this: Lord, give our people internal peace and give and maintain peace abroad. We have experienced in our generation so much fighting that it is natural that we should long for peace. We wish to work; we wish to fashion our Reich. . . .'[4] It was a favourite theme with Hitler, this appealing to the anti-war feelings of old soldiers. He had used it with Ward Price: 'Nobody here desires a repetition of war. Almost all we leaders of the National Socialist Movement were actual combatants. I have yet to meet the combatant who desires a renewal of the horrors of those four and a half years.'[5] He talked in a similar vein to a British Legion delegation, and discussed their war experiences as an old comrade. He returned to the theme again in 1937: he argued that the frontline fighters knew war as a ghastly experience and had no wish to see it recur.[6]

Peace—it was a useful theme for Hitler. It served its purpose; it deluded his enemies. And yet, even at this time, how hollow and specious were Hitler's words was known to some.

---

[1] *Daily Mail*, 19 October 1933.
[2] Speech of 24 October 1933; Baynes, Vol. II, p. 1,120.
[3] Interview with United Press, November 1935: Baynes, Vol. I, p. 668.
[4] Baynes, Vol. I, p. 671.
[5] *Daily Mail* interview, as Note 1.
[6] Address to the International Commission of Front-line Fighters, 17 February 1937 (summary of speech): Baynes, Vol. II, p. 1,348; and see Schmidt, *Statist auf diplomatischer Bühne*, p. 316.

The British Ambassador, Sir Horace Rumbold, reported in April 1933 on Hitler's intentions: 'He declares that he is anxious that peace should be maintained. . . . What he probably means can be more accurately expressed by the formula: Germany needs peace until she has recovered such strength that no country can challenge her without serious and irksome preparations.'[1] Rumbold's words confirm, in essence, what Hitler had said to Ludecke, and they give an accurate forecast of the policy Hitler was about to follow.

Hitler's aim—as he had set it down in *Mein Kampf*, and, in essentials, it was still the same—was an expansion of Germany eastwards by the acquisition of territory belonging to Russia. The Germans must have *Lebensraum*. 'The German people', he wrote, 'must be assured the territorial area which is necessary for it to exist on this earth. . . . When we speak of new territory in Europe today we must principally think of Russia.' The necessary war of conquest would be justified by its results: 'The territory on which one day our German peasantry will be able to bring forth and nourish their sturdy sons will justify the blood of the sons of the peasants that has to be shed today. . . . Today there are 80 million Germans in Europe. And our foreign policy will be recognized as rightly conducted only when, after barely 100 years, there will be 250 million Germans living on the Continent.'[2]

Hitler's eastern policy he expounded to his intimates on several occasions. Rauschning, the Nazi President of the Danzig Senate, afterwards recalled some of these. In 1932 Hitler said to a group in the Brown House at Munich: 'Our great experimental field is in the east. . . . It is true that world empires arise on a national basis, but very quickly they leave it far behind.'[3] Early in 1934, in a conversation with Rauschning, Hitler made clearer both his aim and his flexible, opportunist method of working towards it. Speaking of his policy towards Russia and of those Nazis who thought an alliance with Russia desirable, Hitler said: 'Perhaps I shall not be

[1] *Observer*, 25 May 1941. Cf. his report of 15 March, *Documents on British Foreign Policy*, Second Series, Vol. IV.
[2] See above, p. 114, *Mein Kampf*, pp. 531-49.
[3] H. Rauschning, *Hitler Speaks*, p. 50.

able to avoid an alliance with Russia. I shall keep that as a trump card. Perhaps it will be the decisive gamble of my life. . . . But it will never stop me from as firmly retracing my steps, and attacking Russia when my aims in the west have been achieved. It is naïve to believe that our rise will always move along a straight line. We shall change our fronts from time to time—and not the military ones alone.' That was to be, indeed, precisely Hitler's future policy, in 1939-41. And once more, in his conversation with Rauschning, he emphasized his eastern objective: 'It is still our task', he declared, 'to shatter for all time the menacing hordes of the pan-Slav empire. . . . We alone can conquer the great continental space, and it will be done by us singly and alone, not through a pact with Moscow. We shall take this struggle upon us. It will open to us the door to permanent mastery of the world.'[1]

As Hitler developed his policy successfully in the years 1933-9 it became, for those who had to be taken into his confidence, more precise as to date and as to the use of the final weapon—war. Many people, inside and outside Germany, thought, or hoped, that Hitler would use the great armed forces he was creating merely to exert pressure, to achieve his ends by bluff, and that he would not go as far as war. It was an idle dream. In October 1936 Hitler told the Italian Foreign Minister, Ciano, who had come to Berchtesgaden, that Britain was governed by incompetents, and said: 'German and Italian rearmament is proceeding much more rapidly than rearmament can in Great Britain, where it is not only a case of providing ships, guns, and aeroplanes, but also of undertaking psychological rearmament, which is much longer and more difficult. In three years Germany will be ready, in four years more than ready; if five years are given, better still. . . .'[2]

Next year, on 5 November 1937, at a secret meeting with the War Minister, Foreign Minister, and the three commanders

[1] Ibid., pp. 136-7. It is to be noted that Rauschning's book was published in December 1939, while the German-Russian Pact was in force and nearly eighteen months before Hitler attacked Russia.
[2] *Ciano's Diplomatic Papers*, pp. 56-60.

of the armed forces, Hitler explained his policy, and discussed the circumstances which might favour or hinder it. He stated, according to Colonel Hossbach's minutes of the meeting,[1] Germany's need for space, and declared that the problem could only be solved by force. He warned that Germany would have 'to reckon with two hate-inspired antagonists, Britain and France'. He pointed out that by 1943-5 German armaments, now reaching completion, would begin to become obsolete, and that foreign countries would be catching up. 'Nobody knew today', he said, 'what the situation would be in the years 1943-5. One thing only was certain: that we could wait no longer. On the one hand there was the great *Wehrmacht*, and the necessity of maintaining it at its present level, the ageing of the movement and its leaders; and on the other, the prospect of a lowering of the standard of living and of a limitation of the birth-rate, which left no choice but to act. If the *Führer* was still living, it was his unalterable resolve to solve Germany's problem of space at the latest by 1943-5.' Hitler did not, indeed, foresee the course events were actually to take; he was thinking in terms of a lengthening of the Spanish war and the possible embroilment of France and Britain with Italy. Germany, he declared, would know how to turn such events to her advantage, but in any event he maintained that Germany must first overthrow Austria and Czechoslovakia 'to remove the threat to our flank in any possible operation against the west'.

In May 1939, when his successes with Austria and Czechoslovakia were safely behind him, Hitler revealed to his Service chiefs that the growing pressure on Poland was itself but the prelude to far greater struggles. 'Danzig is not the object of our activities', he said. 'It is the question of expanding our living space in the east. . . . There is no question of sparing Poland, and we are left with the decision: To attack Poland at the first suitable opportunity.' And he continued: 'We cannot expect a repetition of the Czech affair. There will be war. . . .' If Britain or France should interfere, 'then it will

---

[1] *Documents on German Foreign Policy*, Series D, Vol. I, pp. 29-39. Also in *Nuremberg Documents*, 386-PS. Colonel Hossbach was Adjutant to the *Führer*.

be better to attack in the west and incidentally to settle Poland at the same time'.[1]

Although Hitler's words were not known to the Italians, it became quite clear to Ciano that, in spite of Italian anxiety and hesitations, the Germans were bent on war. On 11 August Ciano wrote in his *Diary*: 'The decision to fight is implacable', and, referring to the Nazi pressure on Poland, 'I am certain that even if the Germans were given more than they ask for they would attack just the same, because they are possessed by the demon of destruction'. Next day Ciano referred to Hitler's 'affirmation that the great war must be fought while he and the Duce are still young'.[2] And again, at the end of the *Diary*, Ciano refers once more to the date of 11 August 1939, when he dined with Ribbentrop near Salzburg. He asked Ribbentrop what the Nazis wanted—the Polish Corridor or Danzig. 'Not that any more', said Ribbentrop, gazing with his cold, metallic eyes at the Italian. 'We want war.'[3]

Some days later, on 22 August, Hitler conferred with his Service chiefs at the Berghof. Notes of the meeting survive, and refer to Hitler's call for the most violent action: 'A long period of peace would not do us any good. . . . The destruction of Poland in the foreground. . . . I shall give a good propaganda cause for starting the war. . . . The victor will not be asked later on whether we told the truth or not. In starting and making a war, not the right is what matters, but victory. Have no pity. Brutal attitude. . . . Might is right. Greatest severity.'[4]

But first, to carry out his policy, Hitler must rearm; to cover his rearmament, he talked of peace. With his uncanny sense for feeling the weaknesses of his enemies, Hitler knew that the Western nations were so imbued with the longing for peace that they would willingly accept his words at their

---

[1] Record by Lieut.-Colonel Schmundt of the *Führer's* conference, *Nuremberg Documents*, L-79.

[2] *Ciano's Diary, 1939-1943*, p. 124.

[3] Ibid., pp. 557-8; cf. Schmidt, *Statist auf diplomatischer Bühne*, p. 438, who describes Ribbentrop as 'like a hound straining impatiently to be let loose on its prey. . . . He let himself go in cramped, exaggerated attacks on England, France, and Poland.'

[4] *Nuremberg Documents*, 1,014-PS.

face value and ignore the need for action. At the same time they would cling to their own traditional military security, which would give him an excuse for a measure of German rearmament. He could afford to make a great gesture before Europe; to offer complete German disarmament if other nations would do the same. What Germany asked for was equality; all she wanted was justice. In his peace speech of May 1933, addressed to the Reichstag, but also attracting wide attention elsewhere, Hitler said: 'Germany would be perfectly willing to disband her entire military establishment and destroy the small amount of arms remaining to her if the neighbouring countries will do the same thing with equal thoroughness. But if these countries are not willing to carry out the disarmament measures to which they are also bound by the Treaty of Versailles, Germany must at least maintain her demand for equality.'[1] On these lines, Hitler could score some good debating points, for the treaty had spoken of 'the initiation of a general limitation of the armaments of all nations', which had not come about.

In October, therefore, Hitler declared in a proclamation to the German people that they had suffered 'a bitter disillusionment. . . . Through the resolute refusal to Germany of a real moral and material equality of rights the German people and its governments have been again and again profoundly humiliated.' Thus Germany could no longer belong to the League of Nations and its conference on disarmament, then in session, which were the means of its humiliation. 'Therefore while the German Government asserts afresh its unalterable will for peace, in the face of these humiliating and dishonouring suggestions, to its profound regret it declares that it is forced to leave the Disarmament Conference. And in consequence it must also give notice of its retirement from the League of Nations.'[2] What plausible hypocrisy! For Hitler's pretence of peaceful aims was in direct contradiction of his avowed aim of expansion in Russia. He could not have it both ways: peace in Europe and a war of territorial conquest. He could be equally contradictory in his whole

<hr />

[1] Baynes, Vol. II, p. 1,053.   [2] Ibid., pp. 1,088-9.

attitude to peace—one speech would contradict another.[1] His underlying, irrational conviction in the rightness of his cause made him brush aside as irrelevant the contradictions and double-dealing which his policy involved. Yet Hitler's hypocrisy worked. His pleas for peace impressed the well-intentioned abroad. For example, George Lansbury, the veteran Labour pacifist, during a long interview with Hitler, appeared blind to the *Führer's* signs of boredom and looked at him as if he were a pacifist idealist. 'I return to England', said Lansbury, 'with the conviction that the catastrophe of war will be avoided.'[2] In Germany Hitler's action in leaving the League and demanding equality was approved in November by a plebiscite of over 40 million votes against 2 million.

Hitler proceeded step by step. While the country was still weak, he aimed at limited objectives. 'A clever conqueror will always, if possible', he had written in *Mein Kampf*, 'impose his demands on the conquered by instalments.' At first his main preoccupation must be, therefore, to avoid provoking a general and active European opposition to the development of his policy. It was in keeping with his professedly peaceful policy—though something, nevertheless, of a political sensation—when Hitler announced on 26 January 1934 the making of a ten-year non-aggression pact with Poland.[3] Hitler could claim this pact as a victory for peace. Ever since Versailles there had been friction between Germany and Poland over the Corridor and Danzig; against no people had German feeling been stronger than against the Poles. Yet now, at one stroke, Hitler established more friendly relations. It was a masterly stroke of policy: it strengthened Hitler's peaceful pretensions; it weakened relations between Poland and her ally, France, and so prevented active pressure on Germany by France and Poland together; it gave the Poles a false sense of security; and it prepared the way for a possible German advance against Russia *with* Polish help (for which Hitler worked at first). In any event, Poland was

---

[1] See p. 215, footnote 1.

[2] P. Schmidt, *Statist auf diplomatischer Bühne*, pp. 343-4.

[3] German Text in *Dokumente zur Vorgeschichte des Krieges*, pp. 51-2.

in an impossible position between her powerful neighbours, Germany and Russia:[1] Hitler could deal with Poland later. Meanwhile the non-aggression pact protected his eastern flank, and left him free to turn his attention westwards and southwards.

In Austria, where political tension had been greatly increased by the advent of Hitler to power in Germany, events threatened to move too fast for Hitler. The Austrian Chancellor, Dollfuss, and his Christian Socialist Government felt themselves increasingly pressed by the Communists on the Left and the Nazis on the Right, the Nazis now looking for a speedy *Anschluss*, or union with Germany. The struggle with the Left, however, came first. In February 1934 the bombardment by the Government of the Vienna working-class housing blocks, the imposing, turreted Karl Marxhof and the Goethehof, though it resulted in Government victory, indicated how parlous the position was. In July the Austrian Nazis, with German compliance, staged a *Putsch*: they broke into the Vienna Chancellery and shot Dollfuss. But Dr. Schuschnigg took over the chancellorship and succeeded in suppressing the rebels; Mussolini, who at this stage still regarded an independent Austria as a safeguard for Italy against Germany, mobilized troops on the Brenner. The *Putsch* failed. Hitler held back. It was clear that he was not yet strong enough to brave armed opposition.

Early next year Hitler won his first territorial success—and a peaceful one. On 13 January 1935 the plebiscite was held in the Saar, according to the peace treaty, to decide whether this coal-mining territory should remain under the League of Nations administration or should become German or French. Although the plebiscite was under international control and an international force commanded by a British officer was present to maintain the orderly conditions necessary for a free vote, and although the Saarlanders when they went through the snow to vote on that bleak winter's day had their eyes open to all that had happened in Germany,

[1] See the comments of M. François-Poncet, *The Fateful Years*, pp. 115-16. Cf. F. Hesse, *Das Spiel um Deutschland*, pp. 22-3.

the result was an overwhelming victory for Hitler. Over 477,000 voted to return to Germany; only 46,000 voted for the *status quo*, and 2,000 to join France. It was a singular demonstration of the strength of German nationalism and Nazi feeling as against common sense. It was hailed in Germany as a resounding victory, as indeed it was. Germany regained the valuable industrial area of the Saar, and Hitler now still further strengthened his peace propaganda by stating two days later on the wireless that 'the Germans will make no further territorial claims on France'[1]—that is, Hitler would abandon, to the surprise of many Germans, the claim to Alsace and Lorraine. In a Press interview he pointed to the plebiscite result as a condemnation of the Treaty of Versailles, and stated that the act of renouncing any claims on France 'I do in order . . . to contribute to the pacification of Europe'.[2]

Meanwhile, other nations were making efforts for their own protection. Soviet Russia, seriously alarmed at what had happened in Germany, entered the League of Nations in September 1934. The Western nations negotiated with Hitler and tried to persuade him to bring Germany into an Eastern Locarno. Just as agreement had been reached in the west to guarantee mutually the frontiers between Germany and France and Belgium, so, it was argued, might agreement be reached in the east, and Germany, Russia, Poland, and Czechoslovakia be included in a pact of mutual assistance. But Hitler was anxious not to be drawn into any such agreement.

Instead, early in 1935 Hitler deemed the time was ripe to take a bolder step. In any case, it was becoming clear that Germany was rearming; the creation of an air force and the building of submarines could not be hidden. It was time, therefore, to make an announcement of German rearmament —but at the same time to justify it in terms of the existing situation. In a proclamation of 16 March Hitler announced the introduction of military conscription and the fixing of the

---

[1] 15 January 1935: Baynes, Vol. II, p. 1,195.
[2] Interview with Hearst Press, 16 January: ibid., p. 1,195.

peace strength of the German Army at thirty-six divisions. This action he justified by quoting a speech by Mr. Baldwin on the necessity of self-defence, by pointing out that Russia had an army of 101 divisions and that France had just lengthened the period of military service, and by underlining the fact that Germany had already made assurances to Poland and France and wished 'to make its contribution to the pacification of the world in free and frank co-operation with other nations and their governments'.[1] Next day he said to Ward Price: 'One thing you must know: The German people does not want war. It simply wants equal rights for all.'[2]

The rearmament of Germany was an open breach of the Treaty of Versailles. But no appropriate action followed— only words. Sir John Simon and Mr. Eden visited Hitler in Berlin at the end of March. In April, at the Stresa Conference, Britain, France, and Italy condemned the German action. At Geneva the Council of the League of Nations also condemned it. In May France and Soviet Russia signed a pact for mutual aid in case of attack, and Russia also made an agreement with Czechoslovakia. But meanwhile, Hitler had gained the solid advantage of rearmament. How feeble were the pacts formed to safeguard the nations opposed to him time would show.

To allay premature fears abroad, to which German rearmament might give rise, Hitler made another great peace speech to the Reichstag on 21 May 1935, and an approved translation into English was printed in Berlin for foreign consumption.[3] Hitler showed amazing skill, especially when one remembers that he had not travelled and spoke no foreign language, in the art of beguiling the West and lulling its suspicions. He claimed that he himself, as the result of the plebiscites approving his policy, was the democratically elected representative of the German people, which 'has elected a single deputy as its representative with 38 million votes'. As a result, he said, 'I feel myself just as responsible

[1] *The Times*, 18 March; also Baynes, Vol. II, pp. 1,208-10.
[2] *Daily Mail*, 18 March; Baynes, Vol. II, p. 1,212.
[3] Speech delivered in the Reichstag, 21 May 1935 (approved translation, Müller, Berlin).

to the German people as would any parliament. I act on the trust they have placed in me and I carry out their mandate.' He spoke eloquently on the waste, uselessness, and folly of war. 'National Socialist Germany', he asserted, 'wants peace because of its fundamental convictions. And it wants peace also owing to the realization of the simple primitive fact that no war would be likely to alter the distress in Europe. It would probably increase it. Present-day Germany is engaged in the tremendous work of making good the damage done to it internally. None of our projects of a practical nature will be completed before a period of from ten to twenty years. . . . Germany needs peace and desires peace.'[1] He dealt specifically with objections to German policy by Mr. Eden, and quoted lavishly from English, French, and Belgian statesmen, Lord Robert Cecil, Arthur Henderson, Briand, Paul Boncour, and Vandervelde, who had spoken on the Western nations' failure to disarm. He warned the world against Bolshevism. He went out of the way to declare solemnly that Germany had no intention of annexing Austria, that she would continue to adhere to the territorial clauses of the Versailles Treaty and of Locarno, and that she would respect the demilitarization of the Rhineland. Germany was also willing to agree to any measure limiting the heaviest arms, most suitable for aggression; she was willing to accept air parity, and a limitation of German naval strength to 35 per cent of the British Navy. Hitler closed his speech with renewed appeals, asserting that 'whoever lights the torch of war in Europe can wish for nothing but chaos'.[2]

It was difficult not to be influenced favourably by Hitler's

[1] Speech delivered in the Reichstag, 21 May 1935, pp. 11-12: 'National Socialist Germany wants peace because of its fundamental convictions.' But later on, with equal conviction, Hitler would say the opposite: 'I am a National Socialist, and as such I am accustomed on every attack to hit back immediately.' Speech of 12 September 1938: Baynes, Vol. II, p. 1,495.

[2] Speech of 21 May 1935, p. 48. Passages from the speech also in Baynes, Vol. II, pp. 1,218-47. Cf. the following extract from a personal letter 14 July 1937: 'Germany never would have rearmed if other nations would have disarmed. Hitler proclaimed that again and again . . . Of course Hitler rearmed secretly. But could he do otherwise? Only by rearmament Germany regained equality of rights . . . But it would be fundamentally wrong to conclude from that that Germany is preparing war. No nation needs peace more than Germany'. . . and so on *ad nauseam*.

words; he appealed so adroitly to reason, justice, and common decency. The effect was considerable in England. Ribbentrop arrived in London in June and an Anglo-German naval treaty was concluded which, in accordance with the suggestion thrown out in the Reichstag speech, bound Germany not to build beyond 35 per cent of Britain's naval strength. To the British Government this agreement to limit the German Navy was a success for common sense. It did not seem so to France and Italy, who were not consulted. They saw it as a breach of the Treaty of Versailles, and as a tacit British consent to the creation of a German fleet. At Stresa and Geneva there had been, at least, unanimity in condemning German rearmament. Now Britain, like Poland, had misguidedly made its own private bargain with Hitler. Hitler still harboured his respect for Britain which he had shown in *Mein Kampf*; he still hoped to win her support or neutrality to give him a free hand on the continent of Europe. As a result of the Naval agreement, Hitler succeeded in sowing further distrust among the Western nations and in weakening any common opposition they could put up against him.

Next, Italy's imperial adventure in Abyssinia, which began in October 1935, was a direct threat to the whole League of Nations position, and by occupying European attention gave Hitler an opportunity for another important step towards a position of dominating power. During the period of the Italo-Abyssinian War Germany found a ready market for its coal in Italy, and Germany would not co-operate in the economic sanctions which the League applied against Italian aggression. Germany adopted an attitude of neutrality. Italy was fatally alienated from Britain and France, and was thus drawn towards Germany. While Mr. Eden at Geneva was pressing for an extension of sanctions to oil, and on the very day on which the League's committee of petroleum experts issued its second report, setting out the measures to be taken to apply an oil sanction, Hitler seized the opportunity to act. On 7 March 1936 German troops occupied the demilitarized Rhineland. The discussions about sanctions were set aside. Attention was deflected from the Italo-Abyssinian War to the menace from

Germany. Mussolini gained thereby a free hand to proceed with the conquest of Abyssinia. And serious bad feeling was stirred up between France and Britain. To France it seemed that Britain had mistakenly taken her stand on a minor issue with Italy, and so was driving that country into Germany's arms. But it was, nevertheless, an anxious moment for Hitler; he acted against the advice of his generals; he had not yet sufficient force to maintain his position if the French Army marched. And the French were entitled to act. The German move was a breach of the Treaty of Versailles and of the Locarno Pact, which, unlike the Treaty, had been freely negotiated by Germany. As Mr. Eden pointed out later in the House of Commons, Hitler himself had reaffirmed Locarno. 'We have heard much', said the Foreign Secretary, 'about the *Diktat* of Versailles, but nobody has ever heard of the Diktat of Locarno.'[1]

Hitler's bluff worked, however; no action was taken against him. Hitler covered his action by making the Franco-Russian Pact his excuse—it was, he argued, incompatible with Locarno —and once more he put forward proposals for peace. Belgium now backed out of the Locarno arrangements, and determined to follow a policy of neutrality for the future—a clear indication of the weakening of the Western position. The move into the Rhineland was, indeed, a major victory for Germany. It marked the last occasion on which France and Britain could have checked Germany without war. Hitler would henceforth be too strong. He had safeguarded his eastern frontier by the pact with Poland; now he proceeded to protect himself on the west by building formidable defences along the Rhine and Saar rivers. Before long the Siegfried Line confronted the French Maginot Line, and, in case of war, these opposed systems of defence promised initial stalemate in the west, leaving Hitler free to act elsewhere.

There was only a brief pause before another critical development plunged Europe into new alarms. German pressure on Austria increased, now that Italy was looking elsewhere and

1 *The Times*, 27 March 1936.

was less interested in maintaining an independent Austria. Mussolini completed the conquest of Abyssinia, and on 4 July the League of Nations abandoned sanctions against Italy. Then, on 17 July, the Spanish Civil War broke out. General Franco fought to overthrow the republican Government in Spain and establish a military, fascist dictatorship. From the start Mussolini, and soon Hitler, sent military assistance to Franco. Russia helped the republican Government, while Britain and France tried feverishly and spasmodically to establish a policy of non-intervention. France was, in particular, endangered by the prospect of having yet a third fascist dictator on her frontiers, but in spite of that there was considerable division of French opinion. Bitter political and class differences showed themselves in the fact that the French Left-wing Government of Blum favoured the Spanish republic while the Right sympathized with Franco. These internal French differences were the very means which Hitler needed to follow his clever policy of psychologically weakening his enemies. During the three years of the civil war in Spain, Britain and France cut sorry figures in their ineffective efforts to maintain non-intervention, and the determined and resolute action of Hitler and Mussolini instilled into other nations, if not a sentiment of love for the fascist countries, at least one of fear. The Germans gained economic advantages from Spain, and also experience for men and equipment under war conditions, but most important was the political advantage Hitler achieved. For meanwhile, in spite of the British and French efforts to win over Mussolini now that sanctions had been dropped, the common object of Mussolini and Hitler in their Spanish policy brought their two countries ever nearer.

Official contacts between Germany and Italy became closer. In October 1936 Germany recognized the new Italian Empire of Ethiopia, and on 1 November Mussolini made an important speech at Milan in which he denounced 'Wilsonian illusions' —disarmament, collective security, the idea that peace is indivisible, and the policy of sanctions—and, announcing an agreement between Germany and Italy, he used the expression,

'Rome-Berlin Axis'.[1] This term, which passed into common use, vividly indicated the new alignment of political forces in Europe, which was further strengthened in May 1939 by the so-called Pact of Steel, a defensive and offensive alliance between Germany and Italy. Hitler had written in *Mein Kampf* of the German need for alliances with Italy and Britain. With Italy he had now, in 1936, secured agreement. But Britain, though clearly unwilling to commit herself to any bold policy against the dictators, was also unwilling to be drawn closely into the German net—in spite of the blandishments of Ribbentrop as Ambassador in London and the use made by the Nazis of the common danger of Russian Communism, an argument which had, not unnaturally, an appeal to many people in Britain and France. Instead of with Britain, Germany came to an agreement with Japan. In the November of the Rome-Berlin Axis the Anti-Comintern Pact was signed in Berlin. By this pact Germany and Japan agreed to consultation and collaboration against world Communism as embodied in the Communist International. The pact was open to other states, and Italy adhered to it in the following year.

The broad ideological significance of the Anti-Comintern Pact was clear: it marked a *rapprochement* of the three great aggressor nations, and a common threat to peaceful nations. In fact, in 1937 Japan renewed her earlier policy of aggression against China. Meanwhile, Hitler was still further strengthened. His powers were growing, both political and military. The armaments drive was being pushed ahead with the greatest energy and urgency; Hitler began to feel the new power behind him. During 1937 he pressed German demands with increasing vigour—for example, his claim for the return of German colonies.[2] But Hitler continued, in 1936 and 1937, to reassure

[1] *Le Journal*, 2 November 1936. A French commentator in this issue headed his article, '*Liquider les chimères? Bravo!*' In that, he agreed with Mussolini. The article illustrated how powerful was the hold in France of a purely realist policy against Germany and how different from the attachment of Britain to the idealist principles of the League, although Britain failed to do much to put the principle into action.

[2] Speeches of January and November 1937: Baynes, Vol. II, pp. 1,343-4, 1371. Nor was the British response entirely unfavourable. See Ribbentrop's report of 30 November 1937: *Documents on German Foreign Policy*, Series D, Vol. I, p. 85.

the Poles. He must have security on that eastern flank while he moved elsewhere.

While German strength increased and Hitler was preparing to act, the weakness and demoralization of the Western nations was complete. The dismal weakness of British foreign policy during the years of Hitler's growing strength has not, even now, been altogether explained. In the desperate striving to preserve peace, almost every safeguard was sacrificed, every humiliation accepted, and at length our very existence placed in peril. Whereas in 1919 Germany was defeated and completely disarmed, she had been allowed to rearm under our very noses. Twenty years later she was stronger than ever, able to dominate continental Europe by military power, and to threaten to put an end for ever to the freedom of the Western nations. Above all it was the failure to keep Germany disarmed that was the undoing of the west. And yet, as Sir Winston Churchill has written, it would have been 'a simple policy to keep Germany disarmed and the victors adequately armed for thirty years'. But the victors failed to work together for this common objective. Instead, 'they lived from hand to mouth and from day to day, and from one election to another, until, when scarcely twenty years were out, the dread signal of the Second World War was given'.[1] How had this extraordinary state of affairs come about? How had this fatal malaise settled on the West?

The first and underlying cause of the failure of measures to safeguard peace was the fact that the United States did not enter the League of Nations. President Wilson's great ideal was turned down at home. Thus, from the start, the League was not strong; it did not have the universal support which Wilson, Cecil, and Smuts had intended. Later on Hitler, in his peace speeches, turned the noble ideals of the League inside out, and used the language of Geneva, with the greatest skill, against Geneva. Among the foundation members of the League also, in spite of seeming unity, there was disagreement. There was a marked difference of attitude towards Germany between Britain and France. France in the

[1] *The Second World War*, Vol. I (*The Gathering Storm*).

years following the Treaty of Versailles was, not unnaturally, obsessed with the problem of security against Germany—hence the occupation of the Ruhr and the attempt to extort payment of reparations by force. Britain, on the other hand, viewed more favourably the economic recovery of Germany as a customer for British goods. The difference of attitude appeared again in regard to the League of Nations: France viewed it as an instrument for maintaining French security against Germany; Britain thought of it as a collective means of preventing aggression in other parts of the world as well. Thus Britain and France disagreed bitterly in their attitude to Italy over the Italo-Abyssinian War. Italy was a foundation member of the League, but the principles of Fascism were fundamentally opposed to the democratic spirit of the League, and Mussolini struck it a deadly blow by his aggression in 1935 against Abyssinia, also a member of the League. Mussolini was determined to conquer Abyssinia, as he put it, 'with Geneva, without Geneva, against Geneva'. The democratic nations had failed to use the League to prevent Japanese aggression in Manchuria in 1931; now they failed again with Italy in 1935.

The weakness of Britain and France as props to a system of collective security was revealed. Nothing fails like failure. In the 1930s, years of unemployment and economic depression, England and France suffered a kind of paralysis. In France, one felt the decay of an over-refined civilization, a lack of life and youth; in both France and Britain there was no sense of drive and purpose. Germany, on the other hand, pulsated from end to end with life, vitality, and confidence, even arrogance. The continued successes of Hitler, and Mussolini, confirmed the waverers in their own countries and convinced them that, after all, the dictators were right.

The conviction grew abroad that Britain and France were finished. It was strengthened in 1933 by the famous Oxford Union debate, when the undergraduates resolved 'That this House refuses to fight for King and Country'. The facts were, of course, partially misread abroad. There was in Britain, in spite of her weakness in foreign policy, a considerable movement for resisting aggression; it was demonstrated by the Peace Ballot of 1935, sponsored by the League of Nations Union and the Labour and Liberal parties, which, in spite of being much misrepresented by its opponents, revealed a vote of three to one in favour of *military* sanctions against aggression. But the leadership was lacking; in a vital period, two Prime Ministers, Baldwin and Neville Chamberlain, were temperamentally incapable of realizing the nature of the situation and of giving the required lead. Hitler knew his own strength and his enemies' weakness; he said there was 'on the opposing side, a negative picture. . . . In England and France there is no outstanding personality.'[1] After his greatest diplomatic victory over his opponents later on, Hitler said: 'Our opponents are little worms: I saw them in Munich.'[2] Hitler was not quite right; he never met Churchill. The outstanding personality was there; he gave repeated warnings. But his warnings at this time went unheeded. Churchill was still a voice crying in the wilderness. British politicians refused to take their enemies seriously enough. Bülow many years before had summed up the British attitude, and his judgement still rang true: 'British politicians know little of the Continent. . . . They are naïve. . . . They believe with difficulty that others have bad motives.'[3] Chamberlain fell into this category: he thought he could come to an understanding with Mussolini; he thought he could make an honest bargain with Hitler.

Another difficult factor in the situation, admittedly, was Soviet Russia. Russia was the natural political ally of the West, as in 1914, against Germany. Russia had now joined the League, and had linked up with France in the Franco-Soviet Pact. But there was a profound suspicion of Russia, and not unnaturally. At that time, however, it was exaggerated and ill-timed. The real danger in those years was not Russia, but Nazi Germany. A steady defensive alliance of Britain, France and Russia would have deterred Hitler. Britain and France at

<hr />

[1] *Nuremberg Documents*, 798-PS.
[2] Ibid.
[3] Memorandum of 1899: *German Diplomatic Documents* (trans., E. T. S. Dugdale), Vol. III, p. 113.

last turned to this policy, but only when it was too late. Russian suspicions of the West had grown so strong as to prevent common action to maintain peace.

The decisive event in the decline of the League of Nations and the rise to dominance of the dictators was Italy's war with Abyssinia. Before that the issue was uncertain. Mussolini as well as Hitler had undoubtedly, in spite of their violence and the destruction of democracy, established order and brought certain material advantages and a new national self-confidence to their countries. The question was: would they stop there? The blatant aggression of Italy against Abyssinia showed that they would not. The dream of peace, the dream of the generation which grew up after the First World War, was destroyed. The threat was not merely to Abyssinia, it was to the whole Western conception of life. How clearly the truth was put to the journalists during the last days of Addis Ababa in April 1936 by the Princess Tsahai: 'We are only a small race; but I am seventeen and its leading daughter, and I know, as you know, that if mankind lets armies and gas destroy my country and people, civilization will be destroyed too. We have common cause, you and I. Why do not all do something to drive off this common danger to humanity, this agony, this death by bomb, shell and gas. . . . soon to be spread fatally to your homes and your menfolk too? Italian aggression and gas have set humanity a test. If you fail to help us now, we shall all die.'[1] The Emperor of Abyssinia declared: 'If my tardy allies never come, then I say prophetically and without bitterness: "The West will perish." '[2] Three days later the Emperor was driven from his capital. Mussolini triumphed, and the West was left to face yet more terrible aggressors. Three years later the great failure of the West brought its own nemesis.

It was a lamentable failure.[3] Britain had rallied fifty nations

[1] *Survey of International Affairs*, 1935, Vol. II (Abyssinia and Italy), pp. 355-6.
[2] Ibid., p. 357.
[3] One can easily be accused of being 'wise after the event'. But the author, defending the League of Nations policy, said at the time in an address to Bristol Rotary Club: 'One or other of these dictators has to be taught a lesson . . . if we take on Mussolini, Hitler will take notice. . . . The best way to teach them a lesson is through collective security. . . . Sooner or later we must make a stand, and if we do not make it now, we will have to do it later against greater odds': *Western Daily Press*, 23 June 1936.

at Geneva against aggression. For a brief moment the Foreign Secretary, Sir Samuel Hoare, stirred the democratic and peace-loving forces everywhere by his speech of 11 September 1935: 'The League stands, and my country stands with it . . . for steady and collective resistance to all acts of unprovoked aggression.' But then we recoiled; Baldwin hesitated, and the opportunity was thrown away. As Sir Winston Churchill has expressed it: 'If ever there was an opportunity of striking a decisive blow in a generous cause with the minimum of risk, it was here and now. The fact that the nerve of the British Government was not equal to the occasion can be excused only by their sincere love of peace. Actually, it played a part in leading to an infinitely more terrible war. Mussolini's bluff succeeded, and an important spectator drew far-reaching conclusions from the fact. Hitler had long resolved on war for German aggrandisement. He now formed a view of Great Britain's degeneracy, which was only to be changed too late for peace and too late for him. In Japan also there were pensive spectators.'[1]

[1] *The Second World War*, Vol. I, p. 138. It is perhaps characteristic that Winston Churchill, Eden, Duff Cooper and others who saw through Hitler's peaceful professions, are consistently referred to as the *Kriegspartei* (war party) by F. Hesse, *Das Spiel um Deutschland*. See pp. 40, 58, 61, and 301-2, where Roosevelt is similarly criticized.

CHAPTER XII

GROWING STRENGTH: AUSTRIA AND CZECHOSLOVAKIA

BY the beginning of 1938 Hitler was ready to take bolder action: the period of bluff and preparation was closing, the period of aggression was approaching. Success so far had confirmed his sense of mission. After his occupation of the demilitarized Rhineland in 1936 Hitler declared: 'Neither threats nor warnings will move me from my path. I go with the assurance of a sleep-walker on the way which Providence dictates.'[1] In an address at Augsburg late in 1937 Hitler referred to the ultimate Nazi objective and to the growing strength of Germany: 'Today we are faced with new tasks', he said, 'for the living-space [*Lebensraum*] of our people is too narrow. . . . One day the world will have to pay attention to our demands.' The Nazi leadership, he asserted, 'relying on the common strength of a people of 68 millions expressed in the last resort by its Army, will be able both to defend with success the nation's interests and successfully to accomplish the tasks which are set before us.'[2] Hitler had already decided (as revealed after the war by the captured Hossbach minutes of 5 November 1937) that the first objectives were to be Austria and Czechoslovakia.

In the winter of 1937-8 Hitler shook off a number of restraining hands. Schacht resigned his Ministry of Economics, and was replaced by the more amenable Funk; Neurath was replaced by Ribbentrop as Foreign Minister. Blomberg, the Minister of Defence, was forced to resign as the result of a marriage with a lady of more than doubtful virtue—although the marriage had been encouraged by Göring, and he and Hitler himself were present at it. At the same time, Fritsch,

---

[1] 15 March, Munich: Baynes, Vol. II, p. 1,307.
[2] 21 November: ibid., p. 1,370.

Commander-in-chief of the Army, was compelled to resign on a charge of homosexuality brought against him by the Gestapo. The charge was later proved to be false—but Göring had connived at the making of the charge, and Göring had stood to take over Blomberg's post if he and his likely successor, Fritsch, could be both discredited. And both Blomberg and Fritsch had offended Hitler by offering criticisms of his military proposals of 5 November for action in Austria and Czechoslovakia. However astounding might be the intrigues and corruption revealed in the Nazi State by the Blomberg and Fritsch affairs,[1] Hitler took advantage of the situation to strengthen his own position. He took supreme responsibility for defence himself, suppressed the Defence Ministry and, in its place, created the *Oberkommando der Wehrmacht* (O.K.W.) for all the armed forces, under General Keitel. Göring was, however, consoled by promotion to field-marshal. The outcome of it all was a weakening of the generals as a possible independent force against Hitler, a victory for the Gestapo, and the further concentration of power in the hands of Hitler himself.

To the Reichstag on 20 February 1938 Hitler said: 'Over 10 million Germans live in two of the states adjoining our frontiers . . . it is intolerable for a self-respecting world power to know that across the frontier are kinsmen who have to suffer. . . . To the interests of the German Reich belongs also the protection of those fellow-Germans who live beyond our frontiers.'[2] In other words, as events were soon to show, Hitler was ready to apply first to Austria and then to Czechoslovakia an intolerable pressure which would force them into surrender.

The first Nazi attempt against Austria, in 1934, when Dollfuss was murdered, had failed. But this time there would be no Italian mobilization on the Brenner, though, as Ciano was reported to have remarked, 'No country would want to have Germany as a neighbour', and Mussolini, in spite of the Rome-Berlin Axis, scarcely relished the advance of the Nazis

---

[1] See the account of Gisevius, *To the Bitter End*, pp. 219-65.
[2] Baynes, Vol. II, pp. 1,404-6.

to the Italian frontier. Dr. Schuschnigg had few moments of rest after he took over as Chancellor from Dollfuss. Occasionally with his Foreign Secretary, Guido Schmidt, and Hannes Schneider, the former Olympic ski champion, he would be seen among the winter snows at St. Anton or St. Christoph in the Arlberg. But upon the shoulders of the quiet, grey-haired man, with his horn-rimmed spectacles, there rested the burden of a difficult and unenviable position. As head of the Catholic and patriotic Fatherland Front, he strove to maintain his position as against Socialists and Austrian Nazis inside his own country and, at the same time, to maintain his country's independence as against Nazi Germany outside. In July 1936 an uneasy understanding between the two countries was reached; part was published, part took the form of a secret 'gentlemen's agreement'. Germany publicly recognized the sovereignty of Austria. Germany also relaxed certain restrictions on travel and cultural activities, there was to be a propaganda truce, Austria was to grant an amnesty to Nazi political prisoners, and, most important of all, there was provision for the admission into the Austrian Government of members of the 'National Opposition' (i.e. the Austrian Nazis).[1] Hitler did all he could to stretch the agreement to its uttermost and use it to Nazify Austria from the inside. Schuschnigg struggled to manœuvre, and preserve Austrian independence. Von Papen, German Ambassador in Vienna from immediately after Dollfuss's murder until the *Anschluss*, claimed that he (Papen) was working for union by evolutionary means.[2] But always there was the danger: the Austrian Nazis might stage another *Putsch* or Hitler might become impatient.

During 1937 Nazi acts of terrorism in Austria increased—explosions, the throwing of tear-gas bombs, and street demonstrations—all these with the object of forcing the Austrian police to restore order and so affording Germany the excuse for protesting to Austria against the persecution of the Nazis. By early in 1938 things were serious. The Austrian police had

---

[1] The published clauses and the secret agreement are printed in *Documents on German Foreign Policy*, D, Vol. I, pp. 278-82.

[2] *Memoirs*, p. 341.

discovered documents indicating a Nazi plot; there was said to be a suggestion for the assassination of Papen to give a pretext for German intervention.[1] Schuschnigg was ready to attempt an improvement by a personal contact with the German leader. Papen arranged an interview with Hitler. On 11 February Schuschnigg and Guido Schmidt left Vienna by sleeper secretly for Salzburg; next morning they were driven over the frontier to Berchtesgaden. The last lap of the journey up the icy road was by caterpillar car, and at the Berghof they were received by Hitler—and three generals.

A stormy interview now took place—carefully calculated to intimidate the Austrian Chancellor. When Schuschnigg referred to the fine view from the *Führer's* window, Hitler cut him short with: 'We did not get together to speak of a fine view or the weather.' Schuschnigg persevered in his attempt to be pleasant. 'We have done everything', he said, 'to prove that we intend to follow a policy friendly towards Germany in accordance with our mutual agreement.' 'So you call this a friendly policy, Herr Schuschnigg?' answered Hitler, and continued with what was later described by Schuschnigg as a 'somewhat unilateral' conversation. 'Austria', Hitler shouted, 'has never done anything that would be of any help to Germany. The whole history of Austria is just one uninterrupted act of high treason. . . . And I can tell you here and now, Herr Schuschnigg, that I am absolutely determined to make an end of all this. The German Reich is one of the Great Powers, and nobody will raise his voice if it settles its border problems.' Hitler proceeded to attack the Habsburgs and the Catholic Church. Then he spoke of his own task. 'I have a historic mission', he declared, 'and this mission I will fulfil because Providence has destined me to do so.' In Germany there was now national unity: 'I have made the greatest achievement in the history of Germany, greater than any other German', and 'I am telling you that I am going to solve the so-called Austrian problem one way or the other. . . . You don't seriously believe that you can stop me, or even delay me for half an hour, do you? Who knows? Perhaps

[1] Papen's *Memoirs*, p. 404.

you will wake up one morning in Vienna to find us there—
just like a spring storm. And then you'll see something. . . .
After the Army, my S.A. and the Austrian Legion [i.e. of
Austrian Nazis who had fled to Germany] would move in,
and nobody can stop their just revenge. . . . Do you want
to make another Spain of Austria?' Hitler went on to weaken
Schuschnigg psychologically by placing the entire blame for
any bloodshed or war on his shoulders. 'Do you want to take
this responsibility upon yourself, Herr Schuschnigg?' Schuschnigg stood alone, Hitler avowed; nobody would come to his
aid: 'Italy? I see eye to eye with Mussolini. . . . England?
England will not move one finger for Austria. . . . And
France? Well, three years ago we marched on the Rhineland with a handful of battalions; that was the time I risked
everything. . . . But now it is too late for France.' Schuschnigg
answered as well as he could. Hitler still blustered and
threatened. 'Think it over, Herr Schuschnigg; think it over
well. I can only wait until this afternoon.'[1]

Then, after this two hours of ranting, they went into lunch.
Hitler was by now in excellent spirits, according to Schuschnigg. The Austrian Chancellor, however, according to Papen,
was worried and preoccupied. Later in the afternoon Ribbentrop presented to Schuschnigg a typewritten draft of Hitler's
demands.[2] These included the legalization of National Socialism 'inside the framework of the Fatherland Front'—in
effect, that the Nazi movement should be allowed to carry
on its work openly in Austria; that the Nazi fellow-traveller
(as one might put it today), Seyss-Inquart, should become
Minister of the Interior and thus control the police; an immediate amnesty for imprisoned Nazis and reinstatement in their
former jobs; an exchange of officers between the armies of
the two countries; and a close assimilation of their economic
systems. Schuschnigg realized that this document would mean

---

[1] K. von Schuschnigg, *Austrian Requiem*, pp. 19-26. The dialogue was written
down from memory. Schuschnigg and Hitler were alone. Papen gives a general
account of the meeting and the events at the Berghof, *Memoirs*, Chapter XXIII,
and accepts, in the main, Schuschnigg's account of the dialogue.

[2] *Documents on German Foreign Policy*, D, Vol. I, pp. 513-15, and, for the final
form of the agreement, pp. 515-17.

the beginning of Nazi control in Austria. Ribbentrop went through it with him, paragraph by paragraph, while he waited for another interview with Hitler himself. When he was called into Hitler's study, Schuschnigg found him pacing up and down. Schuschnigg pointed out that though he would sign the document, it would, under the Austrian Constitution, require acceptance by the President, and that he could not guarantee acceptance. On this Hitler appeared to lose control of himself; he ran to the door, and shouted for General Keitel. It looked as though immediate military measures were to start; Keitel, talking outside with Schmidt, immediately changed from a friendly to a hostile attitude. Schmidt thought that he and Schuschnigg would be at once arrested. But no; in half an hour Schuschnigg was called back. Threatened, as it must have appeared to him, by an immediate march into Austria, Schuschnigg signed the paper, with a few minor changes in it, and Hitler became amiable again. Afterwards, according to Papen,[1] Keitel told them that when he had presented himself on hearing Hitler's shout for him, and had asked for his orders, the *Führer* had grinned. 'There are no orders', he said. 'I just wanted to have you here.' Hitler had put on a nicely calculated show of force to intimidate Schuschnigg. Indeed, a successful bluff was always something which gave Hitler great pleasure.[2]

On the way back to Salzburg, Papen assured Schuschnigg of Hitler's good qualities. 'You know', he said, 'the *Führer* can be absolutely charming.' But Schuschnigg was unconvinced. He felt that there would be no more discussions about Austria. 'I also knew', he wrote afterwards, 'that there was little room for hope.'[3]

Indeed, in spite of the Austrian acceptance of the agreement, things grew much worse. The period between 12 February and 11 March Schuschnigg calls 'the four weeks' agony'.

[1] *Memoirs*, p. 417.
[2] Hitler once gave a detailed account of how he won his Iron Cross to Sefton Delmer (*Daily Express*, 11 July 1939). Taking sixteen French soldiers by surprise in a shell crater, Hitler shouted to them, '*Vous êtes prisonniers*', and pretended to call orders to German troops behind him—though there were none there. The bluff worked.
[3] *Austrian Requiem*, p. 32.

Seyss-Inquart in private expressed loyalty to Austria, but his public speeches were ambiguous. The swastika sign appeared, and badges were on sale in the streets. Nazi passive resistance began in the institutions of Government and in the police. Street demonstrations took place; in Graz Nazis stormed the Town Hall and flew the swastika flag. Soon Schuschnigg felt that he must take some drastic action to assert the authority of the Government. At a mass meeting in Innsbruck on 9 March he announced a plebiscite, to be held on 13 March. The people should decide. They would be asked to vote 'for a free and independent, German and Christian Austria'. This the Chancellor hoped would demonstrate popular support for Austrian independence, and disprove Hitler's contention that the majority of Austrians were Nazis. Indeed, during the Berghof meeting Hitler had himself suggested a plebiscite. Reminding Schuschnigg of his (Hitler's) Austrian origin, he asked: 'Why don't you try a plebiscite in Austria in which we two run against each other? You just try that.'[1] But now Hitler feared the result which Schuschnigg's plebiscite might bring.

Hitler had to act quickly. He received the news of Schuschnigg's intention on 9 March. He called his generals and foreign advisers together, and measures were put in hand for the invasion of Austria. He sent a letter to warn Mussolini of what was coming and—Hitler showed some anxiety on this score—to beg for his understanding. He sent his instructions to Seyss-Inquart through Glaise-Horstenau, one of the Nazi ministers in the Austrian Government. Hitler's directive stated: 'I intend, if other measures are unsuccessful, to invade Austria with armed forces in order to establish constitutional conditions and to prevent further violence against the pro-German population.'[2] Early in the morning of 11 March the German armed forces were already moving in Bavaria, and at 5.30 a.m. on that morning Schuschnigg was awakened by his telephone to learn that the German frontier at Salzburg had been closed. Schuschnigg was determined to struggle for Austrian independence by all constitutional and peaceful

[1] *Austrian Requiem*, p. 22.   [2] *Nuremberg Documents*, C-102.

231

means, but he was convinced that there must not be war with Germany—a war *between* Germans of which the outcome could not be in doubt.[1] Before ten o'clock the Nazi ministers brought to Schuschnigg Hitler's orders for the cancellation of the plebiscite. Early in the afternoon Schuschnigg agreed. Then Göring started phoning from Berlin[2] and stepping up the Nazi demands. Schuschnigg must resign—this, too, was agreed. Next, he must be replaced by Seyss-Inquart. Even the Austrian Nazi leaders appeared to be moved by the brutal pressure from Berlin. Seyss was excited, with tears in his eyes; Glaise said: 'I don't know whether one can continue under these circumstances as a gentleman.'[3] President Miklas resisted the German pressure, and refused to have Seyss as Chancellor. The Austrian ministers were in desperation; some were for resistance to the end. But Schuschnigg would not have civil war; he insisted on his own resignation. . . . 'Austria was a German state, and would be a German state when the confusing nightmare of National Socialism was long past, a historical memory of blood and tears. . . . My task was finished. I had done my duty to the best of my knowledge, and I refused to be instrumental—directly or indirectly— in the preparations for Cain once more to slay his brother Abel.'[4]

Attempts to find a Chancellor in place of Schuschnigg failed. More threats came over the phone from Göring. In the evening Schuschnigg broadcast a farewell from the Chancellery—the microphone standing a few paces from where Dollfuss had been shot down—while crowds were gathering outside and Nazis infiltrating into the building itself. He announced: 'We have yielded to force.'[5] Göring telephoned to order Seyss-Inquart to ask Germany to send troops 'to prevent bloodshed'. This was the German excuse—that they

[1] *Austrian Requiem*, p. 47.
[2] A record of these phone calls was captured at the end of the war: *Nuremburg Documents*, 2,949-PS.
[3] *Austrian Requiem*, p. 48.
[4] Ibid., p. 50.
[5] His short speech, broadcast at 7.30 p.m. on 11 March, is printed as an appendix in the English edition of his book, *Farewell, Austria*. (The German original was published in Austria just before he was swept from power.)

were called upon to intervene to maintain order.[1] At last, just before midnight, President Miklas gave up the struggle. He appointed Seyss-Inquart as Chancellor. Even that did not stop the German invasion. At dawn next day, on Saturday, 12 March, German troops crossed the Austrian frontier. That very afternoon Hitler was himself in Austria. To the crowds in Linz, where he had gone to school, Hitler spoke in sentimental terms: 'When years ago I went forth from this town I bore within me precisely the same profession of faith which today fills my heart . . . to restore my dear homeland to the German Reich. I have believed in this mission, I have lived and fought for it, and I believe I have now fulfilled it.'[2] Hitler spoke in similar terms a month later in Vienna: 'I believe that it was God's will to send a boy from here into the Reich, to let him grow up and to raise him to be leader of the nation so that he could lead back his homeland into the the Reich.'[3] Austria became almost immediately a province of the German Reich. There had been, indeed, a considerable popular welcome for the Germans. But the dark work of Nazi oppression went on just the same; Himmler introduced at once the terror of the S.S. and Gestapo. More than 70,000 people in Vienna alone were arrested. In May, Schuschnigg himself was arrested by the Gestapo; the next seven years he spent in prison after prison, concentration camp after concentration camp.

Next came the turn of Czechoslovakia. Hitler, with Austria now part of Germany, enclosed the Czechs as if in the iron jaws of a vice. Strategically, it was clear that Hitler would seize Czechoslovakia. What was more, a similar political technique was followed: the Czech Ambassador was reassured.

---

[1] This excuse was willingly accepted by the German people. One letter to the author put it: 'Ströme von Blut wären geflossen, der Bürgerkrieg, der schrecklichste aller Kriego, wäre ausgebrochen, wenn Hitler nicht so schnell gehandelt hätte.' The German doctor, mentioned in a footnote below, made use of the same excuse.

[2] Baynes, Vol. II, pp. 1,422-3.

[3] Ibid., p. 1,457. Hitler's enthusiasm was reflected among the German people. It was expressed in a letter to the author by a young German doctor: 'How warmly I welcomed this event, for since my early youth I was a strong adherent of the *Grossdeutsche Idee.*'

Göring repeated the assurance to the British Ambassador and, through him, Hitler himself sent the message to the British Government that it was 'the honest desire of his Government to improve German-Czech relations'.[1] But the Czechs were in every way marked out for destruction by Nazi Germany. They were regarded as racial inferiors by Hitler; their country, as a modern state, was the creation of the hated peace treaties; and their constitution was democratic. Czechoslovakia was perhaps the most successful of the new democracies, and she was a strong supporter of the League of Nations. And Czechoslovakia had the means of defence; she had treaties with France and Russia, and she had her own efficient Army, with the Skoda armaments factories and strongly built fortress defences along her frontier with Germany. What was more, Berlin itself was within easy reach of Czech airfields. Czechoslovakia must, therefore, be destroyed.

Once more Hitler found a plausible excuse for action, which would have at the same time a show of reason for the outside world and also be the means of breaking up the Czech state from the inside. Czechoslovakia contained a German minority —something over 3,000,000. These Germans, or Sudetens (from the name of the area, along the frontier, where they lived), had been subjects of the old Austrian Empire, but they had never been subjects of the German Reich. Nevertheless, after the fall of Austria, the propaganda started for 'return home to the Reich', and the Sudeten Nazi Party, assisted and subsidized already by Germany, became of real importance. The Czech Government tried hard to make a satisfactory agreement with the Sudeten leader, Konrad Henlein. But immediately after Hitler's Austrian triumph, at a talk in Berlin with the *Führer*, Henlein was told to demand so much from the Czech Government that the Government could never satisfy him.[2] Thus, though at first to the outside world the Czech affair appeared to be merely an internal matter between the Government and the German minority, Hitler was

[1] Sir Nevile Henderson, *Failure of a Mission*, p. 128.
[2] Henlein's report on his audience with Hitler, *Documents on German Foreign Policy*, D, Vol. II, pp. 197-9.

plotting to make a settlement impossible and to proceed thereby to the disruption of the Czech state.

On 20 May the Czechs were suddenly alarmed; they feared an immediate attack. To meet a surprise, the Government mobilized part of its forces. Hitler, however, was not ready. And Britain, France and Russia made a show of support for Czechoslovakia, to Hitler's surprise, for Britain and France had previously urged the Czechs to reach agreement with the Sudetens. This time, therefore, Hitler had to hold back. But the check to his plans strengthened his determination to destroy the Czech state, and added fuel to the fire of his hatred for the Czech President, Dr. Edvard Beneš. On 30 May Hitler signed a directive[1] to the Supreme Command: 'It is my unalterable decision to smash Czechoslovakia by military action in the near future.' For the purpose he needed 'a convenient apparent excuse, and with it, adequate political justification', and also surprise. October 1 was fixed as the latest date for the operation. Once more Hitler planned to act with suddenness and speed, and to confront the world with a *fait accompli*.

Throughout the summer Hitler continued his psychological weakening of his selected victim. Britain and France were continually pressed by the Germans to realize the alleged obstinacy of the Czechs, and the dangers arising from this obstinate resistance to what were made to appear just claims. The British Government showed, according to the German Ambassador in London, 'the greatest understanding for Germany that is possible in any group of British political leaders of Cabinet calibre. . . . It is showing growing understanding for the demands of Germany in the Sudeten question.' Though the British did make 'the *one* condition that these objectives are sought by peaceful means'.[2] As a result of this understanding for Germany, the British Government sent Lord Runciman to investigate—in itself, under the circumstances, an admission that there might be right on the Nazis' side.

[1] *Documents on German Foreign Policy*, D, Vol. II, pp. 358-62.
[2] Ibid., Vol. I, pp. 1,158-9: report of von Dirksen to German Foreign Minister, 18 July 1938.

The Times on 7 September in a leading article went as far as to suggest the possible 'secession of that fringe of alien populations' which lay contiguous to Germany—though next day the newspaper published a letter from Mr. Vyvyan Adams, M.P., pointing out that this could not be done without giving up the Czech frontier fortresses which were situated in the Sudetenland.[1] The Czechs, naturally, felt a certain isolation, and a doubt of their friends. At the same time, the Nazis encouraged the Poles and Hungarians to bring out the claims, which they too had on Czech territories where there were minorities. Meanwhile German military preparations were going on, with the usual Germanic thoroughness.

Among the generals, however, there was hesitation; they feared that a war against Czechoslovakia would involve Germany in war with Britain and France also, and that Germany was not yet ready for a general conflict. This opposition to Hitler centred on General Beck, the Army Chief of Staff, who was to play a notable and courageous part later. Hitler relied on his intuition, which so far had carried him through; the generals distrusted Hitler's intuition, and relied on their own professional estimates of the situation. Hitler cursed the generals for their caution, and certain of them discussed in secret the possibility of seizing Hitler as soon as he gave orders to invade Czechoslovakia.[2]

Beck had the courage to resign his post as Chief of General Staff. It was a brave gesture, but was kept secret until after Munich, and its effect was thus destroyed. The real trouble about the generals' opposition to Hitler was that they were but individuals with little support behind them. As Halder, Beck's successor, saw it clearly enough, the masses supported Hitler and the soldiers in the army supported him; they owed everything to him. If the generals attempted a coup against Hitler, there was no certainty that they would carry their junior officers and men with them. Halder referred to his five sons-in-law, all captains in the army and all

[1] *The Times*, 8 September.
[2] J. W. Wheeler-Bennett, *The Nemesis of Power*, p. 407. In Part III, Chapter 3, he gives a full account of the generals and their attitude to Hitler.

pro-Hitler. What could the few who saw the danger do? After Munich, of course, it was hopeless. Gisevius declares that Chamberlain saved Hitler. That may be saying too much, for the masses might well have followed Hitler against Czechoslovakia, had it come to war, as they did later against Poland. But certainly, as General von Witzleben explained to Gisevius after Munich, the troops would never revolt against the victorious *Führer*.[1] Some setback would be necessary first. This is indeed the most terrible condemnation of Nazi Germany: people supported Hitler so long as he succeeded and *whatever* the methods he used; only after five years of war, when defeat stared Germany in the face, did the generals have a chance to overthrow him by a coup, and even then the coup failed. So long as Hitler lived, Germans would fight on.

Hitler's luck held. In his speech at the close of the Nuremberg Rally on 12 September, Hitler stirred up excitement to a high pitch. Hitler's words caused a revolt among the Sudetens, and the Czechs were forced to declare martial law. The German newspapers announced a Czech reign of terror, and a campaign of vilification against the Czechs broke out in the Press. Hitler had his excuse for intervention. Later Henlein and a large body of his followers left the country and crossed to Germany.

Hitler's intuition so far had served him well, but at this point the course of events took a dramatic twist which even Hitler had not foreseen. The French Government was indeed in near panic at the prospect of war,[2] but the British Prime Minister, taking things at their face value and hoping that a businesslike, even if painful, settlement would be better than war, proposed to come by plane for a personal meeting with Hitler to seek a peaceful way out of the Sudeten problem. Arrangements were made for the journey to Berchtesgaden. In the afternoon of 15 September Chamberlain arrived at the Berghof and, after tea in the large room in which Hitler

[1] H. B. Gisevius, *To the Bitter End*, pp. 292–326.
[2] *Documents on British Foreign Policy*, 1919–39, Third Series, Vol. II (1938), reports of British Ambassador, Sir Eric Phipps, on his meetings with French Premier, Daladier, and Foreign Minister, Bonnet, pp. 310–14.

had received Lloyd George, conferred with Hitler in his study
—where the stormy meeting with Schuschnigg had taken
place only seven months earlier. Hitler talked;[1] he went over
the old ground of what he had done for Germany and for
peace. He explained his racial theories: that the Germans in
the Sudetenland must logically be united with Germany, but
that he had no wish to incorporate the Czechs in the Reich.
Chamberlain questioned him about the practical issues, the
details involved in a possible transfer of the Sudetenland to
Germany. Hitler grew excited. 'All this seems to be academic',
he cried. 'I want to get down to realities. Three hundred
Sudetens have been killed, and things of that kind cannot go
on; the thing has got to be settled at once. . . . I am determined to settle it in one way or another. [Those words, the
interpreter noted to himself, were an extreme danger signal.]
I am prepared to risk a world war rather than allow this to
drag on.' At this Chamberlain became indignant: 'If the
Führer is determined to settle this matter by force without
waiting even for a discussion . . . what did he let me come
here for? I have wasted my time.' Now Hitler hesitated—
perhaps, after all, if the British Government would accept in
principle a transfer of the Sudetenland, by virtue of the right
of self-determination, there could be further discussion.
Chamberlain, at least, thought he had gained a real con-
cession, and flew back next day to London to consult his
Cabinet before having a second meeting with Hitler.

On 22 September Chamberlain flew again to Germany;
this time he met Hitler at Godesberg, and the conferences
took place in the Hotel Dreesen, with its windows looking
out on the magnificent Rhine panorama.[2] Chamberlain had
a plan for settlement ready. He had, he explained, 'after

---

[1] *Documents on British Foreign Policy*, pp. 338-41, Mr. Chamberlain's notes.
Translation of Herr Paul Schmidt's notes, pp. 342-51. Also his memorandum,
Documents on German Foreign Policy, D, Vol. II, pp. 786-98, and his book, *Statist
auf diplomatischer Bühne*, pp. 394-9. Schmidt was official interpreter, as he had
been to Brüning, Stresemann, and other pre-Hitler ministers. See also his
accounts of Godesberg and Munich.

[2] Minutes by Schmidt, *Documents on German Foreign Policy*, pp. 870-79 and
898-908; notes by Kirkpatrick, *Documents on British Foreign Policy*, pp. 463-73
and pp. 499-508.

laborious negotiations', persuaded the Czechoslovak, French, and British governments to agree to the Berchtesgaden proposal for cession of the Sudetenland. But now Chamberlain ran into difficulty. Hitler had not expected the Czechs to agree, and his military preparations to smash Czechoslovakia were well advanced. When, therefore, Chamberlain told Hitler that the Czechs had accepted, Hitler replied that the original proposal was no longer acceptable. After an embittered discussion, Hitler made it clear that he now demanded an immediate occupation of the Sudetenland by German troops. Chamberlain withdrew across the river to the Hotel Petersburg, where the British delegation resided. Here in his room, No. 109, with its spacious balcony looking down on Hitler's hotel on the opposite bank of the Rhine, Chamberlain could reflect. It was indeed, considered scenically, one of the most dramatic *vis-à-vis* in history. Chamberlain was on the hilltop, Hitler in the valley below, with the splendid river flowing between, and the view of the successive woods and hills of the Eifel stretching into the remote distance. Next day there were more discussions, but Hitler would not budge from his main demand, though he modified the date of occupation from 28 September to 1 October. Hitler must, however, have been divided between his desire to smash Czechoslovakia with his new armies and the more cautious wish to secure, through Chamberlain, very real advantages on the cheap. All Chamberlain could do, at this point, was to return to London with Hitler's Godesberg memorandum (with the details, maps, etc., for the occupation of the Sudetenland by German forces), and lay them before the Cabinet.

With steady perseverance, Chamberlain maintained his contacts with Hitler, sending personal messages by Sir Horace Wilson, who more than once encountered Hitler in his most furious, uncompromising, and irrational moods.[1] To anyone who heard Hitler's speech on 26 September in the Berlin Sportpalast it must have seemed that war was inevitable. The note of personal venom against Beneš, the blasting denunciation of the Czech state, the excitement of the speaker

---

[1] Schmidt, *Statist auf diplomatischer Bühne*, pp. 407-8.

to the point of insane fury were not to be forgotten. 'Now before us stands the last problem', he avowed. 'It is the last territorial claim which I have to make in Europe, but it is the claim from which I will not recede and which, God willing, I will make good.' 'This Czech state', he cried, 'began with a single lie, and the father of this lie was named Beneš. . . . There is no such thing as a Czechoslovak nation.' With gross exaggeration, he attacked the Czechs for the disturbances in the Sudetenland. With skilful twisting of words and meaning, he attacked Beneš for hesitating to accept immediate military occupation of the Sudetenland when he had already accepted its cession in principle: 'Two men stand arrayed one against the other: there is Herr Beneš, and here am I. We are two men of a different make-up. In the great struggle of the peoples, while Herr Beneš was sneaking about through the world, I, a decent German soldier, did my duty. And now today I stand over against this man as a soldier of my people. . . . With regard to the problem of the Sudeten Germans, my patience is now at an end. I have made Herr Beneš an offer which is nothing but the execution of what he himself has promised. The decision now lies in his hands: peace or war. He will either accept this offer and now at last give the Germans their freedom, or we will go and fetch this freedom for ourselves . . . and behind me—this the world should know—there marches a different people from that of 1918.

'We are determined.

'Now let Herr Beneš make his choice.'[1]

How different in tone were Chamberlain's measured words when, on the following night, he made a broadcast speech to the nation. 'I am a man of peace to the depths of my soul', said the Prime Minister, and set out the pros and the cons of the dispute with studied moderation. How simple it all looked back there in London—if only this last great dispute could be peacefully settled. Chamberlain referred to Hitler's promise in his Sportpalast speech: 'He told me privately, and last night he repeated it publicly, that after this Sudeten

[1] Baynes, Vol. II, pp. 1,508-27.

German question is settled, that is the end of Germany's territorial claims in Europe.' Throughout his speech Chamberlain's sincere love of peace was apparent: 'How horrible, fantastic, incredible it is that we should be digging trenches and trying on gas-masks here because of a quarrel in a faraway country between people of whom we know nothing.'[1] But, though those words sounded like common sense to a majority of people at the time, they struck a cold chill to the hearts of those who saw further—who realized that once more, as in the case of Abyssinia, it was not simply the right of 'a far-away country' which was at stake but the security of the whole Western way of life.

But in spite of the violence of his Sportpalast speech, Hitler hesitated a little to launch out into what might prove a general war, in face of the advice of his own generals, in spite of the anxieties of Mussolini, and in face of the news that both Britain and France were making military preparations. He had, too, it was reported, observed the apathetic behaviour of the Berlin populace when a motorized division moved through the Wilhelmstrasse. Chamberlain made another appeal to Hitler: he asked for a conference to find some way of satisfying the *Führer's* demands. Mussolini's support for the proposed conference influenced Hitler, and as a result the famous Munich Conference—of Hitler, Mussolini, Chamberlain and Daladier—opened on 29 September at 12.30 p.m.[2] The conference went on until the early hours of the next morning, by which time agreement had been reached. Hitler's forces were to march into the Sudetenland on the following day, 1 October, and Britain and France were to press upon the Czech Government the necessity for immediate acceptance of the Munich terms. They were, indeed, imposed on them, for neither they nor the Russians had been invited to the Munich Conference. Though Chamberlain and Daladier asked for Czech representation, Hitler would not have it. When the Czech Premier, General Syrový, broadcast to the people the news that his Government was accepting the

---

[1] *Documents on International Affairs*, 1938, Vol. II, pp. 270-1.
[2] Notes by Sir Horace Wilson, *Documents on British Foreign Policy*, pp. 630-5.

Munich terms he said: 'I am passing through the gravest hour of my life, for I am doing the hardest thing which it has ever fallen to my lot to do, and which it would be easier to die than to do. . . . But we were deserted, and we stood alone.'[1] The German occupation duly followed, and the Germans were able conveniently to discount the stipulations and conditions which had been made by Britain and France. Czechoslovakia was broken—her frontier defences were gone, President Beneš resigned, and further territorial losses to Poland and Hungary were soon imposed. Hitler had won his greatest triumph. And Chamberlain returned to England with Hitler's promise of peace. To the crowds which cheered him at Heston Airport Chamberlain read the words of a joint declaration by himself and Hitler: 'We regard the agreement signed last night and the Anglo-German Naval Agreement as symbolic of the desire of our two peoples never to go to war with one another again.'[2]

At home Chamberlain received a great welcome. There was a sudden feeling of relief and relaxation of tension. Only the few perceived the reality behind the apparent success of Chamberlain's policy. Duff Cooper resigned from the Cabinet. Churchill declared on 5 October, in a House of Commons speech, interrupted by ministerial cries of 'Nonsense', that all the Prime Minister had gained for Czechoslovakia was that 'the German dictator, instead of snatching the victuals from the table, has been content to have them served to him course by course. . . . We are in the presence of a disaster of the first magnitude which has befallen Great Britain and France.'[3] 'We had given away', said Mr. Harold Nicolson in the same debate, 'not merely the question of Czechoslovakia, but the whole key to Europe.'

In Germany also there was a popular feeling of relief that war had been avoided; in the Munich streets people had cheered Chamberlain and pressed round to shake his hand. But relief was combined with an intoxicating sense of triumph

---

[1] *Prager Presse*, 1 October, translated in *Documents on International Affairs*, pp. 326-8.
[2] *Documents on International Affairs*, 1938, Vol. II, p. 291.
[3] *The Times*, 6 October.

in Germany's success. The German Reich was now clearly the dominant nation in Europe, and in a position to dictate policy, not only to lesser breeds, but also to the Great Powers.[1] All this was due to Hitler. His personal triumph was immense and clear for all to see, while in the inner circles it was apparent that once more the *Führer's* intuition had been right. The weakness of the opposing nations had been dramatically demonstrated, and the generals' caution and the tentative plans to arrest Hitler were forgotten. Munich, of course, was no genuine agreement. Hitler himself was half disappointed to have been robbed by it of the opportunity of staging a spectacular campaign against the Czechs and a triumphant entry into Prague.[2] Immediately after Munich he was still considering the possibility of attack on the remainder of the Czech state; and Ribbentrop assured Mussolini and Ciano that by September Germany 'could face a war with the great democracies'.[3] Hitler became more, not less, truculent: in a speech early in November he denounced Churchill, Duff Cooper, and Eden as warmongers,[4] and on the night of 5 November an organized pogrom took place which aroused indignation abroad.[5] And even in Britain, when Chamberlain's moment of optimism had passed, Munich led to an increase, not a decrease, in rearmament. Nor were the Russians, though excluded from Munich, unaware of its dangers. Molotov, in a speech in November, made an astute analysis of the situation. 'Despite the allegedly peaceful character of the Munich arrangement', he said, 'all who took part in it are now busily increasing their armaments, expanding their armies, increasing their military budgets. The bargain between the Fascist governments and the governments of the so-called democratic countries, far from lessening the danger

[1] Although one German wrote to the author: 'Old Mr. Chamberlain with his umbrella is a very popular personality in Germany', another, a young doctor, wrote: 'I can't find any pity. It is true our methods were force, but that is the only language you understand.'

[2] Henderson, *Failure of a Mission*, p. 191.

[3] Conversation in Rome, 28 October 1938: *Ciano's Diplomatic Papers*, pp. 242-6; *Nuremberg Documents*, 388-P5, No. 48.

[4] Baynes, Vol. II, p. 1,557.

[5] See pp. 181-2.

of the outbreak of the second imperialist war, has on the contrary added fuel to the flames.' Britain and France, he declared, 'sacrificed not only Czechoslovakia, but their own interests as well. . . . Have they gained greater respect for their rights in the eyes of German and Italian Fascism? There is no sign of it.'[1]

The winter of 1938-9 was an anxious one. It became known to the British Foreign Secretary, Lord Halifax, that Hitler was planning further adventures for early in 1939 and Halifax suspected that there might even be an attack in the west.[2] Hitler was, in fact, making plans to occupy the remainder of Czechoslovakia and to acquire Danzig—which latter operation must bring him into conflict with Poland. His method with the Czechs was to continue to break up their country from the inside, by using the German minority still remaining and also the differences between the Czechs and Slovaks. After Munich the Czech Government had to grant autonomy to its eastern provinces of Slovakia and Ruthenia, and Hitler now did his utmost to intensify Slovak demands for complete independence. Early in March, to counteract the disruptive plans being formed, President Hacha, the new head of the Czech state, dismissed both the Ruthenian and Slovak governments. Hitler's opportunity had come; he put great pressure on the Slovaks, called the dismissed Premier, Tiso, to Berlin, and sent him back to Bratislava to read to the Slovak Parliament on 14 March a declaration of independence. The Slovaks, with a threat of German occupation behind them, had perforce to accept. And this seeming assertion of Slovak independence by the Slovaks themselves gave Chamberlain next day the excuse for avoiding any British obligation to defend Czechoslovak frontiers.

At the same time Hitler dealt with the Czechs. The German Press had suddenly resurrected sensational news of a Czech reign of terror against the Slovaks and the remaining Germans. Black and red headlines appeared: 'Chaos, Unrest,

---

[1] *Pravda*, 9 November 1938. Translated in *Soviet Documents on Foreign Policy* (R.I.I.A.), Vol. III, pp. 308-11.
[2] Lord Halifax to British Ambassador, Washington: *Documents on British Foreign Policy*, Third Series, Vol. IV, 1939, pp. 4-6.

Terror in all Czechoslovakia—Bloody Persecution of Germans.'[1] The Czech Government appealed to Hitler, and Hacha, accompanied by his Foreign Minister, travelled to Berlin. The elderly Czech President was received by Hitler at 1.15 a.m. in the morning on 15 March.[2] He explained that he was not one of the active Czech politicians, and had seldom met Beneš or Masaryk; he pleaded with Hitler to allow his people to retain what was left of their national existence. But Hitler replied that the die was cast: that very morning at 6 a.m. the German Army would invade Czechoslovakia at all points and the German air force would occupy all Czech airports. But perhaps bloodshed could be avoided . . . perhaps Hacha's visit might yet avert the worst. Then the Czechs were taken into another room for discussion with Göring and Ribbentrop; they were threatened with the destruction by bombing of Prague. Hacha collapsed in a faint, but was revived by Hitler's doctor and put into touch with Prague on the telephone; the Czech Government had to agree to offer no resistance to German invasion. There and then— at 4 a.m.—Hacha was again taken to Hitler's room, and signed a communiqué stating that he 'confidently placed the fate of the Czech people in the hands of the *Führer*'.

At 6 a.m. the German forces duly crossed the Czech frontier. That night Hitler slept in Prague and the swastika flag flew over the walls of the castle of the old Bohemian kings. Next day, on 16 March, Hitler issued a proclamation: 'For a millennium the territories of Bohemia and Moravia belonged to the *Lebensraum* of the German people . . . the Czechoslovak state has proved its inability to live its own internal life, and in consequence has now fallen into dissolution.'[3] The Czech provinces were at once formed into the Protectorate of Bohemia and Moravia, in charge of the Sudeten leaders, Henlein and Frank. Slovakia passed under German 'protection'. Ruthenia, in spite of an appeal to Hitler and a declaration of Ruthenian independence, was abandoned to Hungary,

---

[1] *Völkischer Beobachter*, 14 March; see also issues of 12 and 13 March.
[2] German account, signed Hewel: *Nuremberg Documents*, 2,798-PS.
[3] Baynes, Vol. II, p. 1,586.

which was pressing its claims. The state of Czechoslovakia had ceased to exist, and German garrisons were in position to overawe its people. By his methods of intolerable pressure and sudden coups, Hitler had won sensational and vital triumphs. With the acquisition of Austria and the Czech provinces, Hitler had increased and consolidated his military strength and secured his strategic position. In central Europe his position was dominant. By destroying Czechoslovakia he had removed what he had himself called 'the spear in my side'; in the event of war there would now be no threat from the flank. He was now ready for the greatest adventure of all.

CHAPTER XIII

POLAND—AND WAR

HITLER'S policy, with its constant objective, can be traced in a steady sequence of events until 1939, when the attack on Poland launched the general war. War is the continuation of policy by other means, as Clausewitz had said. In the Nazi policy which moved inevitably towards war the occupation of Prague turned out to be, in two senses, a turning-point. It marked for Hitler the end of the period when he could win great triumphs at small cost; from now on he would meet real opposition. For the outside world, Prague was a turning-point in that it was now evident that Hitler had broken the principle of self-determination to which he had appealed when it suited him, and his criticism of the Treaty of Versailles was revealed as hollow. Appeasement had failed, and Britain began slowly and uncertainly to prepare for active resistance. Hitler, after Munich, had called the British and French leaders 'little worms'; he had forgotten that even a worm will turn. Prague was the turning-point.

Chamberlain had now to face the facts of an ugly, a brutal situation. In a speech at Birmingham on 17 March he excused himself for the 'somewhat cool and objective statement' he had made in the House of Commons two days before, when he had first heard the news. He answered critics of his Munich policy by saying that he had gone to Germany 'in an almost desperate situation', and because a personal meeting with Hitler 'seemed to offer the only chance of averting a European war'. But now Chamberlain's eyes were opened to Hitler's duplicity. In view of the seizure of the whole of the Czech provinces, what had become of Hitler's pledges? 'What', Chamberlain asked, 'has become of the declaration of "No further territorial ambition"? What has become of the assurance, "We don't want Czechs in the Reich"? What regard has been paid here to that principle of self-determination on which Hitler argued so vehemently with me at Berchtesgaden when he was asking for the severance of Sudetenland from Czechoslovakia and its inclusion in the German Reich?' Everyone, Chamberlain went on to state, must now be asking a fundamental question: 'Is this, in fact, a step in the direction of an attempt to dominate the world by force?' If such a challenge came, it would be resisted: 'no greater mistake could be made than to suppose that, because it believes war to be a senseless and cruel thing, this nation has so lost its fibre that it will not take part to the utmost of its power in resisting such a challenge if it were ever made'.[1]

It was soon clear that Hitler would next apply his technique of pressure to Poland. Yet, though Prague marked a turning-point, it was so more in the policy of Britain and France than in that of Hitler. Hitler himself continued for some time to move cautiously, feeling his way ahead, planning for war, but still himself uncertain whether it was to be a local or a general war, still ready to achieve great gains at small cost, if possible, by splitting the forces against him and striking down the weaker while maintaining temporary peace with the stronger. Though war might come, before that, if possible, there were still subsidiary actions to be taken, by fraud or force. All was not yet ready for the main action— the attack on Russia. Even in his attitude to Poland, and the policy to be followed, Hitler was uncertain. Events and negotiations had to take their course before Hitler's resolve finally hardened into a decision to destroy Poland by war.

So far, indeed, throughout the period of the Nazi régime Germany had followed a policy of friendship towards Poland. 'Poland', Hitler told the Polish Ambassador at the end of 1933, 'is an outpost against Asia.'[2] The Non-Aggression Pact of 1934 had not been altogether hollow: Poland, whose governing classes were strongly anti-Bolshevik, might be used as an ally against Russia. Göring made a number of visits

[1] *Documents on International Affairs, 1939-46*, Vol. I, pp. 66-71.
[2] *Official Documents concerning Polish-German and Polish-Soviet Relations. 1933-9*, p. 17.

to Warsaw, he attended Marshal Pilsudski's funeral at Cracow, and hinted at common measures against Russia of a far-reaching nature.[1] After Munich the way was open for Hitler to settle with Poland, but the first approaches were still friendly. On 24 October Ribbentrop raised with the Polish Ambassador the questions of the return of the Free City of Danzig to Germany and the creation of an extra-territorial road and railway link across the Polish Corridor to East Prussia, but he made in return a number of friendly proposals, including 'a joint policy towards Russia on the basis of the Anti-Comintern Pact'.[2] Although the conversation took place over lunch, the mention of Danzig (in which Poland had special rights and privileges) was a danger signal to the Poles—it had long been a delicate matter. Further meetings followed, both in Germany and Poland, but the discussions got no further. The Polish Foreign Minister, Colonel Beck, though willing to compromise on matters of less importance, was clear enough that he could not budge on Danzig or a German link through the Polish Corridor. In January 1939 he had an interview with Hitler at Berchtesgaden, and, in spite of the outstanding differences, the *Führer* assured him that there would be no *faits accomplis* in Danzig and nothing would be done to render difficult the situation of the Polish Government.[3] Negotiations continued, and were still friendly.

After the seizure of Prague, however, the fate of Czecho-slovakia stared Poland in the face. What was more, directly after Prague, Germany demanded the return from Lithuania of Memel—a city and strip of territory lost by Germany under the Treaty of Versailles. Lithuania could make no resistance, and the Germans occupied Memel-land at once. In spite of this, the Poles were remarkably bold in standing up to the Germans, and the Ambassador told Ribbentrop that 'the Czech issue

---

[1] *Official Documents concerning Polish-German and Polish-Soviet Relations. 1933-9*, pp. 25-7: minutes and notes on Göring's conversations in Warsaw and with the Polish Ambassador in Berlin.

[2] Ibid., pp. 47-8: letter to the Polish Foreign Minister from the Ambassador, reporting on the lunch conversation at the Grand Hotel, Berchtesgaden.

[3] Ibid., pp. 53-4: minute of Beck's conversation.

was already hard enough for the Polish public to swallow. . . .
But in regard to Slovakia the position was far worse.' The
Ambassador pointed out that Poland had a long frontier with
Slovakia, and that German protection of Slovakia was directed
against Poland.[1] Five days later the Ambassador again complained to Ribbentrop about Slovakia, and referred to the
way the Germans had taken Poland by surprise over Memel
and, though more circumspectly, to the seizure of Prague.[2]
Poland was now caught in the jaws of a German vice almost
exactly, as a glance at a map shows, as Czechoslovakia had
been after the German seizure of Austria. Ribbentrop was
increasing his pressure on Poland by suggesting the unfortunate
possibility that the *Führer* might come to think a friendly understanding with Poland impossible. There were threats and
bluster. Nevertheless, at this time Hitler still did not wish to use
force over Danzig. 'He did not wish', so ran a report of Hitler's
conversation with the Army Commander-in-chief, 'to drive
Poland into the arms of Great Britain by doing so.' Plans must
be prepared, but Hitler would not seek an immediate decision
without very specially favourable political conditions. Hitler
even envisaged the possibility of the Polish Government itself
allowing a German military occupation of Danzig in order,
if they could not get the consent of the Polish people, to confront it with a *fait accompli*. At the same time General Brauchitsch thought that Hitler might shortly abandon his grant
of independence to Slovakia, and use Slovakia as a bargaining counter with Poland and Hungary. The double-dealing
of the Nazis knew no bounds. But in case of war, 'Poland will
be so knocked out that in the next decade it need not be
taken into account as a political factor'.[3]

At this point, however, Chamberlain once more intervened
—but not in the Munich way. In view of the reports of impending German action against Poland, the British Prime Minister
announced in the House of Commons on 31 March that Britain

[1] *Official Documents concerning Polish-German and Polish-Soviet Relations. 1933-9,*
pp. 61-3: Polish Ambassador to Beck, 21 March.
[2] Ibid., pp. 66-9: Polish Ambassador to Beck, 26 March.
[3] Memorandum of Hitler's conversation with General von Brauchitsch, 25
March: *Nuremberg Documents*, R-100.

would give full support to Poland in defending its independence. This was not all, however, for meanwhile, the Italian Dictator was thinking it was time that he too, like Hitler, should score some notable success. On Good Friday, 7 April, Italian troops invaded Albania. Mussolini's occupation of Albania and intermittent German pressure in south-eastern Europe suggested that further moves might be coming in that direction, and on 13 April Chamberlain therefore followed up his unconditional promise to Poland with similar guarantees to Greece and Rumania. A little later England and France made agreements with Turkey for mutual assistance in the Mediterranean. The British guarantees to Poland, Greece, and Rumania marked a momentous departure in British policy; France joined in the guarantees: appeasement was at an end. Hitler was thrown into a fury—and a condition of indecision. He had met with a definite 'No', and he now must search for some new way out of the impasse.

'I'll cook them a stew that they'll choke on', Hitler shouted after he had heard of Britain's guarantee to Poland.[1] What he really wanted from Great Britain, however, was an understanding to allow him a free hand in Europe: let Britain interest herself in the sea and her overseas empire and leave central and eastern Europe to Germany. At home it had suited Hitler very well to drop hints from time to time that he would, in fact, be allowed a free hand. Some of the generals believed that Hitler had a secret agreement with England and France to allow Germany to act against Bolshevism. Thus before Munich, von Witzleben, though he feared that Hitler might bring disaster, was troubled on this point: 'Would it actually come to a war? Or were the diplomatic disturbances . . . just the usual stage thunder? Were not the Western Powers actually aiming at something else entirely? Was some crucial shift taking place behind the scenes about which the initiates had been whispering for so long? Would Hitler be given a clear channel to the east?'[2]

---

[1] Gisevius, *To the Bitter End*, p. 363, reports Canaris' account of Hitler's reaction to the news.

[2] Ibid., p. 305.

Hitler discussed the international situation on 19 April with the Rumanian Foreign Minister, Grigore Gafencu, when he visited Berlin, and the Rumanian has described how, when the conversation touched on Britain, 'the monologue developed into a public speech. Hitler had embarked on the subject which obsessed him: England's resistance. . . . His manner and his countenance were changed, his voice became heavy and threatening, while a strange light shone in his eyes.' 'By what right', Hitler asked in reference to the break-up of Czechoslovakia consequent upon the Munich Agreement, 'did England claim to intervene in order to prevent the normal, natural evolution of the situation in Central Europe?' Hitler realized that all his ill-gotten aims would be in vain, as Gafencu put it, 'unless he succeeded in the final showdown with Britain either by gaining its collusion or by destroying its resistance'. If England wanted war, Hitler shouted, she would have it . . . 'Our air force leads the world, and no enemy town will be left standing'.

Suddenly Hitler became calmer, and asked: 'But, after all, why this unimaginable massacre? In the end, victor or vanquished, we shall all be buried in the same ruins; and the only one who will profit is that man in Moscow.' And he added: 'To think that it is I—I who am accused in Germany of being an impenitent admirer of the British Empire, I who have so often tried to establish a lasting understanding between the Reich and England (an understanding which today I still consider necessary to the defence of European civilization)—to think that it is I who must envisage such a conflict! And this entirely on account of the incomprehension and blind obduracy of the leaders of Great Britain!'[1]

The theme had been repeated again and again since *Mein Kampf*. At Godesberg Hitler had said to Chamberlain: 'Between us there need be no differences. We will not stand in the way of your extra-European interests, and you can, without harm to yourselves, leave us a free hand on the European continent in middle and south-eastern Europe.'[2] Göring, too, had presented

---

[1] Gafencu, *The Last Days of Europe*, pp. 64-6.
[2] Schmidt, *Statist auf diplomatischer Bühne*, p. 407.

the same argument two years earlier in friendly discussion with the British Ambassador (Sir Nevile Henderson). Göring's idea, wrote the Englishman, 'of an understanding between Great Britain and Germany was an agreement limited to two clauses. In the first, Germany would recognize the supreme position of Great Britain overseas, and undertake to put all her resources at the disposal of the British Empire in case of need. By the second, Great Britain would recognize the predominant continental position of Germany in Europe, and undertake to do nothing to hinder her legitimate expansion.' This suggestion was in substance identical with the last proposal Hitler was to make to the British immediately before his attack on Poland. With an altogether different Germany, such an arrangement might have been possible. As Sir Nevile Henderson wrote himself: 'With a Germany prepared to admit the equality of rights of others, and to solve problems by negotiation instead of by force, a gentleman's agreement on such lines would have had much to recommend it.'[1] But Prague had shown Chamberlain himself that such an understanding was impossible. In a man so utterly unreliable, unscrupulous, and ruthless as Hitler, no confidence could be placed. If Hitler had once settled with the European nations, what would hold him back from striking at Britain herself and seizing the Empire overseas?

Hitler's rage against everyone whose interest or conscience stood in his way showed itself in his speech to the Reichstag on 28 April.[2] He repeated his expression of friendship for Britain, but declared that the British had come to think of war with Germany as inevitable. He therefore denounced the Anglo-German Naval Treaty of 1935. In spite of his friendly offers to the Poles, they had shown no willingness to respond to Germany's rightful claims. He, therefore, denounced the German-Polish Pact of 1934 also. In addition, he violently

[1] Henderson, *Failure of a Mission*, pp. 91-2. F. Hesse, *Das Spiel um Deutschland*, repeatedly refers to Hitler's wish for an understanding with England and his admiration for the British Empire. See especially pp. 185, 261, and 264. On p. 261 Hesse says that Hitler *von einer merkwürdigen Hassliebe England gegenüber beseelt war*.

[2] Baynes, Vol. II, pp. 1,605-56.

attacked international warmongers in Europe and America. In particular he gave an answer in bitter and ironic terms to the American President, Roosevelt, who, alarmed by the Italian aggression in Albania, had sent a message in favour of peace to the two dictators. But in spite of his fiery words there was little Hitler could do for the moment. He was in a state of uncertainty,[1] and during the summer there was a lull. Meanwhile, German diplomatic pressure on Poland was maintained, the local Nazis in Danzig were arming and training, and the German Press made play with the argument, for foreign attention, that Danzig was not worth a war. At the same time Germany fostered her contacts with other states in central and eastern Europe—to strengthen her own position by keeping Poland isolated. Leading Hungarian, Yugoslav, and Bulgarian statesmen were entertained in Berlin, and Germany signed non-aggression pacts with Lithuania (now that Memel was part of the Reich), Latvia, and Estonia. And in May the Pact of Steel—a military alliance—was signed with Italy, notwithstanding Mussolini's anxieties about Italy's unpreparedness for a general war.

By 23 May, when he called his Service chiefs to a meeting in the Chancellery, Hitler had decided on war with Poland.[2] Danzig was only the occasion, he explained. The ultimate object was the expansion of *Lebensraum* in the east. To attack Poland was the first step: this meant war, for no repetition of Munich could be expected. War with Poland might involve, though he expected to avoid it, war with the Western Powers. Rightly he saw Great Britain as the motive force in any opposition from the West, for one of Hitler's guiding principles was the weakness of France. Though war with Great Britain would eventually come, he did not want it then. The immediate object was a localized war with Poland. Hitler, then, was bent on war, and during the summer months the Army was busy with detailed preparations—these were to be ready by 20 August.

[1] Hitler's uncertainty of mind is clearly analysed by Mr. Alan Bullock, *Hitler*, pp. 465-6 and 492-3.
[2] See the passage quoted on p. 208, above, from Schmundt's minutes of the conference.

How was this localized war to be achieved? How was British and French support for Poland to be neutralized? The only effective way in which Britain and France could assist Poland would be with Russian support; Russia was the only country which could give direct military aid to Poland in case of attack by Germany. If, therefore, Hitler could secure the neutrality of Russia in any conflict with Poland and the West, he would, it seemed certain, destroy the effectiveness of the British and French guarantees. Either the Western Powers would not fulfil their promises when the time came and would press the Poles to give in to German demands or, if they did intervene, it would be but a nominal intervention and would quickly be dropped, as in the case of sanctions against Italy, as soon as the victim had been devoured by the aggressor. By a strange irony of fate, Germany and Great Britain now entered into competition for the support of Soviet Russia—Britain at the eleventh hour had adopted a policy, with the object of preventing war altogether, which, if adopted earlier, might have achieved that object, while Germany sought the services, in holding the ring for her localized campaign against Poland, of the very nation the Nazis had always decried and against whom Hitler envisaged a future war on the greatest scale.

Soviet Russia, of course, had an inveterate suspicion of all capitalist states, of Germany and the Western democracies alike. Western weakness in the face of the past aggressions, and the tragedy of Munich in particular, had done nothing to give Russia confidence in the effectiveness of co-operation with Britain and France. Just as in the West there were politicians who looked not unhopefully to the possibility of a conflict between Germany and Russia in which each would destroy the other and the democratic West be left intact, and just as in the Far East a war, had it broken out, between Russia and Japan would have seen the whole world cheering to see both sides lose, so the object of Russia was to prevent such a contingency, and if possible play the same trick on the West. But to act alone against Hitler was fatal; only the broadest common front would serve. And both Russia and the West, when war came, were to pay a heavy price for the failure to achieve unity of action against the Nazi colossus which stood between them.

The Western talks with Russia dragged badly. After a British approach in April, it was not until 15 June that talks began in Moscow with British and French representatives. Yet many people expected success. On one occasion the *Daily Express* announced, in its main heading, 'Britain and Russia reach Agreement—Pact Certain'.[1] Meanwhile, in May, Litvinov, the Foreign Minister who had talked of peace being indivisible and had been the strongest Russian exponent of collective security, had been dismissed and replaced by Molotov. These signs were hopefully observed in Germany. In spite of the anti-Bolshevism which had been so consistent a feature in Hitler's speeches and the Nazi Press, there was in Germany a certain tradition favouring a joint policy with Russia—the little German Army of the Weimar days had formed technical and professional links with the Soviet forces. Now to Hitler, for the purpose of his war on Poland, an understanding with Russia offered superlative advantage. Contacts were made; trade talks were undertaken in June and in July; Ribbentrop, as a matter of urgency, pressed the German Ambassador in Moscow to see Molotov to sound him as to the possibility of a political understanding, promising the safeguarding of Russian interests in any Polish development and also in the Baltic.[2] Meanwhile, Ribbentrop himself made things clearer to the Russians in a talk with the Russian chargé d'affaires in Berlin, and wrote, explaining what he had done, to the Ambassador in Moscow: 'In case of provocation on the part of Poland, we would settle matters with Poland in the space of a week. For this contingency, I dropped a gentle hint at coming to an agreement with Russia on the fate of Poland . . . and made it clear that in international politics we pursued no such tactics as the democratic Powers. We were accustomed to building on solid

---

[1] 26 July. On reading below, however, one found that agreement was not certain, but 'virtually certain'!

[2] *Nazi-Soviet Relations*, p. 36: instructions of German Foreign Office to Ambassador in Moscow, 29 July.

ground, did not need to pay heed to vacillating public opinion . . .' and added that conversations such as theirs needed to be 'handled with the discretion they deserved'.[1] The German Ambassador saw Molotov on 3 August for over an hour, and Molotov showed interest. But the Ambassador thought, nevertheless, that Russia would sign with England and France 'if they fulfil all Soviet wishes'.[2] On 11 August British and French military missions reached Moscow in continuance of the work already begun in the talks.

How long could Russia continue to negotiate with both sides? For the pace was quickening. The German Press campaign against Poland was stepped up, wider and wider German claims were made, friction developed between the Nazis in Danzig and the Polish Customs officials, and Hitler told the League of Nations Commissioner for Danzig that 'if the slightest thing was attempted by the Poles he would fall upon them like lightning'.[3] When Ciano, anxious and in the dark, came to Germany in August, he found Ribbentrop and Hitler ready for war. Ribbentrop was certain that Britain would not fight—this certainty was the result of 'his information and above all his psychological knowledge of England'.[4] Hitler, too, attempted to convince Ciano that neither England nor France would intervene. Ciano presented Italy's hesitations, but he became discouraged and said to Hitler: 'You have been right so many times before when others took an opposite view that it is possible that this time also you see things more clearly than we do.'[5] But when he returned Ciano made some scathing comments to Mussolini on the Germans. 'I return to Rome', he wrote in his diary, 'completely disgusted with the Germans, with their leader, and with their way of doing things . . . they are dragging us into an adventure which we do not want and which may compromise the régime

---

[1] *Nazi-Soviet Relations*, telegram, Ribbentrop to Schulenberg, 3 August.
[2] Ibid., telegram, Schulenberg to German Foreign Office, 4 August. A German memorandum of 27 July stated the impression at that time that the Russians 'had not yet decided what they want to do'.
[3] Report by the High Commissioner, Burckhardt, *Documents on International Affairs. 1939-46*, Vol. I, p. 346.
[4] *Ciano's Diplomatic Papers*, p. 297.
[5] Schmidt, *Statist auf diplomatischer Bühne*, pp. 439-40.

and the country as a whole.'[1] Mussolini was worried—yet the hope of future booty drove him to side with Germany.

Hitler now pressed his negotiations with Russia. On 14 August Ribbentrop sent a message suggesting that he should visit Moscow. Molotov delayed. On 20 August Hitler appealed himself with a personal message to Stalin asking if Ribbentrop might go on the 22nd or 23rd.[2] The Russians saw the immediate advantage to themselves in an agreement with Hitler: they could remain neutral in the coming struggle, Hitler's need for haste would enable them to bargain for important advantages, and any territorial gains to Russia at the expense of Poland would put an additional barrier between Germany and Russian vital areas in case of later conflict with Germany. Stalin accepted Hitler's request to let him send Ribbentrop to Moscow, and on 23 August the plane brought the Nazi Foreign Minister to the Red capital.

While Hitler was waiting at the Berghof for news from Moscow, the British Ambassador arrived. He had flown from Berlin with a personal letter to Hitler sent in all haste by Chamberlain. The British Cabinet had met to discuss the reported forthcoming pact between Germany and Russia, and had decided that such an event would not affect their obligation to Poland. Chamberlain's letter to Hitler was an unequivocal warning of what Britain would do in the case of a German attack on Poland:

> It has been alleged that if H.M. Government had made their position more clear in 1914 the great catastrophe would have been avoided. Whether or not there is any force in this allegation, H.M. Government are resolved that on this occasion there shall be no such tragic misunderstanding.
>
> If the case should arise, they are resolved, and prepared, to employ without delay all the forces at their command, and it is impossible to foresee the end of hostilities once engaged.[3]

[1] *Ciano's Diary*, p. 125.
[2] Telegram, Ribbentrop to Schulenberg, setting out Hitler's personal message to Stalin, *Nazi-Soviet Relations*, pp. 66-7.
[3] Henderson, *Failure of a Mission*, Appendix II.

Hitler flew into a fury; he raged against the British and the Poles. The responsibility for war would be England's. At a second meeting that day Hitler was calmer. But in any case, he said, he preferred to fight a war now, when he was only fifty, rather than later on, when he was fifty-five or sixty. He handed Henderson his reply to Chamberlain: Hitler wanted friendship, but if England attacked, Germany was ready.[1]

But although Hitler was worried at the thought of a general war, he was raised to a state of elation by the news from Ribbentrop. While Hitler had been storming at Henderson on the afternoon of the 23rd in the Berghof, Ribbentrop was in the Kremlin conferring with Molotov and Stalin himself. General agreement was reached in the afternoon, and Ribbentrop came back for a sociable evening with his Russian host. Stalin drank a toast to the *Führer*; Ribbentrop felt almost as if he were among his Party comrades: Nazi Foreign Minister and Bolshevik Dictator hit it off, and in the early morning hours of 24 August the documents of the Nazi-Soviet Pact were brought in for signature. The first document, for public announcement, was a non-aggression pact for a period of ten years: in case of war, each country promised to give no help to the enemies of the other, and both countries agreed to consultation and to the settlement of differences by arbitration.[2] But there was another document, a secret agreement. This was not known until after the war, though at the time something of the kind was suspected. Germany and Russia divided eastern Europe into spheres of influence. There was to be a virtual partition of Poland, Lithuania was to be in the German zone, and Finland, Estonia, and Latvia in the Soviet zone. The arrangement confirms the Western suspicions, for Western concern to preserve the freedom of the Baltic republics had been one of the reasons for the failure of the Anglo-French talks with Russia—Russia also staked

---

[1] Henderson, *Failure of a Mission*, pp. 236-7. Ordinary Germans echoed Hitler. As a German teacher wrote in a private letter (22 August) to friends in England: 'Die englische Politik ist so deutschenfeindlich geworden... Jeder Deutsche weiss und Hitler hat es immer wieder gesagt, dass wir nicht gegen England kämpfen wollen ... Wir haben den westwall gebaut. Ist das Angriffslust?'

[2] *Nazi-Soviet Relations*, pp. 76-7, Treaty of Non-aggression.

out a special interest in Rumania.[1] But the details were of lesser importance. The fact of vital significance was that Germany and Russia had come to an understanding: Russia would hold the ring while Germany settled with Poland. The pact was a humiliating rebuff for the West, to Britain and France. It was a startling indication of the cynicism of Nazis and Communists alike, and a demonstration of the ruthless realism of power politics. Stalin gave the signal for the Second World War.

Ribbentrop was elated by his great diplomatic success. But Hitler was not altogether reassured. There was no sign of a weakening of the British attitude. Chamberlain and Halifax had both spoken on Britain's determination to stand by her obligations to Poland. Hitler was visibly impressed by Chamberlain's letter and his speech in the House.[2] Hitler was equally determined now to break Poland, either by her complete surrender to his demands or by war. But it might still be possible, so it seemed to Hitler, to detach Poland from her Western allies. A Swedish businessman, a friend of Göring's, Dahlerus by name, was sent on 25 August to Lord Halifax to assure him, even at this late hour, that Germany still sought agreement with England.[3] On the same day Hitler called Henderson and made an offer: he asked for the free hand in Europe, what he had always wanted, in return for a German guarantee of the British Empire. Hitler wanted with England a pact such as he had just achieved with Russia—that Great Britain as well as Russia would stand aside while Germany dealt with Poland. Henderson flew to London with Hitler's proposal, and Hitler called the French Ambassador also to say to him that there was no issue between France and Germany that could justify their going to war.

[1] *Nazi-Soviet Relations*, p. 78, Secret Protocol.
[2] Schmidt, *Statist auf Diplomatischer Bühne*, p. 449.
[3] B. Dahlerus has described these negotiations in *The Last Attempt*. Dahlerus apparently acted in good faith, not having been informed of Germany's wider plans for attack on Poland. He commented on Hitler's personal behaviour as that of 'a completely abnormal person' (p. 62). Dahlerus had already been an unofficial intermediary in July and earlier in August. He had arranged a private meeting of a group of British business-men with Göring on 7 August. Memoranda on these contacts are in *Documents on British Foreign Policy*, Third Series, Vol. VI, Appendix IV.

At or about this time two items of news reached Hitler: one was the news of the actual signing in London of a mutual assistance pact between Poland and Britain—the outcome and formalization of Chamberlain's guarantee; the other item of news was a carefully worded message from Mussolini that Italy would be unable to give military aid to Germany if the Western Powers attacked. Both items of news were blows to Hitler, and as a result he postponed the invasion of Poland, which had been fixed for the following morning, 26 August.

Hitler hesitated—and Europe trembled on the brink of catastrophe. And yet in the warm sunshine of a fine summer it was difficult to realize how near war was. It was still possible that summer to travel from Berlin to Warsaw by rail through a peaceful countryside, and to look at the sights of the two capitals without seeing the preparations for war—save that in Berlin there were full anti-air raid exercises with bombers zooming overhead and an immediate clearing of streets and balconies and closing of windows, carried out with German discipline and thoroughness. Steamers from Istanbul to Constanza were crowded with Jews from Israel, who were travelling on holiday to see the old folks in Poland—right into the cauldron of war. On the anniversary of the outbreak of war in 1914 the leading article of one of Britain's most popular newspapers stated: 'The *Daily Express* reaffirms its belief that there will be no European war this year.' That theme had been repeated again and again.[1] And three days later, on August Bank Holiday, ten out of twelve of its foreign correspondents in the various countries of Europe assured the readers of the *Daily Express* that there would be no war. A similar assurance was given in mid-August to anxious enquirers at the British Consulate in Istanbul. A large party, over 100 strong, from the British organization the Link, a society for Anglo-German friendship, with an admiral at its head, was at the Salzburg Festival, and Link officials sat in Hitler's box. In Germany the people were as friendly as ever to British visitors. Up to the very end, when the Germans were

[1] *Daily Express*, 4 and 7 August. See also 1 August and 6, 7, 11, 18, and 22 July 1939.

already advancing into Poland, people in France whispered: 'They will arrange something.' They still trusted Chamberlain and Daladier. Another Munich?

It was to the British that Hitler directed his closest and most urgent attention. Of the other Munich figures, Mussolini and Daladier played an insignificant part. The Pact of Steel had proved to be of straw, and Hitler brushed aside Mussolini's offer—made in an attempt to save face over his admission of military weakness—to mediate between Germany and Poland.[1] To Daladier Hitler sent a message repeating what he had said to the French Ambassador. But with Britain it was different: close contact was maintained by the flights to and fro between Berlin and London of Dahlerus and Henderson. Through each of these envoys Hitler sent the offer of a friendly understanding with Britain, though to Henderson he had said little on the Polish problem, while to Dahlerus he offered an agreed settlement with Poland. The British answer to each proposal was virtually the same: Britain wished to come to a friendly understanding with Germany, *but, in any event, Britain stood by its guarantee to Poland.* The official reply, which Henderson brought, stated that the British Government 'could not, for any advantage offered to Great Britain, acquiesce in a settlement which put in jeopardy the independence of a state to whom they have given their guarantee'.[2] The British Government, therefore, asked that there should now be direct discussions between the German and Polish Governments, to which course it had already secured Polish agreement.

Hitler again hesitated, and at that moment Göring, who, unlike Ribbentrop, was not anxious to see Germany rush into war, thought that war might be avoided. Next day, on 29 August, Hitler replied to the British note. He made a show of responding to Britain's willingness for a friendly understanding, but asked that a Polish emissary should come to Berlin with full powers the following day, 30 August.[3] It was a clever trick—a single Pole, in the German capital, under conditions

[1] Minutes of Hitler's talk with Italian Ambassador, 31 August: *Nuremberg Documents*, 1885-PS. Hitler also turned down further proposals by Mussolini on 3 September for a conference: 1,831-PS.
[2] Henderson, *Failure of a Mission*, Appendix V.   [3] Ibid., Appendix VI.

of tension and the threat of war, might have been overawed; an isolated Polish emissary might have stepped into the shoes of Hacha and Schuschnigg. But Chamberlain was not caught a second time. The British Government held the proposal to be completely unreasonable and could not ask the Poles to accept—though wishing that properly conducted negotiations between Poland and Germany might still take place.

At midnight, 30-1 August, there was a dramatic meeting between Ribbentrop and Henderson.[1] It was the stormiest he had ever experienced, said the interpreter, in twenty-three years of work: to him it looked at the critical point as though 'the least that can now happen is that the Foreign Minister of the Reich will throw his Britannic Majesty's Ambassador out of the door'. But Henderson stood his ground. Ribbentrop read out a list of sixteen proposals for settlement—not unreasonable proposals. But when Henderson asked for a copy, Ribbentrop refused. It was too late now, he replied, as the time limit for the arrival of the Polish plenipotentiary had expired. When, under British pressure on the Polish Government, the Ambassador called on Ribbentrop, in the late afternoon of 31 August, to say his Government was favourably considering the British proposal for direct negotiations, one of the briefest official interviews ever known took place. 'Have you authority to negotiate on the German proposals?' asked Ribbentrop. 'No', answered the Polish Ambassador. 'Well, then, there is no point in our continuing the conversation', said Ribbentrop and closed the interview.[2] As for the sixteen points, they made an alibi. On the evening of the 31st the Berlin radio broadcast them to prove to the German people the moderation of Hitler's terms and the insensate obstinacy of the Poles in refusing them. 'I needed an alibi', said Hitler privately, 'especially with the German people, to show that I had done everything to maintain peace. On that account I made this generous offer.'[3] The same night Hitler signed his directive for war.

[1] The final interchanges are vividly described by Schmidt, *Statist auf diplomatischer Bühne*, pp. 456-64.
[2] Ibid., p. 460; *Official Documents concerning Polish-German Relations*, p. 119.
[3] Schmidt, p. 460.

Next morning, 1 September, at dawn the German troops crossed the frontier.

In Berlin, Göring—and Hitler himself—still hoped that Britain and France would do nothing, and this hope was encouraged by apparent hesitation on the part of Poland's Allies. There was a delay of two days, while Britain and France presented warnings. But on 3 September Henderson delivered the final British ultimatum at the Foreign Ministry: unless Germany suspended her aggressive action against Poland and withdrew her troops from that country, a state of war would exist between Germany and Great Britain as from 11 a.m. that day. The document was taken to Hitler in the Chancellery, and when the interpreter had finished translating the message to Hitler there was complete silence. Hitler sat and gazed in front of him, completely immobile. After an unbearable pause, he turned a dark look on Ribbentrop, and asked, 'What now?' It was as though he blamed the Foreign Minister for his ill-founded conviction that England was finished, and all Ribbentrop could do was to say that next would come an ultimatum from France. In the neighbouring room, Goebbels for once was also silent. But Göring let slip the remark: 'If we lose this war, then God help us!'[1] Perhaps he felt at that moment the force of Chamberlain's recent warning to Hitler: 'It is impossible to see the end of hostilities once engaged.'

[1] Schmidt, p. 464.

PART FIVE

Hitler's War

CHAPTER XIV

HITLER CONQUERS EUROPE

AT last Hitler had his war, and launched the first *Blitzkrieg* against Poland. It was, as the German opposition leader, Gisevius, called it, 'Hitler's war';[1] but it was more than that —it was Germany's war. Whatever doubts about its advisability the generals had, whatever fears the man in the street felt as to the possible repercussions on himself which war might bring, when the *Führer* commanded, the generals and the rank and file obeyed, and the mass of the people fell into line behind. Although, as was reported, there were no cheering crowds nor enthusiastic scenes in the Berlin streets on 1 September, the German people offered no opposition to the war. A flagrant act of aggression was committed against a people with whom Germany had lived on friendly terms for the past five years, a nation was broken and its territory overrun—but there was no military coup against Hitler, no general strike, no spontaneous rising of the masses against war. Instead, the new German Army moved to attack and conquest with speed, efficiency and ruthlessness, while behind it there worked a smoothly functioning system of production and supply.

The German Army launched its attacks from Pomerania in the north-west and from Silesia in the south-west, and from East Prussia in the north and the recently acquired German positions in Slovakia in the south. While the mechanized land forces were advancing on all sides, the Luftwaffe opened its attack on Polish towns and airfields. The small Polish Air Force was largely destroyed on the airfields, and air bombing disrupted communications and transport. Although the Poles showed the highest spirit and fought with reckless and devoted courage, they were helpless against the overwhelming German superiority in planes and tanks. The Polish forces

---

[1] *To the Bitter End*, p. 265.

were pinned to the ground they held, and whole units were speedily surrounded and broken up. No help came from the West; England and France did not dare to risk reprisals by attacking Germany from the air, and General Gamelin limited his efforts to patrol activity in front of the Maginot Line. In two weeks the greater part of the fighting was over; on 17 September Russian forces invaded Poland from the other side, and soon Russians and Germans met at Brest-Litovsk; on the 19th Hitler made a triumphal entry into Danzig. In Warsaw the Poles maintained themselves longer; it was only after a desperate and heroic stand that the city surrendered on 27 September. During the last days of the campaign, on 27 and 28 September, Ribbentrop was again in Moscow for talks with the Russians. In spite of the success in Poland, Germany was at war with England and France, and the future uncertain: Stalin could therefore take advantage of the opportunity to bargain. Polish territory was divided between Russia and Germany, and Poland as a state ceased to exist;[1] Lithuania was transferred from the German to the Russian sphere of influence, and such clear recognition of spheres of influence indicated that Russia would deal in her own way with Lithuania and the other Baltic states of Latvia and Estonia.[2] Stalin, that is to say, did all he could to buttress Russia's western flank, and Hitler was ready to pay the price demanded because it allowed him a free hand to settle with the West. To further their alliance, Molotov wrote a note to Ribbentrop outlining an economic policy: 'The Soviet Union will supply Germany with raw materials which Germany will, in its turn, compensate by industrial goods to be delivered over a long period.' In a joint declaration, Germany and Russia stated their determination to work for 'a lasting peace'. If their efforts failed, it would be established thereby 'that England and France bear responsibility for the continuation of the war'.[3]

---

[1] Soviet-German Friendship and Frontier Treaty, 28 September 1939, in *Soviet Documents on Foreign Policy*, p. 377. Also in *Nazi-Soviet Relations*, pp. 105-7.
[2] Secret Additional Protocol to the above.
[3] *Soviet Documents*, pp. 379-80. The joint peace offer won support from Communists abroad, for example, in *Daily Worker*, 30 September and 4 October.

Now came a so-called 'peace offensive'. Many Germans would doubtless have welcomed peace; the generals feared to see Germany plunged further into a general war. Mussolini and Ciano, conscious of Italy's weakness and jealous of Hitler's newly found friendship with Stalin, would have welcomed a compromise. The German newspapers and the wireless gave out that, now the Polish problem was settled, there was no reason for war in the west. The *Völkischer Beobachter* of 30 September published Ribbentrop's message that both Russia and Germany wished for peace and hoped that England and France would now stop 'their senseless war against Germany'. It is interesting to compare at this time the pages of the *Völkischer Beobachter* with those of the *Daily Worker*, which now talked of an 'imperialist war'. One result of Hitler's peace offensive was that it helped to sow doubts and suspicions in England and France. It was a period of confusion; Germans themselves were divided. According to Gisevius, 'Hitler's generals were overcome by fear. Was it absolutely necessary for the war to go on to the end—or was some compromise still possible? . . . Fearful confusion reigned in all authoritative quarters.'[1] Yet at the same time General Thomas admitted to Gisevius that 'the young officers were in a pernicious state of mind. Their confidence in Hitler's leadership had been tremendously fortified by those first victories and by the absence of any threats from the West. Now they were eager for new heroic feats.'[2]

Hitler himself appears to have been in two minds as to what to do next. There are two somewhat conflicting reports of him at this time. 'Hitler', says Gisevius, 'brooded and tormented himself. He instinctively felt that he must take the active role, but he knew that the decision involved total war, irrevocable, all-destructive war. Once he gave the signal, the only remaining alternatives would be victory or ruin.'[3] Ciano reported Hitler on 1 October as seeming 'absolutely sure of himself. The ordeal he has met has given him confidence for future ordeals. . . . What most impressed me is his confidence in ultimate victory. Either he is bewitched or he really is a

[1] *To the Bitter End*, pp. 377-8.   [2] Ibid., p. 384.   [3] Ibid., p. 378.

genius.'[1] Nevertheless, if only as a piece of propaganda, Hitler did make a peace offer. In a long speech to the Reichstag on 6 October, he acclaimed the success of German arms in Poland, but he went on to ask again for an understanding with England and France. 'Why', he asked, 'should this war in the west be fought? For the restoration of Poland? The Poland of the Versailles Treaty will never rise again. This is guaranteed by two of the largest states in the world.'[2] Hitler's speech gave the German Press the opportunity to blazon abroad the so-called peace offer. The day after his speech the *Völkischer Beobachter* carried as its main heading: 'Constructive Peace Plan of the *Führer*: Lasting Security for Europe.'[3] Both France and Britain, however, were unwilling to accept peace on Hitler's terms. And at the same time Hitler was issuing directions to his generals as to 'the war aim. That is and remains the destruction of our Western enemies.'[4]

Indeed, in the outcome, Hitler was strengthened in his resolve to deal with his Western enemies. The pact with Russia covered him on the east and left him a free hand to strike at England and France. But Hitler did not believe in the lasting neutrality of Russia, and therefore he must act soon, before the Russian mood changed. The failure of the British and French to give active help to Poland by attacking in the west confirmed his basic conviction of their weakness and unwillingness to fight. Most of all, the success of his *Blitzkrieg* in Poland suggested that the German Army might win even greater successes elsewhere.[5]

But in spite of Hitler's determination, action was not immediate. The west remained quiet during the winter: this was the period of the 'phoney war', the *drôle de guerre*, or *Sitzkrieg*. In Germany, Gisevius says, 'no one knew what interpretation

---

[1] *Ciano's Diary*, p. 162.

[2] *My New Order*, p. 749.

[3] *Völkischer Beobachter*, 7 October, 'Der aufbauende Friedensplan des Führers'. This and several subsequent issues were largely taken up with the plan and reactions abroad. Cf. *Der Angriff*: '*Muss Krieg im Westen sein*' . . . *Der Führer weist Europa den Weg zu neuem Aufstieg.*'

[4] *Nuremberg Documents*, 52-L.

[5] F. Hesse, *Das Spiel um Deutschland*, p. 236. It was reported to Hesse that Hitler *vor Ungeduld brenne, im Westen loszuschlagen.*

to put on the *drôle de guerre*'.[1] To the outside world it seemed strange that, in view of the swift and crushing German victory in Poland, the Nazis did not attack in the west at once. The reason was that a struggle was going on between Hitler, who was determined to attack at the earliest opportunity, and the generals, who feared disaster and therefore tried to postpone the offensive. Hitler presented a carefully prepared memorandum[2] to his Service chiefs on 10 October, but they were not convinced: they pointed out the size and strength of the French Army, the difficulty of transferring the German forces from Poland to the west, and the dangers of a winter campaign. The doubts and the stalemate revived the hopes of the opposition groups—General Beck, Gisevius, Admiral Canaris and General Oster of the *Abwehr* (military counter-intelligence), General Thomas, Gördeler, formerly Mayor of Leipzig, and Hassell, former Ambassador in Rome. Ever since the events leading to Munich they had worked for a *coup d'état* by the Army; they had pressed the Commander-in-chief, Brauchitsch, and the Chief-of-staff, Halder, to seize Hitler and restrain him by force. Now, when Hitler fixed 12 November as the date of attack—which Brauchitsch believed would bring military disaster—it looked as if the Army would have to act. But bad weather intervened, and the attack was postponed without the necessity of the Army acting against Hitler. Such reasons held up the attack throughout the winter, and thus the opposition groups were thwarted. To their intense surprise, however, on 8 November, there was a bomb attempt on Hitler's life. He had spoken in Munich on the anniversary of the 1923 *Putsch*, and left the Bürgerbraukeller a few minutes before the explosion, which killed and injured a number of his supporters. There are conflicting explanations of this event:[3] it may have been the lone effort

[1] *To the Bitter End*, p. 446.
[2] *Nuremberg Documents*, 52-L.
[3] Gisevius, *To the Bitter End*, pp. 393 and 404-11; S. Payne Best, *The Venlo Incident*. Captain Best was one of two British Intelligence officers captured at the time on the Dutch frontier, and whose activities the Nazis connected with the bomb attempt. Captain Best had been in contact with German officers representing the opposition, and was kidnapped, on Dutch territory, at a supposed rendezvous.

of a Communist carpenter who confessed, or he may have been planted to do the job and the whole incident arranged by the Gestapo to arouse popular feeling for Hitler. The *Führer* himself regarded his narrow escape as a sign of the intervention of Providence on his behalf.

Hitler's mood was well demonstrated when he called the Service chiefs to a conference in the chancellery on 23 November. He explained as he had done previously his reasons for attack in the west. He thought the moment favourable. He himself was irreplaceable: 'I am convinced of the powers of my intellect and of decision', he said. But assassination attempts might be repeated. 'My decision is unchangeable', he said. 'I shall attack France and England at the most favourable and earliest moment. Breach of the neutrality of Belgium and Holland is unimportant. No one will question that when we have won.' Hitler spoke in his inspired mood of mingled mysticism and megalomania: 'No one has ever achieved what I have achieved. My life is of no importance in all this. I have led the German people to a great height, even if the world does hate us now. I am setting this work on a gamble. I have to choose between victory and destruction. I choose victory. . . . As long as I live I shall think only of the victory of my people. I shall shrink from nothing and shall destroy everyone who is opposed to me. . . . I want to destroy the enemy. . . . In the last years I have experienced many examples of intuition. Even in the present development I see the prophecy. If we come through this struggle victoriously—and we shall—our time will enter into the history of our people.'[1]

But the generals were unconvinced; Brauchitsch offered his resignation, but it was not accepted. Several times the date of attack was fixed; each time the generals managed to postpone it, and ultimately to delay it until the spring brought better weather conditions.

Delay in his plans for the west encouraged Hitler to give his attention to another project, for circumstances and events gave both Germany and Great Britain a vital interest in

[1] *Nuremberg Documents*, 789-PS.

Norway. Germany depended on the north of Sweden for high-quality iron ore. In winter the Swedish east coast port of Lulea was frozen, and the iron ore was brought by rail to the Norwegian port of Narvik, to be shipped south through Norwegian territorial waters to Germany. The British Admiralty pressed for the laying of mines to hamper this traffic, but the Cabinet was uneasy about interference with Norwegian neutrality. Germany, on her part, must retain control of this traffic. In addition, as Admiral Raeder pointed out, bases in Norway would give the German Navy a much stronger power of interfering with British shipping in the North Sea. The Russian attack on Finland in November and the winter war, which led to Russia's expulsion from the League of Nations, gave Britain and France the occasion for preparing to send a small force to Finland's aid—though Norway and Sweden were unwilling to allow passage through their territory. If Allied forces could gain a foothold in Scandinavia, they would be on the spot to forestall any German action against Norway. The Germans made their own plans with the utmost care; the commander of the expedition, General von Falkenhorst, was directly responsible to Hitler. The Finns, however, were at last forced to make an armistice with Russia on 12 March 1940, and the landing of British and French forces appeared less likely.

Meanwhile, the British Government was preparing for stronger naval action. A German prison-ship, the *Altmark*, was boarded on 17 February in Norwegian waters, and British prisoners rescued. The Cabinet sanctioned the mining of Norwegian waters, and this took place on 8 April. To meet a possible German reaction, Allied forces were put on shipboard for Norway.

But the German secret had been well kept; their plans were already in operation, and their warships and transports on the way. On 9 April the German attack opened in Norway and Denmark. Denmark was at once overwhelmed. The Norwegians resisted—in spite of the pro-German efforts of Quisling—but Oslo, Stavanger, Bergen, Trondheim, and Narvik fell the first day, and King and Government were forced within two months to escape to England. In spite of considerable losses, the German operations were a complete success and, although Allied troops were landed, they were rapidly driven out of central Norway. It was a spectacular success for Hitler. For Britain was outwitted in what was largely a seaborne landing, and German naval and air bases right along the lengthy Norwegian coast gave to Germany a wide range of operation against Great Britain.[1]

Suddenly, on 10 May 1940 the storm broke in the west. German ruthlessness and German might were now revealed. Without warning and with overwhelming force, by land and air, Germany attacked the neutral countries of Belgium, Holland, and Luxembourg. This was the prelude to the principal attack—on France. The Dutch and Belgian frontier defences were quickly overrun—by parachutists who captured bridges before they could be blown up and by glider troops landed in the rear. Rotterdam was ruthlessly bombed and its airfield captured on the first day. The French troops and the British Expeditionary Force moved out of their positions and into Belgium to meet the advancing Germans, but it was not long before Holland and Belgium were largely in German hands. The Dutch Queen escaped with the Government, and Dutch resistance was almost over by 14 May. On 27 May the Belgian King and Army surrendered. And meanwhile Belgium was fast becoming a trap for the Allied armies.

For a threat to the whole Allied position had quickly developed. Churchill, who replaced Neville Chamberlain as Prime Minister on 10 May (as a result of the failure in Norway), after the first attacks on the Continent, offered the British people 'blood, toil, tears, and sweat'. The main German attack on France came on 14 May at the weakest spot, between Namur and Sedan. Here, as in Poland but on a vaster scale, the strategy of *Blitzkrieg* was put into operation. The idea of mobile warfare, the use of tanks on a great scale, had been put forward in England by General Fuller and

---

[1] Yet it was on the naval side that the Germans suffered a disproportionate loss. See T. K. Derry: *The Campaign in Norway*, p. 231. Their losses in ships, as Dr. Derry points out, hampered their action at Dunkirk, in planning invasion of Britain, and in the Mediterranean.

General Martel, and in France by General de Gaulle, but only in Germany had it been developed to practical reality by the tank expert, General Guderian, with the backing of Hitler, who looked, in warfare as in politics, for new and revolutionary methods. A tremendous force of dive-bombers and armoured divisions, outflanking the main Maginot Line, broke through the French defences and, once through, advanced with incredible speed. Hitler and the German Command did not yet know their own strength; fearful of a French counter-attack, the advance of the tanks was slowed down by orders, but only for a moment. By 18 May the tanks reached Amiens; two days later they reached the sea. The Allied forces were cut in two. In the north the B.E.F. and the French northern army were cut off from their supplies and reserves.

But by an extraordinary stroke of fortune for the British Army the German tanks were again halted.[1] The pause gave the Allied forces in Belgium time to fight their way back to the coast. The evacuation from Dunkirk followed. More than 200 naval and 600 other ships were assembled, and good weather, naval supremacy, and the support of the home-based R.A.F., made possible the evacuation of 335,000 British and Allied troops. Their equipment was lost, but the men were saved. They lived to fight another day. The British Army had slipped out of Hitler's clutches when all else was falling to him.

The French were all but finished. General Weygand tried to form a new line along the rivers Somme and Aisne. But the German armour came on again. On 7 June the tanks crossed the Somme; on 10 June they crossed the Seine near Rouen. On that very day Italy declared war—Mussolini

[1] The exact reason for this has been the subject of some discussion, and it has been suggested by some of the German generals that Hitler interfered, with the intention of saving the British. See B. H. Liddell Hart, *The Other Side of the Hill*, pp. 140 et seq. Blumentritt reported that, the day after the halting of the tanks, Rundstedt and himself were astonished to hear Hitler speak with admiration of the British Empire and of the necessity for its existence. But the German commanders not unreasonably wished to protect their armour after the long advance, and the ditched country near Dunkirk was unsuitable for tanks, though German caution helped the B.E.F. See L. F. Ellis, *The War in France and Flanders, 1939-40*, pp. 347-52. Guderian, *Panzer Leader*, pp. 117-19, blames Hitler and the Supreme Command for their caution.

feared to be left out now that the going was so good. The French saved Paris by not defending it, and the Germans entered the city on 14 June. The country was falling into chaos; civilian refugees and soldiers crowded the roads, German bombers attacked them from the air, and German tanks sped southwards towards the Mediterranean and the Pyrenees. The democratic Government gave way to the rule of Marshal Pétain, and on 22 June France signed an armistice. The ceremony of signature was held in the Forest of Compiègne, at the very place where the Germans had had to sign on 11 November 1918, and Hitler had the old railway coach brought out from the museum in Paris and brought to the spot for the signing of the new armistice. At last Hitler had turned the tables; he literally danced, and slapped his thighs with joy. But, in sober truth, he had achieved so far miraculous success. He had again and again showed himself right and the professional diplomats and soldiers wrong. He had scored some of the most remarkable triumphs, both military and diplomatic, in history.

But what next? Hitler could not stop where he was. Astounding as was his victory in the west, his ultimate objective in Russia was still unachieved. To the French, however, and to many people all over the world, it seemed that Britain also must capitulate. Hitler thought that now, at last, the British Government would make an approach and ask for peace. But no approach came. Indeed, all the indications were soon to the contrary. Churchill spoke out firmly and bravely. General de Gaulle set up his Free French movement in England. The Home Guard was formed. Under the indomitable leadership of Churchill, the nation was organized and braced for resistance to whatever might come. 'This', he declared, 'was their finest hour.' Hitler, on the other hand, in a speech to the Reichstag on 19 July, attacked the British war leaders and their declared intention to carry on the war, if necessary, from Canada. The leaders, he mocked, could escape to Canada, but the people would have to stay in England and suffer. At the same time Hitler made another appeal for peace: 'It almost causes me pain to think that I should have been selected by Fate to deal the final blow to the structure. . . . Mr. Churchill ought perhaps, for once, to believe me when I prophesy that a great Empire will be destroyed—an Empire which it was never my intention to destroy or even to harm. . . . In this hour, I feel it to be my duty before my own conscience to appeal once more to reason and common sense in Great Britain. . . . I can see no reason why this war must go on.'[1]

In reality, Hitler was again in doubt about how to proceed. While the world waited for a German invasion of Britain to begin, Hitler was weighing up alternative courses of action: Must he defeat Britain first and finish with the west before he marched against Russia, or could he ignore Britain and move his forces eastwards towards his ultimate objective? Hitler knew he must avoid a war on two fronts;[2] nevertheless, he was now forced to consider two fronts at the same time—the days when he could concentrate his energies on a single limited objective were over.

In July plans were set on foot for the invasion of England: directives were issued for Operation Sea Lion: there were to be four main landing areas on the south-east coast between Selsey Bill and Folkestone, and preparations were made for the assembling of ships.[3] But, at one point in that same month, Hitler contemplated immediate invasion of Russia in the autumn of 1940. The difficulty, however, of building up quickly enough the great forces required was too great. Hitler postponed his proposal, and turned back to plans in the west. Yet Hitler never showed the same enthusiasm and driving power in preparing for invasion of Britain as he had shown in so many other undertakings. And he realized the dangers —'a defensively prepared and utterly determined enemy faces us and dominates the sea area which we must use'.[4]

A prerequisite to successful invasion of Britain, Hitler

[1] *My New Order*, pp. 836-7.
[2] It was the 'necessity for avoiding a two-front war' which had led Hitler to make the Nazi-Soviet Pact of 1939, as Ribbentrop explained to the Japanese Ambassador in February 1941: *Nuremberg Documents*, 1,834-PS.
[3] *Führer Conferences on Naval Affairs* (reprinted in *Brassey's Naval Annual*, 1948), pp. 110-40.
[4] Ibid., Conference on 21 July 1940.

pointed out, would be 'complete mastery of the air'.[1] If Göring and his Luftwaffe could destroy the R.A.F., then the Germans could bomb British cities by day and destroy them; they could destroy the ports and naval bases, and deprive the British Navy of air cover. An invasion might then be little more than a follow-up operation, an unopposed crossing of the Channel by the German forces. The Battle of Britain began in July, and the aerial conflicts high over south-eastern England went on through August and September. The outcome was in doubt: but the intrepid pilots, the famous few, aided by radar and the technical superiority of the new Spitfire aircraft, turned the scale. The R.A.F. more than held its own. On 7 September the Germans switched from attacks on airfields to night bombing. The change of tactics indicated that the Luftwaffe had lost the first battle. But it might still bomb the nation into submission. A long and hideous ordeal came that winter to London and the great cities. But once more the Luftwaffe failed; the war went on, and although invasion was still under consideration during the winter, the plan was eventually put aside—though not cancelled, in order to keep up the anxiety of Britain. Hitler, indeed, considered he could always deal later on with England and France. In August 1941 he confided to Mussolini 'that once the Russian campaign is over, he intends to deal the final blow to England by invading the island'. Similarly, 'the French question will be re-examined at the end of the war'.[2]

Even while the Battle of Britain was going on, Hitler's planning staffs were working out the details of war against Russia.[3] Everything must be prepared for the great campaign which was to come in the following year. But meanwhile, throughout the winter, the bombing of Britain continued. If Britain could be knocked out or reduced to terms by air bombing, all the better; if not, the campaign against

---

[1] *Führer Conferences on Naval Affairs*; cf. Guderian, *Panzer Leader*, p. 438. He blames Göring severely for the failure of the Luftwaffe over England and, earlier, at Dunkirk.

[2] *Ciano's Diplomatic Papers*, p. 449.

[3] Evidence of General Warlimont, *Nuremberg Documents*, 3,031-PS, 3,032-PS (trans. in *Nazi Conspiracy and Aggression*, Vol. V).

Russia could still be carried out, and Britain, unable to take the offensive, could be ignored. Hitler was thinking in terms of a short war with Russia—a series of overwhelming knockout blows which would cut off and destroy the Russian armies before they could retreat and draw the German forces far into the interior.[1] The directive for Operation Barbarossa, the attack on Russia, was issued by Hitler on 18 December 1940.[2]

Meanwhile, Hitler had to organize the territories he had already conquered and stabilize his position in Europe. After the conquest of Poland and its partition, Hitler had annexed the north and west to Germany; the remainder of his portion he formed into the Government-General and put it under Hans Frank (to be distinguished from the Sudeten leader, K. H. Frank). Towards France Hitler showed a certain moderation in the armistice terms. Mussolini, now that the war appeared to be won, advanced the widest claims on the French Empire; he saw himself as master of the whole Mediterranean area. But Hitler held him back: if he pressed France too hard even the Pétain Government might make war again, from North Africa. Thus the Germans occupied north and west France, but they left a smaller Unoccupied France under Pétain and his Government at Vichy, and they left to France her colonies and her fleet. Then there was the need to safeguard the Mediterranean area—both to close that sea to Britain and increase her difficulties and also to protect himself against any possible later moves by the French, or British, or even the Americans, in North Africa, or from Egypt, or in the Balkans. Hitler held conferences with Mussolini, with Franco, and with Pétain. He hoped that these three would see to the safety of the Mediterranean and North Africa. But all three were pillars of uncertain strength on which to lean. Pétain was outwardly amenable, but played for time; Mussolini had his own plans and ambitions, which would in time involve the Germans in further unwelcome commitments; and Franco—Franco was, in wiliness, a match for Hitler.

[1] From War Diary, O.K.W., *Nuremberg Documents*, 1,799-PS.
[2] *Nuremberg Documents*, 446-PS. Also printed in *Führer Conferences, Brassey*, p. 159.

Hitler made plans for a German-supported Spanish assault on Gibraltar, but Franco suspected that the war was not yet over. He refused to commit himself; he was confirmed in his doubts when Wavell hit out in Libya in December. In a letter in February 1941 to Hitler, Franco expressed his support in general terms but with an excuse making 'the conditions of our economic system the only reasons why it has not been possible up to now to determine the date of Spain's participation'. The Gibraltar plan was set aside, and Hitler's efforts to bring Franco's Spain into the war failed.[1]

With the collapse of France, Germany found herself with a free hand in eastern Europe and the Balkans—except for Russia. Russia, indeed, made haste after the German victories of 1940 to occupy the territories in her sphere of influence; Russian troops moved into the Baltic States in June, and in August incorporated all three, Lithuania, Latvia and Estonia, in the U.S.S.R. Russia demanded from Rumania the border provinces of Bessarabia and northern Bukovina, and added these territories also to the Soviet. But Hitler now took active measures to consolidate and extend German influence in the Balkans. Bulgaria and Hungary both had territorial claims on Rumania, but Hitler was strong enough to override such claims and counterclaims, and imposed a settlement at Vienna in August. By diplomatic means, economic pressure, and the threat of force in the background, Germany built up a strong position: Rumania, Hungary, Bulgaria, and even Jugoslavia were brought into close relations. Particularly was this the case in Rumania, where General Antonescu established a dictatorship, and reached an understanding with the Germans which resulted in the sending of German military and air force missions, of anti-aircraft batteries to protect the oilfields, and of troops with a view to future co-operation against Russia. These moves aroused the suspicions of Molotov, and even of Mussolini.

[1] *The Spanish Government and the Axis*, especially pp. 9-13, notes of conference of 17 September 1940 in Berlin between Hitler and Suñer, Spanish minister of the interior and, shortly afterwards, foreign minister; pp. 21-5, notes of conference of October 23 between Hitler and Franco at Hendaye; and pp. 33-5, letter of 26 February 1941, Franco to Hitler. See also *Nuremberg Proceedings*, Vol. V, p. 2; *Nuremberg Documents*, 1,842-PS and 057-C.

It was indeed not easy for Hitler to make his own plans for German expansion and at the same time hold together his allies and restrain their independent plans which might conflict with his. At the end of September 1940 a new Tripartite Pact was signed by Germany, Italy, and Japan, which Ribbentrop regarded as a great diplomatic success, and which was given great publicity to fortify the morale of the German people. There were many meetings during that winter. Hitler met Mussolini on the Brenner and in Florence. Molotov came to Berlin in November—the famous occasion when he had to take refuge in an air-raid shelter and, as Stalin later told Churchill, Molotov answered Ribbentrop's assurances that Britain was finished with the question: 'If that is so, why are we in this shelter and whose are those bombs which fall?'[1] In the spring of 1941 the Japanese Foreign Minister, Matsuoka, visited Berlin and had a number of talks with Hitler and Ribbentrop. Ribbentrop gave a glowing account of Germany's position—she possessed 'perhaps the strongest military power that had ever existed in the world'. Germany was ready for England, but if necessary she was ready for 'the total crushing of the Russian Army and the Russian state'. 'The war had already been definitely won for the Axis.'[2] Nazi diplomacy was on its toes: to make preparations, and at the same time to camouflage those preparations, for the great undertaking which Hitler was planning.

But before the great undertaking began Hitler's plans suffered a considerable interruption as a result of the combined effect of Mussolini's great ambitions and Italian weakness. The Italian advance into Egypt had begun on 12 September 1940, but had made little progress. Piqued, Mussolini, wanting dearly some Italian triumph to put against German victories, used his bases in Albania to attack Greece on 28 October. The Italians were soon bogged down by the gallant resistance of the Greeks under their national leader, General Metaxas. The attack on Greece at this time had taken place

[1] Churchill, *Second World War*, Vol. II, p. 518.
[2] Memorandum on this meeting, 27 March 1941, *Nazi-Soviet Relations*, pp. 281-98.

against Hitler's wishes, and the *Führer* had now to make military preparations to assist Italy not only in North Africa, but also in Greece, and also to meet a possible landing of British forces in Greece, from which British bombers might attack the Rumanian oilfields and objectives in the south of Italy. The Italian plight increased later in the winter: they were routed by Wavell in Egypt and chased through Libya; they were driven back into Albania by the Greeks. The need for German help became more pressing. Hitler, however, was undaunted by such minor troubles: he made his military plans to meet them at the same time that his preparations were continuing for the grand campaign.

How were the Germans to get to Greece in order to help the Italians? Several countries, Hungary, Jugoslavia, Rumania, and Bulgaria, lay between Germany and Greece. That this obstacle presented little difficulty to Hitler was the measure of German dominance in Europe and also of Nazi diplomacy: how different had been the position of the anti-Nazi nations when the problems of how Russia was to send aid to Czechoslovakia across intervening national frontiers, of how the national security of Poland and the Baltic states was to be squared with the defence of Poland against Germany, of how the West was to send help to Finland without the agreement of Norway and Sweden had all presented insurmountable difficulty. During the winter Hungary, Rumania, and, lastly, on 28 February Bulgaria joined the Tripartite Pact, and German troops occupied positions in all three.

In February and March Hitler applied pressure to Jugoslavia and there were visits to Germany by the Premier and by the Regent, Prince Paul. Agreement was reached: Hitler's path to Greece appeared clear. But on the night of 26 March a group of Jugoslav officers reacted strongly against this policy. They carried out a *coup d'état*. Hitler was so enraged at the news that, at a military conference next day, he decided to punish Jugoslavia without mercy: 'It is especially important that the blow against Jugoslavia is carried out with unmerciful harshness . . . the main task of the Air Force is . . . the destruction of the Jugoslav Air Force ground installations and to destroy the capital, Belgrade, in attacks by waves.'[1] Military measures were immediately improvised. Hitler postponed the invasion of Russia for a term of four weeks.

On 6 April at dawn Germany attacked Jugoslavia and Greece. Belgrade was destroyed by bombing, and over 17,000 people perished. Both Jugoslavia and Greece were overwhelmed; ten days saw the end of the Jugoslav Army, and a few days more and the Greeks also had to capitulate. The small British force, landed previously to assist Greece, was evacuated with considerable loss. Jugoslavia was partitioned; Greece passed under a puppet government. Europe from the North Cape to Cape Matapan was in the hands of, or dominated by, Nazi Germany. Meanwhile Rommel and his *Afrikakorps*, sent to help the Italians in North Africa, had driven the British out of Libya and back to the frontier of Egypt. And late in May the bitterly contested island of Crete was captured by German parachute troops. The way lay open to further successes in the Near East—even perhaps to the destruction of the whole British position in that area. Raeder and Rommel pressed the possibilities of the moment on Hitler. But the *Führer* was now giving his attention to his main interest.

If he could conquer Russia and dominate the great continental land mass of Europe-Asia, he could then either subdue or ignore Great Britain and even the U.S.A. At his military conferences in February and March, Hitler and his military chiefs went over their preparations for the invasion of Russia.[2] He had convinced himself that Russia would attack Germany (though, in fact, there was no evidence of this), and that there was a secret agreement with Britain.[3] The Russian armies must be encircled and destroyed, not allowed to retreat. The war would be finished in two or three months. It must be carried out mercilessly; Himmler and his S.S. were to be given special tasks in the administration of occupied

---

[1] Report of the Conference, *Nuremberg Documents*, 1,746-PS.
[2] Conference of O.K.W. with Hitler, 3 February 1941: *Nuremberg Documents*, 872-PS; cf. 1,799-PS.
[3] Affidavit of General Halder, *Nazi Conspiracy and Aggression*, Vol. VIII, pp. 643-7.

Russian territory,[1] and the territory and resources were to be used for German ends, even though 'as a result millions of people will be starved to death'.[2] The doubts of his generals were brushed aside, though Brauchitsch, Halder, and others were uneasy. Soon all was in readiness; in Great Britain for five weeks there was a welcome, though significant, cessation of bombing. Where was the next surprise attack to come? Through Spain to Gibraltar? Through Turkey to the Suez Canal? One sensational event broke the period of waiting. In the night of 10 May, Rudolf Hess, the *Führer's* deputy and long standing friend, dropped by parachute into Scotland. Was this, everyone asked, a sign of conspiracy and unrest in Germany and impending revolt? Mystery settled over the event—but nothing happened. It seems, in fact, simply that Hess made on his own account one last effort to get Britain to make peace. For the time being, however, Hitler had put away the question of Britain. He believed that, under his leadership, German arms were invincible. He convinced himself that he was about to win his greatest victory, over Russia, in a short campaign as he had done in France. Victory over Russia would ensure ultimate success in the war as a whole, and he would then be able to create the great New Order in Europe for the German race. Meanwhile the world waited.

[1] Top secret directive, O.K.W., 13 March 1941: *Nuremberg Documents*, 447-PS; see also Halder's affidavit.

[2] Memorandum on meeting of under-secretaries, 2 May 1941: *Nuremberg Documents*, 2,718-PS.

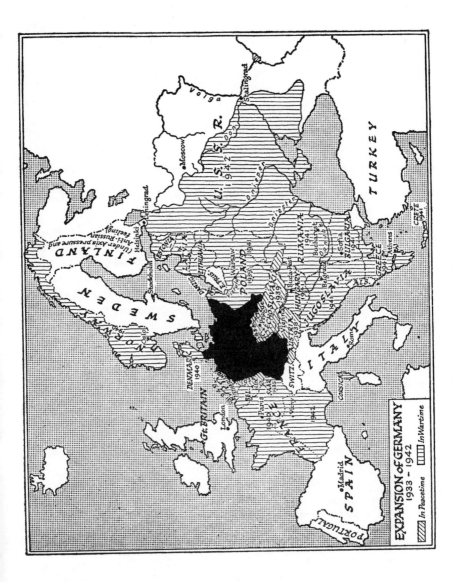

CHAPTER XV

HITLER TURNS EAST

O N 22 June 1941, without declaration of war, the German armies attacked Russia on a front stretching for over 1,000 miles. Brauchitsch was in command—with 140 divisions, nineteen of them armoured divisions, three air fleets, the support of the Rumanian Army, and of, a little later, troops from Slovakia, Finland, Hungary, and Italy. In spite of a personal warning from Churchill, the German attack took Stalin by surprise.[1] For Russia had made great efforts to satisfy the Germans, to meet their economic demands and to do everything to avoid friction or provocation.

Stalin, indeed, had missed a great opportunity when Hitler attacked France. That was the moment the Russian Dictator should have seized, not to attack small countries like Finland, Poland, and the Baltic States, but to have thrown in the weight of the Russian forces against the Nazi menace itself. Stalin was, perhaps, justified in holding back at the time of Munich—in any event, he was not consulted. His suspicion of Chamberlain and the West at that time was not unreasonable. The same suspicion still held good in the summer of 1939, when the West approached him—though it does not really excuse his making of the Nazi-Soviet Pact, which gave the signal for war and the death-knell for Poland. But the campaign in Norway should have opened his eyes. Britain and France were at last committed to war. The moment of Hitler's attack on the Low Countries and France should have been the signal for Stalin to move. Russia might have saved France. If France had avoided collapse, then from that moment in 1940 when Hitler unleashed general war there would have been a war against Germany on two fronts. But Stalin missed his chance and, with the French defeated and

[1] Churchill, *Second World War*, Vol. III, pp. 315-33.

the British driven from the Continent, Russia was left to bear the full weight of a German attack on the largest scale. Russian propagandists then made loud appeals in the West for 'a second front'. But Stalin had himself thrown away the opportunity, in 1940, of creating a second front.

The German advance was rapid at first. The armoured forces moved swiftly into enemy territory, as they had done in the attack on the Low Countries and France. The border territories, which Russian aggression had turned into buffers, —eastern Poland and the Baltic states—were soon occupied. Three great armoured advances were developed: the Northern Army Group moved through the Baltic area towards Leningrad, which Hitler made his immediate objective; the Centre Army Group moved in the direction of Moscow, though Hitler regarded its main task as support for the Northern drive; and the Southern Army Group moved southwards through the Ukraine. But there were differences of opinion between Hitler and his generals: was the main assault to be made on Leningrad, or Moscow, or in the Ukraine?[1] The differences resulted in delay. Hitler now pressed for a wide encircling movement in the south, and great victories were won. Kiev and Kharkov were captured, and over half a million Russian prisoners taken. The Germans pushed on almost to Rostov-on-Don and the Black Sea coast; in the north their armies threatened Leningrad and Moscow. But when the terrible Russian winter set in, what Hitler had warned his generals against had happened, largely, it seems, through Hitler's own direction and interference: the German armies had been drawn deep into Russian territory, but the Russians had avoided any decisive encirclement and still had armies intact, and were building new ones to replace those destroyed. General Halder afterwards maintained that Hitler's decision to strike south was the turning-point: Hitler thereby missed a decisive victory against Moscow.[2]

When the main German pressure was switched back on Moscow, it was just too late. At the beginning of December

---

[1] F. Halder, *Hitler as War Lord*, pp. 44-7.
[2] Ibid., p. 47.

a last attack on the capital was made, and a few Germans got as far as the outlying parts of the city. But, to the surprise of the Germans, the Russians had prepared a counter-attack on the whole central front. It started on 6 December, and pushed the Germans back.

There was acute anxiety in Germany during the winter of 1941-2. In spite of the German advances and victories—loudly acclaimed by Press and radio—it was evident that there had been no decision. The Russian winter had proved the first real setback to the Nazis, and many Germans remembered Napoleon and his Moscow campaign. The German troops were deeply committed and caught without adequate winter clothing, for Hitler had not planned for a winter campaign.[1] Frost-bite as well as battle caused heavy loss. There were other difficulties. Hitler, in a conversation with Mussolini in late August 1941, had admitted that he had been misled by faulty intelligence; he had not been informed of the size and power of the Russian armies, and he had been surprised by the bravery of their soldiers.[2] Ciano noted in November reports from Germany that the generals thought 'the war in Russia as it is being conducted is pure folly, that the German Army is gradually wearing itself out . . . and that he [Hitler] is leading Germany to the brink of ruin. It seems that this is the unanimous opinion of all the military leaders, but that no one dares tell Hitler.'[3] The ordinary German feared the limitless space of Russia with its huge population, so great that a few million would not be missed. '*Viele Hunde sind des Hasen Tod*' (Many hounds spell death to the hare), said old soldiers of the First World War.[4]

The Germans were indeed meeting in Russia very different conditions from those they had met in western Europe. There the strategy of *Blitzkrieg* had brilliantly succeeded: once the aircraft and tanks had broken a way through the defence,

[1] Halder, *Hitler as War Lord*, pp. 42 and 48. The Commander-in-Chief had asked for supplies of winter clothing, but his requests were refused or ignored.

[2] *Ciano's Diplomatic Papers*, p. 449.

[3] *Ciano's Diary*, pp. 393-4.

[4] S. Payne Best, *The Venlo Incident*, pp. 101-2. Captain Best was a prisoner in Germany at the time.

the area to be overrun was comparatively small, and enemy supplies and communications were quickly disrupted. In Russia the Germans had to contend with vast space as well as ice-cold; they fought and advanced, but they did not break through and disrupt. Eventually, also, even a superb fighting machine like the German Army ran up against difficulties of supply: it had to reconstruct many hundreds of miles of Russian railways and fit out huge supply depots in the conquered territory. Hitler's own determination and refusal to admit defeat held the German armies in position throughout the winter, and prevented any panic flight.[1] In the spring they came on again: they moved forward in the south, clearing the Crimea and sending one force into the Caucasus with the objective of the oil wells, and another eastwards to the Volga with the object of cutting the oil route from the Caucasus to the heart of Russia. But final victory eluded the Germans, and meanwhile there were new factors in the situation.

On 7 December 1941 Japan suddenly attacked the United States: carrier-borne aircraft surprised the American Pacific Fleet at Pearl Harbour, Hawaii, and, in less than two hours, put it out of action. This event was perhaps the most important of the whole war: it changed it from a European into a global conflict. Germany and Italy declared war on America, as Britain did on Japan. These events were to prove decisive. Perhaps the scale of the global conflict, coupled with the suddenness of events, prevented a proper grasp by the human mind of its various possible developments. For it would seem that both Hitler and the Japanese leaders committed major errors of political strategy.

The Japs, had they set to work more cautiously, might have acquired bit by bit the French, Dutch, and British possessions in the Far East; neither French nor Dutch, nor even British, were in a position to defend them, and all this might have been done *without* involving America in the struggle.

[1] Mr. Alan Bullock thinks this was Hitler's 'greatest achievement as a war leader', *Hitler*, p. 610. But Walter Görlitz, *The German General Staff*, p. 408, says: 'All high-ranking officers were agreed that Hitler's great decisive mistake was his method of inelastic defence during this winter.... The General Staff favoured an elastic defence, which permitted boldly conceived retreats....' Cf. Halder, p. 51.

The view of the Reich Foreign Minister and of the German Navy was that the Japanese should seize Singapore, thereby striking a grave blow at Britain, but striving at the same time to keep the United States out of the war. Admiral Raeder argued in March 1941 that the U.S.A. was not prepared to wage war on Japan, that the entire British Fleet was tied down, and that the opportunity of taking Singapore was more favourable than it ever would be again.[1] But with the German war in Russia, the German views of what Japan should do became more complicated. Hitler now looked for a Japanese surprise attack on Vladivostok.[2] Ribbentrop had pointed out, in a telegram to the German Ambassador in Tokyo: 'The natural objective is still that we and the Japanese join hands on the Trans-Siberian railway before winter. With the collapse of Russia the position of the Three-Power-Pact states will be so gigantic that the question of England's collapse or the total destruction of the English islands will only be a matter of time . . . then there will be an America totally isolated from the rest of the world.'[3] If Japan had taken either, or both, of these courses it would have been better for Hitler—and Japan—than the attack on America.

Hitler, too, when Japan challenged America, did not need to have Germany declare war; Japan had not declared war on Russia to please Hitler. Hitler might have left Japan to fight the United States, which would have meant no American build-up against Germany. But as it was, America now became fully involved in east and west. Pearl Harbour had an exactly opposite effect from that for which the Japs had hoped. Instead of crippling and discouraging the Americans, it stirred them to immediate action on a gigantic scale. American resources were so great that eventually she must win, if the initial Japanese onslaught could be checked. It was checked, and when once checked, Allied strategy decided first

---

[1] Memorandum, 27 March 1941, meeting in Berlin of Ribbentrop and Japanese Foreign Minister, Matsuoka: *Nazi-Soviet Relations*, p. 287. Conference of 18 March 1941. Similar views expressed at conferences of 27 December 1940 and 20 April 1941. *Führer Conferences on Naval Affairs* (reprinted in *Brassey's Naval Annual*, 1948). Also *Nuremberg Documents*, 1,877-PS and 1,881-PS.

[2] *Führer Conferences*, 22 August 1941.

[3] *Nuremberg Documents*, 2,896-PS (telegram of 10 July 1941).

to deal with Germany and Italy in the west, before moving back east to a final settlement with Japan. Thus Allied strategy ultimately forced on Germany a war on two fronts, and this was fatal to Hitler.

It has become common, in the light of after-events, to regard as a blunder Hitler's action in attacking Soviet Russia. From our own point of view in this country, it did, of course, hold out the first real possibility of eventual victory. Britain was no longer alone; there was now a powerful ally, whose forces did in fact throughout the remainder of the war engage never less than two-thirds of the German Army.[1] But Hitler, if he were to achieve his great design of a New Order for the German race, the policy he had followed ever since *Mein Kampf*, must sooner or later attack Russia. And Hitler was no fool. To defeat Russia appeared possible. Compared with Germany, Russia was inefficient and backward. Anyone who travelled in Nazi Germany and Soviet Russia before the war could judge for himself. The Russian population, however, was more than three times the German; Russian territory was immensely larger. In spite of the vastly greater size of Russia, Germany at first won great victories. But the Russian winter, space, the determination of soldier and civilian alike, and the supplies sent by America and Britain held up the Nazi armies, until a war on two fronts ultimately brought Hitler to disaster. Hitler's main interest was in the Russian campaign. It was fortunate, indeed, for us that this was so, and that he did not listen overmuch to Raeder and Rommel, who pleaded for his attention to the Near East, and that Turkey was not tempted by the Allies into the war, as the Allies had at times hoped. Had that happened, Hitler might have been led, in spite of his overriding concern with Russia, to send his armoured divisions crashing through Asia Minor to clear up the Turkish Army, brave but without effective air defences or armour, to seize the Suez Canal, and to destroy the whole British Near Eastern position. As it was, however, it was the Japanese intervention in the war which was ultimately decisive by bringing in America.

[1] Cyril Falls, *The Second World War*, p. 295.

Hitler had underestimated the strength of the Russian re-action to attack; about America he was largely ignorant. He doubted American ability to interfere in Europe. 'America', he had once said, 'is permanently on the brink of revolution. It will be a simple matter for me to produce unrest and revolts in the United States, so that these gentry will have their hands full with their own affairs.'[1] Thus though Japan's aggression at Pearl Harbour took him by surprise, he appears to have been pleased with the news and to have seen Japan's intervention only as a welcome accession of strength to his own side. Indeed, Hitler saw himself more clearly in the role of a great historical figure, not only on the European stage, but now also on the wider stage of the world. When he announced Germany's declaration of war on America in a speech on 11 December, Hitler attacked President Roosevelt as aiming at unrestricted world domination.[2] But, said Hitler, 'I can only be grateful to Providence that it entrusted me with the leadership in this historic struggle which, for the next 500 or 1,000 years, will be described as decisive, not only for the history of Germany, but for the whole of Europe and indeed the whole world . . . a historical revision on a unique scale has been imposed on us by the Creator.'[3] A few days later Hitler made a still further concentration of mili-tary authority in his own hands. He had lost faith, during the winter crisis, in his generals; he accepted Brauchitsch's re-signation when the Germans were checked before Moscow, and on 19 December Hitler announced that he would him-self be the Commander-in-Chief of the Army in the field (that is, he took over the O.K.H.—*Oberkommando des Heeres*). If up till now Hitler could blame the generals for failing to carry out his policy, now he was assuming direct responsibility himself.

During the summer of 1942 the long-term factors at work were largely hidden, for events were still moving on the whole in favour of Germany. Allied shipping resources were

---

[1] H. Rauschning, *Hitler Speaks*, p. 4. Cf. *Ciano's Diplomatic Papers*, p. 451, where Hitler expressed to Mussolini his distaste for American life.
[2] *Hitler's Words* (ed. G. W. Prange), p. 375.
[3] Ibid., p. 97.

stretched to the limit, particularly Atlantic communications, by German U-boat sinkings; German armies in southern Russia had advanced into the Caucasus and to the Volga to besiege Stalingrad; and in North Africa the position was once more in grave doubt—in June Rommel made his most formidable attack, Tobruk was lost and the British chased right back into Egypt. But now during the autumn and winter of 1942-3 the whole tide of war changed. The Allies at last had something to fight with; planes, tanks, guns, equipment of all kinds were pouring in. Hitler had lost the long start which his planned aggression had given him. On 23 October General Montgomery's Eighth Army attacked at El Alamein; the Germans were heavily defeated, and the long pursuit through North Africa began again, and for the last time. A few days later, on 8 November, General Eisenhower landed large Anglo-American forces in Morocco and Algeria. On 19 November the Russians began their great counter-offensive which saved the ruins of Stalingrad. Hitler had overreached himself in the south by his double advance, which was halted eventually in both places. The Russian counter-offensive, north and south of Stalingrad, in turn encircled the German forces which were besieging the city. Hitler's orders to Rommel in Egypt and to von Paulus before Stalingrad were: Stand fast. But in each case the orders could not be obeyed, and the Germans suffered disaster. By the end of January 1943 the great Russian victory at Stalingrad accounted for twenty-two German divisions destroyed or captured. 'It was', says a German writer, 'a second Jena, and was certainly the greatest defeat in history that a German Army had ever undergone.'[1] Among the generals who surrendered was Paulus—the first surrender of a field-marshal in the history of modern Germany. But there was no general collapse of the German forces in Russia. Nazi Germany was still a long way from defeat. The career of Nazi aggrandisement had been finally checked, but the occupied territories had still to endure a long period of suffering before the Nazi oppressors were at last driven out.

With the double German advance to the Caucasus and

[1] W. Görlitz, *The German General Staff*, p. 431.

Stalingrad the career of Nazi aggrandisement reached its apex. That career, indeed, marked as it had been by successive and ever-greater triumphs, had gone on in peace and war. The outbreak of war in 1939 did not check it; the forces of the nations at war with Hitler were at first too weak to do so, and the series of Nazi aggressions which had taken place in peacetime swelled into a tide of conquest as the war went on. In September 1939 the Germans had conquered and occupied western Poland; in the spring and summer of 1940 they added Denmark, Norway, Holland, Belgium, Luxembourg, and the greater part of France (later, after the Allied landings in Morocco and Algeria, German forces occupied also the remainder of France). In the spring of 1941, having already established military positions in Hungary, Rumania, and Bulgaria, Germany had attacked and overrun Jugoslavia and Greece—the only part of south-eastern Europe then remaining independent was European Turkey. At the other side of Europe, Spain was under German influence. Although Switzerland, Sweden,[1] and Eire preserved a precarious neutrality, the German power in Europe really halted only at the English Channel and the North Sea. German forces in North Africa and in Crete gave a degree of control over the Mediterranean. The vast extent of territory overrun in Russia brought the Germans close to Leningrad, Moscow, and Stalingrad, and deep into the Caucasus. What use was made of, and how were these vast territories administered by, the Nazis?

For propaganda purposes, abroad and also at home, Hitler and the Nazis made great play with the idea of a New Order in Europe. At the Berlin Sportpalast on 30 January 1941, in a speech to mark the eighth anniversary of his coming to power, Hitler said: 'I am convinced that 1941 will be the crucial year of a great New Order in Europe. The world shall open up for everyone. Privileges for individuals, the tyranny of certain nations and their financial rulers shall fall. And, last of all, this year will help to provide the foundations of a real understanding among peoples, and with it the

[1] Hitler had hard words to say to Mussolini about both Sweden and Switzerland, 25 August 1941. Hitler described the Swedes 'as villains'. *Ciano's Diplomatic Papers*, pp. 450-1.

certainty of conciliation among nations.'[1] 'Conciliation among nations'—this on the eve of Hitler's most grandiose campaign, his attack on Russia! Hitler and Mussolini met on the Russian front and were together from 25 to 29 August. They issued a communiqué which was a propaganda counterblast to the signing earlier that month of the Atlantic Charter, when President Roosevelt and Churchill met off the Newfoundland coast and joined in proclaiming their belief in freedom for both individual and nation. The communiqué of the German and Italian dictators stated: 'The new European order which will result from victory is to remove as far as possible the causes which in the past have given rise to European wars. The destruction of the Bolshevist danger and plutocratic exploitation will create the possibility of a peaceful, harmonious and fruitful collaboration of all the peoples of the continent of Europe in the political, economic, and cultural spheres.'[2]

A demonstration of the new international solidarity was organized in Berlin at the end of November, when representatives gathered there from Italy, Japan, Manchukuo, Spain and Hungary to renew adherence to, and representatives from Rumania, Bulgaria, Slovakia, Croatia, Finland, and Denmark to join, the Anti-Comintern Pact, while the Nanking régime in China adhered by telegram. But, as Ciano described it, 'The Germans were the masters of the house, and they made us all feel it even though they were especially polite to us. There is no way out of it. Their European hegemony has now been established.'[3]

In addition to propaganda for the New Order in Europe, Hitler also made glowing promises, along socialist lines, to the Germans themselves. Thus, in a speech towards the end of 1940, he told them: 'The German people will be richly rewarded in the future for all that they are doing. When we have won this war, it will not have been won by a few industrialists or millionaires, or by a few capitalists or aristocrats, or by a few bourgeois, or by anyone else. Workers, you must

---

[1] 30 January 1941, *My New Order*.
[2] Announced from the *Führer's* H.Q., 29 August 1941: *The Times*.
[3] *Ciano's Diary*, p. 402.

look upon me as your guarantor. I was born a son of the people; I have spent all my life struggling for the German people. . . .

'When this war is ended Germany will set to work in earnest. A great "Awake!" will sound throughout the country. Then the German nation will stop manufacturing cannon and will embark on peaceful occupations and the new work of reconstruction for the millions. Then we shall show the world for the first time who is the real master—capitalism or work. Out of this will grow the great German Reich of which great poets have dreamed. . . . Should anyone say to me: "These are mere fantastic dreams, mere visions", I can only reply that when I set out on my course in 1919 as an unknown, nameless soldier, I built my hopes for the future upon a most vivid imagination. Yet all has come true.'[1]

If Germany had won the war, it is probable that a great economic drive would have been made to expand the German race and raise still further its physical well-being and material standards of life. But material advance of that kind would have been purchased at the expense of all the humane and Christian virtues, for German advance and well-being would have been the result of the deliberate destruction of some, and the permanent debasement of other, supposedly inferior races. For to what did all the Nazi talk of a New Order in Europe amount?

In the short run—that is, in wartime—the New Order amounted to the co-ordination of European economic resources to feed Germany's war machine and bring about her domination of the world. For the great additions to German economic and military potential that conquest brought, coupled with the fact that the Nazis were prepared to let conquered peoples starve where necessary to feed the German Army, largely freed Germany from the danger of blockade which had been so great a menace during the First World War. The plans made before the invasion of Russia clearly allowed for the death by starvation of conquered peoples to supply German military needs. Among those plans, one

[1] *My New Order*, pp. 873-99.

memorandum stated: 'The war can only be continued if all the armed forces are fed by Russia in the third year of the war. There is no doubt that as a result many millions of people will be starved to death if we take out of the country the things we need.'[1] Ciano reported Göring as saying: 'We cannot worry unduly about the hunger of the Greeks. It is a misfortune which will strike many other peoples besides them. . . . This year between 20 and 30 millions of people will die of hunger in Russia. Perhaps it is well that it should be so for certain nations must be decimated.'[2] Göring also recounted that Russian prisoners were eating each other; unfortunately, they had also eaten a German sentry. He added that hunger was now so great among the Russian prisoners that it was no longer necessary to send them back to base under armed guard: it was enough to put a camp kitchen at the head of the column, and thousands would trail along 'like a herd of famished animals'. 'And', commented Ciano in his *Diary*, 'we are in the year of grace 1941.'

One of Germany's heaviest demands was for labour—veritable slave labour. Some few of the workers were volunteers or willing collaborators, but the great majority were conscripted, and they often worked under intolerable conditions. At one time, at the beginning of 1945, there were nearly 5 million foreign workers in Germany, somewhat under 2 million being Russians. Including prisoners of war and political deportees, the approximate total of foreigners working in Germany at this time was 6,691,000.[3] Fritz Sauckel, who was in charge of manpower supply, stated that less than 200,000 foreign workers came voluntarily to Germany. He said that since French and Italian workers got better food to eat at home than in Germany they had no incentive to come; he also complained that he was being blamed for stimulating, by his call-up of foreign workers, the formation

[1] Memorandum of 2 May 1941, *Nuremberg Documents*, 2,718-PS. See also report by the Economic Staff on exploiting Russian resources, 23 May 1941, 126-EC.
[2] November 1941: *Ciano's Diplomatic Papers*, pp. 464-5. See also *Ciano's Diary*, pp. 402-3.
[3] Based on German figures and Allied checks of foreigners found at the end of the war: *Nuremberg Documents*, 2,520-PS.

of partisan bands in various occupied territories.[1] Those who were called to work in Germany fled, it was alleged, to the woods and mountains instead. The worst conditions of all were in some of the concentration camps. Certain classes of prisoners were marked as being available 'to be worked to death'.[2] 'The idea of exterminating them by labour is the best', thought Goebbels.[3] Two birds were thus killed with one stone. Cheap labour was attained, and racially unwanted elements were eliminated. At Camp Dora, at first a branch camp of Buchenwald, prisoners worked on making the flying bombs and rockets. Russians, Poles, and French lived and worked in tunnels in the Hartz Mountains, to which research plants were transferred after the Allied bombing of Peenemunde in 1943. Prisoners were driven to work; beatings and hangings were part of the normal round.[4]

In the long run, the New Order was simply the application of Hitler's old policy of *Lebensraum*, the *Mein Kampf* policy of creating living space by conquest in the east and the extermination of the supposedly inferior occupying races, or their reduction to an altogether lower level as serfs, in order to make room for the master race, the Germans. The racial theory was, indeed, not limited to Germans in a narrow sense—theoretically it was the Aryan race which was the master race. In practice, there were in the *Waffen S.S.* many foreigners, and a very large number who were Germans from outside the Reich. And although German control of occupied Europe was strict and ruthless, it did vary in different parts of Europe. In some countries there were puppet governments, or governments under strong German influence, as in France; in other parts German administrators exercised direct control. The treatment of subject peoples was less severe in western Europe; the full German barbarism was reserved for Slavs and Jews.

In Norway an arrested Norwegian member of the S.S. in Trondheim reported after the war to British officers that in

[1] Central Planning Conference, 1 March 1944: *Nuremberg Documents*, 124-R.
[2] Notes on discussion with Himmler: *Nuremberg Documents*, 654-PS.
[3] *Nuremberg Documents*, 682-PS. Notes on discussion with Goebbels.
[4] Report of the American War Crimes Case, *Nordhausen*.

about 70 per cent of S.S. interrogations it was necessary to use torture, and the British officer collected with this information photographs of whips, canes, cat-o'-nine-tails, ox-thongs, thumbscrews, and Nielsson's Patent (an iron bar for suspending a prisoner, with hands tied to knees, to interfere with the circulation of the blood). But the Norwegian explained that Norwegians were better treated than others, and the German chief of the S.D. in Trondheim, though he thought that an Englishman should be treated in a decent manner during interrogation, looked upon Russians and Serbs as little more than animals.

The Nazi policy in Russia was not a wartime improvisation, but the application of Hitler's long-held plan of exterminating Slavs to make way for Germans. Although Hitler had thought that German invasion of Russia would precipitate risings against Stalin and ordered a cunning policy of concealing for the time being his real objects, German policy in practice, by its utter ruthlessness, soon made it apparent that Russians in supporting Stalin were struggling for their very existence. Thus, though in certain parts of Russia the German armies were at first welcomed as liberators, the S.S. destroyed that popular illusion and had the effect of stiffening Russian resistance. Indeed, Hitler's policy for the Slavs was one of utter ruthlessness, and devoted entirely to German selfish interests. Bormann noted Hitler's view that 'the Poles, in direct contrast to our German workmen, are born for hard labour. To our German workers we must give every possible advancement; as for the Poles, there can be no question of improvement . . . the standard of life must be kept low in Poland . . . the Government-General should be our source of unskilled labour. . . . For the Poles there must be only one master, the German . . . therefore all representatives of the Polish intelligentsia are to be exterminated. This sounds cruel, but such is the law of life. . . . The priests must keep the Poles quiet, stupid, and slow-witted. This is entirely to our interests.'[1] As

---

[1] Memorandum by Bormann on conference with Hitler, 2 October 1940: *Nuremberg Documents*, 172-USSR; cf. ibid., 864-PS. Some details of German repression are given by Bor-Komorowski, *The Secret Army*, p. 155. In two weeks of 1943, 177 people were shot publicly in Warsaw.

for the Czechs, 'it would take too long to deport them all; therefore the major part of the intellectual class' was to be 'eliminated, and shipped out of the country by all sorts of methods'. The intellectuals, Hitler clearly saw, could not be converted ideologically and as potential Czech leaders would be dangerous to the Germans: 'Elements which counteract the planned Germanization are to be handled roughly and should be eliminated.'[1]

At a conference in July 1941 of military and civilian leaders, Hitler explained his policy for Russia. The real aim must be concealed, but preparations made nevertheless for a final settlement in Russian territory. According to Bormann's notes, Hitler's policy was as follows:

> What we told the world about the motives for our measures ought to be conditioned by tactical reasons. . . .
>
> Therefore we shall emphasize again that we were forced to occupy, administer, and secure a certain area; it was in the interests of the inhabitants that we provided order, food, traffic, etc., hence our measures. Nobody shall be able to recognize that it initiates a final settlement. This need not prevent our taking all necessary measures—shooting, re-settling, etc., and we shall take them.
>
> But we do not want to make any people into enemies prematurely and unnecessarily. Therefore we shall act as though we wanted to exercise a mandate only. At the same time *we* must clearly know that we shall never leave those countries.
>
> Our conduct therefore ought to be:
>
> 1. To do nothing which might obstruct the final settlement, but to prepare for it only in secret.
> 2. To emphasize that we are liberators.
>
> On principle we have now to face the task of cutting up the giant cake according to our needs, in order to be able:
>
> > first, to dominate it,
> > second, to administer it, and
> > third, to exploit it.

[1] Top secret letter of the commanding general in Protectorate of Bohemia and Moravia, 15 October 1940: *Nuremberg Documents*, 862-PS.

The Russians have now ordered partisan warfare behind our front. This partisan war again has some advantage for us; it enables us to eradicate everyone who opposes us.

Principles:
Never again must it be possible to create a military power west of the Urals, even if we have to wage war for a hundred years in order to attain this goal. . . .
Our iron principle is and has to remain:
We must never permit anybody but the Germans to carry arms!

We have to create a Garden of Eden in the newly occupied eastern territories: they are vitally important to us; as compared with them, colonies play only an entirely subordinate part. . . . Naturally, this giant area would have to be pacified as quickly as possible; the best solution was to shoot anybody who looked sideways.[1]

Hitler and his leaders went on to discuss details of the areas to be annexed and the Germans to be appointed to take charge of them. From these discussions it is clear how personal jealousies were at work and that the rival Nazi leaders—Rosenberg, Ribbentrop, and Himmler—were all trying hard to enlarge their own influence in the new territories. In particular, Bormann threw cold water on Rosenberg's proposals; some were turned down. The jealousy ran even to minor matters, and there seemed a general disinclination to accept Rosenberg's proposals. For example, when he proposed to use a certain Captain von Petersdorff there was 'general consternation, general rejection. The *Führer* and the Reichsmarschall [Göring] both emphasize there was no doubt that von Petersdorff was insane.' Göring, too, made some effort to set limits to the powers of Himmler.

But it was not easy to limit Himmler's power. For Himmler was now, more than ever, the head of a great power complex; he controlled all the police and the S.S. As *Reichsführer* S.S. he was head of the Waffen S.S. (armed S.S.), which was a considerable private army; he had achieved what Röhm had paid with his life for trying to do with the S.A. Through the S.S. also, Himmler controlled the concentration camps and

[1] Bormann's memorandum, 16 July 1941: *Nuremberg Documents*, L-221.

extermination camps, for which guards and extermination squads were given special training. The executions, beatings, torture, and sadism, the tanning of human skin for books, lampshades, and briefcases,[1] the mass extermination by gassing and burning, the so-called medical and scientific experiments on human beings—all these things lay in Himmler's province.[2] By the *Führer's* decree of October 1939 Himmler had been charged with carrying out a principal part of the Nazi racial policy. He was to bring back Germans abroad and resettle them in the newly-acquired territories of the Greater German Reich, and 'to eliminate the harmful influence of such alien parts of the population, which represent a danger to the Reich and German folk community'.[3]

What this meant in practice was vividly described by Himmler in addressing S.S. officers. Speaking at Metz on the deportation of subject peoples, Himmler said: 'Exactly the same thing happened in Poland in weather 40° below zero, where we had to haul away thousands, ten thousands, hundred thousands; where we had to have the toughness— you should hear this but also forget it again immediately— to shoot thousands of leading Poles. . . . We also had to bring in, in this winter of 40° below zero, ten thousands of Germans and had to take care of their needs.'[4] Thus racial Germans from outside were moved into territories newly annexed to Germany, and were cared for. The displaced Poles were destroyed, or moved away into misery and subjection.

Himmler went on to apologize to his soldiers of the Waffen S.S. for the fact that they, as soldiers, must also help with tasks of guard duty and extermination. They must think of the tasks of the S.S. as a whole. To develop the S.S., to carry

[1] Evidence taken from the commandant of Mauthausen Camp (Austria): *Nuremberg Documents*, 3,870-PS.

[2] For a detailed account of the concentration camps and the work of the S.S., see E. Kogon, *Der SS-Staat*, the English edition of which has been appropriately entitled *The Theory and Practice of Hell*. Dr. Kogon suffered seven years as a prisoner, and gives carefully detailed information, which was used by the War Crimes Commission at Nuremberg.

[3] *Erlass des Führers . . . zur Festigung deutsches Volkstums: Nuremberg Documents*, 686-PS.

[4] *Nuremberg Documents*, 1,918-PS. Himmler thought also of bringing back Germans from the Balkans and America, 1,919-PS.

out for it a programme of building apartment houses for S.S. men and their families, money 'will be earned by forcing the scum of mankind, the prisoners, the professional criminals to do positive work. The man guarding these prisoners serves just as hard as the one on close-order drill.' Himmler was thinking also, not only of wartime, but of a final settlement, for he said: 'In peacetime I shall form guard battalions and put them on duty for three months only—to fight the inferior beings (*Untermenschentum*), and this will not be a boring guard duty, but, if the officers handle it right, it will be the best indoctrination on inferior beings and the inferior races. This activity is necessary, as I said, (1) to eliminate these negative people from the German people, (2) to exploit them once more for the great folk community by having them break stones and bake bricks so that the *Führer* can again erect his grand buildings, and (3) to invest, in turn, the money, earned soberly this way, in houses, in ground, in settlements so that our men can have houses in which to raise large families and lots of children. This in turn is necessary, because we stand or die with this leading blood of Germany and if the good blood is not reproduced we will not be able to rule the world.'[1]

In another speech to S.S. major-generals, in October 1943, Himmler still further clarified his views: 'What happens to a Russian, to a Czech, does not interest me in the slightest. What the nations can offer in the way of good blood of our type we will take, if necessary by kidnapping their children and raising them here with us. Whether nations live in prosperity or starve to death interests me only in so far as we need them as slaves for our *Kultur*. . . . Our concern, our duty is our people and our blood. . . . We can be indifferent to everything else. I wish the S.S. to adopt this attitude to the problem of all foreign, non-Germanic peoples, especially Russians.' Himmler went on to speak of 'the extermination of the Jewish race . . . most of *you* must know what it means when 100 corpses are lying side by side, or 500 or 1,000'. Then Himmler spoke of the S.S. as a selected body—'we are a product of the law of selection'—and concluded with the

1 *Nuremburg Documents*, 1,918-PS.

long-term tasks: 'When the war is won . . . our work will start.' Then the S.S. must breed—'to present the whole of Europe with its leading class'. Himmler looked forward to the S.S. holding Germany's most easterly frontier, and pushing out to the Urals; he visualized an area where war would provide perpetual military training. 'I hope that our generation will successfully bring it about that every age-group has fought in the East, and that every one of our divisions spends a winter in the East every second or third year. Then we shall never grow soft. . . . Everyone will know that . . . he [the S.S. man] has contracted in writing that every second year he will not dance in Berlin or attend the Carnival in Munich, but that he will be posted to the Eastern frontier in an ice-cold winter. Then we will have a healthy *élite* for all time. Thus we will create the necessary conditions for the whole Germanic people and the whole of Europe, controlled, ordered, and led by us, the Germanic people, to be able in generations to stand the test in her battles of destiny against Asia, who will certainly break out again.'[1]

Himmler had spoken of 'the extermination of the Jewish race'. That this was aimed at in sober fact was admitted by the Camp Commandant of Auschwitz in Poland, Rudolf Höss. In his sworn statement at Nuremberg, Höss said: 'The "final solution" of the Jewish question meant the complete extermination of all Jews in Europe. I was ordered to establish extermination facilities at Auschwitz in June 1941. . . .' Of the numbers killed there, he said: 'I estimate that at least 2,500,000 victims were executed and exterminated there by gassing and burning, and at least another half-million succumbed to starvation and disease. . . . We executed about 400,000 Hungarian Jews alone at Auschwitz in the summer of 1944.'[2] The total of Jews murdered everywhere by the Nazis cannot be fixed definitely. S.S. Officers put the figures at 6 million—4 million were killed in the extermination camps, 2 million by other methods, mostly shooting by special squads.

[1] *Nuremberg Documents,* 1,919-PS.
[2] Ibid., 3,868-PS.

Himmler, however, was dissatisfied by the total—he thought it should be greater.[1]

In the summer of 1943 Hitler was arguing that 'all the rubbish of small nations [*Kleinstaaten-Gerümpel*] still existing in Europe must be liquidated as fast as possible. The aim of our struggle must be to create a unified Europe. The Germans alone can really organize Europe.'[2] In Hitler's words, scornful and boastful as they were, was implicit the tragedy of Europe and of Germany. With its central position, highly developed industrial system, and great qualities of organization, Germany is qualified to co-operate economically with the agricultural and raw-material producing countries of the Balkans and Russia. And there is an even deeper tragedy. For, as Goebbels reported, 'the *Führer* sometimes asks himself in a worried sort of way whether the white man is going to be able in the long run to maintain his supremacy over the tremendous reservoir of human beings in the East'.[3] He referred to the conquests of the Turks and of Genghis Khan, and their blows, in past history, at the heart of Europe. Our present predicament, over against Russia and China, lends added force to Hitler's words. But the Germans, by reason of their lust for power and domination, their lack of the capacity for conciliation and compromise, have again and again proved themselves fundamentally undesirable as leaders. 'I shall finish off definitely these small states, God help me', Hitler declared at a military conference.[4] A different Hitler might indeed have made a European New Order, the German people helping and co-operating with other European peoples materially less developed than itself. As it was, Hitler narrowly missed establishing a German New Order in which the other European peoples were exterminated or reduced to a lasting slavery.

[1] Affidavit of D. W. Höttl: *Nuremberg Documents*, 2,738-PS. There is an excellent short and clear account of 'The German Treatment of the Jews', by James Parker, in *Hitler's Europe (Survey of International Affairs, 1939-46)*, pp. 153-64.

[2] Quoted in the *Goebbels Diaries*, p. 279. It seemed from a later part of the conversation that, if he had won the war, Hitler would have destroyed the independence of Switzerland also. Cf. *Ciano's Diplomatic Papers*, p. 451, for another indication of the *Führer's* displeasure with Switzerland.

[3] *Goebbels Diaries*, p. 280.

[4] From a badly preserved record (an attempt had been made to burn the papers), probably of May 1943: see Gilbert, *Hitler directs His War*, p. 175.

CHAPTER XVI

WAR ON TWO FRONTS

FROM Alamein and Stalingrad onwards Nazi fortune was on the decline. The Allies had built up sufficient forces and armaments to check the Nazis' career, and they were adding to them steadily until the time would come for massive counter-attack and the final defeat of the German armies in the field. Hitler the strategist could only fight a long, delaying action—unless the Allies against him should themselves fall out, and to this end Nazi propaganda made the differences between the West and Soviet Russia a constant theme. Hitler, with a touch of that intuition which made him often aware of underlying political realities, forecast the 'Cold War'[1]— though it was his own action, in destroying the European balance of forces by plunging into war, which was to bring Russia into the heart of Europe. Of their Russian ally, the British must necessarily have their suspicions, for the British, as Göring put it, entered the war to prevent us from going into the East, but not to have the East come to the Atlantic'.[2] Hitler himself, however, though he withdrew more and more into himself and made few public appearances, still clung to his sense of mission, to his conviction that he was to make 'a historical revision on a unique scale'. The tide of fortune must change again for him, he thought, as it had changed in the past; Providence, which had preserved him on so many occasions, from the dangers of war and assassination, would show its power once more. Hitler placed great hope in new secret weapons—the flying bombs and rockets which were being prepared.

[1] Gilbert (editor), *Hitler directs His War*, pp. 117-18. Military conference of 27 January 1945.
[2] Ibid. Cf. B.B.C. monitoring report of 30 January 1944, quoted Bullock, *Hitler*, p. 664. In 1914 famous German professors, Haeckel and Eucken, had protested against 'England fighting with a half-Asiatic power against Germanism'. Quoted in *War and Democracy*, by R. W. Seton-Watson and others, p. 9.

So the war went on. The German soldiers fought with great discipline and courage, held up their enemies for long periods and hit back on occasion or whenever an Allied weakness showed itself. On the sea the relatively small German Navy had scored some remarkable triumphs, and the sinking by U-boats of Allied shipping in the Battle of the Atlantic had been a major and constant anxiety to Britain and a grave threat to our food supplies. In 1942, their most successful year, the U-boats sank 6,250,000 tons of Allied shipping; they might have won the war for Germany by cutting Britain's vital supply lines to America. But by mid-1943 Allied anti-submarine devices were sufficiently developed to give victory over the German submarines. The German sailors fought as bravely as the soldiers; out of 39,000 who served in the U-boats during the course of the war, 33,000 lost their lives. In the air the menace of the Luftwaffe was at length overcome, and Germany opened up in her turn to aerial bombardment. The first R.A.F. 1,000 bomber raid on Cologne took place on 30 May 1942. Writing in his *Diary* of the heavy raids on Cologne and also on Rostock and Lübeck, Ciano commented on 'the German population, accustomed as it has always been to hit, but never to be hit back. Which leads many Germans, who have devastated half Europe, to weep about the "brutality of the British, who make many innocent Prussian families homeless". The worst of it is that they really feel this way.'[1] As the war went on, the Allied air offensive was stepped up; both the scale of raids and their frequency and also the size and weight of bombs dropped were all much increased. British bombing by night and American bombing by day made life very hard for the Germans, hampered production and communication, and added to the growing shortages affecting the whole German economy. Goebbels noted in May 1943 the precision of the American bombing of Bremen, and commented: 'The population has the paralysing feeling that there really is no protection against such daylight attacks. This again shows that we are purely on the defensive in the air, and even that to a wholly inadequate extent. It will be

[1] *Ciano's Diary*, p. 463.

difficult to make up for our Air Force's failure.'[1] And the air attacks went on; Berlin itself came under heavy and repeated bombing raids.

As the tide of war turned against them, the German armies had also to contend with greater resistance movements in the occupied countries. Governments in exile had their headquarters in London, agents and supplies were parachuted into occupied Europe, and broadcasts by the B.B.C. were used to inform and to encourage. Resistance activities called down terrible reprisals from the S.S., as, for example, the destruction of Oradour in France and Lidice in Czechoslovakia, but the operational importance of the resistance was greatest in the Balkans and Russia. There the Germans had to devote whole divisions to the fight against the Partisans.

But there was no German collapse. The Germans fought hard wherever they were in contact with the enemy. They reacted strongly and effectively to the Allied invasion of Morocco and Algeria in November 1942. With speed and skill characteristic of earlier German operations, a large German force got into Tunisia by sea and air and won some considerable initial success. German troops were ordered into Unoccupied France and also proceeded to seize Corsica; they also occupied the French naval base of Toulon, but the French sailors scuttled the warships. In Tunisia the Germans captured the ports of Bizerta and Tunis before the advancing Allied troops could reach them, and the Allies were repulsed. The German forces were large enough to halt the Allied advance, but not to hold it up indefinitely. The irony of the position for the Germans was that whereas, if such strong forces had been spared earlier to reinforce Rommel, he might have won complete victory in Egypt, now all they could do was to win initial successes in a delaying action. The Germans built up a strong position in Tunisia, facing west. Rommel, after his defeat at Alamein, retreated across Libya to join them and took up positions in the old French Mareth Line, facing east against the advancing Eighth Army. Between January and May 1943 the Allied forces increased their pressure

[1] *The Goebbels Diaries*, p. 277.

on both sides, and slowly pushed the Germans back and
squeezed them in what was now a vast trap. On 7 May the
Germans had to give up Bizerta and Tunis. By 13 May the
last of the German forces were taken prisoner in the Cape
Bon Peninsula—making a total of over 250,000 men. Hitler
thus lost all power in North Africa, and the Mediterranean
was reopened to Allied shipping.

In Russia, too, the defeat at Stalingrad, though a disaster
for the Germans, resulted in no general collapse. The Germans were forced to retreat, but not routed. As a result of
Stalingrad, the Russian forces were able to move forward,
and the whole German position in the Caucasus was threatened in the rear. But the German army there extricated itself
in orderly fashion; part retreated through Rostov, and part
crossed the Kerch Strait into the Crimea. The German retreat
in the south weakened their hold in the north; the Russians
relieved the pressure on Leningrad, and in March captured
Rzhev and Vyazma, two strong German positions which had
threatened Moscow. Nevertheless, with the thaw, the Germans were still strong enough to strike hard into the Ukraine;
in March they recaptured the great city of Kharkov which
they had lost in February.

But in the summer of 1943 Germany suffered great blows,
in east and west. The tables were now turned. Instead of the
rest of the world waiting to see where the aggressors would
attack next, Germany waited for an attack on Fortress Europe.
The Russians had called loudly for a second front. Among
the Western Allies there were some differences of opinion,
however. The United States had agreed, though not without
hesitation, to give priority to the war with Germany as against
that with Japan. The Americans had then inclined towards
an early invasion of France. But the heavy Canadian casual-
ties in the large-scale raid on Dieppe (August, 1942) had
showed how hard invasion would be. Much greater preparation was, in fact, necessary, and eventually the British view
prevailed: to make Sicily a stepping-stone to invasion of Italy
and the attempt to knock Italy out of the war. The Germans
waited: they did not know where the expected attack would

be made. Hitler, in fact, thought the invasion would come in Sardinia.

On 10 July big Allied landings in Sicily took place, with air cover from Malta and Pantelleria (captured from the Italians in June). But the Germans fought hard and the island was not completely conquered until the middle of August. This time the German forces escaped capture. With the aid of air-cover they crossed the Straits of Messina and reached the Italian mainland. But meanwhile the Allied invasion of Sicily had had a resounding repercussion in Italian politics.[1] The Fascist Grand Council met on 24 July and appealed to the King to take over supreme command from the Duce. Next day Mussolini handed his resignation to the King, and was arrested while leaving the royal palace. The King entrusted Marshal Badoglio with the task of government, and Badoglio formed a Cabinet without Fascist ministers and dissolved the Fascist Party.

The Italian action was a slap in the face for Hitler. Not only did it presage the end of any effective Italian co-operation in the war, but it meant the fall of Hitler's comrade-in-arms, the man whom he had always thought of as the first Fascist victor over Communism, the first to purge a disordered democratic system and replace it by Fascist order, and as a man marked, like himself, to play a great historical role in laying the foundations of the New Order. Now Mussolini was gone —without resistance, and without a blow struck in his defence. It was a blow to Hitler personally; it might also be a dangerous object lesson to the German people as to how easily a dictator might be removed. But Hitler did not panic. He realized at once that Badoglio's public statement that Italy would continue to fight at Germany's side was worthless. New German divisions were sent across the Alps, and those already in Italy were regrouped to meet emergencies. The German people were uneasy and disturbed, but there was little the Nazis could say to alleviate their fears—but Hitler ordered Himmler to be ready with severe police measures in case of visible

[1] In January 1943, an Italian colonel back from the Russian front had already painted the darkest picture to Ciano, saying that the only way to save Italy would be a separate peace: *Ciano's Diary*, p. 551.

unrest. Even Goebbels could not speak openly: 'What can one say in the present situation? . . . And we naturally can't say anything about the steps we are taking.'[1]

On 3 September the British Eighth Army landed on the Italian mainland, in Calabria, and on the 9th the Americans at Salerno. On the 8th it was made known that the Italians had signed an armistice. The treachery of the Italians, though expected, was a bitter pill to the Nazis. As Goebbels summed it up: 'The Duce will enter history as the last Roman, but behind his massive figure a gipsy people has gone to rot.'[2] At once the German counter-measures came into operation: the Germans took over control in Rome and disarmed the Italian forces in Italy, as well as in the south of France and the Balkans. The King and Badoglio escaped from the capital, and took refuge with the Allies; the remaining ships of the Italian fleet sailed to Malta. The German forces in the south of Italy put up a strong resistance to the Allied invading armies, and although these made considerable advances and occupied Naples on 1 October, a little further to the north the Germans succeeded in establishing a strong defence line from sea to sea across the peninsula. And here for the time being there was stalemate— in spite of the daring rescue of Mussolini by the S.S. leader, Skorzeny, the Italian declaration of war on Germany by the Badoglio Government on 13 October, and the Allied attempt in January 1944 to turn the whole German position by a landing at Anzio behind their lines. Mussolini himself was a broken man, and showed little interest in resistance to events. Only under Hitler's driving power was Mussolini persuaded to put himself at the head of a new, specially created Italian puppet government, and to punish former Fascist leaders— among them Ciano, who was shot. For the time Hitler's fierce determination had saved the situation in Italy and prevented what might have been disaster.

While Hitler was dealing with Italy, however, the heaviest blows they had so far felt were falling on the Germans in Russia. The Russians defeated a German attack on the Kursk salient in July, and then went over to the offensive. A Russian

[1] *The Goebbels Diaries*, p. 322.   [2] Ibid., p. 349.

offensive in summer was a novelty; previously it had been the Germans who attacked in summer, the Russians counter-attacking only in winter, when the Russian cold gave them the advantage. And now their offensive became a big advance. In August the Russians captured Orel and Kharkov, in September Bryansk and Smolensk; they reoccupied Kiev in November, and by their advance along the Black Sea coast cut off considerable numbers of Germans in the Crimea. The Germans counter-attacked and checked them temporarily, but by the end of December, and in January 1944, the Russians were again advancing, and Russian pressure continued throughout the winter. In January, Leningrad, partially ringed around by the Germans since the autumn of 1941, was at last freed from the danger of capture; the main line to Moscow was reopened. All along the front, and over immense distances, the Russians were advancing. Early in 1944 Russian forces approached the former frontiers of Poland and Rumania.

The German soldiers in the field fought on bravely; nowhere was there panic or collapse. At home the German workers went steadily to their long and arduous labours in factory and workshop, sometimes underground. As soon as a raid was over streets were cleared, public services got going again, and essential repairs put in operation. German discipline and organization seemed proof against every test. The German generals, most of them, realized that the war was lost, but they performed their daily tasks; at the same time a number of them were in touch with opposition leaders, who were still planning the removal of Hitler and were considering the possibility of peace by an approach to either West or East. Many realized that such a move was the only means left of saving Germany. But outwardly the show of national unity was maintained. Among the Party leaders, Göring had given himself too much to luxury and pomp, and was no longer his former self; Martin Bormann, as head of the Party Chancellery and secretary to Hitler, was a powerful figure and something of a rival to Himmler. These men, and Goebbels, were personally loyal to the *Führer*, and, in any case, their fate was inextricably bound up with his. A new man was the architect, Albert Speer, whom Hitler had made Minister for Armament Production; he proved himself one of the ablest of Hitler's servants, and did whatever was possible, under the strain placed on the economic system by the heavy bombing, to organize manpower and factories to meet the voracious demands of total war. But he, like the generals, realized that Hitler would destroy Germany rather than admit defeat, and contemplated removing him—yet Speer felt the effect of Hitler's personal magnetism, and came to regard him as Germany's inevitable destiny, for good or ill.[1]

Germany still had great military power at her command, so long as the German soldier was prepared to fight and die and the German civilian to spend his nights in the air-raid shelter. And Hitler was determined to fight on. More and more he became a recluse, but he did not deviate from his purpose to fight to final victory. Perhaps, inwardly, he realized that the logic of events was now against him. His forces everywhere had been pushed back; he was himself kept going by quack doctors and their drugs. During 1943 Hitler had developed a trembling of the left arm and the left leg. He made few public appearances and few speeches. The old days were over. And now that his fortunes were failing, Hitler's mind went back more and more often to the early days, the days of Party triumph and his spectacular rise to power. Between the attack on Russia in 1941 and November 1944, Hitler spent the greater part of his time at his military headquarters, Wolfsschanze, in East Prussia. His life was a monotonous one; the most important daily event was the *Führer's* Conference each day at noon, which stretched on into the afternoon, and at which the military leaders and others made their reports and Hitler took decisions. Apart from his military conferences, there were his simple vegetarian meals, his tea and cakes, the company of his secretaries, adjutants, and his Alsatian dog, Blondi. 'It is tragic', Goebbels thought, 'that the *Führer* has become such a recluse and leads such an

[1] Speer's Evidence, *Nuremberg Proceedings*, Vol. XVI, pp. 493-504, and Vol. XXII, pp. 405-7.

unhealthy life. He never gets out into the fresh air. He does not relax. He sits in his bunker, worries and broods.'[1] Göring thought the *Führer* had aged by fifteen years. While Hitler devoted himself to the military leadership, there was, Goebbels complained, 'a lack of leadership in our domestic and foreign policy'. He thought Rosenberg and Ribbentrop unequal to their tasks. 'Everybody', wrote Goebbels in March 1943, 'does or leaves undone what he pleases, because there is no strong authority anywhere. The Party goes its own way and won't let anyone interfere.'[2] But, in spite of all, Hitler went on living in his own little world, still apparently believing in his mission, still outwardly confident that he must succeed, still determined to fight on—and, most extraordinary of all, still able to persuade others to follow and obey him, until the end.

Meanwhile, the Western Allies were preparing new attacks which would face Hitler with war on two fronts, war on the greatest scale, which ultimately, though still only after a long and bitter struggle, would press the Germans from west and east until Americans and Russians met in the heart of Germany. Stalin, Roosevelt, and Churchill conferred at Teheran in 1943, and made plans for 1944, when Germany would be attacked on each front: in the east the Russians would make a major offensive; in the west, the Allied army in Italy would attack, and, also in the west, the Allies would launch a new invasion.

The Allied blows fell in the summer of 1944. The first big attack was in Italy on 12 May. After a three-day battle, General Alexander broke through the German lines; Monte Cassino, which the Germans had so long defended against the heaviest artillery and aerial bombardment, was lost; Kesselring's forces were pushed slowly back. On 4 June the Germans abandoned Rome, and the Allies entered the city —the first European capital to be liberated.

At long last the Allies launched their main attack in the west. All through the spring and early summer of 1944, the German positions in the west were subjected to continual bombing; the air over southern England and northern France

[1] *The Goebbels Diaries*, p. 200.   [2] Ibid., pp. 200-1.

was hardly silent by day or night as the great air flotillas swept over. The Allied air offensive was aimed at ensuring air superiority, putting German radar out of action, and systematically disrupting enemy rail and road transport. Vital bridges were knocked out at the last moment, to prevent the Germans making a speedy 'build-up' of their forces at the invasion point before the Allies could land reinforcements and consolidate their positions. On 6 June the invasion took place, in the bay of the Seine between Caen and the Cherbourg Peninsula. Under a vast 'umbrella' of aircraft, over 4,000 ships took part in the crossing of the Channel; airborne divisions were towed over by glider. Assault troops went ashore and, when the beaches were secure, prefabricated harbours were set in position and used for unloading. A large measure of initial surprise and success was achieved. The defence of the whole western coast of Europe was no easy task in any case, and, owing to the prolonged strain of the war in Russia, the German troops in the west were not as numerous, nor the defences of the so-called Atlantic Wall as strong, as they might have been. Coastal batteries and beach defences were, to some extent, neutralized by the air bombing. Nor did the Germans foretell the time and place of the landings. It had been felt that the invaders would make for ports, and therefore a strong German force was kept back, north of the Seine, for the expected task of defending the Calais area. The Allied success in establishing powerful forces on the coast of France faced Hitler with crisis. He in turn blamed his generals, and replaced the Commander-in-chief in the west, Rundstedt, by Kluge. But no general could now hold up indefinitely the Allied consolidation and advance in the west.

Invasion of Normandy on the west was followed by a great new Russian offensive. The Russians attacked on 23 June, and moved forward with spectacular success. The Germans lost twenty-five divisions out of fifty on the central front. Russian forces pushed on towards Latvia and Lithuania, and threatened to isolate the German divisions further north in Estonia. Red forces also advanced south of the Pripet Marshes.

The whole German position in eastern Europe was threatened.

While crisis threatened in east and west, a bomb exploded under Hitler's table when he was conducting a military conference at his Wolfsschanze H.Q. in East Prussia.[1] At last the German opposition struck in a deliberate plan to kill Hitler, and provide an alternative government which could approach the enemy with a view to peace; at last, after its long hesitations and frequent frustration, the opposition made a spectacular attack on the *Führer* himself.

The German opposition, however, was not, and never had been, a closely-knit, organized body or one resting on wide popular support; it consisted instead of various small groups and individuals, but among them were important people, some bearing famous names. These Germans of the resistance groups acted with the greatest courage, but their task was one of cruel difficulty—to struggle in secret against an all-powerful and popular dictator. As soon as discovered by the Gestapo, anti-Nazis were ruthlessly suppressed. The brother and sister, Hans and Sophie Scholl, who had organized a student demonstration in Munich University in 1943, were executed, as were others also at this time. Then there was the *Solfkreis*, the group around Frau Solf, widow of a former Ambassador to Tokyo; this group was broken up early in 1944, some were later executed, and Frau Solf herself, after brutal and exhausting interrogation, was in prison or concentration camp until the end when, in the confusion of defeat, she narrowly escaped with her life. There was the Kreisau circle, so called from a country estate where it met, under the leadership of Count Helmuth von Moltke, who paid with his life. Two others belonging to this group, also executed, were Count Peter Yorck von Wartenburg, of an old and cultured family, and the former Rhodes Scholar at Oxford, Adam von Trott zu Solz. There were many others—individuals: some were ex-ambassadors or diplomats, ex-ministers, lawyers, Catholic and Protestant clergy, and a number of generals, including Field-Marshal von Witzleben. Active throughout—and coming

[1] A detailed account is given by J. W. Wheeler-Bennett, *The Nemesis of Power*, Part III, Chapter 7.

nearest to the description of leaders—were Beck and Gördeler. There was, however, no close identity of view among these different groups and individuals: some did not even want violence against Hitler, others favoured approaching Himmler or some other Nazi leader, some looked to opening negotiations in the East, others looked to the Western Allies. Some were genuine idealists, opposed to Nazism on principle; others, particularly some of the more nationalist and militarist, were against Hitler because he had failed; some of these latter looked to a reorganization of the military leadership which might yet make some partial salvage of Germany's fortunes. But most, especially after Stalingrad, felt that, somehow, Hitler must be removed. There was, however, among the conspirators a strong preoccupation with the moral issue: were they justified in removing by violence the head of the state? It was the old German reverence for the State, for authority, not merely the question of murder.

Several attempts were planned, even put into operation. In March 1943 General von Tresckow and Lieutenant von Schlabrendorff managed to place a bomb in Hitler's plane. But the bomb failed to go off: Schlabrendorff, when he heard of the *Führer's* safe arrival, flew after him and, with exquisite coolness and courage, retrieved the bomb, dismantled it without discovery, and lived to tell the tale.[1]

Later in 1943 a new man began to make himself felt in opposition circles. He was Colonel Count von Stauffenberg, of an old Catholic family, who has been described as 'a natural soldier and a natural leader . . . not only a great man, but a charming one'.[2] He was prepared himself, although badly wounded in North Africa and handicapped by the loss of a hand and an eye, to assassinate Hitler. He made his plans in conjunction with the other men of the opposition; in the background were Beck and Gördeler, who were to form a provisional government on Hitler's death, with Beck as Regent and Witzleben as Commander-in-chief of the Army. Time pressed in 1944, as invasion became more and more threatening:

---

[1] Fabian von Schlabrendorff, *Revolt against Hitler*.
[2] W. Görlitz, *The German General Staff*, p. 432.

if Germany were to be in a position to bargain, Hitler should be assassinated *before* the Allies invaded in the west. But the invasion came first. Then the Gestapo got on the track of the conspiracy—and a number of arrests were made in July; Gördeler had to hide. Stauffenberg was on edge with the strain—with his bomb in readiness—but two occasions in July at the last moment turned out to be unfavourable. Then on 20 July Stauffenberg flew to Hitler's military conference at the Wolfsschanze, set the fuse to his bomb, shook hands with Hitler, and put his briefcase, which contained the bomb, under the table. Then, on the excuse of a telephone call, he left the room. A few moments later, at about 12.30 p.m., there was a loud explosion, roof and walls were blown out, and the hut disappeared in smoke and flame. Convinced that Hitler was dead, Stauffenberg got away in the confusion and took a plane back to Berlin.

In the capital the conspirators had gathered at the buildings of the General Staff in the Bendlerstrasse, in the office of General Olbricht. Beck was there, Witzleben, Yorck von Wartenburg, Gisevius, and others. A wide network had been built up by the conspirators among the higher Army officers and the various commanders. On the news that Hitler was dead, the group in the Bendlerstrasse began to put its plans into operation; but there was some confusion and uncertainty: it had naturally been impossible to arrange beforehand a fixed time for the assassination, and Gördeler, who was on the run from the Gestapo, could not be reached at all. At Hitler's Wolfsschanze H.Q. there was also confusion: at first it was thought that a bomb had been dropped by an aircraft. One man was killed, several mortally wounded; Keitel and Jodl escaped. Hitler was hurt—burns, shock and broken eardrums —but not seriously; the same afternoon he was able to receive Mussolini, who by a strange fate was scheduled to arrive that very day, and point out to the Italian with vivid demonstration that Providence had intervened to preserve the *Führer* for the fulfilment of his mission.

The crucial fact was that Hitler was alive—and that fact alone would most likely have spelt the failure of the conspiracy. But the conspirators failed in another matter also. They had planned to destroy the communications centre at Hitler's H.Q., and so isolate it. But the officer who was to do this was unsuccessful. Thus Keitel was able at once to send out messages saying that Hitler was alive and safe. When the news became known the commanders in the field, those who commanded troops, drew back in alarm, and Beck, a retired general, and the others in the Berlin headquarters offices were left stranded—a group of men without power behind them. Beck, who was in poor health, was somewhat overwhelmed by the situation, but Stauffenberg took charge, and telephoned desperately to the provincial commanders for support. But all was in vain. Only in Paris did the Military Governor win a temporary success. But Field-Marshal Kluge, commander-in-chief in the West, would not openly support him now that Hitler was known to be alive. Once more the loyalty of Germans to Hitler was what destroyed the opposition: Kluge feared that, in the new situation, he could not rely on his officers and troops.[1] The conspirators in Berlin failed to get troops, and by evening their situation was desperate. Officers loyal to Hitler made counter-moves. Troops under a certain Major Remer came to suppress the conspiracy, and the opposition leaders were disarmed. General Fromm, commander of the home army, who had known of the plot and would have joined in had the assassination succeeded, tried to save his own skin by getting the opposition leaders out of the way before the S.S. arrived to ask too many questions. He compelled Beck to shoot himself, and, when the wretched man only wounded himself, he was finished off by an N.C.O. Then Fromm set up a court-martial, and condemned Stauffenberg, Olbricht, and two other officers. During the night they were executed, in the quadrangle outside, by a firing squad. As a German writer has described the grim scene, 'Stauffenberg cried out, "Long live Free Germany!" but the soldiers

[1] H. Speidel, *We Defended Normandy*, pp. 131-2. Cf. B. H. Liddell Hart, *The Other Side of the Hill*, p. 26. German generals reported to Captain Liddell Hart, after the war, the great confidence of the troops in Hitler, unlike the situation in 1916-18 when Socialist propaganda had spread the idea that the war was merely the Kaiser's war.

did their duty in sullen silence. They understood nothing of the meaning of these words.'[1]

'They understood nothing of the meaning of these words.' That was the bitter truth. The brave men of the German resistance gave their lives—but the German masses were unmoved. Hitler lived—and while he lived the people obeyed. They heard his voice on the wireless shortly after midnight of the fateful day. For the Germans who had tried and failed there was no respite. Terrible vengeance followed on all those implicated in the plot. Indeed, those who had been summarily executed were fortunate—for long agony awaited many of the others. Witzleben, Yorck von Wartenburg, and several generals and other officers were executed by slow hanging from meat-hooks; the execution was filmed, and the film shown to Hitler in his private cinema. Gördeler was caught and hanged. Fromm did not save himself by the hurried court-martial; he was beheaded. A list of those executed, of 160 names, has been compiled, but the list is admittedly incomplete, and many more were executed.[2] There was also a number of suicides—the great Rommel, also implicated, though unconscious in hospital at the actual time after R.A.F. fighters had bombed his car, was given, and took, the choice of suicide rather than trial involving the disgrace of his family. And many, many more suspects, families, and friends of the conspirators, including Schacht and Halder, the former Chief of Staff, were arrested and put into concentration camps. Hitler, the corporal, took his own full vengeance on the generals. Himmler was made commander of the home army, and the tank general, Guderian, who had not been involved in the conspiracy, was made Chief of the General Staff. As a non-political, straightforward soldier, Guderian now did his best to reorganize the German commands for the grim task of continuing the war—but his non-political attitude did not prevent his ordering the closest association of Army and Party and the indoctrination of the Army with Nazi beliefs by staff officers.

[1] W. Görlitz, *The German General Staff*, p. 473. There are slightly different accounts of the details of the final scenes. Cf. Wheeler-Bennett, p. 661.

[2] Wheeler-Bennett, *The Nemesis of Power*, pp. 744-52. A pamphlet, *Verräter oder Patrioten*, by K. Strölin (1952), speaks of 4,980 victims.

Once more, then, there was no general collapse of the German fighting forces. The war went on. After their long retreat on the eastern front, the Germans again stood their ground, this time in front of East Prussia and Warsaw. Inside that city the Polish underground movement, which had been active throughout the war, rose against the Germans on 1 August. But after some weeks of desperate fighting, the rising was crushed. The Warsaw Poles looked, in political sympathy, to London rather than Moscow, and the Russians, not far away, gave no help.[1]

In the west, the Allied forces on the French coast were preparing to break out, and the Germans were making use of what time was still left to them to use their coastal launching stations to hurl their new projectiles—the V1 (flying bombs) and V2 (rockets)—against England. Had the Germans had more time to develop and use these weapons, they might have proved a serious threat. But the Allies' advance was soon to clear the coastal areas. The Americans on 25 July broke through the Germans, westwards; General Patton's tanks pushed on to the Loire, cutting off Brittany, and then wheeled back, and in the Falaise pocket pressed the Germans against the British and Canadians to the north. Here at Falaise, a kind of French Stalingrad, the Germans suffered immense losses by bombing and artillery bombardment, estimated by 20 August at 240,000 killed or wounded, 210,000 taken prisoner, and 3,500 guns and 1,500 tanks destroyed or captured.[2] Hitler had set his face firmly against retreat while there was still time; now he had lost France. The German forces were pushed back across the Seine; Paris was liberated on 23 August. At the same time the F.F.I. (Free French Forces of the Interior) were active in many parts of the country, and on 15 August a new Allied army had landed in the south of France and was advancing up the Rhône Valley. In the north British and Canadian forces crossed the Seine and moved on into Belgium; in the first days of September they

---

[1] There is a detailed account, *The Secret Army*, by its commander, General T. Bor-Komorowski.

[2] Montgomery, *Normandy to the Baltic*, p. 112.

captured Brussels, Antwerp, and Liége. The Americans advanced to the south-east of the British and reached German soil on 11 September; by the 14th Aachen was under shellfire. The German front in France had crumbled, and it seemed for a moment as if the Allies might push on and smash their way into Germany. But the failure of the British air-landing at Arnhem, the object of which was to make possible a crossing of the Rhine in the north and the turning of the whole German Siegfried defences, showed what reserves of strength the Germans still possessed. Once more they stabilized their positions, running roughly along the German frontier, and gained a respite for the winter. Indeed, as Lord Montgomery puts it: 'After his defeat in Normandy, the enemy had made a remarkable recovery.'[1]

Then in December the Germans struck back hard. At dawn on 16 December Hitler launched an offensive through the Ardennes. He caught the Allied commanders by surprise, and fog helped to conceal the advance of the German troops. The Germans struck towards Liége, with the further object of capturing the port of Antwerp and splitting the Allied forces, as in 1940. The plan was ingenious and carefully prepared, though Hitler's generals warned him of the difficulties of carrying it through. Actually it was beyond his strength at this stage of the war. But perhaps the attempt was worth making; careful defence could only postpone Germany's defeat. Hitler preferred to gamble on the off-chance of the attack bringing a great German triumph at the expenses of Americans and British. At first the Germans made substantial gains; it was an anxious moment for the Allies. But they collected themselves. The Germans were checked, and then turned back. It was their last offensive.

As the winter went on the Russian advance continued through Rumania, Bulgaria, and Jugoslavia. The Germans resisted grimly, wherever they could make a stand; Budapest held out until February 1945. But, further north, the Russians made three great attacks in January, and poured into Poland. Warsaw was captured, and the Russians—their forces

[1] Montgomery, *Normandy to the Baltic*, p. 181.

estimated at 3 million—moved on into German territory. Now the Germans paid bitterly, and in the same kind, for their savage triumphs of the earlier years. The Russian forces moved into the materially advanced lands of Germany, and brought devastation—murder, rape, and a trail of destroyed and burning villages. Terrible fear gripped the German women—fear of the Mongol beasts from central Asia. Columns of refugees moved out of the threatened cities and towns, though the city of Königsberg was fanatically defended; in the January cold the refugees trudged on foot and in horse-drawn wagons. Red planes bombed and machine-gunned the roads. Ships which carried thousands of refugees were sunk by Russian submarines. Innocent and guilty suffered alike. There were scenes of unspeakable horror, the stories of which arouse pity. But one must remember Poland and Greece, Warsaw, Belgrade and Rotterdam, and the vast destruction Hitler had wrecked on the Russians themselves. Now there was vengeance.

From mid-January on Hitler himself lived in his own quarters at the Reich Chancellery in Berlin. Here he lived more than ever out of touch with reality—still thinking that determination and attack would win him great victories. The retreating German armies stood their ground once more along the Oder, to attempt to defend Berlin. But by 23 April the Russians approached the capital. Vienna had fallen a few days earlier, and now Berlin became the scene of the last of the sieges, marked by bitter street fighting. Hitler's Chancellery was soon under fire.

In the west the Allies were fighting their final battles. They broke through the Siegfried Line and crossed the Rhine in March: at Remagen the Americans found a railway bridge that had not been blown up. In April the Americans reached the Elbe, and on the 25th at Torgau, on the Elbe, between Berlin and Leipzig, Americans and Russians met. The German armies in the field had been defeated, and were now being pressed inwards into the heart of Germany in a vast movement which must bring the unconditional surrender which the Allies demanded.

PART SIX

The End

CHAPTER XVII

THE END OF THE NAZIS

THE closing scenes of the Nazi régime were marked with a special violence and horror, a bizarre and macabre character of their own. As the enemy armies approached from east and west, Germany was more and more battered and broken. Yet Hitler, amid all the scenes of horror, retained his personal ascendancy. While he lived his personality was supreme.

The mighty pressure of its enemies on either side was too great for the German Reich. That was the simple truth, though German generals have attributed much of the blame to Hitler's interference, and in so doing have indicated a number of contributory causes of German failure. Thus General Warlimont has enumerated reasons for German collapse.[1] There was that 'chaos of leadership in the Leader State'—the confusion in a totalitarian State in which the dictator was often remote from the scene of action and had even become remote from reality, and in which rival Party chiefs built up their own, often jealous and conflicting, power complexes. Then it was felt by the military that Hitler, as a layman, was wrong in taking over supreme military command. The Luftwaffe had been allowed to decline—so that during the invasion of Normandy the Allies had a crushing air superiority. Perhaps most serious of all was the policy of inelastic defence. Ever since the first winter in Russia, Hitler, who had once believed in mobility and subtle methods of warfare, had followed a fixed policy of standing fast. Thus, by the closing stage of the war, the Germans had battleworthy divisions scattered and with little to do in many secondary theatres of war—in the Baltic, in Scandinavia, in Greece and the islands, and in fortified cities and areas in western France. If these divisions had been withdrawn earlier,

[1] Summarized by W. Görlitz, *The German General Staff*, p. 452.

if all France south of the Seine had been abandoned, if the line in Russia had been withdrawn and shortened, Hitler could have concentrated his still large available forces for a much stronger defence of Germany itself. But, of course, some of these failings were the inevitable result of a two-front war—indeed, of a many-front war—and it is difficult to believe that the final outcome would have been different so long as the Allies remained united and kept up their pressure on both sides.

General Speidel has made similar criticisms. Of the weakness of leadership during the invasion of Normandy, he says: 'The *Führer* and the High Command of the armed forces directed operations from Berchtesgaden in the first weeks of the invasion, and then from East Prussia. There were grave disadvantages in these distances, particularly as air communications were impossible . . . a chaotic muddle in the chain of command, entirely incompatible with the *"Führer* principle", hampered any attempt to give clear-cut orders and led to divided authority.' Then 'instead of confidence between officers and men, there was compulsion, the lie, political trials and courts-martial'. Speidel thinks there should have been early strategic retreat and drastic shortening of the line in Russia, in Italy, and in France. 'But Hitler, unable to compromise in any of his activities, devoid of any sober thought, ordered the troops to hold their ground at any cost, and abandoned 200,000 men in his "fortresses".' Hitler, Speidel maintains in his most damning criticism, should have recognized the logic of events, and brought the war to an end in the summer of 1944. Hitler, however, 'deceived others, but he deceived himself most terribly of all when he tried to veil the true facts and raise false hopes in his "miracle weapons" instead of facing the political consequences of defeat'. Even in 1944 'Hitler wildly underestimated his Western enemies. . . . Hitler lived upon his rank imagination without any measure of sense, exaggerating his will-power to himself and possessed by a limitless frenzy. . . . Adolf Hitler gave way to illusions, quite consciously refusing to recognize that the war was lost.'[1]

[1] H. Speidel, *We Defended Normandy*, pp. 167-73: quotations from his final chapter, 'After the Battle'.

'The Allied cause', Speidel admits, 'was better than ours. The transgressions of Hitler had created a moral vacuum in the German forces', while, at the same time, 'the Allied armies resembled a massive line that pushed their enemy backwards —in fact, a steamroller that was slowly but surely to crush him.' Yet the German soldier fought on with the greatest courage and tenacity on every front. The manner in which the German troops, late in 1944, withdrew from Greece in the face of British invasion, and struggled through hostile and mountainous Jugoslavia to Hungary was a demonstration of how good German troops still were. But their courage 'was misused and sacrificed for a phantom'.[1] The soldier fought on—that was the miracle of Hitler, the sign of his lasting power over the Germans.

'Fight on'—that was Hitler's fixed determination. At the end of August 1944 he told three of his generals:

> All of the coalitions in history have disintegrated sooner or later. The only thing is to wait for the right moment, no matter how hard it is. Since the year 1941 it has been my task not to lose my nerve, under any circumstances. . . .
>
> I think it's pretty obvious that this war is no pleasure for me. For five years I have been separated from the world. . . . I live only for the purpose of leading this fight, because I know that if there is not an iron will behind it this battle cannot be won. . . .
>
> If necessary, we'll fight on the Rhine. It doesn't make any difference. Under all circumstances we will continue this battle until, as Frederick the Great said, one of our damned enemies gets too tired to fight any more.[2]

Before the Ardennes offensive, Hitler, in the presence of Keitel and Jodl, spoke to the commanders, who had first been carefully stripped of weapons and briefcases, of the political antagonisms among the enemies opposed to Germany: 'If now we can deliver a few more heavy blows, then at any moment this artificially bolstered common front may collapse with a gigantic clap of thunder. . . . Wars are finally decided

---

[1] H. Speidel, *We Defended Normandy*, pp. 167-73.
[2] F. Gilbert (editor), *Hitler Directs His War*, p. 106.

by one side or the other recognizing that they cannot be won. We must allow no movement to pass without showing the enemy that, whatever he does, he can never reckon on a capitulation. Never! Never!'[1] On 28 December, when the German offensive had been checked, Hitler still urged his commanders to new attacks: 'We shall yet master Fate.'[2]

Then, at last when everything was closing in on him, Hitler ordered a policy of scorched earth in Germany itself. Everything in the enemy's path was to be destroyed.[3] If victory was lost, now was the time for final destruction. Hitler gave his orders to Speer, though Speer avoided carrying them out. 'If the War were lost', Speer reported Hitler as saying in the middle of March, 'the nation would also perish. This fate was inevitable. There was no necessity to take into consideration the basis which the people would need to continue a most primitive existence. On the contrary, it would be better to destroy these things ourselves, because this nation will have proved to be the weaker one and the future belongs solely to the stronger Eastern nation. Besides, those who would remain after the battle were only the inferior ones, for the good ones had been killed.'[4] Hitler spoke now as he had spoken in conversation with Rauschning before he was in power: 'We may be destroyed, but if we are, we shall drag a world with us— a world in flames.'[5] The news of the death of Roosevelt on 12 April was seized on by Hitler and Goebbels, for a moment, as a sign that the tide of fortune was turning. But, in reality, nothing had changed to Germany's advantage. The extreme pressure from east and west continued.

While everything he had striven for was disappearing, Hitler's will-power and sense of the historic alone remained. His health and physical powers had seriously declined, and there was an intense nervous strain upon him—so much so that he talked of suicide. During the autumn of 1944 he had

[1] Quoted by Chester Wilmot, *The Struggle for Europe*, p. 578, from the collected fragments of the record of the conference.

[2] Gilbert, p. 174.

[3] Speer's Evidence, *Nuremberg Proceedings*, Vol. XVI, p. 488.

[4] Ibid., p. 498.

[5] Rauschning, *Hitler Speaks*, p. 15.

to spend periods in bed, and in October he underwent an operation for the removal of a polyp on his vocal chords. But he pulled himself together again, and returned to his task. This strange man was alone, without friends and ordinary family relationships. 'His path through the world', writes General Guderian, 'was a solitary one and he followed it alone, with only his gigantic plans for company. He turned night into day with his conferences; to send him to sleep, to waken him, to keep going, he relied on drugs.' When in the middle of January 1945 he moved into residence in the Reich Chancellery, with its substantial underground bunkers, he was a broken man. Guderian, and others, have described his physical condition. 'It was no longer simply his left hand but the whole left side of his body that trembled. . . . He now walked awkwardly, he stooped more than ever, and his gestures were both jerky and slow.'[1] At the same time he was subject to terrifying fits of rage. 'His fists raised, his cheeks flushed with rage, his whole body trembling, the man stood there in front of me', as Guderian described one such occasion, 'beside himself with fury and having lost all self-control. After each outburst of rage Hitler would stride up and down the carpet edge, then suddenly stop immediately before me and hurl his next accusation in my face. He was almost screaming, his eyes seemed about to pop out of his head and the veins stood out on his temples.'[2] No doubt such behaviour was his reaction to the growth of an inner realization that all was lost. But his determination not to surrender endured, and with it his determination to destroy. If he was to fall, then all should fall with him. All that was great and worthwhile about Germany he identified with himself—so great were his egoism and megalomania. He could not conceive of a Germany which could survive without him.

At the eleventh hour it became clear to Hitler himself that the end was at hand. Most of his last month he spent underground. Conferences of the Nazi leaders and the Service chiefs

[1] H. Guderian, *Panzer Leader*, p. 443. Cf. G. Boldt, *In the Shelter with Hitler*, Chapter I. Captain Boldt was one of the German officers interrogated by Mr. Trevor-Roper.
[2] Guderian, p. 414.

took place in the Bunker. Plans were in operation for a with-drawal to Bavaria, where the Nazis could make a last stand in the 'redoubt' of the mountains around Berchtesgaden. Time pressed, if they were to get away from doomed Berlin. But on 22 April Hitler decided at a stormy conference that he would remain in the capital to the end. Those who wished could go to the south, but he would fight on, and then, at the last moment, shoot himself. That was his decision, and to that decision he adhered.

Now the last, gloomy days in the underground fortress of the *Führerbunker*, fifty feet below the level of the chancellery, were reached.[1] Above, by night and day there were the air-raids, and, for the last few days, the Chancellery was under Russian shell-fire. Below, with the *Führer* and his companion Eva Braun, were Goebbels and his wife and children, a num-ber of adjutants and officers, personal attendants, secretaries, and S.S. guards, living in an atmosphere of high psychological tension. Conferences went on in the Bunker, but Hitler's state· of mind was uncertain. He had determined to destroy him-self, and he would destroy anyone else who crossed his path. Now even the highest Nazi chiefs could fall under suspicion, and into peril of execution. Göring had left for the south and, learning of Hitler's fateful decision to kill himself in Berlin, sent a wireless message asking if he, as Hitler's successor designate, was to take over 'the total leadership of the Reich'. There is no evidence that Göring was disloyal, but Hitler, in his disordered state of mind, took Göring's action as treachery; he dismissed the Reichsmarschall from his high offices, and ordered his arrest for treason. But worse was to follow: on the evening of 28 April a message reached Hitler stating that Himmler was attempting to make peace terms through the Swede, Count Bernadotte. This was true—though Himmler's efforts, in this respect, not unnaturally, came to nought. Hitler at once decided on vengeance: a plane was ordered to make the attempt to get out of Berlin, and in it

[1] The story is told in detail by H. Trevor-Roper, *The Last Days of Hitler*. As an Army Intelligence officer, Mr. Trevor-Roper investigated the circumstances of Hitler's end. There is also an American account, based on personal investiga-tion and interrogation; see M. A. Musmanno, *Ten Days to Die*.

were officers to arrest Himmler. Himmler's S.S. liaison officer with the *Führer* had tried to slip away out of the Bunker now that the final scene was in sight, but he was followed into the city, arrested, brought back to the Chancellery, and finally executed. This was Fegelein, and he was not saved by the fact that he was married to a sister of Eva Braun, the *Führer's* friend and companion.

There was still one surprise to come—strangely out of keeping, yet, amid so much that was extraordinary, accepted by those present without difficulty. Hitler got married. And so, after the war was over, there came to light a story which had been carefully concealed in the great days. Hitler, the all-powerful on his lonely pedestal, had, after all, had a mistress. Not a breath of scandal had touched the *Führer*, yet for many years he had kept Eva Braun, at first discreetly in a small house in Munich, later installed in the Berghof itself, but she came very seldom to Berlin and did not appear with Hitler in public. When, however, her sister married Himmler's liaison officer with Hitler, Eva's status in the *Führer's* circle became easier, for she could be introduced to visitors as Frau Fegelein's sister. Eva, who had worked in Hoffmann's photographer's shop, was not outstanding; she took no interest in, and did not interfere in, politics. She was a simple, attractive type of German girl—blonde, pretty, and good-natured, a beautiful physical specimen, good at skiing and climbing. and a fine swimmer and diver. Most at home in a swimming costume sunning herself at the Berghof, she provided a background of relaxation for Hitler.[1] Above all, she was loyal. On 15 April she came, of her own accord, to the menaced capital, determined to share Hitler's fate. 'Poor, poor Adolf', she was heard to say, 'deserted by everyone, betrayed by all. Better that 10,000 others die than that he should be lost to Germany.'[2] But now that Hitler had decided to end his life,

---

[1] Trevor-Roper, *The Last Days of Hitler*, pp. 104-7, and the film, *The Eva Braun and Hitler Story*, based on captured films and photographs.

[2] Interrogation of Fräulein Hanna Reitsch, who was in the Bunker: *Nuremberg Documents*, 3,734-PS (trans. in *Nazi Conspiracy and Aggression*, Vol. VI, p. 5,602). Fräulein Reitsch spoke of Eva's 'rather shallow mentality', but agreed that 'she was a very beautiful woman'.

he did not need to keep Eva in the background any more—
the thought that marriage would harm his political position
was no longer of validity. And so, in the early morning hours
of 29 April, a civil ceremony of marriage was performed in
the Bunker, and with, at long last, the status of wife, Eva
Braun was able to sign the register as Eva Hitler.

While the wedding party in the Bunker were drinking
champagne, Hitler withdrew with his secretary to dictate a
political testament and a personal will.[1] In the political testament the old Hitler of *Mein Kampf* and of the years of bluff
and preparation speaks out unchanged:

> More than thirty years have now passed since I in 1914
> made my modest contribution as a volunteer in the First
> World War, which was forced upon the Reich.
>
> In these three decades I have been actuated solely by
> love and loyalty to my people. . . .
>
> It is untrue that I or anyone else in Germany wanted
> the war in 1939. It was desired and instigated solely by
> those international statesmen who were either of Jewish
> descent or worked for Jewish interests. I have made too
> many offers for the control and limitation of armaments,
> which posterity will not for all time be able to disregard, for
> the responsibility for the outbreak of this war to be laid on
> me. I have, further, never wished that, after the fatal First
> World War, a second against England, or even against
> America, should break out. Centuries will pass away, but
> out of the ruins of our towns and monuments the hatred
> against those finally responsible whom we have to thank
> for everything, international Jewry and its helpers, will
> grow . . . that race, Jewry, which is the real criminal of
> this murderous struggle, will be saddled with the respon-
> sibility.

Of his decision to remain in Berlin to the end, Hitler said:

> After six years of war, which in spite of all setbacks will go
> down one day in history as the most glorious and valiant
> demonstration of a nation's life purpose, I cannot forsake
> the city which is the capital of the Reich. . . . Moreover,

[1] *Nuremberg Documents*, 3,569-PS (trans. in *Nazi Conspiracy and Aggression*,
Vol. VI, pp. 259-63).

I do not wish to fall into the hands of an enemy who requires a new spectacle, organized by the Jews, for the amusement of their hysterical masses. I have decided, therefore, to remain in Berlin and there of my own free will to choose death at the moment when I believe the position of the *Führer* can no longer be held.

I die with a happy heart, aware of the immeasurable deeds of our soldiers at the front. . . . From the sacrifice of our soldiers and from my own unity with them unto death will in any case spring up in the history of Germany the seed of a valiant renaissance of the National Socialist movement and thus of the realization of a true community of nations.

Then he turned to the question of a government after he was gone. He formally expelled Göring and Himmler from the Party and from office in the State. He named as his successor Admiral Dönitz, a man who had been markedly loyal to Hitler, and, by naming an admiral, Hitler indicated his disillusion with his generals. Dönitz was to be President and Supreme Commander, Goebbels Chancellor, and Bormann Party Minister. Finally, in the last paragraph of the typewritten document, Hitler charged the new leaders of Germany 'before all, to scrupulous observance of the racial laws and merciless resistance to the universal poisoner of all nations, international Jewry'.

In his personal will Hitler gave a brief explanation of his late marriage. 'As', he said, 'I did not consider that I could take the responsibility, during the years of struggle, of contracting a marriage, I have now decided, before the end of my life, to take as my wife the woman who, after many years of faithful friendship, of her own free will entered this town, when it was already practically besieged, in order to share my fate. At her own desire, she goes to death with me as my wife. This will compensate us for what we have both lost through my work in the service of my people.' And he added: 'I myself and my wife—in order to escape the disgrace of deposition or capitulation—choose death. It is our wish to be burned immediately in the place where I have carried out the greater part of my daily work in the course of my twelve years' service to my people.'

Later in the same day, 29 April—these were long days with little to distinguish day and night, for Hitler slept at unusual times, and the routine of the whole company depended upon him—came the news that the Duce was dead. Mussolini and his mistress, Clara Petacci, had been shot the day before by the Partisans, and their bodies hung up to be publicly reviled in a Milan square. Hitler's reflections may, perhaps, be guessed, but no comment was recorded. He went on with his own preparations. Blondi and the other dogs were destroyed, and in the early morning hours of 30 April Hitler assembled his staff and said farewell. Now took place an extraordinary scene. A wave of relief passed over those who were in the Bunker when they realized that the *Führer* would soon be gone. In the soldiers' canteen, in the Chancellery, a dance took place; German energy, vitality and brute enjoyment of life, even under the immediate menace of death and destruction, did not fail. So great was the hilarity that, from the *Führer's* quarters, a message came bidding them be quieter.[1] Only a few streets away, meanwhile, the Russians were fighting their way towards the centre of the city. Later in the morning they were reported in the Tiergarten and even the Potsdamer Platz, close by. The end was at hand.

Hitler took his lunch quietly, much as usual, on this 30 April. Then he said goodbye again to Goebbels and Bormann. Soon after three o'clock in the afternoon he went to his own rooms, rejoining his wife there. A little later a single report was heard. Hitler was found shot through the mouth; by his side was Eva, who had taken poison. At once, according to instructions, the two bodies were carried into the garden, soaked in petrol, and burnt. So—according to the accounts afterwards given—died the *Führer* of the Third Reich. On 1 May Hamburg Radio, which still remained in German hands, proclaimed, with a background of solemn music, 'that our *Führer*, Adolf Hitler, has fallen at his command post in the Reich Chancellery, fighting to the last against Bolshevism

[1] Trevor-Roper, p. 217.

and for Germany'. Dönitz announced his own succession to Hitler, and spoke of the *Führer's* 'death as a hero in the capital of the Reich'. The language of myth was thus employed to shroud the suicide's end, which at long last rid Germany of the magician who had first raised the country to the heights of power only to plunge it into destruction. No remains of the bodies were ever found. All that was mortal of Adolf Hitler had vanished—behind him he left defeat and ruin.

From the Bunker a number of persons escaped. Of these Bormann was one; he was never traced. Goebbels on 1 May gave poison to his six children, and ordered an S.S. attendant to shoot him and his wife. Their bodies were burnt, but in this case the remains were found when the Russians entered the Chancellery on the following day. On 2 May Dönitz moved the seat of his government to Flensburg, near the Danish frontier, and set up a non-party government. He sent out letters of dismissal to Goebbels (of whose death he had not yet heard), Himmler, and Rosenberg. Still Himmler lingered on—he also had moved with his staff and attendants to Flensburg—not able to believe that his power was gone. Two weeks later, in disguise as an ordinary soldier, he fell into British hands. He was recognized. Thereupon, while being searched, he swallowed poison and died on the spot.

Just before that had come surrender. Goebbels and Bormann had tried to negotiate with the Russians, Dönitz with the West. But the answer was 'unconditional surrender', the formula agreed on since early in 1943. On 29 April the Germans in Italy capitulated, and on 4 May the German forces in north-west Europe. Finally at Rheims, on 7 May 1945, General Jodl signed the unconditional surrender of all German forces in the presence of representatives of the U.S.A., Britain, France, and Russia. The war in the west was over, and with it the Third Reich.

The German defeat was complete. Hitler had always said that Nazi Germany would never capitulate as in 1918. He was right, but in a way which he had not been able to conceive. The Germany of 1918 had retained a government of its own, and, though small, an army of its own. But the

GERMANY AFTER THE SECOND WORLD WAR

Germany of 1945 retained neither: a totalitarian State suffered totalitarian defeat. The entire armed forces, officers and men, became prisoners of war, and sovereignty in Germany passed from German hands into those of the four Occupying Powers. The Occupying Powers did not recognize the successor government of Dönitz, and on 23 May Eisenhower arranged for the arrest of Dönitz and the members of his Government at Flensburg. Meanwhile, all over Germany the remaining Nazi leaders were being rounded up and put under arrest. Military government was imposed in Germany—according to the scheme worked out at the Yalta Conference in February 1945 and completed later at the Potsdam Conference in August. Power was vested in the four commanders-in-chief in a Control Council, meeting in Berlin. At the same time Germany was divided into four zones of occupation, British, American, French, and Russian, and each commander-in-chief became the governing authority in his own zone. Materially and economically, the country had been reduced to desperate straits. Every city of any size was in ruins, and in the sultry days of summer there was, from beneath the rubble and the piles of masonry, the stench of rotting bodies. Amid such conditions the Allied Powers began to put their policy into operation: disarmament, demilitarization, de-Nazification, and a certain measure of de-industrialization, the last to compensate the Allies by handing to them machinery and equipment and at the same time to prevent their use for possible future German military purposes. The Nazi Party and all its organizations were dissolved, and the Allies set out on the difficult task of reconstructing German political life on a democratic basis.

But there was also the task of putting on trial the Nazi war criminals and of punishing the guilty.[1] The principle of punishment for war crimes was not new. During the war, also, the Allied nations from time to time declared their intention of bringing war criminals to justice, and by the Moscow Declaration of 30 October 1943 it was agreed that accused Germans should be returned for trial and punishment to the countries where the crimes had been committed. But it was clear, of course, that there were directing and responsible hands behind all these crimes, and that for these major war criminals there was no appropriate geographical location with its own national system of law. For their trial a special international tribunal was created,[2] of four members, British,

---

[1] For a discussion of the legal issues involved, see P. Calvocoressi, *Nuremberg*.
[2] The London Agreement of 8 August 1945 (setting up the International Tribunal) and the Charter of the Tribunal are printed in *Nazi Conspiracy and Aggression*, Vol. I, pp. 1-12, and in Calvocoressi, Appendix I. The London Agreement refers back to the Moscow Agreement of 1943.

American, French and Russian. It met at Nuremberg—not because of that city's close association with the Nazi system, but because the Palace of Justice there and the gaol had escaped with little damage. Here, then, in Nuremberg between 20 November 1945 and 1 October 1946 the trial of the major war criminals took place. As a preliminary, over 100,000 documents were individually scrutinized to prepare the prosecution case.[1] In addition, oral evidence was taken at the trial. By means of simultaneous translation and a system of headphones, each lawyer or witness was able to speak in his native language.

The trial provided an elaborate demonstration of the enormity of Nazi crimes, but it was fairly carried out, German lawyers putting forward their case for the defence. In principle, the trial rested on established law; its novelty lay in the international character of the court, and in the fact that 'the Nuremburg trial represents the first time in history that legal proceedings have been instituted against leaders of an enemy nation'.[2] This time it was not only little people who suffered in war; the great were also tried and punished. Twenty-four were selected for trial before the international tribunal: Göring, Hess, Ribbentrop, Rosenberg, Frank, Frick, Funk, Schacht, Sauckel, von Papen, Seyss-Inquart, Speer, von Neurath, Fritzsche, Ley, Streicher, von Schirach, Bormann, Keitel, Dönitz, Raeder, Jodl, Kaltenbrunner, and Gustav Krupp. Ley committed suicide before the trial opened, Krupp was too ill to attend. The men on trial were accused 'of crimes against Peace, War Crimes, and Crimes against Humanity, and of a Common Plan or Conspiracy to commit those Crimes'.[3]

The overriding crime was that of aggressive war. 'The fact of the war', said the American prosecutor, '. . . is history. . . . That attack upon the peace of the world is the crime against international society which brings into international cognizance crimes in its aid and preparation which otherwise might be only internal concerns. It was aggressive war, which the

---

[1] *Nazi Conspiracy and Aggression*, Vol. I, Preface, p. vi.
[2] Ibid., Preface, p. v.   [3] Ibid., p. 14.

nations of the world had renounced. It was war in violation of treaties, by which the peace of the world was sought to be safeguarded. This war did not just happen: it was planned and prepared for over a long period of time and with no small skill and cunning. The world has perhaps never seen such a concentration and stimulation of the energies of any people as that which enabled Germany . . . to come so near carrying out its plan to dominate Europe.'[1] The important Hossbach Minutes of 5 November 1937 made clear Hitler's intention of expanding Germany's frontiers by aggression against her neighbours. By waging aggressive war, Germany had broken each of a long series of international agreements, from the Hague Convention for the Pacific Settlement of International Disputes of 1899 to the Pact of Paris, or Kellogg Pact, of 1928, when sixty-three signatories, including Germany, had declared that 'they condemn recourse to war for the solution of international controversies, and renounce it as an instrument of national policy in their relations with one another.' In preparing for and in waging aggressive war, the Nazis had committed great and terrible crimes against humanity, in the suppression of opposition at home, in the exploitation of slave labour, and in the wholesale extermination of Jews and supposedly inferior races. The prosecution case was concerned with 'twelve million murders'—'twelve million men, women and children . . . done to death. Not in battle . . . but in the cold, calculated, deliberate attempt to destroy nations and races.'[2] And in these crimes each of the guilty men had had an individual share. The common denominator of guilt was well expressed by one of the French prosecutors, who said of each: 'The defendant occupied within the machinery of the State and the Party a position of eminence which endowed him with authority; . . . the defendant complied with, if he did not conceive, the doctrine of the régime —"Conquest of space by any means"; he personally played an active part in the political development of this doctrine.'[3]

[1] *Nazi Conspiracy and Aggression*, p. 119.
[2] Closing speech by British Attorney-General (Sir Hartley Shawcross), *Nuremberg Proceedings*, Vol. XIX, p. 434.
[3] *Nuremberg Proceedings*, Vol. XIX, p. 550.

The trial was no mere formality; its result not a foregone conclusion. When the sentences were announced on 1 October 1946, three of the accused—von Papen, Schacht, Fritzsche—were acquitted. Twelve were sentenced to death, three to life imprisonment, two to twenty years, one to fifteen years, and one to ten years. The executions were carried out on 16 October. Göring, who had shown considerable spirit at the trial and scored several points off the American chief prosecutor, won a final success in that he acquired poison and took his own life a few hours before the time fixed for his execution. Bormann had been sentenced in absence. The other ten sentenced to death—Ribbentrop, Keitel, Jodl, Rosenberg, Frick, Seyss-Inquart, Sauckel, Kaltenbrunner, Frank, and Streicher—were hanged. Thus the Nazi leaders paid at last for their crimes—and many more, tried in the courts set up by each of the Allied nations, paid also. It was a proper retribution.

Yet the crimes of the Nazis, crimes in which so many of the German people had taken part, should not blind us to the fact that there were inside Germany some few who had recognized the evil in their midst and struggled courageously against it. There had been the men who had tried themselves to dispose of Hitler on 20 July 1944. As General von Tresckow said before he took his own life on 21 July to escape the Nazi executioners:

> My conviction is still firm as a rock that we have done right. I hold Hitler to be not only the arch-enemy of Germany, but the arch-enemy of the world. When I appear in a few hours before the Throne of God to render account for my deeds and my omissions, I believe I will be able to answer with a good conscience for all that I have done in the struggle against Hitler.
>
> As God told Abraham that He would not destroy Sodom if ten righteous men were found in the city, it is my hope that for our sake God will not destroy Germany.[1]

[1] H. Speidel, *We Defended Normandy*, pp. 133-4.

CHAPTER XVIII

THE NAZI MYTH AND THE FUTURE

WITH the complete defeat of Nazi Germany all the outward signs of the régime disappeared. At first it seemed like a bad dream. Every German blamed some other German for what had happened: it was the Party, not the Germans, which was responsible. Almost at once Germans extended the hand of friendship to those they had known from abroad before the war. There was no sign of shame, embarrassment, or humility.[1] It was as if the war had been a vast natural cataclysm which had swept over friend and foe alike. Dazed, but ready very soon to set their hands again to the tasks of everyday life, the Germans stepped out of the Nazi era into the period of reconstruction. Vitality began to show itself in many ways, and a cabaret song-hit of the first winter after the war expressed something of the prevailing mood. Dressed as a tramp—a returned soldier or refugee from the East— and with a background of ruins, the young variety artiste sang her *Marschlied*:

> *In den letzten dreissig Wochen*
> *zog ich sehr durch Wald und Feld.*
> *Und mein Hemd ist so durchbrochen,*
> *dass man's kaum für möglich hält.*
> *Ich trag' Schuhe ohne Sohlen,*
> *und der Rucksack ist mein Schrank.*
> *Meine Möbel hab'n die Polen*
> *und mein Geld die Dresdner Bank.*
> *Ohne Heimat und Verwandte,*
> *und die Stiefel ohne Glanz—*
> *ja das wär' nun der bekannte*
> *Untergang des Abendlands!*

---

[1] There were, of course, individuals who admitted the wrongs Germans had done. Thus Helmut Gollwitzer, . . . *und führen, wohin du nicht willst*, p. 14, wrote on 10 May 1945: '*Nun wurden die Deutschen mit dem Masse gemessen, mit dem sie die Juden gemessen hatten.*' (Now the Germans are treated as they treated the Jews.)

343

Eine Grossstadtpflanze bin ich.
Keinen roten Heller wert,
Weder stolz, noch hehr, noch innig,
sondern höchstens umgekehrt.
Freilich, als die Städte starben . . .
als der Himmel sie erschlug . . .
zwischen Stahl—und Phosphorgarben—
damals war'n wir gut genug.
Wenn die andern leben müssten
wie es uns sechs Jahr ' geschah—
doch wir wollen uns nicht brüsten,
dazu ist die Brust nicht da.

Ich trag' Schuhe ohne Sohlen.
Durch die Hose pfeift der Wind.
Doch soll mir der Teufel holen,
wenn ich nicht nach Hause find'.
In den Fenstern, die im Finstern
lagen, zwinkert wieder Licht.
Freilich nicht in allen Häusern
Nein, in allen wirklich nicht . . .
Tausend Jahre sind vergangen
samt der Schnurrbart-Majestät.
Und nun heisst's: von vorn anfangen!
Vorwärts marsch! Sonst wird's zu spät![1]

The 'moustache-majesty' and his 1,000-year Reich had vanished. All around was unimaginable devastation, but God did not destroy Germany, as General Tresckow had feared. Instead there took place, in the next years, a miracle of economic reconstruction in western Germany. German energy and hard work, Allied financial help, and the common threat which developed from Soviet Russia to Western Allies and Germans alike, all contributed to recovery. Germany

[1] As sung by Ursula Herking, 1946. Reproduced in *Nürnberger Nachrichten,* 20 August 1954. 'In the last thirty weeks I tramped with my rucksack through woods and fields, my shirt worn to a thread, my shoes without soles, without home or relations. Yes, this was the famous decline of the West. Now I'm not worth a farthing—certainly, it was otherwise in the bombing and the fighting. There we were useful enough—but there's no good now congratulating ourselves on that. Now I'm returning—the windows which were blacked-out, are showing lights again, although, of course, not all the windows. A thousand years have passed together with the moustache-majesty. And now we must begin again. Forward march, otherwise it will be too late.'

remained divided, for the Western Allies found it impossible to follow a common policy with Russia. But in 1948 a stable currency was created for western Germany, and in 1949 the three western zones of Germany were closely linked up and, later in the same year, the *Bundesrepublik Deutschland*, the Federal Republic of Germany, was instituted, with Bonn as capital. In all this the Germans and the Allies worked together. The new Federal Republic was the only recognized German government—neither it nor the Allies recognized the government created by the Russians in their Zone, because it was not based upon free elections. Ruins were cleared, towns rebuilt, dwellings constructed, industry produced goods in vast quantity once more, the 10 million Germans driven from the lost provinces beyond the Oder-Neisse Line (the provisional frontier between East Germany and Poland) were absorbed, wealth and prosperity were obvious on the streets, wages and the standard of life rose. The wave of strikes during the summer of 1954 was not the result of falling wages, but of the conscious determination of the trade unions to win a larger slice of the economic cake.

With economic prosperity, the Germans could forget politics. That had been the case before, in the good years between 1924 and 1929. But the Allied proposal to rearm Germany inside a European Defence Community—a proposal put forward in 1950 and arising from the threat to the West from Russia—aroused fears, not only outside Germany, but inside as well. And the flight to the east at the end of July 1954 of Dr. John, the head of the German constitutional defence or counter-intelligence service, who made the definite charge of a Nazi revival, rendered those fears acute. To this the Federal Chancellor, Dr. Adenauer, gave a categorical denial in a broadcast speech: 'I declare with all emphasis that there is no revival of National Socialism. I warrant that there will be no revival.'[1]

Dr. Adenauer has staked his whole political position on working with the West for the creation of German democracy

[1] Adenauer's appeal for calm and responsibility had the widest publicity in the Press—for exa.nple, on the front page of *Bild-Zeitung*, 7 August, Germany's cheapest newspaper, with a circulation of over 1 million.

and of a common front against the threat of a new tyranny from the East. One hopes he is right about the disappearance of National Socialism in Germany. The *News Chronicle* reported Adenauer's statement under banner headlines: 'Hitler's Ghost will not Walk—Nazism is dead for Ever.'[1] But earlier, in March, Mr. Sefton Delmer of the *Daily Express* had asked the question: 'How dead is Hitler?' His articles created a great stir in Germany. Remarkable bitterness was shown in some of the German Press. John himself was bitterly attacked, not only for going over to the Russians, but for his part during the war: because he had interrogated German officers in England, had criticized German generals at the Nuremberg trial, had worn English uniform, and given information to the English. 'Also the English journalist, Sefton Delmer, who a short time before started his infamous campaign of hate against the German Republic, was a friend of John.'[2] Another paper described Delmer as a 'devourer of Germans'.[3] Criticism in this tone arouses suspicion. One can scarcely avoid asking if there is after all a Nazi myth, if there are grounds for a Nazi revival in Germany.

Mr. Sefton Delmer, who reported the symptoms before Hitler took power, found similar portents once more. He felt he could say: 'This is where I came in.'[4] He found prominent men who feared to speak their mind, and a patriotic hue and cry against 'traitors'—that is, men who had resisted the Nazis. He alleged that militarists and industrialists saw in proposed German armaments merely a means of getting back their power, and regretted the past only in so far as mistakes in leadership had led to defeat. He pointed to the revival of ex-Servicemen's organizations, and even an association for the S.S., as another sign of reviving military spirit, and thought that General Gehlen, former German anti-Soviet intelligence chief, with his present American-financed secret service organization, must inevitably strengthen the militarist tendency. He

[1] 7 August 1954.
[2] *Deutsche Soldaten Zeitung*, No. 22, August 1954.
[3] *Der Mittag*, 12 August.
[4] *Daily Express*, 22 March 1954. Other articles followed on 23, 25 and 29 March.

pointed out that influential Germans were discussing Germany's prospects of playing off East against West, and he mentioned by name three of the Republic's Cabinet Ministers with Nazi records. Delmer saw in the proposed German rearmament a danger of justifying the Nazis: 'As the inevitable consequence, Nazis and militarists alike today proclaim that this rearmament of Germany is a posthumous justification of Hitler as the champion of the West against Bolshevism—an ever-recurrent German propaganda line during the war.'[1] Dr. John made similar charges against Germany, but he added to them charges against America. Accusing America of preparing a war against the Communist East, he alleged: 'The Americans need German soldiers for their war against the East. The Germans, therefore, most welcome to them are those who learnt nothing from the recent catastrophe and are simply waiting for the hour to revenge their defeat. On that account, the wildest Nazis and militarists are allowed to be active again in Germany.'[2] But whatever the potential dangers in the German situation, by making exaggerated charges against America and himself going over to the East, Dr. John weakened his case and struck a blow, even if unintentionally, against European freedom.

Mr. Wheeler-Bennett, whose studies of Germany both before and after Hitler—*Hindenburg; Brest-Litovsk; Munich; The Nemesis of Power*—have made him perhaps our greatest authority, has expressed his own fears. He, too, has asked the question: 'Is this merely "Where we came in" in the repetitive history of the German Army in politics?' Though he agrees that 'the defence of Western Europe demands a contribution of strength from Western Germany; there can be no doubt of this', he records that, although the downfall of the German Army was such very recent history, 'within a few years the resurgence of the military tradition was in full flood'. As he says, 'provision for an army of some twelve divisions . . . is already afoot. The register of the Officer

---

[1] *Daily Express*, 29 March.

[2] *Frankfurter Allgemeine Zeitung*, 12 August 1954: full report of Dr. John's Press conference in the Russian Sector of Berlin.

THE RISE AND FALL OF NAZI GERMANY

Corps has already been established. The ex-soldiers' leagues are already in the field. The legends of the "stab in the back" are already in circulation. Moreover, the apologists for the German militarists are already active in our own country.'[1] The Western Allies are indeed in a dilemma: they want German military assistance, but they do not want German militarism. The amused irritation of the Germans is not altogether unnatural:[2] on the one hand, they are asked for a military contribution; on the other, they are condemned for making military preparations.

Four stages have been distinguished in what has been called 'Neo-Nazism' or 'Right-wing radicalism'.[3] At first, Nazism appeared crushed. During the tight Allied control of the immediate post-war years, the die-hard Nazis remained in hiding. Secondly, as Allied control relaxed, certain groups emerged, and sought to take advantage of democratic forms. Such was the S.R.P. (Socialist Reich Party), formed under the leadership of Major-General Ernst Remer, the former Major Remer, who had taken a prominent part in suppressing the conspiracy against Hitler of 20 July 1944 and vigorously defended his action in a pamphlet published in 1951. The S.R.P. bitterly attacked the 'criminals of July 1944' and the new German Republic. In Lower Saxony the S.R.P. made considerable headway: in the elections of 1951 the Party polled 367,000 votes, which gave it sixteen seats out of 158 in the Landtag (state legislature of the *Land* of Lower Saxony). But in 1952 Remer was sentenced to three months' imprisonment for slandering the resistance movement of 20 July. Later in the year, while further legal action was pending against the S.R.P., the Party dissolved itself. Shortly afterwards the Federal Constitutional Court declared the Party unconstitutional. As a result, Nazi sympathizers had to exercise more caution. Thus, in the third stage, they tried to infiltrate into the democratic parties of the Right, the German Party (D.P.), the Refugees Party

[1] *Nemesis of Power*, p. ix. On this matter see his Introduction and Epilogue (ii).
[2] '*Der deutsche Soldat wird salonfähig*' (The German Soldier becomes respectable), N. Tönnies, *Der Staat aus dem Nichts*, p. 226.
[3] *Deutsche Tatsachen* (Transatlantik-Brücke, Hamburg), p. 63.

(B.H.E.), and the Free Democrat Party (F.D.P.). In particular, Naumann, a former state secretary in Goebbels' Propaganda Ministry, had tried to work himself and his old comrades into influential positions in the F.D.P. He and several others were arrested early in 1953. After his release he was banned from political activity. The fourth stage was marked by the Bundestag elections of the German Republic in September 1953. The extreme right-wing groups of Neo-Nazis hoped for a come-back. But Dr. Adenauer's Christian Democrats won an overwhelming victory. The two Neo-Nazi groups together polled less than $1\frac{1}{2}$ per cent of the total votes. As the electoral law requires a minimum of 5 per cent. for representation in the Bundestag, the Neo-Nazis gained no representatives. This fate was also that of the Communists. Thus, so far as the present voting strength of Western Germany goes, both Neo-Nazis and Communists—extremes of Right and Left —appear negligible. As a result of Adenauer's victory Germany was represented as 'a strong centre for European stability'.[1]

But, of course, the Nazi ideology which had been completely dominant in Germany and had its roots stretching into the distant past could not completely lose its influence all at once. The Nazi outlook had worked its way even into the language and the way of thought. Many simple words or expressions had taken on a political implication. *Neudenken* and *altdenken* came to mean to think after and before 1933. *Parteitreu* was used for loyalty to one party only, the Nazi Party. *Fanatisch*, which before 1933 had been used in its usual sense of fanatical, of something to be avoided, took on a positive sense as of devotion or loyalty. What was horrible and bad was turned to make it appear, to the ordinary person, as if it were good. Thus *Schutzhaft*, or protective custody, which might mean torture or concentration camp, sounded innocent enough as something intended, as it were, for the benefit of the recipient. *Die Partei hat immer recht*—there was a twisting of men's minds, reminiscent of the conditioning imaginatively pictured by George Orwell.[2]

[1] *Salzburger Nachrichten*, 8 September, 1953.
[2] These influences on the language were pointed out in a lecture, *Die deutsche Sprache der Gegenwart*, by Professor W. Betz of Bonn University.

Outwardly, of course, the German authorities have tried hard to show Nazism in its true light.[1] Monuments have been erected to the victims of the Nazis, wreaths are laid in public places in memory of the resistance fighters of 20 July, the German President, Professor Heuss himself, dedicated in 1952 the memorial on the site of Belsen. 'Stones can talk', he said of the message on the memorial, but 'it rests with the individual, with you, to understand this language, this special language in stone, for your own sake and for the sake of us all.'[2] He spoke noble and timely words. The Bonn Government has through its Press and information services done its utmost to present the truth about the Nazis to the German people. Yet an independent publication of 1952 complains that people are still found who condemn the resistance and especially the men of 20 July as traitors. 'There are still', it says, 'supporters of National Socialism. They even dare once more to make their National Socialist ideas known in public.'[3]

When, on 1 May 1945, Admiral Dönitz announced on the Hamburg Radio the *Führer's* 'death as a hero in the capital of the Reich, fighting to the last against Bolshevism and for Germany', he used language which could well form the basis of a Hitler or Nazi myth.[4] In a farewell message to the Officer Corps, Dönitz wrote: 'We have been set back for 1,000 years in our history. . . . Therefore the political line we must follow is very plain. It is clear that we have to go along with the Western Powers and work with them in the occupied territories in the West, for it is only through working with them that we can have hopes of later retrieving our land from the Russians. . . . Whether we want to create another form of National Socialism, or whether we conform to the life imposed upon us by the enemy, we should make sure that the

---

[1] Three supplements were published in May and June 1954 to the Government-sponsored weekly, *Das Parlament*. They dealt with *Die Vollmacht des Gewissens*—the authority of conscience, asserting a right to resistance. As Father Pribilla, S.J., one of the contributors, put it: '20 July failed as revolt, but triumphed as symbol . . . it was a sign of protest before the world, to show that not the whole German people had gone to rot.'

[2] *The Memorial*, p. 13, a translation in pamphlet form of President Heuss's speech.

[3] *Die Wahrheit über den 20 Juli* (Budde und Lütsches), Preface.

[4] See p. 337.

unity given to us by National Socialism is maintained under all circumstances.'[1] Admiral Dönitz was later sentenced and imprisoned for his share in war crimes. But his sentence is running out, and some feel that he could make a popular figure around whom former Nazis would gather.

Two different theories have already found expression to explain the defeat of the German Army. Some of the German generals, notable among them Halder,[2] have accused Hitler himself of blunders and failures in leadership. The inference is that the professional soldiers, if left to themselves, would have avoided these errors, and would not, like Hitler, have brought Germany to disaster. Though such writers generally now condemn the Nazi régime, they do not appear clear as to whether they regard Germany's military errors as a bad thing or a good. If the professional soldiers had had their way, would they have won the war and thereby perpetuated the Nazi system? For them, however, it was Hitler's intuition which let them down. The other theory is even more blatant and offensive. It is the contention of General Remer and his Neo-Nazis that 20 July was another stab in the back.[3] Just as the Social Democrats betrayed Germany in November 1918, it is claimed, so the men of the resistance betrayed Germany in July 1944. The defeatism of his generals let Hitler down; the secret opposition to Hitler explains his defeat. Such is the theory—otherwise, without the traitors, the *Führer* would have triumphed.

Germans, like people elsewhere, feel a natural disinclination to rethink and reconstruct their basic ideas. And as in the old Germany nationalism and German-centred thinking were powerful, so still today these ideas are active below the surface. Their strength helps to account for the popular success of a book like Ernst von Salomon's *Fragebogen*. Two German professors, on the other hand, have stated their belief that the only possible *creative* reaction for Germans to take to the events of the past fifty years is the 'inexorable recognition of the frightful rôle which the Germans played in them'. But

[1] Quoted by Wheeler-Bennett, *Nemesis of Power*, p. 699.
[2] F. Halder, *Hitler as War Lord*, pp. 44-7.
[3] Wheeler-Bennett, *Nemesis of Power*, p. 700, refers to a pamphlet, *Gegen eine neue Dolchstosslüge*, written in 1947 as a warning by one of the survivors of 20 July.

of such a reaction there is not very much evidence. Many of the memoirs of German generals and officials serve rather to explain, justify, and whitewash.

Voices are to be heard in Germany which explain the Nazi period in such a way as to exonerate the German people. Such justification makes impossible the necessary 'creative reaction' and precludes the requisite rethinking of the recent past. Thus some excuse the Nazi aggression against Soviet Russia as both a necessary move in self-defence and as an action undertaken in the defence of Europe. They blame the West for its alliance with Communist Russia, for thwarting Hitler in his aim to destroy the Communist menace in the East, and for allowing Stalin's forces to enter the heart of Europe. Thus a new legend arises of Hitler's Germany as a bulwark of Christendom against Communism—and Hitler was stabbed in the back by the Allies and the men of 20 July. One of the evil effects of Dr. John's defection to the East is that it has created a new 'guilt by association'; it enables German nationalists to suggest that others who were in the plot against Hitler are also smeared with Communism. It makes possible a campaign of defamation against democracy.[1] Yet the argument that Hitler defended European civilization against Communism is spurious. Stalin sought by every means to avoid war with Germany; he was an appeaser to the last moment. Hitler and Stalin joined in destroying European civilization in Poland and the Baltic republics. By his attack on Poland, Hitler struck down a Christian nation and destroyed a useful screen against Russia; it was his attack on Russia which resulted in bringing Bolshevism into central Europe. It was Hitler himself who, by his war, destroyed the old Europe and thereby made possible the menacing domination of Soviet Russia in the Europe of today.

[1] *N.R.Z. am Wochenende*, 21 August 1954, points out this danger. Thus the *Deutsche Soldaten Zeitung*, August 1954, speaks of Dr. John and his friends: '*Sie haben sich nach dem Zusammenbruch in der Maske der Widerstandskämpfer in unser Leben wieder eingenistet. Sie nehmen heute für sich in Anspruch, Feinde des Nationalsozialismus gewesen zu sein und waren in Wirklichkert nur Spiessgesellen Moskaus.*' They crept back after the collapse in the guise of members of the resistance movement. Today they claim to have been enemies of National Socialism but in reality they were accomplices of Moscow.

Other Germans, again, try to excuse the past by alleging the stupidity and error of the Allies in 1945 and afterwards;[1] or they blame the Western Powers for not having intervened to stop Hitler before he was too strong; or they draw attention away from the fact of German aggression in 1939 by pointing to other cases of aggression, or seek to excuse the war crimes, the concentration camps, and extermination camps by underlining Russian cruelties and the horrors of their labour camps.

Yet others stress the extent to which pernicious trends in modern Germany were common to the general development in Europe. Thus they can make National Socialism in Germany one example of a European tendency towards dictatorship which showed itself in Italy, Spain, Greece, Poland, and—with Mosley, Colonel de la Rocque, and Degrelle—even in the Western democracies themselves. It is possible to go even further back and to attempt to explain Hitler as the result of the French Revolution and the Industrial Revolution, which produced the upsurge of the masses, to see Hitler as the new-type dictator in the age of the mass-man. Hitler can be made to appear as not essentially German; indeed, as an Austrian, and something of a bohemian—the lazy, ne'er-do-well—he was the antithesis of the rigid, efficient Prussian. Thus the attempt is made 'to present the rise of National Socialism as an event within the context of "objective historical necessity", to which moral categories are not applicable.' In this way the German people might escape moral responsibility for actions thrust upon it by the necessity of history. But the German exponents of such an argument forget that what were only isolated or partial trends elsewhere became dominant, all-embracing—totalitarian—in Germany, and were accepted uncritically by the majority. The Germans *did* accept Hitler, whereas elsewhere comparable ideas were not generally accepted, in spite of similar tendencies and dangers in our common civilization. Another argument—different but also evading moral responsibility—places the Germans in a special predicament which allows the use of special measures to deal

[1] Professor F. Grimm's *40 Jahre Dienst am Recht* on these lines is analysed in the *Wiener Library Bulletin*, Vol. VIII, 1954.

with it. 'The powerful auto-suggestion', it has been said, 'of having been wronged by history—in comparison with the Western nations—created a sense of living in a unique situation which justified unique measures.'[1]

In private conversation, the Hitler myth is sometimes produced in a simpler but more complete form. This is all the more likely to happen with the man of about forty, whose youth and manhood were moulded by the Nazi régime and who fought fanatically in the German Army for the Nazi creed. Such a one argues as follows: Hitler attacked Poland to save the Germans in the Corridor from Polish atrocities. Hitler had no wish for war with England; he held up the tanks at Dunkirk to allow the British Army to escape, and he still hoped for an understanding with England. Even if the Germans had invaded England, it would have been for our good; the Nazis would have developed the country in our common interests. Hitler attacked Russia to save Europe from Communism; England should have fought with Germany against Russia. A question about concentration camps will be brushed aside by a reminder that 'the English started concentration camps in the Boer War'. And then will follow some Neo-Nazi additions: Even now England and Germany must get together. The Americans (this, of course, for English consumption only) are no good; they will collapse when the first H-bomb is dropped in America. Only the British and the Germans are really tough; they must work together for a new Europe. How common such ideas are it is impossible to say. But they do exist. Something of the old spirit appears in the popular welcomes accorded to released war criminals. In the light of past events, one must necessarily expect to find something of the old Nazi mentality lingering on. The important thing is that those ideas should not again come to the top.

The truth probably is, indeed, that Germany is passing again through a period comparable to the years 1924-9. Once more there is a struggle for the German soul—a struggle between the new forces of democracy and good-neighbourly

---

[1] Hans Kohn, *German History—Some Recent German Views*, p. 25. See his Introduction and chapter on 'Rethinking Recent German History'.

understanding and the much older forces of nationalism and militarism. Once more, as far as Germany's western neighbours are concerned, there is the same problem: how to provide for the German people equality of rights without allowing them dominant power. (In other respects, however, Germany's international position—to which we must return in a moment —is very different from what it was after the First World War.) Inside Western Germany there is a striking parallel: once again there is going on a German experiment in democracy. The Weimar Constitution is matched by the Bonn Basic Law. The fundamental human and democratic rights are guaranteed once again—though these liberal rights are something exotic rather than something won in a political struggle by the people themselves. Democratic machinery has been re-created—though with the conscious intent of avoiding, so far as possible, the earlier mistakes. Thus larger powers are given to the *Land* governments, as contrasted with the earlier trend towards governmental centralization. So far, then, as its system of government goes, the German Republic is democratic, and as yet no Neo-Nazi party exists in the central parliament to challenge democracy, although it will be recalled how strong the democratic forces of Social Democracy and the Centre Party appeared in the Weimar days before 1929 and how rapidly thereafter the Nazis grew into a dominant political force. But this time democracy has a rather better chance. Last time it was associated with defeat and the Treaty of Versailles. This time Germans could see that Hitler had led them to disaster; they could blame him for defeat and blame the Occupying Powers for the inevitably disagreeable measures which followed. But at the same time Germany needed help, immediate large-scale help—and she got it, from the Western Occupying Powers. The air-lift saved Berlin from the Russians. Good relations developed between Germany and the West. Dr. Adenauer has had warm and friendly co-operation instead of the cold-shouldering which was given to Weimar. The Bonn democracy came a little later; it did not have to bear the odium of defeat and post-war suffering. It marked instead a great advance towards independence; and it came in times of economic prosperity. To this extent the auguries were good.

The great majority of Germans are going about the tasks of everyday life and are absorbed by them, as are the masses elsewhere. There has been a great break in tradition, an orgy of destruction, and now there is a resultant conservative tendency. People want to safeguard and maintain what they have, to rebuild and restore. This trend perhaps partly accounts for the paucity of good modern literature in Germany—there was a break in the cultural life for which there has not yet been compensation. But there are many hopeful signs. There is much honest reporting and sober comment in newspapers, such as the *Frankfurter Allgemeine* and *Die Welt*; there are good periodicals, such as *Gegenwart, Frankfurter Hefte,* and *Deutsche Rundschau.* Among the young, especially among those who have come under American and British influence, there is a serious attitude and a balanced optimism. Such young people look forward to a strong, democratic Germany taking her part with the democratic nations of the West. Yet there are fears, freely expressed in conversation, of what the effect of German rearmament may be. For above all Germany needs peace— a period of peace in which a peaceful attitude of mind can become general and normal.

What would now, ideally, be best for Germany and the world would be a period of German neutralization. If East and West could reach sincere agreement, Germany could be reunited on condition that she remained indefinitely disarmed. That would give the Germans every opportunity to concentrate their great qualities and energies on economic development. In that way they would develop the conditions of peaceful industry and contented life which make for a calm and tolerant attitude in international affairs. Neutralization and disarmament would be best not only for Germany's neighbours, but for the Germans themselves. The disarmament of Germany for an indefinite period in the future was the original Allied intention. By the Potsdam Agreement in August 1945, the four Allied Powers agreed to 'the complete disarmament and demilitarization of Germany and the elimination or control of all German industry that could be used for military production'. A Four-Power agreement in September and later orders of the Allied Control Council contributed to this end. And when, in 1949, the Western German Republic was set up, the disarmament provisions were carefully safeguarded. But the dream of a permanently disarmed Germany was not, once more, to be realized.

The reason was the attitude of Soviet Russia: in 1945 Russia was our ally, but as the time passed she came to be more and more hostile and difficult, more and more suspect of aggressive intentions. Russia was already preparing and training military forces in her Zone of Germany. As Mr. Wheeler-Bennett has put it so clearly: 'Events played into the hands of the guardians of militarism. The ever-increasing menace of Soviet aggression compelled the Allied governments, against their will and, perhaps, against their better judgement, to consider the rearmament of Germany as an integral part of the defence of Western Europe. . . . There are perhaps few who view with equanimity the re-creation of German military power, in however limited a degree, but all will welcome the participation of Germany in a system of Western security if by this means the system can be effectively strengthened. In such matters Man is but the prisoner and plaything of Fate.'[1] Dr. Adenauer has himself expressed his understanding of the anxieties in Germany and abroad, but spoke of 'the policy of the lesser evil'. A greater evil would be isolation in face of Russia.[2]

By her attitude to her non-Communist neighbours, Communist Russia casts a heavy shadow over Germany, Europe, and the world. The whole world is affected by insecurity, and in the Far East the West rearms a reluctant Japan just as in Europe the West overrides its own and German fears to rearm Germany. Europe is divided by her fears, and France long hesitated on the brink of decisions which must make or

[1] *Nemesis of Power*, p. 701.
[2] *Die Hauptsache ist: Europa* (pamphlet reproducing broadcast discussions of 5 March 1952 between Dr. Adenauer and Ernst Friedländer), p. 8.

mar the future. Germany is brought once more face to face with militarism, a danger greatest of all to Germany itself, for Hitler brought suffering to many peoples, but, as much as to any people, to the Germans themselves—3 million soldiers killed, half a million civilians killed, 7 million prisoners, over 12 million driven from their homes, and their country devastated. Yet how can the Germans forget their lost territories beyond the Oder-Neisse line—the eastern parts of Pomerania and Brandenburg, Silesia, and East Prussia—which have passed under Polish and Russian administration, from which the German populations have been expelled, and which show every sign of being resettled and permanently annexed?[1] Every map reminds them. How can they overlook Russian control as far as the Elbe, and the isolation of Berlin in the Russian Zone? Little placards in their railway trains recall its loss: they see the Russian Bear with its paw on Berlin, 'heart and head city of Germany'.—*Berlin—immer dran denken!* And the hostility of East and West puts off German reunification to the Greek Kalends. Free elections in the Russian Zone would most probably give an overwhelming vote for parties looking West, and therefore could never be allowed by the Russians; a linking of Western Germany to the German Democratic Republic (so called—the former Russian Zone) would extend Communist control over the whole of Germany, and could never be tolerated by the West.

Germany, therefore, remains divided, and is now threatened by the prospect of an armaments race, *inside* Germany, between East and West. The Soviet-dominated East already has its military forces. The rearming of Western Germany would lead to their further increase, and to acute competition between the two parts of Germany—so is it suggested in one newspaper in Germany. The paper suggests, too, that in Washington these developments may well prove disappointing in the highest degree: 'in the matter of German rearmament,

---

[1] '*Noch gibt es viele Wünsche zu erfüllen: kein Tag, da wir nicht von der Wiedereinigung träumen, der Schwestern und Brüder drüben gedenken, für unsere Gefangenen bitten . . .*', N. Tönnies, *Der Staat aus dem Nichts*, p. 245. (Still there is much to be fulfilled: no day passes when we do not dream of reunion, when we do not think of our sisters and brothers over there, when we do not pray for the prisoners . . .)

as in many other matters also, things turn out very differently from what was expected'.[1] Already, indeed, the struggle is going on in the field of espionage and intelligence. Russian spy organizations are notorious. On the Western side the controversy over the rearmament of Germany has given a certain notoriety to the Gehlen organization. General Gehlen is said to have, working for the Americans, an organization of 4,000 men, agents in Russia and the satellite countries, with headquarters in the old S.S., later American, camp at Pullach, near Munich, and the cover-name of *Süddeutsche Industrieverwertung*.[2] But, though Gehlen was formerly head of a German Army anti-Soviet intelligence organization, he contributed valuable material to the Americans after the war, and entered their service. It is not surprising that he should now be active in the 'Cold War'; it is not necessary to exaggerate his importance or make him a sinister figure in the present phase of German rearmament.

In spite of all difficulties the leaders of the Western Powers and of the German Republic persevered in their efforts to create a common front in face of the peril from the East. On 5 May 1955, after the necessary treaties had been ratified by Germany, the U.S.A., France, and Great Britain, West Germany became a Sovereign State with the right to an agreed measure of rearmament, the Allied occupation came to an end (their troops in future to be guests not occupying forces), and the Allied High Commissioners became ambassadors. At the same time West Germany was admitted into the Western European Union and into the North Atlantic Treaty Organization. All this marked a notable triumph for the West. But at the same time, Soviet Russia created her own rival to NATO—a unified command under the Soviet Marshal Koniev, for Russia, Poland, Czechoslovakia, Hungary, Albania, Rumania, Bulgaria and East Germany. And by an equally notable reversal of her previous policy, Russia suddenly showed herself willing to negotiate a treaty

[1] *Neues Europa,* 15 August 1954.
[2] *Neue Rhein Zeitung*; a series of articles appeared in the issues, 18-24 August 1954.

of peace with Austria; the treaty was signed on 15 May, by Russia, Austria, the U.S.A., France, and Great Britain, on the basis of the withdrawal of their forces by all four Occupying Powers. Speculation was at once rife as to how far 'the Kremlin's objective was to create a suggestive model with the intention of arousing in Germany the desire for a similar solution'[1] and thereby breaking down West Germany's new position as a member of NATO. *Moscow hat mit Wien gesprochen, aber es hat Bonn gemeint.*[2] Meanwhile the possibility of four-power talks with Russia at the highest level aroused wider hopes of a general settlement.

So long as the Cold War continues it must poison the European situation. What can be hoped for in the immediate future is that the common threat from the East to Western Europe, West Germany and America will further understanding and genuine co-operation among them. Most dangerous of all would be any tendency to isolate Western Germany. Dr. Adenauer and the Federal Republic need friendly support, understanding and co-operation. Hitler was a symbol of German isolation—of cutting loose from the culture, the restraints, the morality of European civilization. More than ever is it important that Germany should form part of a European Community. Nazi ideas—unless they are revived —will tend to die away as the generation which was most influenced by them grows older and dies. Germany of the future must look to its youth who are being trained under the aegis of democracy. If a truly democratic spirit can grow to maturity in time, Germans may take rearmament in their stride. A strong European Community, with German help, may yet offer a better future to the German youth of today, and enable the generations to come to escape from the shadow of the swastika.

[1] *The Bulletin,* 21 April 1955 (German Press and Information Office.)
[2] *Welt am Sonntag* (Hamburg), 17 April 1955—Moscow spoke to Vienna but was thinking of Bonn.

BIBLIOGRAPHY

THIS bibliography is arranged as follows:

PART I. THE BACKGROUND

1. The German Problem
2. German History
3. German Thought

PART II. NAZI GERMANY

A. Sources

1. Collections of Documentary Material
2. Newspapers
3. Nazi Writings and Speeches
4. Memoirs, etc.

B. Secondary Works

1. General
2. The Weimar Republic and the Rise of the Nazi Party
3. Hitler
4. Germany under Hitler—the Third Reich
5. Foreign Affairs
6. The War
7. The End of the Nazis

Part I lists a number of books which are useful in the study of the background of Nazi Germany. For German history there is a select bibliography in Flenley's *Modern German History* (1953). Dahlman-Waitz, *Quellenkunde der deutschen Geschichte* (1931) is the standard German guide to historical sources. See also G. Franz, *Bücherkunde zur deutschen Geschichte* (1951). Alan Bullock and A. J. P. Taylor, *Select List of Books on European History 1815-1914,* and G. P. Gooch, *Bibliography of European History 1918-1939* (Historical Association Pamphlet, 1940), contain sections on Germany. A. J. P. Taylor, *The Struggle for Mastery in Europe, 1848-1918* (Oxford History of Modern Europe, 1954), gives full bibliographical information for diplomatic history during its period.

For German thought, further reference may be made to the bibliographies in Butler's *Roots of National Socialism* (1941) and Coole and Potter, *Thus Spake Germany* (1941).

Part II indicates the principal sources for the study of Nazi Germany and gives also a selection of the secondary works. The Wiener Library in London is devoted to the subject of National Socialism, and its catalogues provide the fullest bibliographical information. Two parts, No. 1, *Persecution, Terror and Resistance in Nazi Germany*, and No. 2, *From Weimar to Hitler, Germany, 1918-1933*, have been published. *The Speeches of Adolf Hitler*, edited by Norman H. Baynes (1942), contains a very full bibliography of Nazi Germany. There is also *A Short List of Books on National Socialism*, by Norman H. Baynes (published by the Historical Association, 1943). Alan Bullock, *Hitler* (1952), and J. W. Wheeler-Bennett, *The Nemesis of Power* (1953), both have lengthy bibliographies. *The Foreign Affairs Bibliography* (Council on Foreign Relations, New York) is a large-scale guide to books on international relations, in two parts: *1919-1932* (edited by W. L. Langer and H. Fish Armstrong) and *1932-1942* (edited by R. G. Woolbert).

PART I. THE BACKGROUND

1. *The German Problem*

W. Röpke: *The German Question* (1946); F. W. Foerster: *Europe and the German Question* (1941); 'Verrina': *The German Mentality* (1946); J. A. Cramb: *England and Germany* (1914); *The German Mind and Outlook* (by G. P. Gooch, Morris Ginsberg, etc., under the auspices of the Institute of Sociology, 1945); Hermann Levy: *England and Germany* (1949); K. Otten: *A Combine of Aggression* (1942); A. L. Rowse: *The End of an Epoch* (1947); R. H. Lowie: *Toward Understanding Germany* (1954).

The following were contributions to a wartime controversy centring around the views of Lord Vansittart:

Lord Vansittart: *Black Record: Germans Past and Present* (1941); H. N. Brailsford: *Germans and Nazis—A Reply to 'Black Record'* (1944); Victor Gollancz: *Shall our Children Live or Die?—A Reply to Lord Vansittart* (1942); Harold J. Laski: *The Germans—are They Human? A Reply to Sir Robert Vansittart* (1941); H. Fraenkel: *Vansittart's Gift to Goebbels: a German Exile's Answer to 'Black Record'* (1941); D. Koffler: *Vansittartitis* (1943).

Two recent books by Germans which throw light on the problem are M. J. Bonn, *Wandering Scholar* (1949), and F. W. Foerster, *Erlebte Weltgeschichte 1869-1953* (1954). See also the excellent review article dealing with F. W. Foerster and the German edition of Bonn (*So macht man Geschichte*) in *Times Literary Supplement*, 24 September, 1954.

2. *German History*

G. Barraclough: *Factors in German History* (1946); *The Origins of Modern Germany* (1949); R. Flenley: *Modern German History* (1953); Veit Valentin: *The German People* (from Holy Roman Empire to Third Reich, 1946); *Germany—History and Administration* (published by H.M.S.O. from material prepared in 1944); S. H. Steinberg: *Short History of Germany* (1944); E. Stern Rubarth, *Short History of the Germans* (1941); A. J. P. Taylor: *The Course of German History* (1945); Roy Pascal, *Growth of Modern Germany* (1946); J. A. Hawgood: *The Evolution of Germany* (1955); K. S. Pinson: *Modern Germany—Its History and Civilization* (1955).

E. Eyck: *Bismarck and the German Empire* (1950); *Bismarck after Fifty Years* (Historical Association Pamphlet, 1948); E. Brandenburg: *From Bismarck to the World War* (history of German foreign policy, 1927); A. J. P. Taylor: *Bismarck* (1955).

J. Ellis Barker: *Modern Germany* (1909); H. Lichtenberger: *Germany and Its Evolution in Modern Times* (1913); W. H. Dawson: *Evolution of Modern Germany* (1919; first edition, 1908); *The German Empire 1867-1914* (2 vols., 1919); G. P. Gooch: *Germany* (1925); E. Vermeil: *Germany's Three Reichs* (1944); *L'Allemagne contemporaine* (1952-3; Vol. I, Kaiser Wilhelm II; Vol. II, Weimar, Hitler); Hans Kohn (editor: *German History—Some New German Views* (1954).

3. *German Thought*

R. D'O. Butler: *Roots of National Socialism 1783-1933* (1941); W. W. Coole and M. F. Potter: *Thus Spake Germany* (1941); S. D. Stirk: *The Prussian Spirit* (1941); E. Vermeil: *Doctrinaires de la Révolution Allemande 1918-1939* (studies of Rathenau, Keyserling, Thomas Mann, etc., and of Spengler and Moeller van den Bruck, as well as of Hitler and the Nazis; useful bibliography, 1939); H. W. C. Davis: *Political Thought of Heinrich von Treitschke* (1914); M. Boucher: *Les Idées politiques de Richard Wagner* (1947); G. P. Gooch: *Studies in German History* (1948); L. L. Snyder: *German Nationalism: The Tragedy of a People* (1952).

The following are among the more important works which illustrate some of the dangerous tendencies in German thought: Fichte: *Addresses to the German Nation* (Eng. trans. by R. F. Jones and G. H. Turnbull, 1922); Hegel: *Philosophy of Light* (trans. by T. M. Knox, 1942); H. von Treitschke: *Politics* (trans. by Blanche Dugdale and T. de Bille, 2 vols., 1916); Nietzsche: *Works* (trans. edited by O. Levy, 1909-13), especially *The Will to Power*, *The Antichrist*, *Beyond Good and Evil*, *The Genealogy of Morals*, *Thus Spake Zarathustra*; E. Dühring: *Die Judenfrage als Racen-, Sitten-, und Kulturfrage* (1881); Count de Gobineau: *Essai sur l'inégalité des races humaines* (1853-5, 2 vols.); Houston Stewart Chamberlain: *Foundations of the Nineteenth Century* (Eng. trans. by J. Lees, 1911, from Chamberlain's German *Grundlagen des Neunzehnten Jahrhunderts*, 1889); F. von Bernhardi: *Germany and the Next War* (trans. A. H. Powles, 1912); *Britain as Germany's Vassal* (trans. J. Ellis Barker, 1914); *The New Bernhardi* (collected articles, with a Preface by S. W. Sprigg, 1915); *The War of the Future* (trans. F. A. Holt, 1920); Prince von Bülow: *Imperial Germany* (trans. M. A. Lewenz, revised edition, 1916); Oswald Spengler: *Preussentum und Sozialismus* (1932); Moeller van den Bruck: *Das Dritte Reich* (1923; Eng. trans. by E. O. Lorimer, 1934).

PART II. NAZI GERMANY

A. Sources

1. *Collections of Documentary Material*

   The Trial of the Major War Criminals before the International Military Tribunal (Nuremberg, 1947-9):
   Proceedings, Vols. I-XXIII.
   Documents in Evidence, Vols. XXIV-XLII.
   In *Documents in Evidence* is printed the material in German collected for the trial at Nuremberg in 1945-1946. This collection which covers the whole Nazi period is of the first importance; it provides information on and illustrates the whole Nazi story.
   Nazi Conspiracy and Aggression (10 vols., Washington, 1946-8). Contains translations of many of the more important German documents, and is most valuable.
   The Trial of German Major War Criminals (23 parts; the trial proceedings published by H.M.S.O., 1946-50).
   Law Reports of Trials of War Criminals (Vols. 1-15; selected and prepared by the United Nations War Crimes Commission, H.M.S.O., 1947-9). These are reports of the trials other than that of the major war criminals. For further guidance to the vast mass of material collected for these trials, see the *Guide to the Records of the United Nations War Crimes Commission, 1943-1948* (U.N. Archives Reference Guide No. 19, August 1951).
   The German Constitution (Eng. trans. of the Weimar Constitution. H.M.S.O. 1919).
   The Treaties of Peace 1919-1923 (Versailles, St. Germáin, etc. 2 vols. Carnegie Endowment for International Peace, 1924).
   Der Hitler-Prozess vor dem Volksgericht in München (2 parts in one volume. Knorr und Hirth, Munich, 1924).
   Der Hitler-Prozess—Auszüge aus den Verhandlungsberichten (Deutscher Volksverlag, Munich, 1924). This edition of the proceedings

contains a Preface by 'A.R.', presumably Alfred Rosenberg, a number of whose writings published by the same firm are listed on the back cover.

Brown Book of the Hitler Terror and the Burning of the Reichstag (World Committee for the Victims of German Fascism, London, 1933).

The Reichstag Fire Trial. Second Brown Book of the Hitler Terror (as above, 1934).

The Treatment of German Nationals in Germany 1938-9 (Cmd. 6120. H.M.S.O., 1939).

Dokumente der deutschen Politik, Vol. I, 1933, and subsequent years to 1940. (Berlin, 1935-1943.) A Nazi production, but giving the text of official documents.

Organisationsbuch der N.S.D.A.P. (edited by the Party, Munich, 1940).

Nationalsozialistisches Jahrbuch (edited annually by the Party).

Documents on International Affairs. 1928 onwards (Royal Institute of International Affairs. 1929-   ).

Documents on British Foreign Policy, 1919-1939. Edited by Sir Llewelyn Woodward and Rowan Butler. First, Second, and Third Series (H.M.S.O., 1947-   ).

Documents on German Foreign Policy 1918-1945, Series D. (H.M.S.O., 1949.)

Ciano's Diplomatic Papers. Edited by Malcolm Muggeridge (1948).

Documents concerning German-Polish Relations and the Outbreak of Hostilities between Great Britain and Germany (Cmd. 6106, H.M.S.O., 1939).

Final Report by Sir Nevile Henderson . . . termination of his mission to Berlin (Cmd. 6115. H.M.S.O., 1939).

French Yellow Book. Diplomatic Documents 1938-1939 (Eng. edition, Hutchinson, 1939).

Polish White Book. Official Documents concerning Polish-German and Polish-Soviet Relations, 1933-1939 (published for the Polish Government, Hutchinson, 1939).

Polish Black Book. The German Invasion of Poland (as above).

German *Weissbücher* (German Foreign Office, Berlin, 1939-41): 1. *Urkunden zur letzen Phase der deutsch-polnischen Krise;* 2. *Dokumente zur Vorgeschichte des Krieges;* 3. *Polnische Dokumente zur Vorgeschichte des Krieges;* 4. *Dokumente zur englisch-französischen Politik der Kriegsausweitung;* 5. *Weitere Dokumente zur Kriegsausweitungspolitik der Westmächte;* 6. *Die Geheimakten des französischen Generalstabes;* 7. *Dokumente zum Konflikt mit Jugoslawien und Griechenland.*

Nazi-Soviet Relations, 1939-1941 (documents from the German Foreign Office archives; published by the Department of State, U.S.A., 1948).

Soviet Documents on Foreign Policy (3 vols., R.I.I.A., 1951-3).

The Spanish Government and the Axis: Official German Documents (Department of State, U.S.A., 1946).

Hitler Directs His War (records of his military conferences; edited by Felix Gilbert, 1951).

Führer Conferences on Naval Affairs (collected in *Brassey's Naval Annual, 1948*).

Axis Rule in Occupied Europe (collection of laws, regulations, etc.; edited R. Lemkin, 1944).

2. *Newspapers*

Day-to-day reports in the German, British, and other newspapers of the events in the rise and fall of Nazi Germany, articles, and accounts of interviews with leading figures can be conveniently followed in the files at the British Museum Newspaper Library, Colindale, London. Among the German newspapers see especially the *Frankfurter Zeitung*, *Berliner Tageblatt*, *Vorwärts* (the Social Democrat paper), and the two principal Nazi papers, the *Völkischer Beobachter* and *Der Angriff*.

3. *Nazi Writings and Speeches*

Adolf Hitler: *Mein Kampf* (2 vols. in 1; unexpurgated English edition, trans. by James Murphy, Hurst and Blackett, 1939). (See also the illustrated edition, Hutchinson & Co.)

Speeches of Adolf Hitler, 1922-1939 (edited by Norman H. Baynes, 2 vols., 1942). Professor Baynes's collection is a work of fundamental importance for the study of Nazi Germany.

My New Order (Hitler's speeches, 1922-41, edited by Count Raoul de Roussy de Sales, New York, 1941).

Hitler's Words (speeches, 1922-43; edited by Gordon W. Prange, Washington, 1944).

Hitler's Table Talk, 1941-44 (trans. by N. Cameron and R. H. Stevens; Introduction on 'The Mind of Adolf Hitler', by H. R. Trevor-Roper; 1953).

Gottfried Feder: *Hitler's Official Programme and Its Fundamental Ideas* (1934, Eng. trans. of fifth edition of Feder's *Das Programm der N.S.D.A.P.*, first published in 1927).

Germany Speaks (by Nazi authors; preface by Ribbentrop; 1938).

Collections of the speeches of the other Nazi leaders were published in Germany, including those of Göring, Goebbels, Hess, Rosenberg, and Gregor Strasser, and works dealing with the Nazi ideology by Gottfried Feder, Rosenberg, Himmler, and Darré. Among the best known of these works was Alfred Rosenberg's *Der Mythus des 20 Jahrhunderts* (1930).

4. Memoirs, etc.

German:

P. Scheidemann: *Memoirs of a Social Democrat* (1929); Carl Severing: *Mein Lebensweg* (2 vols., 1950); Otto Braun: *Von Weimar zu Hitler* (1940); Prince Max of Baden: *Memoirs* (1928); *Gustav Stresemann, His Diaries, Letters, and Papers* (ed. Eric Sutton, 1935-40). There are also volumes by Bernstorff, Curtius, Dirksen, Noske, and Rathenau.

A. C. Grzesinski: *Inside Germany* (1939).

Anton Drexler: *Mein politisches Erwachen* (1923); Otto Dietrich, *Mit Hitler in die Macht* (1934); T. Düsterberg: *Der Stahlhelm und Hitler* (1949); F. von Papen: *Memoirs* (1952); F. Thyssen: *I Paid Hitler* (1941); Hjalmar Schacht: *Account Settled* (1948); Joseph Goebbels: *My Part in Germany's Fight* (1935); *The Goebbels Diaries* (edited by Louis P. Lochner, 1949); Kurt G. W. Ludecke: *I Knew Hitler* (1938); Hermann Rauschning, *Hitler Speaks* (1939); *Makers of Destruction* (1942); Ernst Röhm, *Die Memoiren des Stabchefs Röhm* (1934); Otto Strasser: *Hitler and I* (1940); *The Ribbentrop Memoirs* (introduction by Alan Bullock, 1954); *The Bormann Letters* (ed. H. R. Trevor-Roper, 1954); O. Meissner: *Staatssekretär unter Ebert-Hindenburg-Hitler* (1950); *Memoirs of Ernst von Weizsäcker* (1951); Erich Kordt: *Wahn und Wirklichkeit* (1947); *Nicht aus den Akten* (1950); P. Schmidt: *Statist auf diplomatischer Bühne* (1949); *Hitler's Interpreter* (trans. of much of Schmidt by R. H. C. Steed).

H. B. Gisevius: *To the Bitter End* (1948); *The Von Hassell Diaries 1938-1944* (1948); F. von Schlabrendorff: *Revolt against Hitler* (1948).

The Other Side of the Hill (German generals' views on the war; edited by B. H. Liddell Hart, 1951); Otto Dietrich, *Auf den Strassen des Sieges* (1940); General H. Guderian: *Panzer Leader* (1952); General F. Halder, *Hitler as Warlord* (1950); General Hans Speidel: *We Defended Normandy* (1951); *The Rommel Papers* (edited B. H. Liddell Hart, 1953); Field-Marshal A. Kesselring: *Soldat bis zum letzen Tag* (1953).

Austrian:

K. von. Schuschnigg: *Farewell Austria* (1938); *Austrian Requiem* (1947); Prince E. R. von Starhemberg: *Between Hitler and Mussolini* (1942).

British:

Winston S. Churchill: *The Second World War* (1948-53): Vol. I, *The Gathering Storm*; Vol. II, *Their Finest Hour*; Vol. III, *The Grand Alliance*; Vol. IV, *The Hinge of Fate*; Vol. V, *Closing the Ring*; Vol. VI, *Triumph and Tragedy*.

An Ambassador of Peace—Lord D'Abernon's Diary (period 1920-26; 3 vols., 1929-30); G. Ward Price: *I Know These Dictators* (1937); Sir Nevile Henderson: *Failure of a Mission* (1940); Lord Norwich (Duff Cooper): *Old Men Forget* (1953); Viscount Templewood (Sir Samuel Hoare): *Nine Troubled Years* (1954); Viscount Simon: *Retrospect* (1952); Sir Walford Selby: *Diplomatic Twilight, 1930-1940* (1953); Thomas Jones: *A Diary with Letters 1931-1950* (1954); Viscount Maugham: *At the End of the Day* (1954).

Major-General E. L. Spears: *Assignment to Catastrophe* (2 vols., 1954); S. Payne Best: *The Venlo Incident* (1950); Field-Marshal Montgomery: *El Alamein to the River Sangro* (1948); *Normandy to the Baltic* (1947); General F. W. de Guingand: *Operation Victory* (1947).

American:

Ambassador Dodd's Diary, 1933-1938 (1941); William Shirer: *A Berlin Diary* (1941); Sumner Welles: *A Time for Decision* (1944); *Memoirs of Cordell Hull* (2 vols., 1948); General D. D. Eisenhower: *Crusade in Europe* (1948); H. C. Butcher: *Three Years with Eisenhower* (1946).

French:

A. François-Poncet: *Souvenirs d'une ambassade à Berlin, 1931-1938* (1946; Eng. trans., *The Fateful Years*, 1949); P. E. Flandin: *Politique française 1919-1940* (1947); General M. G. Gamelin: *Servir* (3 vols., 1946-7); Paul Reynard: *La France a sauvé l'Europe* (2 vols., 1947); General de Gaulle: *L'Appel* (Vol. I, 1954); *The Unpublished Diary of Pierre Laval* (1948).

Italian:

Mussolini: *Memoirs* (ed. R. Klibansky, 1949); *Ciano's Diary, 1937-1938* (1952); *Ciano's Diary, 1939-1943* (1947); D. Alfieri: *Dictators Face to Face* (1954).

Polish:

General W. Anders: *An Army in Exile* (1949); General T. Bor-Komorowski: *The Secret Army* (1950).

Yugoslav:

V. Dedijer: *Tito Speaks* (1953).

Rumanian:

G. Gafencu: *The Last Days of Europe* (1947). A fascinating account of the Rumanian Foreign Minister's meetings with the leaders of Europe on the eve of war.

Czech:

Memoirs of Dr. Eduard Beneš. From Munich to New War and New Victory (trans. by Godfrey Lias, 1954).

Hungarian:

Mémoires de l'Amiral Horthy (1954).

Swedish:

Count Fulk Bernadotte: *The Curtain Falls* (1945); B. Dahlerus: *The Last Attempt* (1948).

Spanish:

R. Serrano Suñer: *Entre les Pyrénées et Gibraltar* (1947). Notes and reflections on Spanish foreign policy since 1936.

B. SECONDARY WORKS

1. *General*

A very important work on the whole Nazi period is J. W. Wheeler-Bennett, *The Nemesis of Power—The German Army in Politics, 1918-1945* (1954).
General accounts of international affairs during this period can be found in E. H. Carr: *International Relations between the Two World Wars* (1947; originally published as *International Relations since the Peace Treaties* in 1937); F. Lee Benns: *Europe since 1914* (Seventh Edition, 1949); R. W. Seton-Watson: *Britain and the Dictators* (1938); T. K. Derry and T. L. Jarman: *The European World 1870-1945* (1950).

2. *The Weimar Republic and the Rise of the Nazi Party*

G. Scheele: *The Weimar Republic* (1946); Arthur Rosenberg: *Birth of the German Republic* (1931); *History of the German Republic* (1936); H. G. Daniels: *Rise of the German Republic* (1927); H. Quigley and R. T. Clark: *Republican Germany* (1928); R. T. Clark: *The Fall of the German Republic* (1935); A. Brecht: *Prelude to Silence* (1944); Erich Eyck: *Geschichte der Weimarer Republic* (1954); E. Vermeil: *L'Allemagne contemporaine*, Vol. 2 (see under 'German History'); R. G. L. Waite: *Vanguard of Nazism* (1952)—the Free Corps movement, 1918-1923.

F. Hartung: *Deutsche Verfassungsgeschichte vom 15 Jahrhundert bis zur Gegenwart* (1950); J. R. Brunet: *The German Constitution* (trans. from French, J. Gollomb, 1923); E. Vermeil: *La Constitution de Weimar et le Principe de la Démocratie allemande* (1923); Agnes Headlam Morley: *The New Democratic Constitutions of Europe* (1928);

J. A. Hawgood: *Modern Constitutions since 1789* (1939); J. Mattern: *Principles of the Constitutional Jurisprudence of the German National Republic* (1928); F. F. Blackley and M. E. Oatman: *The Government and Administration of Germany* (1928).

F. S. Marston: *The Peace Conference of 1919* (with full bibliography, 1944); H. W. V. Temperley: *A History of the Peace Conference of Paris* (6 vols., 1920-4); K. F. Nowak: *Versailles* (1929); J. M. (afterwards Lord) Keynes: *The Economic Consequences of the Peace* (1920); E. Mantoux: *The Carthaginian Peace* (1946); T. E. Jessop: *The Treaty of Versailles: Was it Just?* (1942).

F. Tuohy: *Occupied 1918-1930* (1931); P. Tirard: *La France sur le Rhin, Douze Années d'Occupation Rhénane* (1930).

General J. H. Morgan: *Assize of Arms* (disarmament and rearmament of Germany 1919, Vol. I, 1945).

Konrad Heiden: *History of National Socialism* (1934); E. A. Mowrer: *Germany Puts the Clock Back* (1933); Vernon Bartlett: *Nazi Germany Explained* (1933); C. B. Hoover: *Germany Enters the Third Reich* (1933); H. Powys Greenwood: *The German Revolution* (1934); H. Wickham Steed: *Hitler, Whence and Whither?* (1934); W. M. Knight-Patterson: *Germany from Defeat to Conquest, 1913-1933* (1945); Douglas Reed: *Insanity Fair* (1938); J. W. Wheeler-Bennett: *Hindenburg, The Wooden Titan* (1936); O. Dutch: *The Errant Diplomat* (life of von Papen, 1940).

3. Hitler

Alan Bullock: *Hitler—A Study in Tyranny* (1952). A comprehensive and brilliant 700-page account of Hitler's whole career. Konrad Heiden: *Der Fuehrer* (1944) and an earlier life, *Hitler* (1936). Heiden's *Der Fuehrer* gives the most detailed account of the earlier part of Hitler's career. R. Olden: *Hitler the Pawn* (1936). Kurt G. W. Ludecke, *I Knew Hitler* (1938) is an illuminating book which re-creates the authentic atmosphere of the Nazi struggle for power. A. Kubizek: *The Young Hitler* (1954)—Hitler's boyhood and youth by a personal friend. H. Hoffmann: *Hitler was my Friend* (1955).

4. Germany under Hitler: The Third Reich

The Third Reich (essays by leading European scholars, commissioned by U.N.E.S.C.O. 1955). *Germany—History and Administration* (H.M.S.O., from material prepared in 1944); S. H. Roberts: *The House that Hitler Built* (1937); H. Lichtenberger: *The Third Reich* (1938); F. L. Schumann: *Hitler and the Nazi Dictatorship* (1936); F. Neumann: *Behemoth, the Structure and Practice of National Socialism* (1942); Hermann Rauschning: *Germany's Revolution of Destruction*

(1939); J. K. Pollock: *The Government of Greater Germany* (1938); F. M. Marx: *Government in the Third Reich* (1937); O. Koellreuter: *Volk und Staat in der Weltanschauung des National Sozialismus* (1935); Carl Schmitt: *Nationalsozialismus und Völkerrecht* (1934); F. Roetter: *Might is Right* (1939); E. Kogon: *Der S.S. Staat* (1946); G. d'Alquen: *Die S.S.* (1939); J. K. Pollock and Homer Thomas: *Germany in Power and Eclipse* (1952).

C. W. Guillebaud: *The Economic Recovery of Germany 1933-1938* (1939); W. F. Bruck: *Social and Economic History of Germany from William II to Hitler* (1938); O. Nathan: *The Nazi Economic System* (1944).

A. S. Duncan Jones: *The Struggle for Religious Freedom in Germany* (1938); Nathaniel Micklem: *National Socialism and the Roman Catholic Church* (1939); Pastor F. Hildebrandt: *Pastor Niemöller and His Creed* (1938).

Ewan Butler and G. Young: *Marshal without Glory* (1951); W. Frischauer: *Göring* (1951); *Himmler* (1953); Curt Reiss: *Joseph Goebbels* (1949); E. Ebermayer and H. O. Meissner: *Evil Genius* (Goebbels, 1954); J. R. Rees (editor): *The Case of Rudolf Hess* (1947).

5. *Foreign Affairs*

Survey of International Affairs (R.I.I.A., 1925-). The series begins with the volume for 1920-3, and continues for each of the subsequent years. It was preceded by Temperley's *History of the Peace Conference of Paris* (see above). The series of annual volumes was interrupted by the outbreak of war in 1939, and began again in 1947. The period of the war is now being covered by a new series of volumes, known as *Survey of International Affairs, 1939-1946*. Of these volumes, see especially *The World in March 1939*; and *Hitler's Europe*.

F. L. Schumann: *Europe on the Eve* (the crises of diplomacy from 1933 to 1939; 1939); Fritz Hesse: *Das Spiel um Deutschland* (1953); W. N. Medlicott: *British Foreign Policy since Versailles* (1942); E. H. Carr: *Britain, Foreign Policy* (from Versailles to the war; 1939); A. François-Poncet: *De Versailles à Potsdam* (France and the German problem, 1919-45; 1948); W. M. Jordan; *Great Britain, France and the German Problem 1918-1939* (1943); W. H. Dawson: *Germany under the Treaty* (1933); R. Martel: *The Eastern Frontiers of Germany* (1930); L. Kochan: *Russia and the Weimar Republic* (1954); E. H. Carr: *German-Soviet Relations 1919-1939* (1952); Max Beloff: *Foreign Policy of Soviet Russia 1929-1941* (2 vols., 1947-9); A. Rossi: *The Russo-German Alliance* (1950); S. Wambaugh: *The Saar Plebiscite* (1940); M. Bullock: *Austria 1918-1938* (1939);

G. E. R. Gedye: *Fallen Bastions* (1939); Sheila Grant-Duff: *Europe and the Czechs* (1938); R. W. Seton Watson: *Munich and the Dictators* (1939); J. W. Wheeler-Bennett: *Munich, Prologue to Tragedy* (1948); L. B. Namier: *Diplomatic Prelude, 1938-1939* (1948); Keith Feiling: *Life of Neville Chamberlain* (1946); Elizabeth Wiskemann: *Czechs and Germans* (1938); *Undeclared War* (1939); *The Rome-Berlin Axis* (1949); L. B. Namier: *Europe in Defeat* (1950); Prince Constantine of Bavaria: *The Pope* (Pius XII; 1954); G. A. Craig and F. Gilbert: *The Diplomats, 1919-1939* (1953).

6. The War

Cyril Falls: *The Second World War* (3rd edition, 1950); General F. J. C. Fuller: *The Second World War* (1948); P. E. Schramm and H. O. H. Stange: *Geschichte des Zweiten Weltkrieges* (1951, from Ploetz, *Auszug aus der Geschichte*); W. Görlitz: *The German General Staff* (Eng. trans., 1953); *Der Zweite Weltkrieg 1939-1945* (2 vols., 1951); K. von Tippelskirch: *Geschichte des Zweiten Weltkrieges* (1951); F. H. Hinsley: *Hitler's Strategy* (1951); Milton Shulman: *Defeat in the West* (1949); Chester Wilmot: *The Struggle for Europe* (1952); D. Young: *Rommel* (1950); A. Martienssen: *Hitler and His Admirals* (1948); *History of the Second World War: United Kingdom Military Series* (in progress)—volumes by T. K. Derry: *The Campaign in Norway* (1952); L. F. Ellis *The War in France and Flanders 1939-1940* (1953); I. S. O. Playfair: *The Mediterranean and Middle East* (Vol. I 1954); S. W. Roskill: *The War at Sea 1939-1945* (1954).

Gunther Weisenborn (editor): *Der lautlose Aufstand* (account of the German opposition movement, 1953); W. Foerster: *Generaloberst Ludwig Beck—Sein Kampf gegen den Krieg* (1953); A. W. Dulles: *Germany's Underground* (1947); Ian Colvin: *Chief of Intelligence* (Canaris, 1951); *Das Gewissen steht auf* (edited by Annedore Leber and others, 1954); *Die Wahrheit über den 20 Juli* (edited E. Budde P. Lutsches, 1952); K. Strölin: *Verräter oder Patrioten* (1952); Inge Scholl: *Six against Tyranny* (1955).

Hitler's Europe (R.I.I.A., 1954; see above; see also the corresponding volume of documents, under the same title, in *Documents on International Affairs*); G. Reitlinger: *The Final Solution: The Attempt to Exterminate the Jews of Europe, 1939-1945* (1953); Lord Russell of Liverpool: *The Scourge of the Swastika* (1954); R. Hewins: *Count Folke Bernadotte* (1949).

W. L. Langer: *Our Vichy Gamble* (1947); W. L. Langer and S. E. Gleason: *The World Crisis and American Foreign Policy* (2 vols., R.I.I.A., 1952-3): (1) *The Challenge to Isolation, 1937-1940* and (2) *The Undeclared War, 1940-1941*.

7. *The End of the Nazis*

H. R. Trevor-Roper: *The Last Days of Hitler* (Second Edition, 1950)—the detailed account based on the author's official investigations as an intelligence officer; M. A. Musmanno: *Ten Days to Die* (1951)—an American account of the end of Hitler.

P. Calvocoressi: *Nuremberg* (1947); A. von Knierim: *Nürnberg—Rechtliche und Menschliche Probleme* (1953); F. J. P. Veale: *Advance to Barbarism* (1953); J. Fishman: *The Seven Men of Spandau* (1954).

A. G. Dickens: *Lübeck Diary* (1947); H. J. Morgenthau (editor): *Germany and the Future of Europe* (1951); *Germany Reports* (German Press and Information Office, 1953); *Deutsche Tatsachen* (Transatlantik-Brücke, Hamburg, 1953); N. Tönnies: *Der Staat aus dem Nichts* (1954).

INDEX

ABYSSINIA, Italian conquest, 216-17; Powers' failure to help, 223

Adams, Vyvyan, 236

Adenauer, Dr., Christian Democrat victory, 349; co-operation with, 355, 360; rearmament, 357; revival of National Socialism, 345

Africa, North, German defeat in, 309; military position in, 1942-3, 293

Albania, Italian invasion of, 251

Alexander, General, 314

Algeria, Allied invasion, 1942, 308

Ali Akbar, S., 20n

Allied Powers defeated in Norway, 274; Germans blame Allies, 353; Peace Conference, Paris, 74-5; plans for attack, 1944, 314; policy after Peace Treaty, 80; strategy, 291

Alsace-Lorraine, 75, 213

Altmark boarded, 273

Amann, Max, 92, 99n, 125, 174

Anglo-Saxons, 30-1, 35, 58

Angriff, Der, 126, 137

Anti-Comintern Pact, 219, 249, 295

Anti-Hitler plots. *See* Hitler.

Anti-Semitism. *See* Jews.

Antonescu, General, 280

Antz, Joseph, 48n

Appeasement, policy of, 247, 251

Arbeitsfront, 197, 199, 200

Armaments increased after Munich Conference, 243; limitation of, 215

Army, defeat of, theories for, 351; importance of, 52-3; S.A., Army jealous of, 160

Arnhem, 322

Arnold, Matthew, 18-19,

Aryan race theory, 57-60, 115-16, 298

Atlantic Charter, 295

Auschwitz, camp at, 304

Aust, Hermann, 93

Austria: Austro-German Agreement, 1936, 227; Germanic Confederation, 41; independent state, 39; Nazi attempt, 1934, 226; Nazi demonstrations, 231; Nazis, Austrian terrorism of, 227; *Putsch*, 1934, 212;

Germany and: Customs union, 131; Hitler denies intention of annexing, 215; pressure on and invasion, 208, 217-18, 225-6, 229, 231, 233

Autobahnen, 192

B.H.E. (REFUGEES PARTY), 348

Badoglio, *Marshal* Pietro, 310-11

Baldwin, Stanley (later Earl Baldwin), Prime Minister, 214, 222, 224

Balfour, Arthur J. (later Earl), 54

Balkans, German influence in, 280

Baltic States, Russian move into, 280

Barraclough, G., 35n

Barter system, 195

Bauer, Chancellor, 84

Bavaria, Communist rising, 84; Government, changes in, 94; attitude to Nazi Party, 92; struggle against central government, 97-9; nationalist forces united, 96-7; Nazi control, 154; *Putsch* called off, 94; revolution in, 73; state of emergency, 1923, 97; state and federal politics, 95

Baynes, N. H., 74n, 86-7n, 89n, 95n, 135n, 142n, 148-9n, 157-8n, 161n, 164n, 166n, 167n, 169-70n, 191n, 199n, 205n, 210n, 213n, 214n, 215n, 219n, 225n, 226n, 233n, 240n, 243n, 245n, 253n

Bechstein family, 92

Beck, Colonel Jozef, Polish Foreign Minister, 249

Beck, General Ludwig, 271; conspiracy against Hitler, 317-18; death of, 319; resignation of, 236

Belgium, German attack on, 274; invasion of, 15; Locarno Agreements, withdrawal from, 217; neutrality of, 217, 272

Belgrade destroyed, 283

Belsen, memorial at, 350

Beneš, Edvard, Czech President, 235; Hitler's attack on, 240; resignation, 242

Bennett, G., 64n

Berlin, bombing of, 308; general strike, 1920, 84; revolutionary outbreaks, 84
Berliner Arbeitszeitung, 125
Berliner Illustrirte Zeitung, 175
Berliner Tageblatt, Peace Treaty, 1919, 77-8
Bernadotte, Count, Peace negotiations, 332
Bernhardi, General Friedrich von, 66-7
Best, S. Payne, 23-4, 271n, 288n
Betz, W., 349n
Bibel Forscher, 180
Bismarck, Prince Otto von, German Chancellor, 29; dropped, 65; methods, 109; personality and influence of, 45; political system, 46; policy of, 41-2, 44-5, 48; progress under, 18; Second Reich proclaimed, 42; social insurance, 19; socialism, failure against, 119
Black Front, 129
Bloch, Paul, 77n
Blomberg, Field-Marshal, Minister of Defence, 148, 150, 161, 225
Blum, Léon, French Premier, 218
Blumentritt, General, 275n
Bohemia, Protectorate of, 245
Boncour, Paul, 215
Bonn Basic Law, 355
Bonn Government, 350
Bor-Komorowski, T., 299n, 321n
Bormann, Martin, 172, 300-1; escape of, 337; loyal to Hitler, 312; named as Party Minister, 335; Poles, treatment of, 299; trial of, 340
Bose, von, 163
Boucher, Maurice, 61
Bouhler, Philip, 172
Brailsford, H. N., 14n, 131n
Brauchitsch, Field-Marshal, Walter von, 250, 271-2, 284, 286, 292
Braun, Eva, with Hitler at the end, 332; marriage to Hitler, 333-4; status and character of, 333; death, 336
Bredow, General von, 163
Brest-Litovsk, 80, 268; Treaty of, 74
Briand, 123, 215
Brinton, Carl, 57n
British race, 64
Broadcast to resistance movements, 308
Brownshirts, origin of, 91

Bruck, W. F., 191n
Bruckmanns, Nazi supporters, 93
Brunet, René, 83n
Brüning, Dr., German Chancellor, 133, 135-6
Bryce, 37n
Buch, 174
Buchheim, K., 44n, 49n
Bülow, 222
Building and town-planning, 18
Bulgaria joins Tripartite Pact, 282
Bullock, Alan, 254, 289n, 306n
Buna, synthetic rubber, 194
Bund Oberland (Oberland League), 97
Bundestag elections, 1953, 349
Burckhardt, 257n
Bürgerbräu Keller meeting, November 1923, 98-9

CABINET COMPOSITION AND STATUS OF, 172-3
Caird, E., 51
Calvocoressi, P., 339
Canaris, Admiral, 271
Carlyle, Thomas, 18
Catholic Centre Party. See Centre Party.
Catholics shot, 163
Cecil, Lord Robert, 215, 220
Centre Party, 82, 132-3, 136, 148, 151, 154
Chamberlain, Houston Stewart, 57, 61-5, 67, 93
Chamberlain, Sir Austen, 17n, 123
Chamberlain, Joseph, Colonial Secretary, 64
Chamberlain, Neville, Prime Minister, broadcast speech, 240-1; conference, appeal for, 241; free hand agreement, suggestion for, 252; guarantees to Greece and Rumania, 250-1, 260; Hitler, visits to, 1938, 237-9; leadership of, 222; Munich Conference, 241-3; Munich policy, 247-8; Poland, British firm stand, 258-9; speech at Birmingham, March 1939, 247-8; Stalin's suspicions of, 286
Charlemagne, 35-6
Charles V, 1519-56, 38
China; Japanese aggression, 219
Christian Democrats, 349
Christianity, Nazi attitude to, 182-3; Nietzsche's views, 55-6

Churchill, Rt. Hon. Winston S., Prime Minister, 220n, 222, 224, 281; Atlantic Charter, meeting with President Roosevelt, 295; 'blood, toil, tears and sweat', 274; Conference at Teheran, 1943, 314; Czechoslovakia, 242; disarmament of Germany, 220; leadership, 276; Stalin, warning to, 286

Ciano, Count Galeazzo, 207, 209, 226, 257, 258n, 269, 270n, 278n, 288, 294n, 295, 297, 305n, 307, 310n, 311

Clemenceau, Georges, French Premier, 114; Peace Conference at Paris, 74; Weimar Republic, 83

Clovis, 35

Coburg, demonstration at, 91

Cold War, 306, 359-60

Collective security, 221, 223n

Cologne, 307

Colonies, German, 73, 75, 219

Communists, 147; danger of, 219; Deputies arrested, 150; Germany, bulwark against, 205; menace of beaten, 186; Nazi policy towards, 149-50, 156, 204; Party, increase of, 132-3; property seized, 154; Reichstag, membership, 140; revolution, alleged, 149; risings, 1919-20, 73, 84; West blamed for Russian alliance, 352

Concentration camps, 176, 179-80, 298, 302

Conference on Disarmament, 210

Congress of Vienna, 1815, 40

Council for Defence, 172

Customs Union, 1834, 41

Crete captured by Germans, 283

Crowe, Sir Eyre, 66

Curtius, Dr., 135n

Curzon, Lord, Viceroy of India, 64

Czechoslovakia, Munich Conference, 241; position of, 234; Sudeten Germans, 234-6; British, French and Russian support, 235; British understanding of Sudeten problem, 235-6; Germany, generals' attitude towards a war, 236; Hitler's attitude and policy, 208, 225, 233-5, 240, 243; military preparations, 236; occupation, 242, 244-5; German treatment of Czechs, 300; Russian agreement with Czechoslovakia, 214

D.P. (GERMAN PARTY), 348

D'Abernon, Lord, 130n

Dachau, 180

Dahlerus, B., 260, 262

Daily Express, 150, 151n, 256, 261, 346, 347n

Daily Mail, 205n, 214n

Daily Worker, 268n, 269

Daluege, 178

Daladier, Edouard, French Premier, 241, 262

Danzig, 209, 211; annexation of, 73; Germany plans to acquire, 244; Hitler enters, 268; Hitler, no wish to use force, 250; Nazis arming and training, 254; Polish discussions with Germany, 250

Darré, Walther, 172-3

Davis, H. W. C., 54n

Dawes Plan, 123

Defeat of Germany, Germans blame Allies, 353; stab in the back legend, 49, 74, 102, 348, 351-2

Delmer, Sefton, 151n, 230n, 346-7

Democratic Party, 82, 133, 154

Democracy, 118

Denmark, German attack on, 273

Dernburg, Dr., Finance Minister, 78-9

Derry, T. K., 274

Deutsche Arbeiterpartei. See German Workers' Party.

Dieppe raid, 1942, 309

Dimitroff, Georgi, 150

Dirksen, von, 235n

Disarmament Conference, Germany withdraws from, 193

Dolfuss, Engelbert, Chancellor of the Austrian Republic, 212, 226

Dönitz, Admiral Karl, announcement of Hitler's death, 337, 350; announces his succession, 335, 337; Government set up, 337-8; trial of, 340, 351

Drexler, Anton, 88-90, 92

Dual Alliance, 48

Dühring, Eugen, 57

Duesterberg, T., 68, 163-5n

Duff Cooper, Sir A. (later Viscount Norwich), 224n, 242

Dunkirk, evacuation of, 275

Dutch, Oswald, 162n

EBERT, FRIEDRICH, REICH PRESIDENT, 72, 80-1, 84, 98, 124

Eckart, Dietrich, 88, 92-3, 122

Economic policy, 193-4; recovery, 1938, 195; slump, 129-34
Education, 18-21
Eden, Rt. Hon. Anthony, British Foreign Secretary, 160, 214-17, 224n
Egypt, Italian advance into, 281
Eire, neutrality of, 294
Eisenhower, General Dwight D., 293, 338
El Alamein, 293
Ellis, L. F., 275n
Enabling Bill, 152-3
English people, affinities and differences, 15-17
Entente Cordiale, 1904, 48
Epp, Franz X., Ritter von, 92, 127, 154, 174
Ernst, Karl, 163
Ersatz goods, 194
Erzberger, Matthias, 49, 85, 94
Esser, Herman, 94, 122
Estonia, non-aggression pact with Germany, 254; Soviet Zone, 259; Russia and, 268; incorporated in Russia, 280
Ethiopia, Italian Empire of, 218
Eucken, Professor, 306n
Expansion of Germany, 206-7
Exports, efforts to increase, 194
Extermination camps, 302, 304
Eyck, Erich, 45, 46n

Falaise, 321
Falkenhorst, General N. von, 273
Falls, Cyril, 291
Faulhaber, Cardinal, Archbishop of Munich, 182-3
Feder, Gottfried, 88-90
Federal Republic of Germany, 345
Federal States under control, 154
Fegelein, Herman, 333
Fichte, 50, 55
Finance, expansion of credit, 190; financial policy, 194
Finland, Allied aid, 273; Russian attack on, 273; Soviet Zone, 259
Fisher, H. A. L., 18
Flag, Nazi, 91
Flexner, A., 20n
Foch, Marshal, 83
Foerster, F. W., 48n
Ford, Henry, 93
Foreign policy, 203 et seq.
Four-Year Plans, 190, 195-6
Fraenkel, H., 14n

France, League of Nations, attitude to, 221; weakness of, 221
Germany and: General relations with, 14, 40-1, 114, 205; German-Russian agreement, 260; Hitler's message, no issue between, 260, 262; Italo-Abyssinian conquest, 217; Poland, attitude to German action, 208-9, 256-7; Ruhr, occupation of, 77, 95-6, 123
Poland and: French attitude, 256-7
Spain and: French attitude to Civil war, 218
Russia and: Pact for mutual aid, 214, 217
Turkey and: Mediterranean Agreement, 251
War: Allies landing, 1944, 315; armistice signed with Germany, 276; armistice terms, 279; disbelief in war, 1939, 262; Free French Forces of Interior, 321; German attack, 1940, 274
Francis II, Emperor of Austria, 40
Franco, General, 218, 279-80
Franco-Prussian War, 1870, 42
François-Poncet, A., 120, 212n
Frank, Hans, 166, 245, 279, 340, 342
Frankfort Parliament, 1848-9, 41
Frankfurter Allgemeine Zeitung, 347n
Frederick Barbarossa, 36
Frederick the Great, 29, 40
Free Democrat Party (F.D.P.), 349
Freikorps, 84, 92
French Revolution, 39-40
Frick, Wilhelm, 99, 127, 134, 147, 149, 154-5, 172-3, 180, 340, 342
Frischauer, W., 149
Fritsch, General Werner, 225-6, 340, 342
Fromm, General Fritz, 319-20
Führer: German attitude towards, 16; Führerprinzip, 166. See Hitler, Adolf.
Fuller, General, 274
Funk, Walther, 225, 340

Gafencu, Grigore, 252
Galen, Count von, Bishop of Münster, 183
Gamelin, General, 268
Gaulle, General de, 275-6
Gehlen organization, 359
Gehlen, General, 346
German Freedom Movement, 122

German National Party, 128, 133
German Workers' Party, 88-90
Germanic Confederation, 41
Germany, *general:* European hege-
  mony, 295; frontierless, 37;
  German Empire, the Second
  Reich, 1871, 29, 42, 109;
  German people, 13-31, 305;
  German thought, 50; greatness
  of, 49; Imperial Constitution,
  46; open country in 1933-9, 187;
  Parliament, Frankfort, 1848-9,
  41; policy of in pre-war years,
  48; strength of, growing, 220,
  225; Thirty Years' War, 38;
  weakness and insecurity of, 40;
  world position, 1941, 294
Germany, *1918-19:* armistice of
  1918, 72, 74; general strike in
  Berlin, 1918, 72; military collapse inevitable, 74; revolutionary outbursts, 72-4, 80-1, 84;
  Peace Treaty, 1919, reactions
  to, 73, 75
Germany Constitution and Government:
  Weimar Republic, 28, 71-2, 81-7,
  94, 150, 166, 355; Nazi Government, *see* Nazi Party.
Political conditions: Constitution suspended, 150; Government to
  make laws without Reichstag,
  153; political development of
  Germany, 35, 39, 50; parties,
  143, 147; political revolution,
  71, 81; political system, 46
Economic and social conditions, German
  Policies: Bolshevism, bulwark
  against, 204-5, *see also* Communism. Conquered people,
  treatment of, 296-7; democracy,
  30; economic depression, 1930,
  28; economic policy of conquest,
  296; economic prosperity, 345;
  economic recovery, 124, 188-9;
  expansion, views on, 66-7; expansion of credit, 190; financial
  crisis, 131; food problems, 296-7;
  housing, 19; imports, restriction
  of, 194; industrial progress, 18;
  inflation, effect of, 95-6, 123;
  insurance, social, 19; labour
  problems, 297; Labour Front,
  154; leadership, 23-4; megalomania, 50 *et seq.*; nationalism,
  50, 57 *et seq.*, 65, 71; Papacy,
  relations with, 36; peace offensive, 269; prisoners, treatment of,

297-8; Prussianism, 42, 52-4;
  racial policy, Himmler in charge
  of, 302; reparations, 75-7, 96;
  Tripartite Pact, 1940, 281; unemployment, 130, 188-91; unity
  achieved by force and war, 46-7;
  wages and prices, 191; *Winterhilfe,* 189
Armaments, rearmament: armaments
  drive, 1937, 219; armaments
  race, threat of, 357-8; military
  assistance wanted, dilemma of
  the Allies, 348; military conscription, 1935, 213-14; military
  organizations, 348; Rearmament
  of Germany, 193, 203-4, 209,
  216, 345, 347
War and militarism, German attitude:
  aggressive war, the charge
  against Germany, 341; guilt,
  avoidance of, 27; Hitler post-
  pones attack, 1939, 271; programme towards war, 207-8;
  militarism, 30, 44, 49, 194, 346-7,
  358; nationalistic writers, 66;
  Nietzsche on, 56; responsibility
  for, 27, 47-8, 73-4; threat to
  Europe, 49; Treitschke's views
  on, 52-3
War, campaigns and countries: Germany,
  general: Austria and Czechoslovakia, objectives, 225; collapse of Germany, causes, 327-8;
  opposition leaders' peace moves,
  1943-4, 312; policy of 'Fight on',
  313, 329-30; scorched earth
  policy, 330; *Western Front:* Allied
  advance, 1944, 321; Ardennes
  offensive, 322; Allies defeated
  1940, Belgium and France, 274-
  5; armistice with France, 276;
  German front crumbled, 322;
  Hitler plans attack in the West,
  272; tank warfare, 275-6; V1
  and V2, use of, 321; winter of
  1939, 270-1. *Germany:* Allied
  advances to Berlin, 323; Luftwaffe overcome, 307; R.A.F.
  raids, 307. *Great Britain:* Air
  Force, Battle of Britain, 278;
  invasion planned, 277. *Poland:*
  German troops across frontiers,
  264, 267; peace or compromise
  suggested, 269; plans against
  Poland, 248. *Russia:* plans and
  policy against Russia, 277-9,
  288, 300-1; progress of attack,

Germany—cont.
287-8; winter, effect of, 288-9; German stand in East Prussia, 321. *Two fronts:* war on two fronts, 276-7, 291, 306 *et seq.*: surrender signed, 337
Germany after surrender: democracy, experiment in, 355; dictatorship, tendencies towards, 353; Dönitz Government not recognized, 338; Hitler or Nazi myth, 337, 350, 354; lost territories, 358; Nazi and Neo-Nazism, 347-8; neutralization and disarmament solution, 356; Power's occupation policy, 339; reactions after the war, 343, 351; reconstruction, 344-5; reunification difficulty, 358; right-wing radicalism, 348; Russian policy, 357-8; Sovereign State, 359

Gesler, Minister of Defence, 98
Gestapo, 176, 178-80, 226, 233
Gibraltar, 280
Gilbert, F., 305*n*, 306*n*, 329*n*, 330*n*
Gisevius, H. B., 226*n*, 237*n*, 251*n*, 267, 269, 271, 318
Glaise von Horstenau, E., 232
Gobineau, Count de, 57-60
Godesberg, Hitler-Chamberlain conversations, 252
Goebbels, Joseph, 125-7, 134, 148*n*, 158, 162, 170-3; bombing of Germany, 307; Chancellor, 335; election under State facilities, 148; Germans as leaders, 305; Hitler, relations with, 312-14; Italian situation, 311; labour and concentration camps, 298; Nazi electioneering, 1932, ▶137-8; Papen's speech banned, 162; Roosevelt, death of, 330; wife and children in the Bunker at the end, 332; death of, 337
Gördeler, Karl, 271, 317-18, 320
Göring, Reich Marshal Hermann W., 122, 127, 134-5, 171-3, 180, 225-6, 232, 301, 314; Anglo-French intervention, 264; Bürgerbräu Keller meeting, 99; British ultimatum, 264; character of, 312; concentration camps, 180; Chancellorship, negotiations on, 142; dismissed by Hitler, 332, 335; election activities, 148-9, 151; Enabling Bill, 153; Four-Year Plans, 172,

195-6; 'free hand' understanding, 252-3; made a General, 161; Hacha's visit to Hitler, 245; letter to Hitler upon taking over, 332; Luftwaffe, failure of, 278; Minister without portfolio, 147; Nazi Party, joins, 93-4; November *Putsch*, 101; police reorganized, 178; Polish-German discussions suggested, 262; Prussia controlled, 154; Reichstag fire, 150; S.A. leaders killed, 163; Secret Police, 156; starvation of Greeks and Russians, 297; suicide at Nuremberg, 342; trial of, 340, 342; visits to Warsaw, 248-9
Görlitz, Walter, 289*n*, 293*n*, 317, 320*n*, 327
Gollancz, Victor, 14*n*
Gollwitzer, Helmut, 343*n*
Graf, Ulrich, 94
Great Britain: Foreign policy, failure of, 220; League of Nations, 221; military position of, 33; nationhood, growth of, 32-33; political development of, 34-35; racial affinity with Germans, 30; wars of defence, 33; weakness of, 221
Germany and: general relations, 112, 204-5, 222, 224; Anglo-German Naval Treaty, 1935, 216, 253; economic recovery of desired, 221; German need for alliance with, 219; Hitler's hope for neutrality or understanding with, 216, 251-3, 260, 262; German-Russian agreement a rebuff, 260; war with envisaged by Bernhardi, 67
Germany, war with: Battle of Britain, July-September, 278; invasion postponed, 1941, 278; Norwegian waters mined, 273
Poland and: possibility of war, 208-9; British change of policy, 247-8; would support Poland, 251-2, 256-8; mutual assistance pact signed, 261; guarantee to Poland, 262; suggestion of direct discussions, 262; British ultimatum, 264; appeal by Hitler for peace, 276-7
Spain and: attitude to Civil War, 218
Greece, British guarantees, 251; Germany conquers, 283; Italian attack, 1940, 281-2

Grimm, Professor F., 353
Gröner, General Wilhelm, 135n, 136
Grzesinski, A. C., 84n
Guderian, General Heinz, 275, 278n, 320, 331
Gürtner, Franz, 102
Guillebaud, C. W., 188n, 195, 196n

HABSBURGS, 38
Hacha, Emil, President of Czechoslovakia, 244-5
Haeckel, Professor, 306n
Hague Convention, 1899, 341
Haldane, Lord, 18
Halder, General Franz, 236-7, 271, 283n, 284, 288n, 320, 351
Halifax, Viscount (later Earl), 244, 260
Hanfstängl, Putzi, 93
Hanseatic League, 37
Harrer, Karl, 88, 92
Hasse, Professor Ernst, 65
Hassell, Ulrich von, 271
Headlam-Morley, A., 82n
Hegel, 50-1, 55
Heiden, Konrad, 89n, 125n, 127n, 149n
Heimpel, H., 35n
Heines, 163
Henderson, Arthur, 215
Henderson, Sir Nevile, 234, 243n, 258n, 259; British ultimatum, 264; free-hand understanding with Germany, 253, 260; Polish negotiations, 262; Ribbentrop, meeting with, 263
Henlein, Konrad, 234, 245
Herking, Ursula, 344n
Herrenvolk, 23, 200
Hess, Rudolf, 93, 170, 172-3; effort for peace, 284; S.A. leaders killed, 163; trial of, 340
Hesse, F., 115n, 212n, 224n, 253n, 270n
Heuss, Professor, 350
Hewel, 245n
Heydrich, 178, 182n
Himmler, Heinrich, 134, 171-4, 283, 298n; Commander of the home army, 320; concentration and extermination camps, 302; in Austria, 233; influence and power of, 301; Jews, extermination of, 304; Nazi racial policy, 302; peace negotiations with Count Bernadotte, 332; arrest ordered, 332-3; expelled, 335; death of, 337; police and S.S.,

178, 301; S.A. leaders killed, 163; S.S., 177-8; S.S., address to 302-3; duties and responsibilities of, 303-4
Hindenburg, Oskar von, 135, 142
Hindenburg, Field-Marshal Paul von Benckendorf und: 29, 49, 135; armistice negotiations, 72; ceremony at Potsdam, 152; death of, 165; elected President, 124; election opposed by Hitler, 136; Hitler's policy towards, 139, 142
Hitler, Adolf: 1889-1945, Reich Chancellor and Führer, his family and private life: domestic affairs, 124-5; family and early life, 105-6; farewell and death, 336; health and habits, 1944, 330-1; life in Reich Chancellery in Berlin, 323; Wagner's operas, 111; end at hand, 331; marries Eva Braun, 333-4; political testament and will, 334-5; expels Göring and Himmler, 333, 335; appoints new leaders, 335; suicide, 332
Character and personality of: Christianity, attitude towards, 182-3; Churches, attitude to, 183; eccentricity, 105; emotionalism, 110; history, a favourite subject, 111; Iron Cross award, 230n; megalomania, 68; methods of, similarity to Bismarck, 46; Nietzschke, admiration for, 57; personality of, 28, 90, 104-7, 110, 313-14; power, belief in, 108; Roman Catholic Church, attitude to, 183; superiority of, 26; war, interest in, 110; women, charm over, 105
Elsctioneering, propaganda, policy, speeches, Mein Kampf: ceremony at Potsdam, 152; election propaganda, 148; *Führer,* speeches by, 167; *Mein Kampf,* 103-4, 107 *et seq.,* 125; policy outline in *Mein Kampf,* 113, 291; Nazi electioneering, 132, 137-8; New Year's message, 141; oratory, effect of, 107; peace speech, 1935, 214-15; policy of, 140; Speeches at Linz and Vienna, 233; speech in Reichstag, July, 1934, S.A. leaders killed, 164; speech in Berlin Sportpalast, 1938, 239-41; in Reichstag 28 April 1939, 253;

Hitler—*cont.*
speech, Service Chiefs, 23 November, 1939, 272
Political ideas, mission: Bolshevism, policy against, 204: Communism, attitude to, 150-1, 352; conquers Europe, 267 *et seq.*; *coup d'état* by Army planned, 172; Democracy, dislike of, 118; fundamental aims, 108; *Gleichschaltung*, policy of, 152-3, 156; *Lebensraum*, 114, 225; Marxism, hatred of, 116-18; National Socialism, necessity for, 118-19; Nationalism, 71, 90; Nazi objective, 225; new territories to be acquired, 112; mission, belief in his, 107, 306; parliamentary institutions, dislike of, 118; revolution in permanence, 157-8; reward to the German people, 295-6; success not inevitable, 28; Third Reich, 29; Weimar Republic attacked, 86-7; *Weltschauung*, 111, 117
Economic, social, racial questions: anti-Semitism, 115, 181-2, 334; Aryan race theory, 115-16; capitalism, 204; Germanism, 111; population, 112; social problems, 116-17; *Volkisch* conception, 116
Foreign policy, peace and war, New Order: aggression, period of, 225; declaration, no further territorial ambition, 247; disarmament offered, 210; Eastern policy, 206-7; German foreign policy, 112-13; hatred of Germany's enemies, 104-5; Locarno Pact reaffirmed, 217; Munich Conference, 241; New Order in Europe, 294-6, 305; peace, pacific policy, 191; peace speeches, 205, 270; peace and war, 205-7; Peace Treaty, 1919, attacked, 86-7, 105; policy after Poland, 269, 277; war, programme towards, 207-9; war, responsibility for, 73-4; world rôle, 292
Personal career: banned as a speaker, 123; Bürgerbräu Keller meeting, 99-100; Chancellorship, 138-43, 147; Coalition Government, 142, 147; Commander-in-Chief of Army in the field, 292; *coup d'état* planned, 97; defence, responsible for, 226; dictator, 153, 155, 168; Enabling Bill passed, 153; *Führer und Reichskanzler*, 165-6; German citizenship conferred, 136; German Workers' Party, membership of and programme, 88-90; growing strength of Hitler, 1937, 219; hospital, 104; imprisoned, 102, 121; leadership accepted, 27; military service, 106-7; Munich, 1913, 106; Munich trial, 101-2; Nazi Party, unlimited power in, 92, 94; *Oberkommando der Wehrmacht*, 226; progress, step by step, 211; régime, establishment of, 13, 23, 28; Socialist May Day demonstration, 97; support by educated Germans, 20; triumphs, military and dramatic, 276; November *Putsch*, 100-1; Nuremberg, Rally, 1923, 97; personal control, a cause of the collapse, 327; policy after prison, 121-2; Presidential election, 135-6; Vienna, 106, 111
Opposition and attacks on: bomb attack on, 1939, 271-2; opposition to, small groups and individuals, 316-17; Staffenberg attempt, 316-19; Tresckow and Schlabrendorff, 317; vengeance for, 320
Hitler or Nazi myth, 337, 350, 354
Hitler Youth, 175, 199-200
Hoare, Sir Samuel, 224
Hobhouse, Professor L. T., Hegelian State, 51-2
Höss, Rudolf, 'final solution' of Jewish question, 304
Höttl, D. W., 305*n*
Hofer, Dr. Walther, 50*n*
Hoffmann, Heinrich, 94
Hohenzollerns, rise of, 38-9
Holland, German attack on, 274; neutrality of, 272
Holy Roman Empire, 29, 32, 36-8, 40
Hoover, President, 131
Horst Wessel Lied, 134
Hossbach, Colonel, 208, 225, 341
Hugenberg, Alfred, 128, 148; bargain with Hitler, 147; negotiations for a coalition, 142; Nationalist Party liquidated, 154; Reichstag fire, 150; resigns, 154
Hungary: joins Tripartite Pact, 282
Huns: Germans as, 15

INDEPENDENT SOCIALISTS, 81
Italy: Allies enter Rome, 314; Armistice signed, 311; British landing in Calabria, 311; declaration of war, 1940, 275-6; Fascist Grand Council, 310; Mussolini, head of the Government, 94-5, *see also* Mussolini; Tripartite Pact, 1940, 281
 Abyssinia and: 216-17, 223
 Albania and: 251
 Germany and, 204; coal supplied to Italy, 216; closer contacts between, 1936, 218; agreement, Rome - Berlin Axis, 218-19; military alliance, Pact of Steel, 254; Italy unable to give military aid, 261; German reaction to Italian armistice, 310-11; German campaign, capitulation, 337
 Poland and: Italian agreement with Germany, 257-8
 Spain and: military assistance sent, 218
 U.S.A. and: Italy declares war on, 289; landing at Salerno, 311

JAPAN: Japanese objective, policy upon intervention, 290; re-armament, 357; Tripartite Pact, 1940, 281; Germany, agreement with, 204, 219; Great Britain, war declared on, 289; Manchuria, aggression in, 1931, 221; U.S.A., Japan and attacks Pearl Harbor, 289
Jarman, T. L., 20n
Jehovah's Witnesses, 180
Jews: anti-Jewish laws, 199; anti-Semitic thought, 57; Chamberlain, racial views of, 63; concentration camps, 180; extermination of Jews, 341; 'final solution' of Jewish question, 304; German attitude to, 26, 298; Himmler on extermination of, 304; Hitler, anti-Semitism, 112, 115, 181-2, 334; Wagner, anti-Semitism, 60
Jodl, General Alfred, present at attempt on Hitler, 318; signs surrender of Germany, 337; trial, 340; death, 342
John, Dr., 345-7, 352
Jugoslavia, German attack on, 282-3

Jung, Edgar, 163
Junkers, 43-4

KAHR, GUSTAV VON, 97-100, 102, 163
Kaltenbrunner, Ernst, 340, 342
Kampfverband Niederbayern, 97
Kapp, Dr., 84
Keitel, General Wilhelm, 226, 230, 318-19, 340, 342
Kellogg Pact, 128
Kerensky, 81
Keynes, J. M., 75-6
Kharkov, 287
Kiaochow, 73
Kiel, mutiny at, 72
Kiev, 287
Kipling, Rudyard, 64
Klausener, Dr., 163
Kluge, Field-Marshal Günther von, 315, 319
Knight-Patterson, 80n, 83n
Kogon, E., 302
Kohn, Hans, 50n, 354n
Koniev, Marshal, 359
Kraft durch Freude, 197-8
Kreisau circle, 316
Krieck, Ernst, 168n
Krupp, Gustav, 340
Krupps, 149

LABOUR FRONT, 197, 199-200
Lammers, Dr., 172
Language, Nazi influence on, 349
Lansbury, George, 211
Laski, H. J., 14n, 16
Latvia, Germany, non-aggressive pact, 254; Russia, incorporated in, 259, 268, 280
League of Nations, 79, 123; disagreement between members, 220-1; German rearmament, 214; Germany leaves, 210-1; Italy and Abyssinia, effect of, 216, 218, 221, 223; Japan, aggression in Manchuria, 221; Russia joins the League, 213; U.S.A., failure to join, 220
Leipzig trial, Reichstag fire, 150
Lenin, 81
Leningrad threatened, 287
Levy, H., 17n, 19n
Ley, Robert, 171, 173-4, 197, 340
Lebensraum, 114, 206-8, 245, 254, 298
Libya: campaign in, 308-9; Wavell's success in, 282

Liddell Hart, B. H., 275*n*, 319*n*
Lidice, 308
Liebknecht, K., 81
'Link' party visit, 1939, 261
Linz, Hitler's speech at, 233
Lithuania, non-aggressive pact with Germany, 254; German zone, 259; incorporated in Russia, 268, 280
Litvinov, Maxim, 256
Lloyd George, David (later 1st Earl), health insurance, 19; interviews with Hitler, 187-8; Peace Conference of Paris, 74
Locarno Pact, 123, 215, 217
Lossow, General Otto von, 97-100, 102
Lowie, R. H., 22*n*
Lubbe, Marinus van der, 149-50
Ludecke, Kurt G. W., 91*n*, 93, 99, 107, 114*n*, 115*n*, 122*n*, 124*n*, 138*n*, 139, 140*n*, 149*n*, 156*n*, 158, 159*n*, 161*n*, 180*n*, 204*n*. 206
Ludendorff, Field-Marshal Erich, 49, 122; armistice negotiations, 72; Bürgerbräu Keller meeting, 99; defeated as President, 124; March offensive, 74; Munich trial, 101-2; November *Putsch*, 100-1; Nuremberg Rally with Hitler, 97; victory or defeat, 74
Ludwig, E., 14*n*
Lulea, port of, 273
Lutheran Church, 182
Lutze, Victor, 174
Luxembourg, German attack on, 274
Luxemburg, Rosa, 81

Mackensen, Field-Marshal August von, 47, 152
Maginot Line, 217, 275
Marriott, J. A. R., 43*n*
Martel, General, 275
Marx, Dr. F. M., 167
Matsuoka, Yosuka, 281
Max, Prince, of Baden, 72-3
Mediterranean, Hitler's organization, of, 279
Mein Kampf, 91*n*, 103-4, 107 *et seq.*, 125, 206-7, 216, 219, 291, 298
Meissner, Dr. Otto, 172
Memel, 249-50
Metaxas, General, 281
Miklas, Wilhelm, President of the Austrian Republic, 232-3
Moeller van den Bruck, A., 85

Molotov, Vyacheslav M., Russian Foreign Minister, 256, 280; Munich Conference, 243; Russo-German understanding, 259; talks over Poland, 257; visits to Berlin, 281
Moltke, Graf Helmuth von, 316
Mommsen, 49
Montgomery, Field-Marshal Viscount, 293, 321*n*, 322
Moravia, Protectorate of, 245
Morocco, allied invasion, 1942, 308
Moscow, threatened, 287
Moscow Declaration, 1930, 339
Müller, Hermann, German Chancellor, 133
Müller, Reichsbischof, 182
Müller-Graaft, C. H., 45*n*
Mundella, A. J., 20
Munich, Bürgerbräu Keller meeting, 98-100; civil war, 1919, 73, 84; Conference on Czechoslovakia, 241-3; German Art Museum, 191; *Putsch*, 1923, 140
Musmanno, M. A., 332*n*
Mussolini, Benito, Duce, 280; Abyssinia, conquest of, 218; Albania, invasion of, 251; France, claims on, 279; death of, 336; Germany sides with over Poland, 258; Italy unable to give military aid, 261; head of the Government, 94-5; Hitler, Mediterranean Conferences, 279; Hitler, meetings with, 281, 288, 295; League of Nations, 221; mediation offered, Germany and Poland, 262; mobilizes troops on the Brenner, 212; Munich Conference, 241; resignation and puppet government, 310-11; Spain, attitude towards civil war in, 218; speech, Wilsonian illusions, 218

Napoleon, 40
Narvik, port, 273
National expansion, 204
Nationalism, 15, 90
Nationalist organizations, 1922, 94
Nationalist Party, 77-8, 147, 154
Nationalsozialistische Briefe, 125
Nationalsozialistische Deutsche Arbeiterpartei. See Nazi Party.

Nato, 359-60
Naumann, 349

Nazi Party, beginnings of the party, 27-8, 71 *et seq.*, 88 *et seq.*; brutality of, 176; Christianity, attitude towards, 182; Communists attacked, 149, 154, 156; continuity of with past, 29; control, coercion and destruction, 176; electioneering campaigns, 137-8, 140, 148-51; end of Nazi Party, 327 *et seq.*: *Führerprinzip*, 127; funds, 92-3, 128, 134-5, 148-9, 174; German acceptance of Nazism, 27; Hitler strengthens his hold over, 92, 169; Hitler's imprisonment, party weakness, 121-2; housing policy, 192; Jews, persecution of, *see* Jews; leaders, independence of, 171; marriage, attitude toward, 199; Marxism, combated, 118-19; mass movement created, 91; membership of Nazi Party, 175; mercy killing, 199; Nazi fortune on decline, 306 *et seq.*; Nazi ideology, influence of, 349; Nazi myth, Hitler's death, 337, 343-50; Nazi-Nationalist Coalition, 148; Nazism, new spirit of Germany, 185 *et seq.*; opposition to, 156; order and discipline re-established, 186; organization, 127, 170-6; Party rallies, 126; police forces, 178-9; politics, only party, 154; policy two faced, 203; positive side of régime, 185 *et seq.*; Post Office, development of, 192-3; propaganda, 203; public works, 190; racial policy, 199, 298; railways, 192-3; Reichstag elections and membership, 122, 127, 138, 142-3, 147; revolution, in permanence, 147 *et seq.*, 156-7; roads, 192; Social Democrats' property seized, 154; sterilization, 199; strength of the Nazi Party, 28, 126; Strength through Joy, 197-8; popular successes of, 1931, 135; supporters of, 1952, 350; suppression of Party, 1923, 101; task of, 86; terror and brutality, 91; theatres and concerts, 198; torture, use of, 299; trade unions taken over, 153-4; trial of war criminals, 339; *Völkischer Beobachter*, 92; war, aggressive, 341; women, policy for, 189, 198; youth, 198

Near East position, 291
Neo-Nazi parties, 349; 'Stab in the back' theory, 351
Neumann, Dr. Franz, 167-8
Neurath, Constantin, Freiherr von, 147-8, 173, 225, 340
New Order in Europe, 294-6
News Chronicle, 346
Nicolson, Harold, 242
Niemöller, Pastor, 182
Nietzsche, philosophy of, 54-7
Nitti, Francesco, 34n
North German Confederation, 42, 66
Norway, German attack on, 273-4; bases in, 273-4
Noske, 84
Nuremberg Laws, 181, 199
Nuremberg Rally, 97, 200, 205, 237
Nuremberg Trials, 339-40, 342

OLBRICHT, GENERAL FRIEDRICH, 318-19
Olden, R., 106n
Olympic Games, 1936, 200
Oncken, Harman, 47
Oradour, 308
Orwell, George, 349
Oster, General, 271
Otto I, 36
Oxford Union Debate, 1933, 221

PACT OF STEEL, 219, 254, 262
Pact of Paris, or Kellogg Pact, 1928, 341
Pan-German League, 65-66; Pan-Germans, 78-9, 89
Papacy, Concordat, 1933, 182; relations with Germany, 36
Papen, Franz von, German Chancellor, 133, 136-7, 142n, 190, 227-30; acquitted, 342; arrested, 163; elections, 139; Chancellorship, negotiations with Hitler, 141-2, 147; negotiations with Schleicher, 140-1; pushed aside in Prussia, 154; Reichstag fire, 150; speech at Marburg, 162; trial of, 340
Paris entered by Germans, 276; liberated, 321
Parker, James, 305n
Parliamentary institutions, 118
Parties in Germany: disappearance of, 169
Pattison, Mark, 19

Patton, General, tank advance, 321
Paul, Prince of Jugoslavia, 282
Paulus, General Freidrich von, 293
Peace and democracy, 86
Peace Ballot, 1935, 222
Peace Conference at Paris, 74-7;
    Peace Treaty, 79-80
Peace, dream of, 223
Pearl Harbor, 289-90, 292
People's Party, 133, 154
Percy, Lord Eustace, 20
Petacci, Clara, 336
Pétain, Marshal Philippe, 276, 279
Petersdorff, Captain von, 301
Phipps, Sir Eric, 237n
Playfair, Lord, 20
Pöhner, Ernst, 99
Pohl, General, 181
Poincaré, Raymond, French Premier,
    96
Poland: *Germany and:* policy and
    relations; discussions, 249-50;
    policy of friendship, 205, 248-9;
    Ten-year non-aggression pact,
    1934, 211-12, 217, 248, 253;
    sixteen points for settlement, 263;
    war and threats of war, 208, 247
    et seq., 254-5, 257-8, 263, 352;
    organization of Poland, 279;
    Poles, treatment of, 299, 302;
    Polish Corridor, 209, 211, 249
    Germany and Russia: understanding
    desired, 256; partition between,
    259, 268
    Intervention of the Powers, 255
    France, 208-9, 264
    Great Britain, 264; guarantees, 251,
    258
Poncet, M. François, 120n
Posen, 75
Potsdam ceremony, Reichstag open-
    ing, 152
Potsdam Agreement, 1945, 356-7
Potsdam Conference, 339
Prague, 245, 247, 250
Prange, G. W., 292n
Preuss, Minister of the Interior, 82
Pribilla, Father, 350n
Price, G. Ward, 17, 205, 214
Prussia, early history of, 39-43;
    dominant state, 46; Göring's
    control, 154
Prussians, characteristics of, 26

RAEDER, ADMIRAL ERICH, 273, 283,
    290-1, 340

Ranke, von, 34n
Rantzau, J. A. von, 52n
Rathenau, Walter, Minister for
    Foreign Affairs, 85, 94
Raubal, Angela, 125
Raubal, Geli, 125
Rauschning, Hermann, 184n, 203n,
    206-7, 292n, 330
Redesdale, Lord, 65
Reichsflagge, 97
Reichsleiter, 173
Reichstag elections, 1919-33, 130-1,
    143; fire of, 149-50; function of,
    46, 169; Kroll Opera House, 153
Reichstatthalters appointed, 154
Reitsch, Hanna, 333n
Remer, Major-General Ernst, 319,
    348, 351
Rentenmark, 123
Reparations, Dawes Plan, 123; effect
    of, 95-6
Resistance movements, 308
Rhineland, demilitarization of, 215;
    evacuation of, 123; occupied by
    Germany, 216-17
Rhodes, Cecil, 64
Ribbentrop, Joachim von, 173, 209,
    216, 219, 225, 229-30, 314;
    British ultimatum, 264; Danzig
    question, 249; German position,
    1941, 281; German-Polish con-
    versations, 249-50; German-
    Russian agreement, 259-60;
    Hacha's visit to Hitler, 245;
    Henderson's meeting with, 263;
    influence and power of, 301;
    Japanese objective, 290; peace
    suggestions, 269; Poland, British
    intervention, 257; Russia, talks
    and understanding with, 256,
    268; trial and death, 340, 342;
    Tripartite Pact, 1940, 281; two-
    front war, 277n; visit to Moscow,
    258; war, German preparedness
    for, 243
Roberts, S. H., 171n, 199n
Robertson, C. Grant, 43n
Röhm, Ernst, 92-3, 134-5, 170, 174,
    301; German Workers' Party,
    88; Hitler, discussions with,
    160-1; killed, 163; nationalist
    organizations, alliance, 96-7;
    November *Putsch,* 101; resigna-
    tion, 122; S.A., Communist
    recruits, 156; S.A., 158-60, 176-7
Röpke, Wilhelm, 27, 43-4
Roetter, F., 166n

Rotterdam, 274
Rowse, A. L., 14n
Roman Catholic Church, Hitler's attitude to, 183
Roman Empire, 30-1
Rome liberated, 314
Rome-Berlin Axis, 218-19, 226
Rommel, Field-Marshal Erwin, 308; advice of, 291; operations in North Africa, 293; possibilities of action in Near East, 283; success in Libya, 283; suicide of, 320
Roosevelt, Franklin D., President of the U.S.A., Conference at Teheran, 314; death of, 330; Hitler's attack on, 292; meeting with Mr. Churchill, Atlantic Charter, 295; message to the dictators, 254; New Deal, 130, 191
Rosenberg, Alfred, 93, 122, 172-3, 314; German Workers' Party, 89; influence and power of, 301; pagan teachings of, 182; trial and death of, 340, 342
Ruhr, French occupation of, 77, 95-6, 123
Rumania, British guarantees, 251; German action in, 280; joins Tripartite Pact, 282; Russian special interest in, 260, 280
Rumbold, Sir Horace, 131-5n, 206
Runciman, Lord, 235-6
Rundstedt, Field-Marshal Karl R. G. von, 275n, 315
Rupprecht, Crown Prince of Bavaria, 100
Russia, League of Nations entered, 213; policy in relation to German rearmament, 357; unified command, 1955, 359; British and French talks over Poland. 256-7; Franco-Soviet Pact, 222
  Germany: Hitler's policy of expansion in Russia, 113-14, 206-7, 276, 297, 301-2; Russian agreement, urgency of, 258; economic policy, 268; efficiency and strength of Russia, 288, 291-2; expansion in Russia, 206-7; Friendship and Frontier Treaty, 1939, 268, 277n, 286; opportunities for intervention, 286-7; understanding with Russia, 256, 259-60
  War with Russia: preparations for invasion, 283; belief in a short campaign, 284; Russian attempts to avoid provocation, 286; Germany attacks, 286-7, 291; winter, anxiety during, 287-8; Russian counter-attack, 288, 293; German campaign, 293, 309; treatment of Russians, 298-9; Russian offensive, 311-12, 315-16; peace overtures by Nazis, 337; Russians enter Berlin, 337; Russia and Poland, 255; Poland invaded, 269
Ruthenia, autonomy for, 244; to Hungary, 245

S.A. (Sturm Abteilungen), 91, 149, 176-7, 199; Army jealous of, 160; ban on lifted, 137; dissolved by Reich Government, 136; election meetings, 1932, 138; Göring commander of, 94; Hitler, attitude to, 126, 160-1; leaders killed, 1934, 162-3; mutiny of, 134; political force, 97; revolutionary policy of, 160; Röhm, Chief-of-Staff of, 158
S.S. (Schutz Staffeln), 134, 149, 176-8; concentration camps, 180; Himmler's address to, 302-3; duties and responsibilities of, 138, 302-4; methods of, 299; reviving military spirit, 346
Saar Valley, 73, 75, 212-13
Saarbrücken theatre, 191
Sadler, Michael, 19
Salomon, Ernst von, 351
Salute, Nazi, 91
Sauckel, Fritz, 297, 340, 342
Schacht, Dr. Hjalmar: 123; arrested, 320; Barter system, 195; currency manipulations, 194; financial support to Nazis, 149; President of the Reichsbank, 190-1; resignation, 225; trial, 340, 342
Scheele, G., 143n
Scheidemann, P., 80-2, armistice negotiations, 72; 'Stab in the back' legend, 74
Schicklgruber, Alois, 105
Schlabrendorff, Lieutenant Fabian von, 317
Schleicher, General Kurt von, Reich Chancellor, 135, 137, 161, 163, 190; Chancellorship, 141-2; elections, 1932, 139; negotiations with Papen, 140-1; policy of, 136

Schleswig, 75
Schmidt, Guido, 227-8, 230
Schmidt, Paul, 209n, 211n, 238n, 239n, 252, 257, 260n, 263n, 264n
Schmidt, Willi, 163
Schmitt, Carl, 170n
Schmundt, Lieut.-Colonel, 209n, 254
Schnabel, Franz, 45n
Schneider, F., 20n
Schneider, Hannes, 227
Scholl, Hans and Sophie, 316
Schröder, von, Chancellorship conversations, 141-2
Schumann, F. L., 155n, 171n
Schuschnigg, Kurt von, Austrian Chancellor, 212, 227-33
Schwartz, Franz Xavier, 174
Second front, Allies, discussions, 309
Second Reich, 29, 42, 109
Seeckt, General von, 98
Seisser, Commander of State Police, 98-100, 102
Seldte, Franz, 148, 154
Seton-Watson, R. W., 14n, 157n, 160n, 306n
Seyss-Inquart, Arthur, 229, 231-3, 340, 342
Shirach, Baldur von, Reich Youth Leader, 172, 174, 340
Sicily, Allied landings in, 309-10
Siegfried Line, 217
Silesia, 75
Simon, Sir John, 214
Singapore, Japan and, 290
Skorzeny, Otto, 311
Slovakia, autonomy for, 244; Polish anxiety over, 250; under German protection, 245
Smuts, General, League of Nations, 220
Social Democrats, 15, 46, 72, 80, 82
115-17, 132-3, 180; arrested, 150; clashes with Communists, 81; election results, 151; Enabling Bill, 153; Peace Treaty, 1919, 78; property seized by Nazis, 154; Reichstag, strength of in, 147; strength of Party, 1928, 127-8
Socialist Reich Party, 348
Solf, Frau, 316
Solfkreis, 316
Solz, Adam von Trott zu, 316
Spain: Civil War, 218; military assistance to France, 218; participation in war deferred, 280

Spartacus Group (later Communists) 81
Speer, Albert, 313, 330, 340
Speidel, H., 319n, 328-9, 342
Spengler, Oswald, 79-80, 85
Sport, 198
'Stab in the back' legend, 49, 74, 102, 348, 351, 352
Stahlhelm, 148-9, 154
Stalin, Josef, 260, 281; bargains with Germany, 268; Conference at Teheran, 1943, 314; German attack on Russia, 286; sought to avoid war, with Germany, 352; policy towards Germany, 286-7; Russo-German agreement, 258-9
Stalingrad, German defeat at, 309; military operations around, 293
State, Nazi Party relationship with, 170; theory of the State, 51; State parliaments abolished, 155
Stauffenberg, Colonel Count von, attempt on Hitler, 317-19
Steed, Wickham, 43n, 65n, 67n
Stern-Rubarth, E., 14n
Strasser, Gregor, 122, 125-7, 139, 163; quarrel with Hitler, 141; revolutionary policy, 158; Schleicher's approaches, 141
Strasser, Otto, 125-6, 129, 158
Streicher, Julius, 122; Der Stürmer, 94, 181; trial, 340, 342
Stresa Conference, 214
Stresemann, Gustav, German Chancellor, 97, 123-4, 128-9
Strölin, Dr. Karl Emil, 320n
Stürmer, Der, 94, 181
Sudeten Germans. See Czechoslovakia.
Suñer, Spanish Foreign Minister, 280n
Swastika, 91
Sweden, iron ore from, 273; neutrality of, 294
Switzerland, neutrality of, 294
Syrový, General, 241-2

TANNENBERG, O. R., 66n
Taylor, A. J. P., 27n
Teutonic Knights, 37, 39, 113
Teutonic peoples, 63
Third Reich, 29
Thirty Years' War, 38-9
Thomas, General, 269, 271
Thomson, Malcolm, 188n

Thyssen, F., 93, 128n, 135n
Times, The, 83, 214n, 217n, 236, 242
Tiso, President of Slovakia, 244
Tobruk, 293
Todt, Dr., 192
Tönnies, N., 348n, 358
Torgler, Ernst, 150
Trade unions, 153
Treitschke, Heinrich von, 42-3, 52-5, 57
Tresckow, General von, 317, 342, 344
Trevor-Roper, H., 332n, 333n, 336n
Tripartite Pact, 1940, 281
Triple Alliance, 48
Tsahai, Princess, 223
Tunisia, campaign in, 308-9
Turkey, Mediterranean agreement, 251

U-BOATS, 307; sinkings, 293
Ullstein Verlag, 174-5
Union of Revolutionary National Socialists, 129
United States of America: economic slump, 129 et seq.; League of Nations, failure to join, 220; war, involved in east and west, 290
  Germany and: bombing of, 307; Germany declares war on, 289, 292; loans to Germany, 77; priority for war against Germany, 309
  Italy and: declares war on U.S.A., 289
  Japan and: Japanese objective, 289-90

VANDERVELDE, 215
Vansittart, Lord, 14-16
Vaterländische Vereine Munchen, 97
Versailles, Treaty of, 71, 215, 217
Vichy Government of France, 279
Vienna, bombardment of housing blocks, 1934, 212
Völkischer Beobachter, 92, 98, 125, 137, 142, 174, 269, 270
Vorwärts, 78, 80

WAFFEN S.S. See under S.S.
Wagners, Nazi supporters, 93
Wagner, Richard, 55, 57, 60-1
Warlimont, General, 278n, 327
Warsaw, Polish underground movement, 321
Wartenberg, Count Peter Yorck von, 316, 318, 320
Wavell, Field-Marshal Earl, action in Libya, 280; success against Italians, 282
Weber, Christian, 94
Weber, E., 66n
Weimar Republic. See Germany.
Wells, H. G., 19
Wels, Otto, 153
Weltanschauung, 25, 166
Western Powers, German policy to work with, 350; failure to work together, 28, 220; weakness of, 220
Weygand, General, 275
Wheeler-Bennett, J. W., 236n, 316n, 320n, 347, 351n
Wilhelmine era, 46, 65
William II, German Emperor, 48, 65, 72
Wilmot, Chester, 330n
Wilson, Sir Horace, 239, 241n
Wilson, President of U.S.A., armistice negotiations, 1918, 72; League of Nations, 220; Peace Conference of Paris, 74; Saar, 73
Witzleben, General von, 237, 251, 316-18, 320
Workers' Travel Association, 187
World War, 1914: responsibility for, 47-8

YALTA CONFERENCE, 339
Young, Owen, D., Young Plan, 128

ZIMMERN, A., 14n
Zirkus Krone, 91
Zollverein, 1834, 41, 66
Zweig, Stefan, 43n